THE GUARDIAN OF THE CONSTITUTION: HANS KELSEN AND CARL SCHMITT ON THE LIMITS OF CONSTITUTIONAL LAW

This volume provides the first English translation of Hans Kelsen's and Carl Schmitt's influential Weimar-era debate on constitutional guardianship and the legitimacy of constitutional review. It includes Kelsen's seminal piece, 'The Nature and Development of Constitutional Adjudication', as well as key extracts from the 'Guardian of the Constitution' which present Schmitt's argument against constitutional review. Also included is Kelsen's review of Schmitt's 'Guardian of the Constitution', as well as some further material by Kelsen and Schmitt on presidential dictatorship under Article 48 of the Weimar Constitution. These texts show Kelsen and Schmitt responding to one another, in the context of a debate focused on a concrete constitutional crisis, thus allowing the reader to assess the plausibility of Kelsen's and Schmitt's legal and constitutional theories.

LARS VINX is an assistant professor in the Department of Philosophy at Bilkent University, Ankara, Turkey. His main areas of interest are legal and political theory, constitutional theory and the history of political thought.

The aim of this series is to produce leading monographs in constitutional law. All areas of constitutional law and public law fall within the ambit of the series, including human rights and civil liberties law, administrative law, as well as constitutional theory and the history of constitutional law. A wide variety of scholarly approaches is encouraged, with the governing criterion being simply that the work is of interest to an international audience. Thus, works concerned with only one jurisdiction will be included in the series as appropriate, while, at the same time, the series will include works which are explicitly comparative or theoretical - or both. The series editors likewise welcome proposals that work at the intersection of constitutional and international law, or that seek to bridge the gaps between civil law systems, the US, and the common law jurisdictions of the Commonwealth.

Books in the series:

The Guardian of the Constitution: Hans Kelsen and Carl Schmitt on the Limits of Constitutional Law
Translated by Lars Vinx, with an introduction and notes by Lars Vinx

Parliamentary Bills of Rights: The Experiences of New Zealand and the United Kingdom Experiences
Janet L. Hiebert and James B. Kelly

Lawyering for the Rule of Law: Government Lawyers and the Rise of Judicial Power in Israel
Yoav Dotan

Balancing Constitutional Rights: The Origins and Meanings of Postwar Legal Discourse
Jacco Bomhoff

Judges on Trial: The Independence and Accountability of the English Judiciary
Shimon Shetreet and Sophie Turenne

Proportionality and Constitutional Culture
Moshe Cohen-Eliya and Iddo Porat

The Politics of Principle: The First South African Constitutional Court, 1995–2005
Theunis Roux

The New Commonwealth Model of Constitutionalism, Theory and Practice
Stephen Gardbaum

Searching for the State in British Legal Thought: Competing Conceptions of the Public Sphere
Janet McLean

Judging Social Rights
Jeff King

Proportionality, Constitutional Rights and their Limitations
Aharon Barak

Parliamentary Sovereignty: Contemporary Debates
Jeffrey Goldsworthy

THE GUARDIAN OF THE CONSTITUTION: HANS KELSEN AND CARL SCHMITT ON THE LIMITS OF CONSTITUTIONAL LAW

Translation, introduction, and notes by

LARS VINX

CAMBRIDGE
UNIVERSITY PRESS

CAMBRIDGE
UNIVERSITY PRESS

University Printing House, Cambridge CB2 8BS, United Kingdom

Cambridge University Press is part of the University of Cambridge.

It furthers the University's mission by disseminating knowledge in the pursuit of education, learning and research at the highest international levels of excellence.

www.cambridge.org
Information on this title: www.cambridge.org/9781107092686

First published in English by Cambridge University Press 2015

A catalogue record for this publication is available from the British Library

Library of Congress Cataloguing in Publication data
The guardian of the constitution : Hans Kelsen and Carl Schmitt on the limits of constitutional law / edited and translated by Lars Vinx.
pages cm – (Cambridge studies in constitutional law)
ISBN 978-1-107-09268-6 (Hardback)
1. Kelsen, Hans, 1881–1973 – Correspondence. 2. Schmitt, Carl, 1888–1985 – Correspondence. 3. Constitutional law – Philosophy. 4. Executive power – Germany. I. Kelsen, Hans, 1881–1973, author. II. Schmitt, Carl, 1888–1985, author. III. Vinx, Lars, editor translator
K339.G83 2015
342.001–dc23
2014029908

ISBN 978-1-107-09268-6 Hardback

CONTENTS

ACKNOWLEDGEMENTS

The publication of this volume would not have been possible without the generous support of Professor David Dyzenhaus and of Finola O'Sullivan at Cambridge University Press. I am very grateful to the Hans Kelsen-Institut in Vienna, to Duncker & Humblot in Berlin, and to Professor George Schwab in New York for giving me permission to make use of the texts that are translated in this volume. I am also indebted to the two referees of the initial proposal for Cambridge University Press who made a number of very valuable suggestions and to Simon Wigley who read a draft of the introduction. Finally, I would like to thank my copy-editor Jeremy Langworthy for helping to improve the quality of the English text.

A NOTE ON THE TEXTS

The translations in this volume contain the page numbers of the German source-texts in square brackets. References to the translated texts in the introduction, cross-references in and between the translated texts, and references in the notes at the end of the volume all use these bracketed page numbers. The ellipses in chapters 2 and 3 indicate the beginnings of passages of Schmitt's *Guardian of the Constitution* that are not included in this volume.

An asterisk in the translated text indicates an editorial note that provides background information on a point discussed in the translated text. These editorial notes can be found at the end of this volume, starting on p. 254. They are likewise identifiable by reference to the bracketed page numbers.

The bibliography lists all literature cited in the introduction and in the editorial notes. Kelsen's and Schmitt's works are referred to by the year of original publication.

Introduction

I The *Preussenschlag*

On 20 July 1932, the conservative chancellor of the Weimar Republic, Franz von Papen, made use of an emergency decree that the president, Paul von Hindenburg, had drawn up a few days before. This decree authorized the chancellor to depose the government of Prussia, the largest German *Land* or state, then under the leadership of the social democratic prime minister Otto Braun, and to appoint federal commissioners to take over the business of the Prussian ministers serving with Braun. The alleged goal of the so-called '*Preussenschlag*' (the 'strike against Prussia') was to restore public security and order in the state of Prussia. There had been serious unrest and violence in the streets of the Prussian town of Altona a few days before, as a result of clashes between communists, Nazis, and police. But von Papen's federal government was as responsible for this breakdown of public order as the Prussian government. It had recently lifted the ban on the SA[1] and thus helped to precipitate violent clashes between Nazis and communists. The real goal of the *Preussenschlag* was to wrest control of Germany's largest state from the social democrats and to make Prussia's executive power available to the conservative federal government.[2]

The emergency-decree that authorized the *Preussenschlag* was based on article 48 of the Weimar Constitution. That article gave the president the power, in its first paragraph, to compel the states of Germany, if need be by the use of armed force, to fulfil their obligations towards the *Reich* under the federal constitution and under federal laws. Moreover, it authorized the president, in its second paragraph, to take all necessary measures to restore order in case of a severe threat to public security. The president's decree appealed to both of these provisions. It claimed that the replacement of the Prussian government with a government

[1] The *Sturmabteilung*, i.e. the paramilitary organization of the Nazi-party.

[2] Clark (2007), 640–54; Mommsen (2009), 529–48; Kolb and Schumann (2013), 142–3, 264–7.

appointed by the chancellor of the *Reich* was necessary to restore public security and order in Prussia, and it also accused Prussia of having violated its legal obligations toward the *Reich*, though the decree itself did not specify this charge in any way.[3]

Article 48 of the Weimar Constitution, in its last paragraph, determined that the president was required to inform the federal parliament, the *Reichstag*, immediately of any measures taken under article 48. The president had an obligation to suspend emergency measures at the request of the *Reichstag*. This restriction of the president's powers under article 48, though, was no longer fully operative in July 1932, as the *Reichstag* had long ceased to function in the way intended by the constitution.

The parties in the *Reichstag* had been unable, since 1930, to form a legislative majority willing to support a parliamentary government. Germany had instead been governed on the basis of presidential emergency decrees issued by appeal to article 48 paragraph 2. The chancellor, as a result, came to depend more on the president's trust than on parliament.[4] The first of these presidential governments, that of Heinrich Brüning, in office from 1930 to 1932, had still enjoyed the toleration of parliament, or more precisely of the parties of the 'Weimar Coalition' that had formed the last pre-crisis government. While there was no majority willing to legislate for Brüning, there was no majority either, due to the tacit support of the democratic parties, for a vote of no confidence against him that would have forced new elections.

The centrist Brüning, however, had been dismissed by Hindenburg at the end of May 1932, for reasons unrelated to the lack of direct parliamentary support for his government. Hindenburg had then appointed the ultra-conservative Franz von Papen as chancellor. Von Papen and his supporters were keen to rid the presidential government of its dependence on the democratic parties, and in particular of its dependence on the social democrats. The new government dissolved the *Reichstag*, a move that triggered federal elections within sixty days. In the interim, von Papen tried to win the support of the NSDAP,[5] which was expected to make large gains in the coming elections, for his government. The plan – which eventually came to naught due to

[3] The decree is printed in Brecht (1933), 481.

[4] Mommsen (2009), 329–82, 431–82; Rossiter (1948), 31–73.

[5] The *Nationalsozialistische Deutsche Arbeiterpartei*, i.e. the National Socialist German Worker's Party led by Adolf Hitler.

Hitler's stubborn insistence that he be appointed chancellor of the *Reich* – was not to return to parliamentary government, but rather to get the Nazis to tolerate von Papen's presidential government. The ban on the SA, which had been put in place under Brüning, at the demand of the interior ministers of the states, had been lifted to attract the support of the Nazis. The *Preussenschlag*, then, was also intended as a conciliatory move towards the NSDAP, as it promised to get Prussian police off the Nazi party's back.[6]

Though the legality of the *Preussenschlag* was very much in doubt, the Prussian government under Otto Braun chose not to actively resist von Papen's measures. The constitutional situation in Prussia did not look much better, in July 1932, than that in the *Reich*.[7] The governing coalition in Prussia, led by the social democrats, had lost its parliamentary majority in the elections to the Prussian legislature in April 1932. But the NSDAP, which had won the election and become the strongest party, as yet did not have enough votes in parliament to elect a new government. The old parliamentary majority had, in advance of the elections, changed the parliamentary rules of procedure for the election of a new government, by introducing the requirement that a new government could only be elected with an absolute (and not, as had previously been the case, with a relative) majority of votes. Since the communists were equally unwilling to support the election of a social democratic or a national socialist prime minister of Prussia, the new Prussian *Landtag* failed to elect a prime minister and Braun's government continued in office in a caretaker role.

There are indications that some members of the Prussian government were not in principle averse to the appointment of a federal commissioner to take control of Prussia's police force. Such a move had already been contemplated by Brüning, not least to ensure that it would not fall into the hands of the Nazis.[8] Von Papen's *Preussenschlag*, however, went much further. As we have seen, the decree of 20 July 1932 was justified not merely on the ground that federal intervention was necessary to restore public order. It accused the Prussian government of having violated its legal duties towards the *Reich*. Moreover, the decree did not only put Prussia's executive power temporarily into the hands of the *Reich*. It envisaged a complete transfer of all competences of the Prussian government to the *Reich*, and thus appeared to eliminate Prussia's independence as guaranteed by the federal system of the

[6] Mommsen (2009), 529–91. [7] Clark (2007), 640–54. [8] Seiberth (2001), 37–58.

Weimar Constitution. The decree, accordingly, also empowered von Papen to remove all Prussian ministers from their offices, a power that he used to the full on 20 July 1932.[9]

Though the Prussian government chose not to resist the *Preussenschlag* through violent means, it challenged the legality of the decree with an appeal to the *Staatsgerichtshof* (literally the 'court of justice in matters of state') in Leipzig. It was supported in this appeal by several other German states that feared that von Papen's *Preussenschlag* would turn out to be the first step in a general abolition of federalism.[10] The *Staatsgerichtshof* was not a full constitutional court, endowed with a non-incidental and exclusive authority to review and to annul unconstitutional legislation and acts of government. It was a special tribunal that was convened upon occasion at the *Reichsgericht* (the Weimar Republic's highest civil and criminal court) and empowered, by article 19 of the Weimar Constitution, to adjudicate conflicts between the federal government and the states.

In its decision of the case, which was issued on 25 October 1932,[11] the court rejected the claim that the Prussian government had violated any duties towards the *Reich* and it ruled that the federal government did not have the power permanently to depose the Prussian ministers or to take over all competences of a Prussian government. At the same time, the court held that the *Reich's* assumption of Prussia's executive power was justified as a measure to protect public security, and thus refused to interfere with the federal government's momentary control over Prussia's administrative apparatus.

This attempt to split the difference left all parties unsatisfied. Though the federal government kept control of the Prussian executive, the judgment blocked its suspected attempts to turn Germany into a politically centralized state, by making it clear that the powers of the president under article 48 could not be used to permanently infringe on the principle of federalism. Nevertheless, the *Preussenschlag* did succeed in wresting political control of the Prussian state from the hands of the social democrats and their coalition partners who supported the continuing existence of the Weimar Republic. When Hitler was appointed chancellor in January 1933, Hermann Göring took over the post of federal commissioner for Prussia. Goebbels quipped that von Papen had purged the Prussian state so carefully of republicans and democrats that there was nothing left for the Nazis to do.[12]

[9] Brecht (1933), 481–6. [10] Seiberth (2001), 111–79.
[11] Printed in Brecht (1933), 492–517. [12] Mommsen (2009), 543.

The *Preussenschlag* was not just a key event in the disintegration of the Weimar Republic and the rise to power of the Nazis. It also marked the culmination of two of the most important jurisprudential debates that took place in the Weimar era: the discussion on the nature and limits of executive powers of emergency under article 48 and the debate on the legitimacy and desirability of constitutional adjudication.[13] These two debates intersected in the context of the *Preussenschlag*.

There were those, on the one hand, who, like Carl Schmitt, advocated an extensive reading of the president's powers under article 48. In a situation of constitutional crisis, Schmitt believed, only a political power capable of taking a decision on the exception,[14] to suspend the law altogether, would be able to restore the situation of normality that, in Schmitt's view, must underpin all legal governance. The power of constitutional guardianship, therefore, must belong to the head of the executive and not to a court, as implicitly acknowledged, according to Schmitt, by article 48 of the Weimar Constitution.[15] Other influential constitutional theorists, among them Hans Kelsen, favoured the view that constitutional guardianship ought to be the preserve of a constitutional court, i.e. of a court empowered to control all acts of legislation and of high-level executive action for their conformity with the constitution, and explicitly endowed with the authority to invalidate acts deemed unconstitutional.[16]

Unsurprisingly, Kelsen and Schmitt came to different assessments concerning the role of the *Staatsgerichtshof* in the aftermath of the *Preussenschlag*. In Kelsen's view, the judgment of the *Staatsgerichtshof* had failed – out of undue deference to the president, who was constitutionally responsible for executing the judgments of the *Staatsgerichtshof* – to annul the legal effects of an emergency decree that the court itself appeared to regard as unconstitutional. This confusing outcome, Kelsen suggested, could have been avoided if the case had been decided by a proper constitutional court.[17] Schmitt, who acted as counsel for the federal government at the trial in Leipzig,[18] expressed the opinion, by contrast, that the president's decree ought not to have been subject to substantive judicial review in the first place.[19]

[13] Stolleis (2002), 114–18. [14] Schmitt (1922), 5–15.
[15] Schmitt (1924); Schmitt (1931a). [16] Stolleis (2002), 117–18.
[17] Kelsen (1932a), 65–91. Translation in ch. 6 of this volume.
[18] Seiberth (2001), 78–110; Mehring (2009), 281–302. See also Schmitt (1932c).
[19] See Schmitt (1931a), 59; Schmitt (1934b), 44–7; Schmitt (1932d), translated in ch. 5 of this volume.

These differing assessments of the judgment on the *Preussenschlag* were only the parting shots in a longer debate between Kelsen and Schmitt on the problem of constitutional guardianship.[20] In 1929, Kelsen had published a paper entitled '*Wesen und Entwicklung der Staatsgerichtsbarkeit*' ('On the Nature and Development of Constitutional Adjudication') that systematically laid out the case for a constitutional court as a guardian of the constitution.[21] Schmitt, in turn, had challenged Kelsen's advocacy of a constitutional court in a number of articles that were eventually integrated into a book-length treatment, which appeared in 1931 under the title *Der Hüter der Verfassung* (*The Guardian of the Constitution*).[22] Kelsen responded to Schmitt's book with a review – '*Wer soll der Hüter der Verfassung sein?*' ('Who Ought to be the Guardian of the Constitution?')[23] – that is one of the most incisive criticisms of Schmitt's constitutional theory ever written.

The aim of the present volume is to make these texts available, for the first time, in English translation.

II The Kelsen–Schmitt debate

As pointed out above, the constitution of the Weimar Republic did not provide for the institution of a constitutional court. But there was a lively debate as to whether the competences of the *Staatsgerichtshof*, created to arbitrate in conflicts between the *Reich* and the *Länder*, ought to be strengthened so as to turn it into a full-blown constitutional court. In particular, scholars and politicians debated the question whether the *Staatsgerichtshof* should be endowed with the power to annul unconstitutional legislation.[24]

The *Reichsgericht* in Leipzig, in a much noted decision in 1925, had claimed that the courts of the Weimar Republic possessed an incidental right of judicial review of legislation: a right not to apply statutes which they considered to be unconstitutional to a particular case at hand.[25] What is more, a highly developed system of constitutional adjudication

[20] See Dyzenhaus (1997); Diner and Stolleis (1999); Beaud and Pasquino (2007); Gümplová (2011). For the background of the debate in German public law theory see Caldwell (1997).

[21] Kelsen (1929a). Translation in ch. 1 of this volume.

[22] Schmitt (1931a). Chapters 2 and 3 of this volume offer a partial translation.

[23] Kelsen (1931). Translation in ch. 4 of this volume.

[24] See Schmitt (1931a), 3–7; von Hippel (1932), Stolleis (2003); Hartmann (2007).

[25] Schmitt (1929b).

had already been put in place in the Republic of Austria, where the constitutional court had been given the power, under the constitution of 1920, to strike down unconstitutional federal and local legislation, upon appeal by the federal or by regional governments.[26] The Weimar debate on a constitutional court, thus, was often phrased in terms of whether Germany should adopt the 'Austrian solution'.[27]

In 1928, two presentations at the annual meeting of the *Vereinigung der Deutschen Staatsrechtslehrer* (the Association of the German Teachers of Public Law) by Heinrich Triepel and by Hans Kelsen engaged with the topic of constitutional review.[28] Both authors affirmed the need for a constitutional court, though Triepel much more hesitantly than Kelsen. Kelsen's presentation is regarded as the classical plea for a special constitutional court endowed with an exclusive authority of abstract or non-incidental control of general legal norms issued by parliament or government. It has been extremely influential in the Continental European context,[29] while it has so far been largely neglected in Anglo-American debates on judicial review. Apart from offering arguments *de lege ferenda* for the introduction of a constitutional court, Kelsen's paper also put forward a host of 'legal-technical' reflections, i.e. of recommendations as to the best institutional design of a constitutional court. These recommendations were to some extent influenced by the model of the Austrian Constitutional Court. Kelsen served as a judge on that court from 1920 to 1929, and he had, through his involvement in the drafting of the Austrian Constitution of 1920, helped to create it.[30]

Kelsen's argument for the introduction of a constitutional court is based on the so-called *Stufenbaulehre*, the theory of legal hierarchy, which Kelsen adopted from his pupil Adolf Julius Merkl.[31] According to the theory of legal hierarchy, the process of the creation of law is to be understood as a step-wise sequence of enactments in which the creation of any legal norm is authorized by higher-level legal norms. A judicial decision, for instance, is seen as the enactment of a particular norm that is authorized by the statute which it applies. The enactment of a statute,

[26] Heller (2010), 139–234; Paulson (2003); Öhlinger (2003). See also Kelsen (1942).

[27] See Schmitt (1931a), 6. [28] Triepel (1929) and Kelsen (1929a).

[29] Stone-Sweet (2000), 32–8.

[30] See Schmitz (1981); Olechowsky (2009); Lagi (2012). For Kelsen as a judge see Walter (2005). Kelsen was removed from the court in the wake of the constitutional reform of 1929. See Neschwara (2005).

[31] Compare Kelsen (1934), 55–75. See also Koller (2005).

in turn, is understood as authorized by the constitutional norms that determine the proper procedure for the process of legislation and that perhaps lay down material limitations for the production of general legal norms.

According to Kelsen, any norm-enactment on any level of legal hierarchy is partly discretionary: the fulfilment of the constitutional conditions, procedural and substantive, for the enactment of a statute typically leaves the legislator with a wide range of legislative choices. Similarly, a judge deciding a particular case typically enjoys a certain degree of discretion in applying a statute. As we move down the legal hierarchy from constitutional norms towards particular judicial or administrative decisions the level of discretion enjoyed by the relevant decision-takers will tend to decrease. Kelsen argues, however, that there is no qualitative difference, only one of degree, between the activity of a legislator and that of a judge or an administrator. Just as a judge applies a statute in enacting a particular norm that will decide a particular case, legislators, though they have greater freedom of choice, apply constitutional norms in enacting statutes.[32]

If that is the case, Kelsen concludes, there is no good reason to hold that the activity of legislators cannot or should not be subject to constitutional review. No one would doubt that the actions of lower-level legal authorities, of subordinate executive agencies or judges of first instance, should be subject to review, in order to guarantee the legality of the relevant particular norm-enactments. But if legislation (or high-level executive action) is also a form of the application of law, it is as possible and as necessary to offer a guarantee that legislators or government will abide by the constitutional norms that authorize and limit their activity. If there are no guarantees of constitutional legality, Kelsen argues, then the constitution, as the highest and most important level of legal order, will remain a form of second-rate law that lacks full legal force. And a sufficient guarantee of constitutional legality, in Kelsen's view, can only be provided by a constitutional court endowed with the power to annul unconstitutional legislation as well as unconstitutional acts of government.[33]

A constitutional court, moreover, is of special importance in a democratic and federal state. Its guarantees of constitutional legality protect minorities against the potential excesses of the rule of a majority; a rule

[32] Kelsen (1929a), 1485–7.

[33] *Ibid.*, 1524–6. See Troper (1995); Nino (1996), 189–96; Vinx (2007), 145–75.

that will become tolerable, according to Kelsen, only if it is bound to the rule of law. A federal state is in need of a constitutional court, since it is to be understood as a system in which two mutually independent authorities are legally co-ordinated on the basis of a constitutional division of competences. Such co-ordination requires an impartial arbitration of conflicts of competence between the central and the local authorities that can only be offered by a constitutional court.[34]

Though Kelsen's argument was on the whole received favourably at the meeting of the *Vereinigung der Deutschen Staatsrechtslehrer*, his plea for the creation of a proper constitutional court in Weimar Germany also called forth strong opposition. Schmitt's 1931 monograph *Der Hüter der Verfassung* (*The Guardian of the Constitution*) is in large part a reply to Kelsen's arguments on constitutional adjudication.

Schmitt's argument against Kelsen builds on the claim that constitutional adjudication exceeds the legitimate powers of a court.[35] A judicial tribunal called upon to adjudicate on the constitutional legality of legislation or of acts of government would, Schmitt argues, typically have to take decisions that are contestable and subject to reasonable disagreement. Constitutional provisions, in contrast to ordinary statutes, are often too vague and open-textured to allow for uncontroversial application. As a result, a constitutional court would be forced to take political decisions, decisions that are no longer justifiable as applications of determinate legal norms. It would have to act as a constitutional legislator and thus violate the separation of powers. The introduction of a constitutional court, Schmitt concludes, would not de-politicize constitutional conflict but rather politicize the courts and thus undermine the legitimacy of judicial activity.

Schmitt, however, was as opposed to parliamentary sovereignty as he was to constitutional adjudication. Schmitt held that modern parliaments, as a result of pluralist division, are no longer capable of taking genuinely political decisions in the name of a people as a whole.[36] In the constitutional monarchies of the nineteenth century, Schmitt claims, parliament could claim to be a representative of the people as a whole because it opposed a monarchical executive the sovereignty of which was still, in principle, uncontested. Parliament acted as the defender of a non-

[34] Kelsen (1929a), 1526–9. See also Kelsen (1927), 162–7.
[35] Schmitt (1931a), 12–48; Schmitt (1967).
[36] Schmitt (1931a), 73–91. See also Schmitt (1938), 65–77.

political social sphere against the incursions of an administrative state that possessed an undoubted monopoly of political decision.

With the establishment of a parliamentary system of government, and due to the accelerating process of modernization, the legislature has, in Schmitt's view, come to occupy a very different position. The traditional distinction between state and society has disappeared, in modern society, together with the limitation of the state's sphere of activity that it implied. The state is now, at least potentially, a total state.[37] There can no longer be any principled limits to the state's interference with society and the economy. At the same time, the state has lost its transcendent position above the fray of party-political conflict. It is now controlled by parliamentary majorities that act in pursuit of their own sectional interest. The state, even while seemingly having grown more powerful, no longer expresses the political identity of the people as a whole. It has become an instrument in the hands of parliamentary leaders whose bickering has thrown it into political paralysis. Schmitt concludes that parliament cannot function as a guardian of the constitution.

Schmitt's reaction to the perceived threat of a pluralist disintegration of the state was twofold. On the one hand, Schmitt championed the claim, despite his hostility to constitutional review, that the Weimar Constitution put absolute limitations on the powers of parliamentary majorities.

In Schmitt's interpretation, the Weimar Constitution, as the expression of a constituent choice of the German people, contained an intangible core of fundamental political decisions that are legally immune to change by any constituted power, including parliament's power of constitutional amendment.[38] This view was not supported by the text of the Weimar Constitution, which does not mention any material limits of amendment. Schmitt tried to justify it, rather, on the basis of a general theory of what a constitution is. According to this theory, a constitution is not to be identified with the constitutional laws that are contained in the written constitutional text. Rather, a constitution, first and foremost, is a 'concrete' social order or 'positive constitution', which is put in place by an exercise of constituent power and which embeds a number of fundamental social values. The written constitution, in Schmitt's view, is no more than an attempt to codify this antecedent concrete social order endorsed by the popular sovereign. Its norms and procedures, therefore,

[37] See Scheuerman (1999), 85–112; Cristi (1998), 179–99.
[38] Schmitt (1928), 72–4, 79–81, 150–8; Schmitt (1932a).

are to be regarded as binding only as long as they help realize and protect the positive constitution.[39]

The constituent choice that affirms a concrete order or 'positive constitution' manifests an antecedent political unity of the people, a unity that Schmitt claims is prior to the politics that takes place under the regulation of constitutional norms. Schmitt's constitutional thought has a tendency to identify the authentic will of the people with the decisions of a pre-legal constituent power, allegedly unaffected by the pluralist division into several competing political parties. True democracy, as a result, is held to exist only in the realm of constitutional politics, while constituted democracy is denigrated as the scene of pluralist disintegration.[40] The function of the constitution, in this perspective, is to hedge in parliamentary politics, through an appeal to popular sovereignty, even while the legal illimitability of constituent power is enthusiastically affirmed.[41]

Schmitt's second, related reaction to the perceived threat of pluralist disintegration was to play up the role of the president of the *Reich* under the Weimar Constitution. The constitution had indeed endowed the president, who was directly elected by the people, with a fairly impressive array of competences.[42] The most important of these were the president's powers of dictatorship under article 48 paragraph 2 of the Weimar Constitution, which, as we have seen, were used by President Hindenburg to legislate by emergency decree and thus to prop up presidential governments that did not have the explicit support of a parliamentary majority. Schmitt had, in an earlier piece, criticized that practice.[43] But in the *Guardian of the Constitution*, he came around to defending it.[44] Schmitt argued that the Weimar Constitution had put the president into the position of a neutral power above party politics that was to form a counterweight against parliament. The president, hence, was to assume legislative power in case of parliamentary dysfunction. In thus preserving orderly government, the president, in Schmitt's view, showed himself to be the true guardian of the constitution.[45]

In calling the president a neutral power, Schmitt did not mean to suggest that presidential guardianship of the constitution would not be

[39] Schmitt (1928), 75–88. [40] *Ibid.*, 79, 138–9. [41] *Ibid.*, 125–35. See Vinx (2013b).

[42] The president had the power to dissolve the *Reichstag* (art. 25), to initiate a popular referendum on a statute approved by the *Reichstag* (art. 73), and to appoint the chancellor (art. 53).

[43] Schmitt (1924), 213–18. [44] Schmitt (1931a), 128–31. [45] *Ibid.*, 132–59.

political. Rather, his point is that it would not be party-political. This claim is in line with Schmitt's general interpretation of article 48, which holds that the president, in using his powers of emergency, exercises a residue of 'sovereign dictatorship'.[46] According to Schmitt, the application of all law, including constitutional law, requires a condition of normality that can only be secured, if it is threatened, by extra-legal acts of dictatorship.[47] Since the constitution had made the president responsible for the exercise of powers of dictatorship, and since it had imposed no real constraints, in Schmitt's view, on the discretion of the president in the exercise of those powers, it fell to the president to secure the condition of normality requisite to the functioning of the Weimar Constitution. In deciding whether and how to use his powers of emergency, the president thus became the highest interpreter of the Weimar Constitution. In contrast to parliament, the president, elected directly by the people, was supposedly legitimized by the unified popular will that also stood behind the constitution as a whole.[48]

Schmitt's argument here is a development of certain ideas of Max Weber's, whose advocacy for a strong president had been influential in the making of the Weimar Constitution.[49] But Schmitt gives a peculiar accentuation to Weber's call for a strong executive supported by plebiscitary legitimacy. One way to read the *Guardian of the Constitution* is to understand the president's powers, as described by Schmitt, as essentially remedial.[50] The president, under such a reading, is to step in and preserve the functioning of the constitutional system in the event that the parties in parliament turn out to be unable to form a stable governing majority.

But while it is true that parliamentary government had broken down by 1931, it should be noted that Schmitt had tried to limit the powers of parliament already in his *Constitutional Theory* of 1928, well in advance of the outbreak of the final crisis of the Weimar Republic. His argument in the *Guardian of the Constitution*, moreover, suggests that a president as a neutral power should be regarded as a necessary and permanent feature of a parliamentary-democratic constitution.[51] Schmitt's historical analysis of the alleged process of the pluralist disintegration of

[46] Schmitt (1924), 202–7. See McCormick (1997), 121–56; McCormick (1998); Dyzenhaus (2006), 34–54.

[47] Schmitt (1922), 13. See Scheuerman (1999), 1–180; Hofmann (2002), 34–77; Croce and Salvatore (2013), 11–76.

[48] Schmitt (1931a), 156–9. [49] Mommsen (1984), 381–9.

[50] Compare Schmitt (1931a), 130–1. [51] *Ibid.*, 132–40.

parliament, which portrays the trend towards the dysfunction of parliamentary government as a natural consequence of the disappearance of a sharp distinction between state and society and of a transcendent state, implies that one should expect a purely parliamentary system of government to become dysfunctional.

Parliamentary government, Schmitt appears to suggest, has turned out to be incapable of providing Germany with strong and coherent political leadership. It can be allowed to continue to exist only under the supervision of a strong president who has a standing power to appoint a presidential government and to shield it, if need be, from accountability to parliament. Though Schmitt presents his argument in the *Guardian of the Constitution* as an interpretation of the powers of the president under the Weimar Constitution, the implicit aim, clearly, is to establish a political system that resembles a constitutional monarchy, with the difference that the position of the monarch is to be occupied by a popularly elected president whose decisions will provide the people as constituent power with the necessary political leadership.[52]

The political subtext of Schmitt's *Guardian of the Constitution* was not lost on Kelsen, who responded to Schmitt's book with a long review entitled *Who Ought to be the Guardian of the Constitution*. Kelsen refused to pass judgement on what he took to be Schmitt's political goals. But he argued, in the course of a defence of his own plea for constitutional review against Schmitt's criticism, that these goals could not be supported by way of an interpretation of the Weimar Constitution and that they ought not to be regarded as democratic.

Kelsen's response to Schmitt points out that it is impossible to uphold a strict separation between legal and political decisions or between adjudication and legislation. Every judicial decision, not just those taken by a constitutional court, must be regarded as discretionary, and thus as political, to some extent, as Schmitt himself had conceded in an earlier publication.[53] The theory of legal hierarchy explicitly incorporates this insight, in holding that all legal decision-taking is partly discretionary. It therefore makes no sense, Kelsen argues, to issue a blanket rejection of constitutional adjudication on the ground that it would have to be political. If it shares that feature with all adjudication, the question ought to be whether it is advisable, in the

[52] See Cristi (2011) and compare Schmitt (1927), 31–54. On Schmitt's involvement with plans of constitutional reform in the late Weimar Republic see Seiberth (2001); Mehring (2009), 281–302; Berthold (1999).

[53] Schmitt (1912).

interest of legality, to have conflicts over the constitutionality of legislation or the constitutionality of acts of government settled by a constitutional court. Schmitt's negative argument, in Kelsen's view, simply refuses to address that question.[54]

Kelsen's engagement with Schmitt's positive claim that the president is the guardian of the constitution under the Weimar Constitution is grounded in a realistic view of democratic politics. Schmitt's argument, as we have seen, assumes that there is a unified will of the people as a whole, above and beyond the legislative will that is formed through the deliberations and negotiations of parliamentary parties, a will that is expressed in constituent choices and actualized by the dictatorship of the president. According to Kelsen, this assumption is plainly false. The Weimar Constitution, Kelsen dryly observes, was enacted by a parliament staffed with party representatives, and presidents are elected, by majority vote, in a campaign that can hardly be free from party-political influence.[55]

In Kelsen's view, Schmitt's assumption is not just fictional. It also carries autocratic implications. If there is in fact no authentic and unified popular will above and beyond the will that is formed within the constitutionally constituted political system – through the deliberation, negotiation, and bargaining of different parties and interest groups – then any attempt to declare one particular organ of the constitution the representative of such a will can be little more than a way to mask the political self-empowerment of a particular group. Hence, the claim that the president can act as a neutral power is to be rejected as a piece of implicitly authoritarian ideology.[56]

Democracy, according to Kelsen, is the ongoing peaceful search for political compromise among different social groups that are all entitled to participate in the game of democratic politics under conditions of equality. Democratic compromise, in Kelsen's view, maximizes the freedom of all under the system of coercive constraint that we call the law or the state. It assures, in contrast to any form of autocracy, that the largest possible number of citizens will see their own political preferences realized, while it holds out the promise to the outvoted that they may be able to form part of a future majority.[57] Democracy is essentially

[54] Kelsen (1931), 1539–53. [55] *Ibid.*, 1561–6.

[56] *Ibid.*, 1572 n. 13. See also Kelsen (1929b), 35–46.

[57] Kelsen (1929b). See on Kelsen's theory of democracy Dreier (1990); Herrera (1997), 118–37; Jestaedt and Lepsius (2006); Vinx (2007), 101–44; Ehs (2009); Baume (2012); Lagerspetz (forthcoming).

constitutional, since the peaceful search for compromise requires the acknowledged supremacy of a system of procedural rules and minority rights that give voice and standing to all groups in society. A constitutional court acting as an impartial guardian of these procedures and rights, therefore, is especially important in a democratic state.[58]

Kelsen points out that, in making a parliament staffed by representatives of political parties the centre of gravity of the political system, the Weimar Constitution clearly sides with democracy, so understood, and against autocracy. Schmitt's argument for presidential constitutional guardianship, since it is a covert plea for autocracy, is therefore indefensible, Kelsen argues, as an interpretation of the Weimar Constitution. Schmitt's conception of constitutional guardianship seems less concerned with the goal of offering guarantees of democratic constitutional legality than with the creation of elbow-room for a transcendent state unbound from constitutional law.[59] Kelsen, by contrast, believed that properly enforced democratic constitutional law can help pacify political conflict. He therefore held it to be desirable to subject political competition as far as possible to the rule of constitutional law.[60]

Kelsen did not deny, however, that there are potential limits to the legalization of politics. A political conflict, he conceded, may undoubtedly become so intense that there is no longer any possibility of a legally regulated resolution of the dispute.[61] But Schmitt, as Kelsen realized, does more than to point to the evident possibility of such conflicts.[62] He argues, in effect, that a judicial guardianship of constitutional legality will always inhibit and pervert democracy, as it will inevitably tend to prevent the expression of the unified constituent will of the people that Schmitt holds to be the only authentically democratic will.

According to Schmitt, a people's 'political existence' is manifested in its willingness to assert itself, under the leadership of a sovereign dictator, against existing constitutional (and international) legality. Schmitt's reply to Kelsen's claim that the unified will of the people is a mere fiction would be to point out that such a will in fact exists for as long as a people is willing to take (or rather to support) genuinely political decisions; decisions on the exception that constitute political community, in an extra-legal space, by drawing the line between friend and enemy.[63]

[58] Kelsen (1929a), 1526. [59] Kelsen (1931), 1570–3.

[60] See Vereinigung der Deutschen Staatsrechtslehrer (1929), 123; Kelsen (1926), 139–42; Kelsen (1929b), 76.

[61] Kelsen (1931), 1533–4. [62] Compare Kelsen (1926), 146–8. [63] Schmitt (1932b).

To preserve its political existence, which Schmitt elevates into the status of a supreme political value, a people must avoid becoming ensnared in a legality that will forever postpone a truly political decision. Kelsen's strategy of pacification through law is therefore to be rejected, according to Schmitt, even where circumstances would render it feasible.[64]

It is wrong, then, to portray Kelsen as a mere 'normativist' who was oblivious of the limits of legality, and Schmitt as a hard-headed realist who was courageous enough to reflect on the political basis of law. The disagreement between Schmitt and Kelsen, rather, reflects differing assessments of the relative value of constitutional legality. Kelsen advocates for a legal peace that provides an umbrella for social difference, while Schmitt demands the extra-legal creation and protection of a substantive social homogeneity that he declares to be the basis of true democracy.

III Kelsen, Schmitt, and the limits of constitutional legality

These differing assessments of the value of constitutional legality are reflected in Schmitt's and Kelsen's reactions to the *Preussenschlag*. Arguing as counsel for the *Reich*, Schmitt claimed that it had not been the aim of the *Preussenschlag* to permanently abolish the independence of the state of Prussia or to turn the Weimar Republic from a federal into a unitary state by presidential decree. However, Schmitt did argue that the mere fact that the caretaker government in Prussia was not politically aligned with the federal government, and that it was indirectly dependent on the tolerance of the communists in the Prussian *Landtag*, constituted a threat to public order that permitted the president to temporarily assign all the competences of the Prussian government to a federal commissioner.[65] At any rate, the presidential assessment of the state of public security, Schmitt argued, as well as of the measures needed to protect it, should not be subject to judicial review, provided there was no abuse of discretion.[66]

If Schmitt's position had prevailed with the *Staatsgerichtshof*, the independence of the states in the Weimar Republic's system of federalism would clearly have been severely compromised. The governments of the *Länder* would have been put under a standing threat of suspension or removal at the president's discretion. This would have made it

[64] See Vinx (2013a). [65] See Brecht (1933), 39–41, 177–81 and ch. 5 in this volume.
[66] Brecht (1933), 130–4, 291.

impossible for the *Länder* to rely on the constitution's system of federalism to protect their interests against a federal government of a competing political stripe. The court, apparently, was concerned to avoid such an outcome, and it tried to limit the consequences of the *Preussenschlag* for the constitution's system of federalism by claiming that the Prussian caretaker government could not be stripped, under article 48 paragraph 1, of its right to represent Prussia in the *Reichsrat*, the federal council where states exercised influence on the federal process of legislation. The court also ruled that the Prussian caretaker government had not, at any rate, been guilty of violating any legal duties towards the *Reich*, and it consequently held that the president lacked the power to permanently remove members of the Prussian government from their offices.[67]

Nevertheless, the court affirmed the president's judgement that there had been a threat to public order and security in Prussia, and it concluded that the president did have the right, under article 48 paragraph 2, to temporarily assign the competences of the government of Prussia relating to the internal governance of the *Land* to a federal commissioner, in order to restore public security.[68] In effect, the *Staatsgerichtshof* read down the president's decree, and held it to be constitutional insofar as it focused on the restoration of public order in Prussia.

Both Kelsen and Schmitt were scathingly critical of the judgment of the *Staatsgerichtshof*, though for slightly different reasons. Kelsen argued, in his assessment of the judgment, that the court's own reasoning in support of the judgment implied that the decree was unconstitutional in its entirety. The court, in Kelsen's view, therefore ought to have ordered the president to rescind the decree. In trying to split the difference between the parties to the dispute, the court's judgment had failed to give clear instructions to the president, who was constitutionally responsible to execute the decisions of the *Staatsgerichtshof*, and thus to stop an emergency action that the court itself appeared to regard as unconstitutional. But the court was not to blame, in Kelsen's view, for its failure to act decisively in the defence of the democratic republic. The problem, rather, was the lack, in the Weimar Constitution, of a fully developed constitutional court, explicitly endowed with the power to annul unconstitutional legislation and acts of government through its own decisions. Kelsen blamed this legal-technical deficiency of the

[67] *Ibid.*, 493. [68] *Ibid.*, 493.

Weimar Constitution – which, in his view, contrasted unfavourably with the Austrian constitution's relevant provisions – on the prevailing German theory of public law that continued to be too deferential to political power.[69]

Schmitt showered with ridicule the suggestion that the establishment of a proper constitutional court might have helped preserve the Weimar Republic.[70] In a later retrospective assessment of the trial in Leipzig, Schmitt claimed that the *Staatsgerichtshof's* interference with the *Preussenschlag* helped the Nazis take power. The court's decision cast a cloud of suspicion on the law-abidingness of President Hindenburg and thus increased the latter's desire to return to parliamentary government. This desire, according to Schmitt, ultimately overcame Hindenburg's apprehensions against permitting the formation of a government under the chancellorship of the 'Bohemian corporal' Adolf Hitler. Schmitt's own defence of the *Preussenschlag* could now be made to appear as a defence of the Weimar Constitution. To strengthen the presidential government would have been the only feasible way in 1932, Schmitt argued, to prevent a national socialist government.[71]

The question which of these two assessments of the *Staatsgerichtshof's* judgment, and of the value of legality in general, is more appropriate cannot be definitively decided in the space of an introduction to the present volume. It should be clear, though, that the debate between Kelsen and Schmitt on the problem of constitutional guardianship is of crucial importance to any assessment of their constitutional theories.

Though Schmitt threw in his lot with the Nazis in 1933, it is often argued that he was not a supporter but rather an opponent of National Socialism before 1933. What is more, it is argued that his constitutional theory contained the resources to prevent the formally legal destruction of Weimar democracy, to turn it into a militant democracy capable of defending itself against its adversaries. Schmitt's understanding of the constitution as a substantive order that is more than a mere collection of constitutional laws would have justified, so the argument goes, a temporary presidential dictatorship designed to keep the Nazis away from power and eventually to restore the Weimar Constitution.[72] Any such dictatorship, of course, would have required the violation of some constitutional law or other and would thus likely have been rejected as illegal

[69] Kelsen (1932a), 89–91; Kelsen (1927), 167–75; Dyzenhaus (1997), 123–32.
[70] Schmitt (1934b), 44–7. [71] Schmitt (1958), 345–50.
[72] See Kennedy (2004), 154–83, Berthold (1999), Seiberth (2001).

by the majority of Weimar public lawyers who, like Kelsen, understood constitutional legality as conformity with constitutional laws. As a result, Kelsen's attempt to develop a purely descriptive and value-neutral science of law that distinguishes sharply between the law as it is and the law as it ought to be is sometimes accused, even by authors who harbour little sympathy for Schmitt, of having unwittingly facilitated Hitler's pseudo-legal *Machtergreifung*.[73]

Kelsen's critique of Schmitt's *Guardian of the Constitution* should give rise to second thoughts about such assessments. To present Schmitt as a defender of the Weimar Republic, one has to accept Schmitt's constitutional theory, as well as the rather peculiar interpretation of the Weimar Constitution that flows from it; an interpretation that was roundly rejected by the majority of democratic constitutional lawyers in Germany at the time[74] and that, as Kelsen makes clear, intends a transformation of the parliamentary system into a constitutional monarchy in plebiscitarian guise. It may well be true that Schmitt was not a supporter of Nazism before 1933 and that he hoped, instead, for the indefinite continuation of a conservative presidential dictatorship unaccountable to parliament that might have been justified on the basis of his theory of constitutional guardianship and that would have been able to reconstruct a strong state holding firm control of society. But that obviously doesn't imply that Schmitt aimed to defend what we would recognize as a truly democratic constitutional order. It also doesn't imply that his constitutional theory didn't, in effect, help to destroy the Weimar Republic and pave the way for Nazism.[75]

There can be little doubt, on the other hand, that Kelsen understood his advocacy of constitutional adjudication as an attempt to help realize a democratic republic's promise of a peaceful and equitable resolution of social conflict, which he took to be dependent on sufficient respect for constitutional legality. Kelsen's argument is addressed to the friends and not to the enemies of liberal democracy, whom it aims to enlighten on the institutional or 'legal-technical' conditions of liberal democracy's proper functioning. It is true that Kelsen did not think that the preference for democracy over autocracy is capable of legal-scientific justification. But he did not desert the cause of democracy. Kelsen's attitude

[73] See Dyzenhaus (1997), 157–60; Radbruch (1946).
[74] See e.g. Anschütz (1933), 404–6; Grau (1932), 274–95.
[75] See Dyzenhaus (1997), 70–101; Cristi (1998), 179–99; Scheuerman (1999), 1–180; MacCormick (2004), Breuer (2012), 143–71.

towards the crisis of democracy in the 1930s is summed up well in a short piece entitled '*Verteidigung der Demokratie*' ('Defense of Democracy'):[76]

> In the light of this situation, the question also arises whether . . . democracy should not defend itself, even against a people that does not want it any more, even against a majority that is united in nothing more than in the will to destroy democracy. To pose this question is already to answer it in the negative. A democracy that attempts to maintain itself against the will of the majority, possibly even by the use of violence, has ceased to be a democracy . . . he who is in favour of democracy must not allow himself to be drawn into a fatal contradiction and reach for the method of dictatorship in order to save democracy. One has to stay loyal to one's flag, even if the ship is sinking; and, while sinking into the depths, one can only hold on to the hope that the ideal of freedom is indestructible and that it will come to life again the more passionately the deeper it has sunk.[77]

Endowed as we are with historical hindsight, we may be inclined to take issue with this sentiment. Surely, in light of the horrors of National Socialism, it would have been much better if Kelsen and the majority of positivist Weimar-era public lawyers had understood the concepts of 'democracy' and 'constitutionality' differently, more 'substantively', so as to allow for a more forceful defence of democracy?

Still, Kelsen's claim that it will likely turn out to be impossible to maintain a democratic political system if a majority of the people emphatically reject it turns out, on reflection, to be rather plausible. Would we want to call a political system democratic in which an absolute majority of the voters are denied the right to vote for a party of their choice, because the parties in question have been banned as unconstitutional? What would we say if the system had turned into an executive dictatorship, bolstered by the threat of the use of military force, where laws are made by the president and not by a parliament in which different social groups are represented? Perhaps there are situations in which an elitist dictatorship of the kind advocated by Schmitt in 1931–2 is necessary to prevent a form of pseudo-popular rule that is even worse. But in that case it would be preferable, arguably, not to sell that alternative under the label of democracy or to claim that it is constitutional; if only because it will become rather difficult to put up principled intellectual resistance to a fascist system if one has already convinced oneself that there is no essential difference between democracy and populist dictatorship.[78]

[76] Kelsen (1932b). [77] *Ibid.*, 237. [78] See Schmitt (1926a), 16–17.

Constitutional guardianship for a democracy becomes irrelevant if democracy has already failed, by losing the support of the majority of the people. What is to be done in that case, as Kelsen acknowledged, is a purely political question, not one of democratic constitutional law. As long as democracy still enjoys the people's support, on the other hand, the reasons for vesting the power to guard it in a judicial institution, and not in the executive, would appear to be strong indeed. Though Kelsen favoured the greatest possible extension of constitutional legality he may well have had a sounder understanding of its political limits than Schmitt. This suggestion may come as a surprise to some readers, but only because Kelsen's political and constitutional-theoretical works do not yet, in contrast to Schmitt's, receive the attention they deserve.

1

Kelsen on the nature and development of constitutional adjudication

Translation of Hans Kelsen (1929a) 'Wesen und Entwicklung der Staatsgerichtsbarkeit' in Hans R. Klecatsky, René Marcic, and Herbert Schambeck (eds.), *Die Wiener rechtstheoretische Schule. Schriften von Hans Kelsen, Adolf Merkl, Alfred Verdross*, 2 vols. (Vienna: Verlag Österreich, 2010), II, 1485–531.

THE NATURE AND DEVELOPMENT OF CONSTITUTIONAL ADJUDICATION

I The problem of legality

Adjudication in matters of state is constitutional adjudication and, as such, a judicial guarantee of the constitution. It is a limb of the system of legal-technical measures whose purpose it is to secure the legality of the state's functions. The functions of the state themselves have legal character; they appear as legal acts. They are acts through which law (and this means legal norms) is created, or through which created law (legal norms already enacted) is executed. Consequently, the functions of state are traditionally divided into legislation and execution, and the application of law, as a mere reproduction, is contrasted with legislation, as the genesis, the creation, or the production of law.

The problem of the legality of execution, in the sense of its conformity with statute, and thus the problem of guarantees of this form of legality, is on the whole well-recognized. The legality of legislation, by contrast, understood as the demand for the legality of the creation of law, as well as the idea of guarantees of this form of legality, seems to run into certain theoretical difficulties. Does it not amount to a *petitio principii* to want to measure the creation of law by the use of a standard that is only produced together with the object to be measured? And the paradox that seems to be contained in the idea of the 'legality of law' becomes the greater the more – following the traditional view – one identifies legislation with the creation of law and thus statute with law as such; so that the functions that are comprised under the name of execution, namely adjudication (judicature) and administration, and in particular the latter, appear to stand outside of the law, so to speak, and not to be genuine legal acts, to represent nothing more than applications or reproductions of a law whose production is somehow already finished, whose creation has been brought to completion, in advance of acts of execution. [**1486**] If one takes the view that the law is exhausted by statute, the meaning of the idea of legality will reduce to conformity with statute. And in that case, an extension of the concept of legality will hardly be self-evident.

This conception of the relationship between legislation and execution, however, is false.* The two functions are not opposed to each other in the sense that there is an absolute contrast between the creation and the application of law: rather, each of them, on closer inspection, turns out to be both creation as well as application of law. The relevant contrast is a relative, not an absolute, contrast. Legislation and execution are not two co-ordinate functions of the state, but only two different levels of the process of the creation of law, a process which neither begins nor ends at the level of statute, that stand in a relationship of subordination and superiority. This process continues to the bottom via the level of the administrative decree, the level of the judicial decision, and of the individual act of administration until it arrives at the acts that put the latter two into effect (these are the acts of so-called enforcement). It continues to the top until it arrives at the level of the constitution, in order eventually to reach, transcending the area of domestic legal order, the sphere of the order of international law that stands above all particular domestic legal orders. With this succession of levels, which is relevant, for now, only insofar as it unfolds itself within the area of a particular state, we of course intend to do no more than to offer a schematic representation of the major steps of the process through which the law, while concretizing itself, regulates its own creation; and through which the state, together with the law, continuously recreates itself. Constitution, statute, decree, act of administration, judicial decision, and enforcement: these are simply the steps in the formation of the will of community that are typical, given the way in which positive law organizes the modern state. Reality may of course depart from this ideal type. For instance, it is not necessary for a decree, i.e. for a general norm issued by an administrative agency, to interpose itself between a statute and the act of enforcement; and it is therefore possible, under certain circumstances, for a decree to be issued directly on the basis of the constitution, instead of being enacted as a means for the execution of a statute, and thus to stand alongside the statute, as a general norm enacted by a representative, parliamentary body. And other modifications of the typical process of the creation of law are similarly possible. But for now, the discussion will presuppose the most common type.

Since the constitution largely determines the way in which statutes come into existence, legislation is an application of law, if seen in relation to the constitution. In relation to the decree, however, as well as in relation to other acts standing below the level of statute, legislation is creation of law. And a decree, similarly, is application of law in relation to statute, and it is creation of law in relation to the judicial decision or administrative act that applies the decree. This decision, in turn, is application in relation to the levels above, but creation of law in relation to the level below, to the matter of fact that constitutes its enforcement. The route that the law travels, on its way from the constitution to the matter of fact that enforces a judicial or administrative decision, is one of continuous concretization. While the constitution, statute, and the decree represent the general norms of the law, [**1487**] which are progressively more saturated with content, the judicial decision or administrative act are to be regarded as individual legal norms. A legislator, who stands only under a constitution that determines his procedure of legislation, is bound by law only to a relatively limited extent. His freedom, his opportunity to engage in creative design, is relatively large. With every further step downwards, the relation between freedom and constraint shifts towards the latter. In other words, of the two components, which determine the respective function, the application of law is strengthened, and that of free creation of law is weakened. Every level of legal order does not just represent a production of law, in relation to the level below, but also a reproduction of law, in relation to the level above. And insofar as it is application of law, reproduction of law, the idea of legality is applicable to it since legality is nothing more than the relation of conformity in which the lower level of legal order stands to the higher. Hence, the demand for legality, and for specific legal-technical guarantees of legality, exists not just with respect to the act of enforcement, in its relation to the individual norms of the administrative command, of the administrative decision, and of the judicial decision, or with respect to these acts of execution in their relation to the general norms of the decree or the statute. The demand applies as well with respect to the relationship of the decree to the statute, and with respect to the relationship of the statute to the constitution. Guarantees of the conformity of a decree with statute and of the conformity of a statute with the constitution are therefore as possible as guarantees of the legality of individual legal acts. A guarantee of the constitution, hence, is a guarantee of the legality of the levels of law that stand immediately below the constitution. That is, first and foremost, a guarantee of the constitutionality of statutes.

That the demand for guarantees of the constitution is still raised today – or rather, that it has not been raised before today, and has therefore only recently acquired urgency and become a subject of scientific discussion – is due not merely to the mistaken theory we characterized earlier on, which lacked a full insight into the hierarchical structure of the law or, what amounts to the same thing, into the thoroughly legal nature of the functions of the state* and of their respective relations to each other. The fact that the legal orders of modern states exhibit an abundance of institutions that ensure the legality of execution, while they do not provide for any, or only for very poor, guarantees of the constitutionality of statutes (as well as of the conformity of decrees with statutes), is to be attributed to political motives. These motives, in turn, do not remain without influence on juristic theory, which, after all, would have to take the principal initiative in enlightening the public on the possibility and necessity of such guarantees. This observation is valid in particular for those modern parliamentary democracies of Europe that grew out of constitutional monarchies. The doctrine of public law of constitutional monarchy is still of great influence today, though this form of state has largely been pushed into the background. The constitutionalist doctrine still determines the juristic theory of the state to a high degree – in part consciously, where one wants to develop the republic, after the pattern of monarchy, in the direction of strong presidential power, and in part unconsciously. Constitutional monarchy [**1488**] developed from absolute monarchy, and its doctrine is therefore often guided by the aim to make the reduction of power that the formerly unlimited monarch had suffered as a result of the change of the constitution appear as small or insignificant as possible, or even to veil it altogether. Even in an absolute monarchy, it is theoretically possible to distinguish between the levels of the constitution and that of statute. But this distinction is practically insignificant, for the reason that the constitution exhausts itself in the basic principle that every expression of the monarch's will is a binding legal norm. And since the legal order therefore lacks a determinate constitutional form, that is, since there are no differentiating legal norms that regulate the enactment of statutes in a way that differs from the procedure for changing the constitution, the constitutionality of statutes is not a problem of any importance whatsoever. With the transition to a so-called constitutional monarchy, a decisive change takes place precisely at this point, which is signalled in a very characteristic way by the designation of the new system as a *Verfassungs-Monarchie* or 'constitutional' monarchy. The decisive legal shift expresses itself in the strengthened significance that is now accorded to the concept of constitution: in the legal norm that statutes may only come about in a certain way (namely with the participation of a body of representatives of the people), and in the fact (and this is the rule of the constitution) that this norm cannot be changed as easily as other general rules of law, namely the statutes, i.e. in the fact that a change of this norm necessitates observance of a special, more difficult form, the constitutional form (heightened majority, repeated decision, special constituent assembly, etc.), which differs from the ordinary form of statute. One would think that constitutional monarchy, in particular, should have been the ground on which the problem of the constitutionality of statute, and thus of the guarantees of the constitution, ought to have made itself felt with the greatest imaginable energy. The case was precisely the opposite! The constitutionalist doctrine veiled the legal shift so threatening to the position of power of the monarchies. In contradiction to the legal reality of the constitution, it presented the monarch as the unique or decisive factor of legislation, by declaring statute to be the sole will of the monarch, and by portraying the function of parliament as that of a mere 'assent' – more or less marginal, inessential, and inferior. To give an example of the method that was employed here: the well-known 'monarchical principle',* which is not deduced from the positive constitution, but imposed on it from the outside, as it were, in order to interpret it in a particular political light, or more correctly in order to reinterpret the positive law with the help of an ideology alien to it; or the famous distinction between the statutory command, which issues solely from the monarch, and the content of statute, which is agreed upon between the monarch and the representatives of the people. The fruit of this method: that it is no longer considered to be a technical imperfection, but rather seen as its deeper meaning, that a statute is to be regarded as valid once it appears in the official gazette, with the signature of monarch, and irrespective of whether the prescriptions relating to the involvement of parliament in legislative decision-taking [**1489**] are satisfied or not. The decisive progress from absolute to constitutional monarchy is thus, at least in theory, almost completely nullified; at any rate, the problem of the constitutionality of statutes and of its guarantees is altogether avoided. The unconstitutionality of a statute signed by the monarch, or even its nullification on grounds of unconstitutionality, cannot even penetrate into juristic consciousness as a practical legal question. What is more, the constitutionalist doctrine – based less on the letter of the constitution than on its aforementioned ideology – claims for the monarch not only the sanction of legislative decisions but also, with it and in it, the exclusive right to promulgate statutes. In signing the decision of parliament, the monarch is to confirm the constitutionality of the process by which the statute came about. According to this doctrine, then, there is at least one part of the process of legislation that is protected by a kind of guarantee. However, the function of control is claimed precisely by the one power that is itself most in need of being controlled. Admittedly, the act of the monarch is put under responsibility, by virtue of the requirement of ministerial countersignature. But ministerial responsibility,* insofar as it is directed against acts of the monarch, is without practical significance in a constitutional monarchy. And it is altogether irrelevant where defects of the process of legislation must be attributed to parliament, since it can only be enforced by parliament itself.

The view, still widely accepted today, and still defended with the greatest diversity of arguments, that any scrutiny of the constitutionality of statutes must remain off-limits to the organs tasked with the application of law, that the courts may at most claim the right to inquire whether a statute has been duly published, that the constitutionality of the genesis of a statute is sufficiently guaranteed by the right of promulgation of the head of state, as well as the realization of this legal-political view in the positive law of the constitutions of the republics of today, all this derives not least from the theory of constitutional monarchy, whose political ideas, more or less consciously, still influenced the design of modern democracies.

II The concept of constitution

If the question is to be answered whether and in what way the constitution can be guaranteed, i.e. whether and how it is possible to ensure the legality of the levels of legal order that stand directly below the constitution and are immediately related to it, then it is necessary, above all, to gain a clear concept of the constitution.* And it is precisely the insight developed here – that the structure of legal order is hierarchical – which is alone capable of fulfilling this task. We do not go too far if we claim that the immanent meaning, the meaning that was from the beginning intended by the fundamental concept of constitution, as it was already in use in the legal and political theory of antiquity, [**1490**] is accessible only if one starts out from the theory of legal hierarchy, since the idea of a succession of steps in the creation of law is implicit in the concept of constitution.

If, peeling off the many modifications that the concept of constitution has undergone, one isolates its firm and intangible core, what results is the idea of a highest principle that determines the whole legal and political order, a principle that is decisive for the nature of the community constituted by that order. However one defines the concept of constitution, it always appears with the claim to encompass the foundation of the state, on which the rest of its order is constructed. If one looks more closely, it becomes apparent that the concept of constitution, which, in this respect, overlaps with the concept of form of government, primarily and always refers to a foundational principle in which the distribution of political power finds its legal expression. It is the rule that determines the genesis of statutes, of the general norms whose execution constitutes the activity of the organs of state, namely of the courts and administrative agencies. This – the rule for the generation of the legal norms that primarily form the order of the state, the determination of the organs and of the procedure of legislation – is the essential, original, and narrow concept of constitution. The positing of this basic rule is the indispensable condition for the genesis of the legal norms that regulate the reciprocal behaviour of the human beings that form the community of the state, as well as for the genesis of those legal norms that determine the organs and procedures that are necessary for the application and the enforcement of those rules. The idea that the basic rule of the constitution forms the foundation of all order of the state, and that it is therefore to be as firm and unchanging as possible, leads to the view that it is necessary to differentiate between constitutional norms and statutory norms; the former are not to be as easily changeable as the latter. This gives rise to the concept of constitutional form, as distinct from the ordinary form of statute: the procedure of constitutional legislation (or constitutional amendment) that differs from the ordinary procedure of legislation, insofar as it is tied to special, inhibiting conditions. In the ideal case, this specific form is restricted to the constitution in the narrower and essential sense, with the result that – as we tend to say, though not very felicitously – the constitutional in the material sense, and only the constitution in the material sense, is also the constitution in the formal sense.*

Once positive law provides for a specific constitutional form that differs from the form of ordinary statute, nothing stands in the way of using this form also for norms that do not fall under the concept of constitution in the narrow sense; first and foremost, for norms that do not determine the mode of creation but the content of statutory norms. In this way, a concept of constitution in a wider sense comes into existence. This wider concept is in play when modern constitutions contain not merely norms that concern the organs and the procedure of legislation, but also a catalogue of basic rights and rights of freedom. The primary, though perhaps not the exclusive purpose of such a catalogue is to put up basic principles, guidelines, and limitations for the content of statutes to be enacted in the future. If the equality [**1491**] of citizens before the law, the freedom of the expression of opinion, the freedom of religion and of conscience, and the inviolability of property are enacted in the typical form – the form of a constitutional guarantee of the subjective rights of subjects to equality, freedom, property, etc. – this means, above all, that the constitution determines that statutes must not merely come about in the prescribed way, but, in addition, must not have a content that violates equality, freedom, property, etc. The constitution, in that case, does not merely have the character of a law of process or procedure, but also the character of material law. The unconstitutionality of a statute can consist not only in the fact that the procedure by which the law came about was defective, but also in the fact that the content of the statute contradicts the basic principles or guidelines laid down in the constitution, or that it exceeds the limitations imposed by it. If one wants to distinguish, in consideration of this point, between the material and the formal unconstitutionality of a statute, one should be mindful that this is permissible only with the qualification that any material unconstitutionality is also a formal unconstitutionality, insofar as a statute that, by virtue of its content, comes into conflict with the relevant provisions contained in the constitution will lose the defect of unconstitutionality once it is enacted as a constitutional statute.* The issue, hence, always reduces to whether a norm has been enacted in the form of an ordinary statute or in constitutional form. Of course, if there is no differentiation, in positive law, between constitutional form and statutory form, only the observance of the latter can ever be at issue. And in that case, the proclamation of basic principles, guidelines, or limitations for the content of law will be meaningless from the legal-technical point of view; it will be no more than a misleading appearance created for political ends. Such is the case with freedoms that are guaranteed in specific constitutional form as soon as the constitution, as is often the case, authorizes the ordinary legislator to restrict these freedoms.*

The constitutional provisions that relate to the procedure of legislation, as well as those that put up basic principles for the content of statutory law, can only concretize themselves in statutes. Guarantees of the constitution are therefore – given this scope of the constitution – nothing but means for the prevention of unconstitutional statutes. However, as soon as the concept of constitution – through the mediation of the idea of constitutional form – is extended to objects other than the procedure of legislation and the basic determination of the content of statutory law, there is a possibility for the constitution to concretize itself in forms of law other than statute; in particular in decrees, and even in individual legal acts. The content of the constitution can make the level of statute superfluous, just as the statute may be drawn up in such a way that it does not stand in need of a decree in order to be applied through individual adjudicative or administrative acts. A constitution could determine, for example, that general legal norms may, under certain determinate conditions, be enacted not through a decision of parliament but rather through an act of government, as in the case of the so-called 'emergency-decrees', which stand immediately below the constitution, alongside statutes, replacing or modifying the latter, and are endowed with the same legal force. [**1492**] Hence, such decrees are immediately related to the constitution (by contrast to decrees that merely execute a statute), and they can therefore be directly unconstitutional, just like statutes, so that the guarantee of constitutionality has to direct itself against them as much as against unconstitutional statutes. Nothing, moreover, rules out the possibility that norms are enacted in constitutional form that are not just basic principles, guidelines, or limitations for the future content of law which can be concretized only by a corresponding statute. It is possible for norms enacted in constitutional form to regulate a subject matter so comprehensively that they can be immediately applied to concrete cases, through acts of adjudication and in particular through administrative acts. Such is the case if the constitution in this extended sense determines how certain of the highest organs of the executive, the head of state, ministers, or the members of the highest courts, etc., are to be selected, and does it in such a way that the creation of these organs can proceed without any further norms (statutes or decrees) that explicate the constitutional provisions in more detail, so that the constitution is immediately executed in the act of appointment, be it a nomination, an election, or a selection by lot. These subjects indeed appear to have been admitted into the concept of constitution typically used by legal theory. One traditionally understands by a constitution (in the material sense) not just the norms concerning the organs and the procedure of legislation, but also those which concern the position of the highest executive organs, and in addition those that determine the basic nature of the relationship of subjects to the authority of the state or, in other words, the catalogue of basic rights and rights of freedom, a catalogue that, to put the matter in juristically correct form, amounts to certain basic principles, guidelines, and limitations for the content of statutes. The practice of modern states, whose constitutional charters, as a rule, exhibit these three elements, typically conforms to this understanding of constitution. If this is the case, not only general norms, like statutes or decrees, but individual acts as well can have the character of being immediate to the constitution, and may therefore turn out to be immediately unconstitutional. The class of individual acts that are immediate to the constitution can, of course, be extended as far as we please, as long as legal norms directly applicable to the concrete case are – for one political motive or another – clothed in constitutional form; so, for instance, if the legal norms that govern the law of associations, or those that regulate the position of religious denominations, are enacted as constitutional statutes. Despite the fact that a guarantee of the legality of acts that execute such statutes formally exhibits the character of a guarantee of the constitution, it is nevertheless evident that the specific form of guarantee of the constitution whose legal-technical design is to be presented in what follows, namely constitutional adjudication, will not easily find a place here. The concept of constitution has now been extended too far beyond its original scope that we derived from the theory of legal hierarchy. The individual character of the unconstitutional act would give rise to an open competition of constitutional adjudication with the administrative courts, which form part of a system of measures that is to guarantee the conformity of execution, and in particular of administration, with statute.

In all cases discussed thus far, we dealt exclusively with acts immediate to the constitution, and therefore with cases of immediate and direct [**1493**] unconstitutionality. There is a clear contrast between such acts and acts that are not immediate to the constitution, and that can therefore only be mediately or indirectly unconstitutional. If the constitution explicitly lays down, in general terms, the principle of the legality of execution, and especially if it raises the demand for a conformity of decrees with statute, the legality of execution will at the same time – indirectly – constitute a form of constitutionality, and vice versa. Let me highlight in particular, because we are dealing with general norms, the decree that executes a statute. The aim to secure the legality of such a decree, for reasons to be discussed later on, can still be included in the tasks of constitutional adjudication. Apart from this, it should be noted that direct and indirect unconstitutionality cannot always be sharply separated from one another, for the reason that there may occur mixed or transitional forms between both types: for example, if the constitution immediately authorizes all or some organs of administration to enact decrees within their sphere of responsibility, in the course of the concrete implementation of the statutes that they are to apply. The administrative organs, in that case, have the authority to enact such decrees of implementation directly from the constitution. That they are at all permitted to enact decrees directly results from the constitution. However, what they have to decree, i.e. the content of their decrees, is determined by the statutes that stand between the constitution and the decrees through which they are implemented. (It probably does not have to be especially emphasized that these decrees of implementation – especially with regard to their proximity to the constitution – differ from the aforementioned decrees which replace or change statutory norms. The latter are immediate to the constitution and can only be unconstitutional, but cannot violate a statute.) A different case: if the constitution posits basic principles, guidelines, or limitations concerning the content of statutes to be enacted in the future, for example in the form of the aforementioned catalogue of basic rights and rights to freedom, then it will be possible for administrative acts to be unconstitutional in a different sense than the indirect one according to which every administrative act that violates a statute is unconstitutional. If the constitution, for instance, determines that an expropriation may only take place in return for complete compensation, and if an expropriation takes place, in a concrete case, pursuant to a statute of expropriation that conforms to the constitution in demanding full compensation, but in violation of the statute's as well as the constitution's determinations concerning compensation, the relevant administrative act will not merely be unconstitutional in the normal, indirect sense, namely as violating a statutory norm. The administrative act in question violates not only a statute, and thus the general constitutional principle of the legality of administration, but also a special principle explicitly enshrined in the constitution: the demand for full compensation in cases of expropriation. The act, hence, oversteps a special limit that the constitution itself imposes on legislation. It would therefore make sense to mobilize an institution that serves to guarantee the constitution as well against unlawful acts of this kind.

The constitutional principle of the legality of execution does not merely demand that every executive act must be in conformity with statute. Above all, it implies that [**1494**] an act of execution may only take place pursuant to a statute, only as authorized by statute, and thus never without a statutory basis. Hence, if a public authority, a court or an administrative agency, posits an act without any statutory basis, the act in question is not really in violation of a statute, as there is no statute, after all, that could be used to check the act's conformity with statute. Rather, the act is lawless and thus immediately unconstitutional. It makes no difference here whether the lawless act in question does not even appeal to a statute or whether the appeal is evidently made in bad faith, as for instance in a case where an administrative agency expropriates an urban apartment building pursuant to a law that authorizes the expropriation of agricultural property for the purpose of a land reform. Though this case clearly differs from the case we mentioned earlier of an expropriation that, in violation of statute, takes place without full compensation, one must not overlook that the distinction between acts that are altogether lawless, and thus immediately unconstitutional, and acts that violate a statute, and are thus only mediately unconstitutional, is not, in general, a sharp one.

International treaties – in addition to statutes, certain kinds of administrative decrees, and particular acts of execution – are to be regarded, in particular, among the legal phenomena that are immediate to the constitution. As a rule, constitutions contain prescriptions concerning the creation of international treaties. They authorize the head of state to sign treaties, grant to parliament the right to consent, be it to all or only to some international treaties, prescribe the transformation of international treaties into the form of statute as a condition of domestic validity, and so forth. Since the basic principles of the constitution that determine the content of statutes also apply to the content of international treaties, or at least can be made to apply to treaties (it is also conceivable that treaties might be exempted by positive law from the demand for conformity with these determinations of the constitution, so that the latter would apply only to legislation) international treaties must be regarded as being in the same position as statutes, as far as their relationship to the constitution is concerned. They can be immediately unconstitutional both formally – with respect to the way in which they come about – and materially – with respect to their content. It does not matter here whether the treaty in question has a general or an individual character.

However, the position of the international treaty cannot be determined in a completely unambiguous way, from the point of view of the hierarchy of legal order. The conception of a treaty as a method of the will-formation of the state that is determined by the state's constitution, and immediately subject to the latter, proceeds from a standpoint that regards the constitution as the highest level of legal hierarchy, from a standpoint that one might describe as that of the primacy of an individual state's legal order.* If one elevates oneself above this point of view, if one assumes the validity of an international law that stands above the legal orders of the particular states or, in other words, the primacy of international legal order, the international treaty will appear as a partial legal order that stands above the contracting states, and that is created, in accordance with a legal norm of international law, by a specific organ [**1495**] of the international legal community, an organ which is composed of the representatives of the contracting states. To determine the mode of appointment of the partial organ (head of state, foreign minister, parliament, etc.) that functions as a member of the complete, international organ that enacts the treaty-based order, international law refers to the respective national legal orders or their constitutions. From this point of view we must conclude that the treaty takes precedence over national statute, and even over the national constitution, insofar as neither an ordinary statute nor a constitutional amendment can derogate from an international treaty, whereas the reverse is possible. An international treaty can – according to the principles of international law – lose its validity only through another international treaty or other matters of fact that are specially qualified as having that legal consequence by international law; but not through a unilateral act of one of the contracting parties, i.e. not through a national statute. If a national law, and be it a constitutional amendment, comes to contradict an international treaty, it is a legally defective law, and perhaps a legally defective constitutional law, as it fails to conform to international law. Such a law immediately violates the international treaty, and mediately the legal rule of contract, the rule of international law: *pacta sunt servanda*. Of course, statutes are not the only acts of state that may be in violation of international law. Other acts of state can be as well, and this not only by virtue of violating the principle of contract, mediately or immediately, but also by virtue of violating other rules of general international law. If one accepts, for instance, that it is a norm of international law that foreigners may be expropriated only in return for full compensation, any national constitution, any national statute, any national administrative act, or any national judicial decision that expropriates a foreigner without compensation is in violation of international law. We must observe, however, that international law itself does not provide for a sanction of annulment of legal acts of individual states that violate international law. International law has not yet developed a procedure through which such legally defective acts can be annulled by an international forum. If they are not quashed in a domestic legal procedure, they will retain their validity. The only available sanction under international law, in the last instance, is war against the state that refuses to remove its act in violation of international law. This, however, does not change the fact that international law – once we presuppose its primacy – is capable of providing a standard of the legality of all national legal acts, the highest, the constitution, included.

III The guarantees of legality

Now that the concept of constitution and thus the nature of constitutionality and unconstitutionality have been sufficiently clarified, we can examine the question of what guarantees are available for the protection of the constitution. These are the general guarantees that modern legal technique has developed with a view to the legality of acts of state in general. [**1496**] They are of a preventative or a repressive and of a personal or a material nature.

The guarantees of a preventative nature want to prevent the occurrence, from the beginning, of legally defective acts; those of a repressive nature want to react against the legally defective act that has already taken place, to prevent its future repetition, to make good the damage that it caused, to remove the legally defective act, and perhaps to replace it with a lawful act. It is possible for both of these moments to combine in one and the same protective measure. One of the possible preventative guarantees, whose number is of course very large, which is of special relevance in the present context, is the organization of the law-making public institution as a court; that is, the independence of the institution, which is guaranteed in a specific form (through protection against dismissal or transfer to another position), and which consists in the fact that the organ, in the exercise of its function, cannot be legally obligated by any individual norm (command) issued by another organ, and in particular not by the norms of any organ otherwise superior, or by those of an organ that belongs to another branch of public administration. It follows from this that the judicial organ is bound only to general norms, and, above all, only to statutes and to decrees that have a statutory basis. (The review of statutes and decrees that is granted to courts is another issue.) The idea, still frequently encountered, that it is only the legality of adjudication that can be guaranteed in this way rests on the mistaken assumption that there is some sort of essential difference between adjudication and administration, from a juristic, legal-theoretical, or legal-technical point of view. However, such a difference between adjudication and administration – or, for that matter, between execution and legislation – is not to be found, in particular with regard to the relation to the respective higher-level norm, which is decisive as far as the demand for the legality of the function is concerned. The difference between adjudication and administration consists exclusively in the organizational position of courts. The proof for this claim: the system of administrative adjudication, which either consists in the fact that acts of administration – that is, acts that would normally be performed by administrative agencies – are performed by courts, i.e. by organs that are organized as courts, or else in the fact that these acts, after they have been set by an administrative agency, are reviewed for their legality by a court, and are invalidated in case of legal defectiveness, and in some cases even reformed, i.e. replaced with a lawful act. The whole traditional opposition of jurisdiction and administration, and the whole dualism of the state's apparatus of organs based on it, i.e. of the state's apparatus of organs of execution, can only be explained historically, and it will – unless all symptoms mislead, symptoms that already indicate a growing similarity between judicial and administrative organs – disappear in the course of future development. And it also can only be explained historically why we regard the independence of an organ from the individual norm of another as a guarantee of the legality of the former's function.

The organization of the law-making organ as a court is not only the characteristic preventative guarantee of the legality of the act to be enacted, but also the first in [**1497**] the group of what we have called personal guarantees. The others are the responsibility under criminal or disciplinary law and the civil liability of the organ that enacted the legally defective act. The material guarantees which exhibit, at the same time, a clearly accentuated repressive character, are the nullity or the annullability of the legally defective act.*

Nullity means that an act that claims to be a legal act – i.e. an act whose subjective meaning it is to be a legal act, and in particular an act of state – objectively fails to be such, for the reason that it is legally defective because it does not conform to the conditions that a higher-level legal norm prescribes for it. An act that is null lacks any legal character from the beginning, so that there is no need for another legal act to strip it of its pretended legal quality. If such a second legal act is required, we are faced with annullability, and not with nullity. If faced with an act that is null, everyone, a public organ as much as an ordinary subject, is entitled to inquire into the act's legality, to recognize it as legally defective, and accordingly to treat it as invalid and non-binding. Only where the positive legal order restricts the power to inquire into the legality of any act that carries the subjective meaning of a legal act, by reserving this power, under certain determinate conditions, to specific authorities, as opposed to leaving it to everyone under all circumstances, can an act that exhibits some defect of legality be regarded as merely annullable, and not as already null *a priori*. In the absence of such a restriction, every act that exhibits some legal defect would have to be regarded as null, i.e. as a non-legal act. As a matter of fact, positive legal orders contain very far-reaching restrictions of the competence – which originally pertains to everyone – to treat legally defective acts as null. In general, private legal acts and legal acts set by public institutions are treated differently in this respect. By and large, there is a tendency to treat a legal act that has been set by a public institution as valid and binding, even if it is legally defective, for as long as it has not been removed by another legal act of a public institution. The question whether a legal act set by a public authority is legally defective or not is not to be decided, without further ado, by the subject or by the public institution to which this act, demanding obedience, is directed. Rather, it is to be decided by the institution itself that enacted the act the legality of which is impugned, or else by another public institution whose decision can be brought about by going through some specified procedure. This principle, which is by and large accepted by the positive legal order, and that one might call the principle of the self-legitimation of the acts of public authorities, is subject to certain limits. No positive legal order can determine that absolutely every act that claims to be a legal act proceeding from a public authority is to be regarded as such as long as it has not been invalidated, due to legal defectiveness, by another act of public authority. If such an act was posited by a human being who in no way possesses the quality of a public authority, it would evidently be meaningless to have to initiate a procedure with a public authority [**1498**] in order to bring about the annulment of the act. On the other hand, it is equally impossible to regard every act posited by a public authority that lacks competence or that is not properly constituted, or every act enacted through a defective procedure, as *a priori* null. Though the problem of absolute nullity is a very difficult one from the legal-theoretical and the legal-technical point of view, it is of interest to the question of guarantees of constitutionality only insofar as it must be stated that the possibility of nullity, which can never be altogether excluded by positive law, also applies to those acts that are immediate to the constitution, and that the possibility of the nullity of these acts, in a certain sense, represents a guarantee of the constitution. Not every act that describes itself as a statute has to be regarded as a statute by subjects or by law-applying public institutions. There can, without a doubt, be acts that merely have the appearance of a statute. But if we ask for the boundary that separates the enactment of a rule that merely appears to be a statute, and which is *a priori* null, from a defective but valid legislative act, i.e. from a statute that fails to conform to the constitution, legal theory is incapable of answering the question with a general formula. The positive legal order alone could undertake this task, but, of course, it usually refuses to do so, or does not do so in a conscious and precise way. It usually leaves the answer to this question to the public authority that must decide in case someone has refused, as a subject or organ of state, to pay obedience to the act that is under consideration, claiming that it merely appears to be a statute but isn't. At that point, however, the act in question already moves from the sphere of absolute nullity into the sphere of mere annullability, since the decision of the competent public authority that the act to which obedience was refused was not a legal act can only be regarded as an annulment of the act, with effectiveness *ex tunc*.* Things are no different in cases where the positive legal order lays down the minimum conditions that must be satisfied in order for the legal act not to be null *a priori*; for instance, where the constitution determines that everything that is promulgated as a statute in the official gazette must be regarded as a statute, notwithstanding other legal defects, as long as it is not annulled by the authority empowered to do so. After all, the determination of the question whether the minimal condition is satisfied or not must, at the end of the day, be made by the competent public authority, and authentically, since it would otherwise be possible for everyone to withdraw from obedience to every statute on the basis of the mere claim that the minimal condition is unfulfilled. From the point of view of the positive law, the position of someone to whom an act addresses itself, demanding obedience, is invariably this: he can, if he takes an act to be null, refuse to pay obedience, but he does so at his own risk, i.e. under the threat that he will be made responsible for disobedience, and that the public authority in front of which he is made responsible will not judge the act to be null, but will declare the minimal conditions prescribed by the positive legal order for the validity of the act to be satisfied, regardless of the possibility of later annulment. If, on the other hand, the authority in question assumes the minimal condition not to be satisfied, then its decision amounts to the annulment of the act with retroactive effect extending back to the time of its enactment. This interpretation is mandated by the fact that the [**1499**] decision is the outcome of a procedure, a procedure which judges the nullity of the act – a nullity at first only claimed by the party accused of disobedience – so that the nullity cannot at all be regarded as given in advance of the conclusion of the procedure, since there is still a possibility that the procedure might lead to a decision that denies the nullity of the act, and since the decision must necessarily have a constitutive character, even if, in its wording, it pronounces the nullity of the act. From the point of view of positive law – that is, from the point of view of the public authority that decides on the act that is allegedly null – the question is therefore only ever one of annullability; and only in the sense that the fact of nullity can be represented as a limiting case of annullability (annulment with retroactive effect).

The annullability of a legally defective act signifies the possibility of removing it, together with its legal effects. An annulment can exhibit several different degrees, and this with respect to its material as well as with respect to its temporal extension. With respect to the first aspect, there are the following possibilities: the annulment (cassation) of the legally defective act remains restricted to a concrete case. If the act in question is an individual act, this restriction will of course apply automatically. Things are different if we are faced with a general norm. The cassation of a general norm remains restricted to a concrete case if the legal order determines that the public authority (court or administrative institution) which is to apply the norm is entitled or obliged to refuse application in the concrete case, should it judge the norm to be legally defective, and that it is thus to decide or to decree, in the concrete case at hand, as though the general norm that it judges to be legally defective did not exist. Apart from this, however, the general norm remains valid and is to be applied in other cases by other public institutions, if these are either not authorized to investigate into and to decide on the legality of a norm they are to apply, or if they, though authorized to do so, hold the norm to be legal. Since the public authority which is called upon to apply the general norm can remove the norm's validity for the concrete case through its judgment of legal defectiveness, it has the power to annul the general norm, as the removal of the validity of a norm and its cassation are one and the same thing. It is only that the cassation is a partial one that is restricted to the individual case. This, in effect, is the position which courts (but not administrative agencies), under many modern constitutions, hold towards administrative decrees, and in some states (for example in the United States of America) also towards statutes. However, such a far-reaching authority of the courts towards statutes is by no means the rule. In most cases, courts are not permitted to engage in a comprehensive review of the legality – that is, of the constitutionality – of statutes. As a rule, their power of review is fairly restricted. The courts are permitted only to inquire into the proper promulgation of a statute and may, accordingly, refuse to apply it to a concrete case only on the ground of a legal defect in its promulgation. [**1500**]

The shortcomings and the insufficiency of a cassation of legally defective norms that remains restricted to the individual case are self-evident. It is above all the lack of consistency and the lack of legal security that results from it that make themselves felt very uncomfortably, if the one court refuses to apply a decree or even a statute as legally defective, whereas another court does the opposite, while administrative institutions – if they are also tasked with the application of the same decree or statute – are in no way permitted to refuse to do so. A centralization of the competence to review the legality of general norms is surely justifiable in every respect.

Should one decide to transfer the power of review to one single public authority, it will likewise become possible to extend the cassation beyond the individual case. We would then be faced with the annulment of a general norm as a whole, i.e. for all possible cases to which the norm, according to its meaning, would have to be applied. That such a far-reaching power can only be vested in a supreme and central authority should be self-evident.

With respect to the temporal dimension, the effect of a cassation can be restricted to the future, or it may extend to the past. In other words, the annulment of the legally defective act may take place with or without retroactive effect. This differentiation, of course, is meaningful only with regard to acts that have a lasting legal effect; it is therefore relevant, above all, with reference to the cassation of general norms. Out of consideration for the ideal of legal security, one should, in general, make the cassation of a general legal norm on the ground of legal defectiveness effective only *pro futuro*, i.e. starting from the time of the cassation. Here, one even has to take into account the option of letting the cassation take effect at a later point in time. Just as the coming into effect of a general legal norm, such as a statute or a decree, is preceded, for good reason, by a *vacatio legis*, it might appear desirable, for analogous reasons, to let a general norm lose its validity only after the expiry of a certain period of time from the decision to annul. Circumstances can, nevertheless, make it necessary for the cassation of a general norm to have retroactive effect. In this context we have to think not only of the extreme case, already mentioned above, of the unrestricted retroactive effect in cases where the annulment of an act is an acknowledgement of its nullity, and where the legally defective act must be recognized, according to the free discretion of the authority empowered to annul, or according to the minimal conditions for the validity of the act prescribed by positive law, as a mere appearance of a legal act. Above all, we here have to consider the possibility of restricting the retroactive effect of an annulment that, in principle, is effective only *pro futuro* to certain individual cases or to a specific category of cases, i.e. to provide for a limited retroactive effect of the annulment; a question to which we will have to return in a later context. [**1501**]

For the legal-technical implementation of the annulment of an act it is of importance, moreover, whether the cassation can only be performed by the organ that posited the legally defective act, or whether another organ is empowered to do so. Considerations of prestige, in particular, lead to the choice of the first of these two modalities. One is concerned to avoid the danger that the authority of the public institution that enacted the legally defective norm, and that is regarded as a highest organ, or that enacted the norm under the supervision and responsibility of a highest organ (especially if the norm at hand is a general norm), will suffer, by virtue of the fact that some other institution appears to have the power to annul its acts, and thus to put itself above it, though it is supposedly to be regarded as the 'highest'. Appeal is made not only to the 'sovereignty' of the organ that posited the legally defective act, but also to the dogma of the 'separation of powers', in order to avoid the cassation of the act of the one public authority by that of another. This argument is invoked especially in cases that concern acts of the highest administrative institutions, where the authority empowered to annul would therefore have to stand outside of the administrative organization of the state and would, with respect to its function as well as with respect to its position, have to have the character of an independent judicial authority or, in other words, of a court. Given the more than doubtful character of the distinction between jurisdiction and administration, the reference to the 'separation of powers' is as unsound, in this context, as the appeal to the 'sovereignty' of an organ. Both arguments, however, play a special role when it comes to the question of guarantees of constitutionality. Under the pretext that the 'sovereignty' of the organ that enacted the legally defective act or the 'separation of powers' are to be preserved, one leaves the annulment of the legally defective act to the discretion of the enacting organ itself and permits nothing more than a non-binding petition for annulment on the part of the affected party (the so-called 'representation'). Or else, there is a regular procedure that is supposed to lead to the annulment of the legally defective act by its author, but the motion that initiates the procedure obliges the authority only to go through the procedure, but not to end it in a certain way, namely with the cassation of the impugned act. The cassation thus remains subject to the discretion of the organ that enacted the legally defective act, a discretion which, though bound by statute, is not controlled by any higher organ. Finally, a third case should be mentioned, though it already forms the transition to the second type of guarantee presented here: Another institution is empowered to decide on the question of the legality of the act, but the cassation of the legally defective act nevertheless remains reserved to the organ that enacted the act. The latter organ, however, may be put under a legal obligation, as a result of the finding of the former, to annul the act that has been judged to be legally defective. The fulfilment of this duty may even be subject to a deadline. That this modification is equally incapable of offering a sufficient guarantee hardly requires any further proof. A sufficient guarantee is given only if the cassation of the legally defective act is to be performed directly by an organ that is altogether distinct from and independent of the organ that enacted the legally defective act. [**1502**] If one holds on to the typical division of the functions of state into legislation, jurisdiction (judicature), and administration, as well as to the consequent classification of the organism of the institutions of the state into three groups of organs – one legislative, one jurisdictional (or judicative), and one administrative branch – one must distinguish whether the cassation of the legally defective act remains within the same branch of public authority; whether, for instance, an act of administration or a judicial decision will, in turn, be annulled only by another act of administration or jurisdiction, i.e. through the act of an authority that belongs to the same group of organs, a higher administrative organ in the one case, a higher court in the other, or whether the authority empowered to annul belongs to another group of organs. The guarantee of the legality of acts of state that consists in the possibility of going through successive stages of appeal within one branch of public authority belongs to the first of these types; a system of administrative justice is an instance of the second. It is characteristic for modern legal orders that the legality of the acts of courts is guaranteed, almost without exception, through means of the first type alone. It is widely believed that the so-called independence of the courts is already by itself a guarantee of the legality of the decision that is to be taken.

The cassation of a legally defective act gives rise to the question of its replacement with an act that is lawful. In this regard, we have to distinguish, from a technical point of view, between two possibilities. The public authority empowered to annul the legally defective act may also possess the competence to put a lawful act in the place of the impugned and defective act. It may have the competence, in other words, not just to annul, but also to reform. But it is also possible to leave the enactment of a lawful act to the public authority whose legally defective act was annulled. If the latter authority, in doing so, is bound by legal opinion articulated in the findings of the authority empowered to annul – for instance in the form of reasons of decision – its own independence is thereby restricted; which, in the case of the annulment of a judicial decision, is not without significance for the assessment of the independence of judges as a specific guarantee of the legality of execution.

IV The guarantees of constitutionality

Of the legal-technical measures that serve the purpose of ensuring the legality of the functions of the state which have been presented in the preceding pages, one above all is to be regarded as the most effective guarantee of the constitution: the annulment of the unconstitutional act. This is not to say that other means should not be used as well in order to secure the legality of acts standing under the constitution. Of course, the preventative, personal guarantee, namely to organize the organ enacting the act as a court, is out of the question from the start. The power of legislation, which is the most relevant here, cannot be vested in a court; not so much because of the difference in the respective functions of legislation and [**1503**] adjudication, but rather for the reason that the organization of the legislative organ is inevitably determined by considerations other than that of the constitutionality of its function. Here, the fundamental opposition between democracy and autocracy alone is decisive. The repressive guarantees of the responsibility of the organ that enacts the legally defective act, under criminal or civil law, however, may usefully be taken into consideration. Of course, insofar as we are dealing with the process of legislation, this kind of guarantee cannot be applied to the parliament as such, or to all those of its members who participated in the decision. There are several different reasons why a collegial organ is not a suitable subject of criminal or civil legal responsibility. But it is possible to make the individual organs that participate in the process of legislation, such as the head of state or the ministers, responsible for the constitutionality of a statute, the more so if the constitution determines that the head of state, or the ministers only, assume responsibility for the constitutionality of the legislative process, with their countersignature or their promulgation of the statute. It is indeed the case that the institution of ministerial responsibility, peculiar to modern constitutions, also stands in the service of the constitutionality of statute. It is self-evident that the personal responsibility of the organ can also be used in order to provide a guarantee of the legality of decrees, and in particular of the legality of individual acts that stand immediately under the constitution. In this last respect, the liability for damage caused by the legally defective act is particularly relevant. However, ministerial responsibility – as can easily be established from constitutional history – is in and of itself not a very effective means; all personal guarantees, moreover, are insufficient insofar as they leave the continuing validity of the legally defective act, and in particular also that of the unconstitutional statute, untouched. Where a legal state of affairs of this kind persists, one cannot, strictly speaking, say that the constitution is guaranteed. That is the case only once there is the possibility of annulling the unconstitutional act.

1 *The constitutional court*

In no other case of a guarantee of legality does it appear to be as natural as in the case of a guarantee of the constitution that the annulment of the legally defective act should be left to the organ itself that enacted the legally defective act. And in no other case would this modality be as inappropriate as it is precisely here. The only form in which it could still be regarded as a somewhat effective guarantee of legality – namely the determination of the legal defectiveness of the act by another organ, and an obligation, on the part of the organ that enacted the legally defective act, to annul it – is impracticable here, for the reason that parliament, by virtue of its whole nature, cannot successfully be made subject to obligations. To expect a parliament to annul a statute that it enacted, **[1504]** on the ground of a pronouncement of legal defectiveness made by another organ, would be politically naïve. For understandable reasons, the legislative organ, in reality, feels that it is nothing but the free creator of the law, and not a law-applying organ that is bound by the constitution, although that is what it is according to the idea. If legal restraints on the legislature are to become effective, one must not make the parliament itself the guarantor of this idea. An organ that is distinct from the legislator and independent of it, and thus of any other public authority, must be empowered to annul the unconstitutional acts of the legislator. This is the institution of a constitutional court. The first objection that one is understandably inclined to make against such an institution is that it is incompatible with the sovereignty of parliament or – where there is direct popular legislation – even with the sovereignty of the people. However, even leaving aside for the moment that one cannot coherently talk of the sovereignty of a single organ of state, and that sovereignty, if it exists at all, must be an attribute of the order of the state,* this whole argument must collapse as soon as one is forced to concede that the process of legislation is determined by the constitution, for the most part, in no other way than the procedures of courts and administrative agencies are determined by statutes, and that the constitution does not stand above the process of legislation in any other sense than that in which legislation stands above jurisdiction and administration, and that the demand that statutes be constitutional, therefore, does not differ, from a legal-theoretical and legal-technical point of view, from the demand that jurisdiction and administration conform to statute. If there are those who, contrary to this insight, hold on to the claim that constitutional adjudication is incompatible with the sovereignty of the legislator, then their claims simply conceal the tendency of the political power that expresses itself in the organ of legislation to reject – in flagrant contradiction to the positive law – any restriction by the norms of the constitution. One might, under certain circumstances, hold such absence of restriction to be desirable; but such a standpoint cannot be defended by juristic arguments.

Things do not look so very different when it comes to the second objection that one needs to face if one aims to defend the institution of constitutional adjudication: the appeal to the principle of the separation of powers. One should concede, at the outset, that the annulment of an act of legislation by an organ other than the legislative organ itself amounts to an interference with the legislative power, as we normally tend to put the matter. But we can see how problematic this whole argumentation is, once we consider the fact that the organ tasked with the annulment of unconstitutional statutes, even if it is referred to as a 'court', and even if, by virtue of its 'independence', it is a court from an organizational point of view, is nevertheless, as a result of its function, engaged in an activity that makes it into something more than a mere court. Insofar as it is at all possible to separate adjudication and legislation on functional grounds, the difference between the two functions is to be seen, initially, in the fact that legislation creates general norms, whereas adjudication only creates individual norms. [**1505**] The fact that even this difference is not one of principle, and that the legislator, in particular, and especially the parliament, can also posit individual norms, shall not be considered here. If a 'court' is endowed with the competence to annul a statute, it is thereby authorized to enact a general norm, since the annulment of a statute has the same general character as the enactment of a statute. The annulment, after all, is nothing but the inverse of enactment. The annulment of statutes is therefore itself a legislative function, and a court empowered to annul statutes is itself an organ of legislative power. Hence, one might as well regard the annulment of a statute by a court as a result of a transfer of legislative power to two organs, instead of portraying it as an 'interference' with the legislative power. And in the case of a transfer of legislative power to two organs, one does not always feel pressed to assert that there is a contradiction with the principle of the separation of powers. So, for instance, if the constitution of constitutional monarchies, as a rule, vests the legislative power – that is, the creation of general legal norms – in the parliament acting together with the monarch, but, for certain cases of exception, reserves to the monarch (in conjunction with his ministers) a power to enact emergency decrees that replace or that change statutes. It would take us too far afield to discuss in this context the political motives that gave rise to this whole principle of the separation of powers, although the true meaning of this principle, adapted above all to the distribution of political power in a constitutional monarchy, becomes apparent only in this way. If the principle is to make reasonable sense for a democratic republic, only one of its different meanings is relevant, the one that is better expressed in terms of a 'division' rather than a 'separation' of powers. It is the idea of a distribution of power across several different organs, not so much for the purpose of their mutual isolation, but rather for the purpose of the mutual exercise of control. And this not only with a view to preventing a concentration, dangerous to democracy, of all too great a power in one organ, but in particular to guarantee the legality of the functioning of the several organs. If the principle of the separation of powers is understood in this way, the institution of constitutional adjudication does not only fail to contradict the principle, but it represents, precisely to the contrary, a confirmation of it.

In light of this state of affairs, the question of whether an organ charged with the annulment of unconstitutional statutes can be a 'court' turns out to be altogether irrelevant. Its independence from parliament as well as from government is a self-evident requirement, since parliament and government are the very organs that, as participants in the process of legislation, are to be controlled by the constitutional court. At most, one might ask whether the fact that the annulment of statutes is itself to be regarded as a legislative function implies any special consequences for the composition and the appointment of the constitutional court. This, however, is not the case. All those political considerations [**1506**] that are determinative of the question of how the organ that forms the will of the state in the process of legislation ought to look like are not really relevant in the context of the annulment of statutes. Here, the difference between the enactment and the mere annulment of a statute makes itself felt. The annulment of a statute on the ground of its unconstitutionality is for the most part an act of the application of constitutional norms. Here, the moment of obligation is preponderant; here, the moment of free creation that is characteristic of legislation recedes very far into the background. The positive legislator, parliament, perhaps in conjunction with government, is bound by the constitution only with respect to its procedure. With respect to the content of the laws to be enacted by it, the positive legislator is bound only in exceptional cases, and only by general principles, guidelines, and the like. The negative legislator, however, the constitutional court, in the exercise of its function, is substantially determined by the constitution. And precisely in this respect its function resembles that of courts in general; it is mostly application of law, and thus it is, in this sense, true adjudication. To construct this organ we therefore need not look to principles very different from those which apply to the organization of courts or of administrative organs.

It is not possible to make a proposal, in this respect, which is equally practicable for all constitutions. The specific design of the constitutional court will have to adapt itself to the peculiarities of the respective constitution. Only this much can be noted: that, since its judicature will mostly deal with questions of law and since the court is going to have to perform the purely juristic work of constitutional interpretation, the number of its members should not be too large. Apart from that, it must suffice here to point to some particularly characteristic forms of appointment. Neither the simple election by parliament, nor an appointment by the head of state alone or by the government alone, can be fully recommended. It may be valuable to consider some combination of the two, for instance election by parliament, on the basis of a proposal of the government that names several candidates for every position to be filled, or the other way around. It is of the utmost importance that legal experts be given due consideration in the composition of the court. This could be ensured, for example, by conceding to the faculties of law, or to a joint commission of all faculties of law in the country, the right to propose candidates for at least some of the positions to be filled. It would also be effective, to this purpose, if the court itself were given the right to make a proposal for every position that is to be vacated, or the right to fill this position through election by the sitting members of the court (co-optation). The court itself has the greatest interest in strengthening its authority through the admission of outstanding experts. It is also important to exclude from membership in the constitutional court members of parliament or of government, because their acts are the acts that are to be controlled by the court. However desirable it would be to keep all party-political influences away from the judicature of the constitutional court, it is particularly difficult to achieve the realization of this postulate. One cannot close one's eyes to the fact [**1507**] that even experts – consciously or unconsciously – are motivated by political concerns. Whenever this danger is especially large, it is almost better to accept the legitimate participation of political parties in the formation of the court, instead of having to deal with non-official and uncontrollable party-political influence. This could take place, for instance, by filling a part of the seats on the court through election in parliament, and to organize this election in a way that takes account of the relative strength of the parties. If the other positions are filled with experts, the latter will have much greater freedom to give consideration to purely juristic matters, since their political conscience will then be relieved by the participation of those who are appointed to protect political interests.

2 *The object of the review exercised by the constitutional court*

(a) The object of the judicature of the constitutional court is formed primarily by those statutes which, for one reason or another, are claimed to be unconstitutional. By statutes we understand the acts of the legislative organ that are referred to as such, hence, in modern democracies, the acts of central parliaments, and in a federal state not only the federal statutes, but also the statutes of the several *Länder* or constituent states. Every act that exhibits the form of a statute ought to be subject to the review of the constitutional court; even if its content is not really a general but rather an individual norm; for example, the budget, or other acts that traditional theory is inclined, for whatever reason, to characterize as acts of administration despite their statutory form. If the legality of the latter is to be subject to some form of control, no authority other than the constitutional court is available to perform this task. Other acts of parliament that, according to the constitution, have a legally binding character of some kind, without having to take the form of statutes (for instance, because they do not need to be promulgated in the official gazette), for example parliament's autonomous order of business or the consent to the budget (in case it is not supposed to take statutory form), ought also to be reviewable for their constitutionality by the constitutional court.

Likewise, all acts that subjectively appear with the claim to be statutes, but that objectively lack that character, due to their failure to fulfil some essential requirement, ought to be made subject to constitutional review, assuming, of course, that they pass the threshold of absolute nullity, and are thus made the object of a legal procedure evaluating them. We have to add, finally, acts that, according to their subjective meaning, are not intended to be statutes, but that, according to the constitution, ought to have been statutes, and that have taken a different form in violation of the constitution, such as the form of a non-promulgated parliamentary decision or of a decree, perhaps in order to avoid the control exercised by the constitutional court. If, for example, the constitutional court was endowed only with the power to review statutes, and if the government was [**1508**] to regulate through decree a matter that, according to the constitution, can only be regulated by statute, because it is unable to get the relevant regulation enacted as a statute, then this decree, which replaces a statute in violation of the constitution, would have to be open to challenge in the constitutional court. A case where a parliament – the parliament of a constituent state of a federal system – tried to regulate a certain matter through a non-promulgated parliamentary decision, because a statute with similar content would have been annulled by the constitutional court, has in fact occurred. It must therefore be possible to challenge such acts as well in the constitutional court, if a circumvention of constitutional adjudication is to be prevented. And this principle must, in an analogous way, apply to all other objects of constitutional review.

(b) The competence of the constitutional court should not be restricted to a review of the constitutionality of statutes. As is clear from our earlier explications, all decrees that can, according to the constitution, be enacted in lieu of statutes belong to the group of acts immediate to the constitution, of acts whose legality consists solely in their constitutionality. The so-called emergency decrees, in particular, belong to this class. The fact that every violation of the constitution, in this context, constitutes a breach of the politically all-important dividing line between the government's and parliament's sphere of power, makes a control of the constitutionality of such decrees all the more necessary. The narrower the conditions the constitution imposes on the enactment of decrees of this kind, the greater is the danger of unconstitutionality in the use of these regulations, and the more necessary is constitutional adjudication. Experience attests that wherever the constitution permits the enactment of emergency decrees, the legality of such decrees, in particular cases, tends to be passionately contested, whether rightly or wrongly. The possibility of having such controversies decided by a highest authority whose objectivity is beyond doubt must be of the highest value; especially where circumstances are such that important areas of life have to be regulated by such emergency decrees.

The review of the constitutionality of decrees that replace or that modify statutes should be uncontroversial, as such decrees, with respect to their rank in the hierarchy of legal phenomena, are on a par with statutes, and are consequently sometimes called 'statutes' or decrees with 'the force of statute'. However, it is advisable to subject to the judicature of the constitutional court not just the constitutionality of such decrees, but also the constitutionality of decrees that implement statutes, i.e. of so-called decrees of execution. That these decrees are no longer acts immediate to the constitution, and that their legal defectiveness is immediately a failure to conform to statute, and only mediately unconstitutionality, is clear from our earlier discussion. If it is proposed here that constitutional adjudication should be extended to these acts, this proposal is made not so much in consideration of the relativity of the contrast of direct and indirect unconstitutionality that was established above, [**1509**] but rather with a view to the natural boundary that exists between general and individual legal acts.

In determining the competence of constitutional adjudication we must, above all, give consideration to a workable delimitation of constitutional adjudication from the system of administrative adjudication that already exists in most states. From a purely theoretical point of view, it would be possible to determine the competence of a constitutional court, in line with the concept of a constitutional guarantee, in such a way as to empower it to decide on the legality of all acts immediate to the constitution. In doing so, however, one would undoubtedly transfer to the constitutional court the jurisdiction over a number of matters that today, in many states, belong to the competence of administrative courts; for instance, when the issue is one of the legality of individual acts of administration which, for reasons that have been expounded in an earlier context, bear the character of acts immediate to the constitution. The control of a number of legal acts that typically do not belong to the jurisdiction of administrative courts today would, on the other hand, not be provided by constitutional adjudication either, if the latter was indeed restricted solely to the review of acts immediate to the constitution. The decrees of execution, in particular, give rise to this problem. If the cassation of a legally defective decree is to be possible, a constitutional court is surely the most appropriate institution to perform it. And this not only because it would, in so doing, not compete with the hitherto accustomed competence of the administrative courts, whose jurisdiction is usually restricted to the annulment of individual acts of administration, but particularly for the reason that there is an inner affinity between the decision on the constitutionality of statutes and that on the conformity of decree with statute, which results from the general character of the act that is to be reviewed. There are therefore two considerations that compete with one another in the determination of the scope of the jurisdiction of the constitutional court: the pure concept of a guarantee of the constitution, according to which all acts immediate to the constitution would have to be brought into the forum of the constitutional court, and the contrast between a general and individual act, according to which decrees, alongside laws, ought also to be subject to cassation by the constitutional court. One should, while avoiding all doctrinaire prejudice, try to combine both principles, in accordance with the needs of the concrete constitution at hand.

(c) If one includes decrees in the constitutional court's sphere of jurisdiction, certain difficulties for the delimitation of its competence are going to result, as there are several types of general norms that are not easy to distinguish from decrees. To mention a few: the general norms that are enacted in the area of municipal autonomy, either by the decisions of the municipal assembly or the municipal government; general legal transactions that become binding only as a result of an act of public authority, for instance the railway tariffs of private companies, statutes of joint stock corporations, collective agreements between employers and employees, which all [**1510**] require a ministerial permission; and so on. A wealth of intermediate forms are possible in between the general legal norm that proceeds exclusively from a public and central administrative agency – that is, the decree in the narrowest and most proper sense of the term – and a general legal transaction between private persons. Any delimitation of these two must, therefore, always have a more or less arbitrary character. With this reservation, I would advise subjecting to the review of the constitutional court only those general norms as 'decrees' that exclusively proceed from public institutions, regardless of whether the enacting authority is central or local, and regardless of whether we are dealing with organs of state in the narrower sense of the term, such as provincial or state authorities, or with municipal authorities. The municipality is only a limb of the state, and its organs are only decentralized organs of state.

(d) As has been pointed out in the foregoing, international treaties are – from the point of view of the primacy of the individual state's legal order – to be regarded as acts of state that are immediate to the constitution. They typically have general character. If their legality is to be controlled, a constitutional court is certainly an institution that is a serious candidate for this task. There are no juristic obstacles to having the constitution of a state transfer the competence to review the constitutionality of international treaties, as well as the competence to annul such treaties in case of their unconstitutionality, to the constitutional court. The arguments that would speak for such an extension of constitutional adjudication to international treaties are by no means insubstantial. Since the international treaty is a source of law on a par with statute, and in particular since treaties can derogate from statutes, the form of treaty offers an opportunity to create norms that modify statutes. That this is only to happen in a constitutional way is certainly of eminent interest; a due consideration of the principles of the constitution that determine the content of statutes and treaties is of special importance here. Likewise, there are no obstacles in international law to a control of international treaties exercised by a constitutional court. If international law, as one has to assume it does, empowers the individual states to determine, in their own constitutions, the organs that are alone capable of entering into valid international treaties, i.e. that are alone capable of binding the state as a party to the treaty, then it cannot contradict international law for a constitution to create institutions that are supposed to guarantee the proper execution of the norms, themselves permitted by international law, that concern the valid conclusion of international treaties. The legal rule that a treaty may not be annulled unilaterally by one of the two contracting states is irrelevant here, since it is subject to the self-evident presupposition that the treaty has been validly concluded. If a state wants to enter into a treaty with another state, then it has to concern itself with the latter's constitution. If a state is itself responsible for the consequences in case it entered into a treaty with an organ of the other state that is incompetent, then it must also assume responsibility if the treaty that it entered into conflicts with the partner's constitution in some other way, [**1511**] and is therefore null or annullable. Even if one was to assume that international law immediately determines the organ of state that is competent to enter into a treaty, in the person of the head of state, and that there is a rule of international law according to which no contracting state is under an obligation to accept a review of the legality of the treaty and a complete or partial annulment through some institution of the other state, this would not affect the validity of the constitutional provisions that conflict with the treaty. From the point of view of international law, a cassation of the treaty would amount to no more than a breach of the treaty, a breach that is subject, in the last instance, to the sanction of war. It is, of course, a completely different question, not a juristic, but rather a political one, whether it is in the interest of a state's capability to enter into treaties if the international treaties that it enters into are subject to the risk of annulment at the hands of a constitutional court. If one weighs the domestic political interests that speak for an extension of constitutional adjudication to international treaties against the foreign policy interests that exert pressure towards an exclusion of international treaties from constitutional adjudication, the latter may certainly, under some circumstances, outweigh the former. It would surely be useful, from a point of view that looks not merely to the interests of a particular state but to the interests of the whole community of states constituted by international law, to transfer the control of the legality of international treaties (together with the jurisdiction over their implementation) to an international institution, and to exclude as one-sided all national jurisdiction in this matter. But this is a question which is outside of the scope of this report, and perhaps also outside of the possibilities offered by the legal-technical development of contemporary international law.*

(e) Finally, in regard to the question of the extent to which individual legal acts should be subject to the jurisdiction of the constitutional court, all judicial acts are to be ruled out from the beginning. As already mentioned above, the fact that a legal act was posited by a court is commonly regarded as a guarantee of its legality that is in and of itself sufficient. That the legality of an act presents itself, mediately or immediately, as constitutionality, is in general no sufficient occasion to direct the procedure out of the sphere of ordinary adjudication and into a special constitutional court. Similarly, individual legal acts posited by administrative agencies ought not to be made subject to the jurisdiction of the constitutional court – even in cases where they are immediate to the constitution – but should, at least in principle, find the control of their legality in the sphere of administrative adjudication. This, in particular, is in the interest of a clear delimitation of the competences of constitutional and administrative adjudication, so as to prevent conflicts of competence and dual competences, the occurrence of which is not a small danger, given the highly relative nature of the contrast between direct and indirect constitutionality. This leaves only the individual legal acts that are set by parliament for constitutional adjudication. If the latter bear the form of a statute or of an international treaty, they fall [**1512**] under the competence of the constitutional court insofar as the latter is entitled to review acts with that form. But it would be possible to extend the competence of the constitutional court to such acts even if they lack the form of statute or treaty, or even immediacy to the constitution, as long as they have legally binding character, since there would otherwise be no possibility at all of a control of their legality. The number of cases that might be of concern here, by the way, should be very small. Of course, there is no harm in putting certain individual acts of the head of state or the government – so far as a legal control of these acts is at all desired – into the competence of the constitutional court, and not into that of the administrative courts, for reasons of prestige or other such considerations. Finally, it should be pointed out that it may be useful, depending on the circumstances, to transfer to the constitutional court the power to decide on the impeachment of ministers, to use it as a central institution to resolve conflicts of competence, or to give it other functions in order to alleviate the need for the creation of special courts (for instance, electoral courts). In general, it is advisable to keep the number of the highest organs tasked with adjudication as small as possible.

(f) It seems to be self-evident that only norms that are still valid at the time of the constitutional court's decision can come into consideration as an object of the judicature of the constitutional court, since a norm that has already been invalidated no longer needs to be annulled.

However, a closer inspection shows that it is possible for norms that have already been invalidated to become subject to the review of the constitutional court. If a general norm – and only such norms are at issue here – is invalidated without any retroactive effect of the invalidating norm, the annulled norm must still be applied by public institutions, even after its annulment, to all the facts that took place while the annulled norm was in force. If such application is not to take place, due to the unconstitutionality of the annulled norm – it is presupposed here that the norm in question was not annulled by the constitutional court – then an authentic determination of this unconstitutionality and an annulment of the last remainder of the validity of the norm that has been invalidated only *pro futuro* is still needed. This can happen only through a judgment of the constitutional court.

The cassation of an unconstitutional norm by a constitutional court – and here we intend to refer primarily to general norms – is needed, strictly speaking, only if the unconstitutional norm is younger than the constitution. If it is not the younger statute (the younger general norm) that puts itself in opposition to the older constitution, but rather the younger constitution that puts itself in opposition to an older statute, the constitution, according to the principle *lex posterior*, derogates from the statute; a cassation of the statute therefore appears to be superfluous, and even logically impossible. This means that the law-applying public authorities, the courts as well as administrative agencies, in the absence of any restriction introduced by positive law, have to assess whether there is a contradiction between [**1513**] the younger constitution and the older statute, and to decide according to the outcome of their inquiry. The situation of public authorities, in particular of administrative agencies, to whom the constitution typically denies any opportunity to undertake a review of statutes, is, in this case, a rather unusual one. And this is particularly the case in a period of constitutional changes, especially in a period of changes of such a fundamental nature as have occurred in a number of states after the Great War. The constitutions of the new states that came into being after the war, in particular, for the most part incorporated the old material law – civil law, criminal law, and administrative law – that used to be in force in their territory, but subject to the proviso that it must not stand in contradiction with the new constitution. Since the incorporated law often consists of very old statutes that came into being while completely different constitutions were in force, the possibility of a contradiction of these statutes with the new constitution is far from negligible. Of course, this problem tends not to arise with respect to the constitution in the narrowest sense of the term.

The way in which the older statutes were created is no longer at issue, only that of how they can be changed. However, conflict is possible, to a high degree, with respect to those principles of the younger constitution that determine the permissible content of statutes. If the new constitution determines, for instance, that there must not be any privileges based on gender, and if this provision cannot be interpreted so as to apply only to statutes to be enacted in the future, but not to the older statutes incorporated by the new constitution, and if one has to assume that the constitution intends an immediate derogation of conflicting older statutes which does not require the enactment of new statutes that change the old, then the question of the compatibility of old laws with the new constitution may turn out to be juristically very difficult and politically highly significant. It would appear to be problematic to leave the decision, in that case, to the perhaps very unstable legal opinion of a multitude of law-applying authorities. It is therefore certainly a good idea to consider whether the review of the compatibility with the constitution of older statutes not explicitly annulled by the constitution should be taken away from the ordinary law-applying organs and be transferred to a central constitutional court. This means nothing other than depriving the new constitution of its power to derogate from older statutes that it incorporated, permitted, and did not explicitly annul, and to replace it with a power of annulment vested in a constitutional court.

3 *The standard of the review exercised by the constitutional court*

After the question of the object of the judicature of the constitutional court, i.e. of what legal acts the constitutional court ought to be made competent to review, we must also raise the question of the standard according to which this review is to take place, of what norms the constitutional court is to rely on to take its decisions. This question can already be answered, for the larger part, by considering the object of review. It is self-evident [**1514**] that acts immediate to the constitution are to be reviewed for their constitutionality, and acts mediate to the constitution, and in particular decrees, for their conformity with statute. Put in general terms, all acts must be reviewed for their conformity with the relevant higher-level norm. It is equally self-evident that the review must make reference both to the procedure by which the act that is to be reviewed was produced, as well as to the content of the act, if higher-level norms, in addition to imposing procedural requirements, also restrict the act's permissible content.

Two points, however, stand in need of more detailed discussion. The first concerns the possibility of employing norms of international law as a standard of review. It may turn out to be the case that one of the acts that is to be reviewed for its legality neither stands in contradiction with a statute, nor with the constitution, but with an international treaty or with a rule of general international law. If an ordinary statute contradicts an older international treaty, this is to be seen as a legal defect even from the point of view of the constitution of an individual state, which, by authorizing certain organs to conclude international treaties, sets up the international treaty as a form of the will-formation of the state. According to this kind of constitution, an international treaty – and this follows from the concept of treaty that the constitution has accepted – may not be annulled or changed by an ordinary statute. A statute that conflicts with a treaty, therefore, is at least indirectly unconstitutional. The view that even a statute that amends the constitution is legally defective if it violates a treaty can only be maintained from a higher point of view than that of the domestic constitution, from a point of view that accords primacy to the order of international law. This alone is the standpoint that allows us to recognize the international treaty as part of a legal order that stands above the contracting states. And the point of view of the primacy of international law – as has been pointed out above – also entails, without further ado, that it is possible not only for the particular international law of a treaty, and thus indirectly for the rule of contract, but also for other legal norms of general international law, to be violated by legal acts of individual states, in particular by the statutes, decrees, etc. that are subject to the review of the constitutional court. Is the constitutional court, then, to have the competence to annul the acts of state subject to its power of review in case they fail to conform to international law? No serious objection can be raised against the cassation of domestic statutes that violate a treaty, at least as long as we are considering ordinary statutes (and the lower legal acts that are put on a par with the latter). Such a judicature of the constitutional court clearly remains on the ground of the constitution, which is – this must not be overlooked – also the ground of the constitutional court itself. The cassation of statutes (and of acts of state on a par with or subordinate to them) for the reason that they violate a rule of general international law is equally possible, provided that the general rules of international law – as in some recent constitutions – are explicitly recognized by the constitution (under the designation of 'generally accepted' rules of international law), i.e. that they are adopted as a part of the state's legal order. In this case, it is the will of the constitution that these norms [**1515**] of international law be respected by the legislator. A statute that fails to conform to international law is to be judged in the same way as a statute that fails to conform to the constitution. It does not matter here whether the legal norms of international law that are incorporated by the constitution are thereby endowed with the rank of constitutional statutes or not. Their incorporation, at any rate, is intended to shield them against unilateral removal by a domestic statute. The incorporation, after all, is supposed to express respect for international law, and one would express the total opposite if it was possible, in spite of the solemn incorporation, for every ordinary statute to violate international law, without therefore being regarded as legally defective, and thus open to annulment, from the point of view of the constitution that incorporates general international law.

The legal situation, however, is different if a state's constitution does not contain such a recognition of general international law. For an organ that, like a constitutional court, functions as an organ of an individual state, the ground of the validity of the norms of international law it is to employ when it reviews acts of state can only be the constitution of its own state that incorporates these norms, i.e. that validates them for the internal sphere of the individual state; the very constitution by which the constitutional court itself is appointed and through which it can, at any time, be abolished. As much as one might hope that all constitutions – following the example of the German and the Austrian – will come to incorporate the rules of general international law, in order to make possible their application by a state's constitutional court, one nevertheless has to concede that, where this is not the case, the constitutional court lacks the legal basis for declaring a statute to be in violation of international law. Even where the rules of general international law have been incorporated by the constitution, the competence of the constitutional court can be brought to an end by a constitutional amendment, in case the change of the constitution consists in a repeal of the recognition of the general rules of international law, or of the instruction to the constitutional court to apply them. In the face of other constitutional amendments, however, the power of the constitutional court to apply the rules of general international law that have been incorporated by the constitution will persist. To be sure, the factual possibility cannot be excluded that a constitutional court will apply the rules of general international law to the acts of state which it is to review even where these rules have not been incorporated by the constitution. But a constitutional court that wanted to annul a statute, in spite of the absence of an incorporation of the rules of general international law, for its violation of the latter, could juristically no longer be regarded as an organ of the state by whose constitution it was created. It would, rather, have to be regarded as an organ of a higher legal community standing above that of the state; and even this only in intention. The constitution of the international legal community does not contain any norms by which an organ of an individual state might come to be appointed to apply the rules of general international law. [**1516**]

If the possibility of the application of norms of international law by the constitutional court is thus restricted in the way just outlined, the application of norms other than legal norms, of meta-positive norms of some sort, must be regarded as out of the question. One occasionally encounters the claim that there are natural legal rules of some sort, superior to the constitution of every state, which ought to be respected by the law-applying authorities of the state. If the latter are principles that are given effect in the constitution, or in some other level of the legal order, and that are derived from the content of positive law by way of a procedure of abstraction, their formulation as independent legal rules will be a rather inconsequential affair. Their application takes place in the course of, and only in the course of, the application of the legal norms by which they are given effect. But if the norms in question have not been positivized in any way, if they are norms, rather, that are yet to be turned into positive law (though the proponents of these principles, in a more or less clear conception, already hold them to be 'law'), because they represent 'justice', they are nothing more than demands, directed towards the organs that are tasked with the creation of law, that are not yet legally binding (and that, in truth, are simply the expression of certain group-interests).* Demands of this sort, of course, are not only directed towards the organs of legislation, which enjoy an almost unrestricted possibility to realize such postulates, but also towards the organs associated with the lower levels of the creation of law, where this possibility decreases to the extent that their function bears the character of application of law, but nevertheless continues to exist to the extent that there is free discretion; as far as jurisdiction and administration are concerned, consequently, to the extent that there is a choice between different possibilities of interpretation. Precisely the fact that the employment or the realization of these principles – principles which have, despite all efforts, so far not received a determination that is even remotely unambiguous – in the process of the creation of law does not have the character of an application of the law in the technical sense of the word – and, for the reasons given above, cannot have that character – provides the answer to the question whether they may be applied by a constitutional court. And the difference is only formal and fictitious if the constitution itself – as is sometimes the case – contains a reference to such principles, by making appeal to the ideals of 'justice', 'freedom', 'equality', 'equity', 'decency', and so on, without any further determination of what is meant by that. If something more is to be found behind such formulas than the usual political ideology, with which any positive legal order tries to adorn itself, then the reference to justice, freedom, equality, equity, and decency, in the absence of a more detailed explication of these values, simply means that the legislator, as well as those who execute the law, are authorized to make use of the latitude that is left by the constitution and by statute as they see fit. The views about what is just, free, equal, decent, etc. depend on people's point of view, which is always defined by this or that interest, and are so different that, in the absence of a determination by positive law, any odd legal content is [**1517**] justifiable on the basis of one of the possible views. At any rate, the appeal to the values in question does not mean and cannot mean that the organs of legislation and execution tasked with the creation of law are freed from their abiding obligation to apply the positive law if the latter conflicts with their subjective view of equality, etc. The formulas in question, therefore, are in general not very significant. The real legal situation does not change in any way if one abstains from putting them into the constitution.

What is more, the formulas in question can play a highly dangerous role, especially in the sphere of constitutional adjudication, in particular when it comes to the review of the constitutionality of statutes. If the constitution makes the demand that the legislator unfold his activity in harmony with 'justice', 'freedom', 'equity', 'decency', and so forth, one might be tempted to regard these words as guidelines for the content of future statutes. But this would certainly be wrong, since guidelines can be said to exist only if a determinate direction is given, if some objective criterion or other is provided by the constitution itself. Nevertheless, the difference between such formulas, which serve only to adorn the constitution politically, and the usual determination of the content of future laws in the catalogue of basic rights and rights of freedom, will be easy to blur; and the possibility is therefore not at all excluded that a constitutional court, if called upon to decide on the question of the constitutionality of a certain statute, might annul that statute on the ground that it is unjust, while claiming that 'justice' is to be regarded as a constitutional principle that ought to be applied by the constitutional court. This, however, would concede to the constitutional court a fullness of power that must be regarded as altogether intolerable. What the majority of the judges on this court regard as just may completely contradict what the majority of the state's inhabitants hold to be just, and it undoubtedly contradicts what the majority of the parliament that enacted the statute in question held to be just. It is self-evident that it cannot be the purpose of a constitution to make every statute enacted by parliament dependent, through the use of an ill-defined and highly ambiguous word like 'justice', or some other equally vacuous term, on the free discretion of a college whose members are as arbitrarily chosen, from a political point of view, as the members of a constitutional court. Such a shift of power from parliament to an extra-parliamentary institution, one that may turn into the exponent of political forces completely different from those that express themselves in parliament, is certainly not intended by the constitution and highly inappropriate politically. If it is to be prevented, the constitution must, if it appoints a constitutional court, abstain from all phraseology of this kind; and if it wants to put up basic principles, guidelines, and limitations for the content of the statutes that are to be enacted, it must make sure to determine them as precisely as possible. [**1518**]

4 *The result of the review exercised by the constitutional court*

Now that the object and the standard of the review that is to be undertaken by the constitutional court have been circumscribed, we need to determine the result. It follows from our discussion so far that an effective guarantee of the constitution can only be attained if the act that is put under review, in the case it is held to be legally defective, is immediately destroyed by the judgment of the constitutional court. This judgment must, even if it is about general norms – and that is of course the core case – have the character of an annulment. Given the far-reaching significance of the annulment of a general norm, and in particular of a statute, it is to be considered whether the constitutional court should not be authorized to perform the annulment for formal reasons, i.e. for a legal defectiveness of procedure, only in cases where the procedural defects are particularly grave or 'essential'. The judgment as to what counts as an essential defect is then best left to the free discretion of the court, since it is not advisable to draw the very difficult distinction between essential and inessential defects, in general terms, in the constitution itself. In the interest of legal security, it is to be considered whether the possibility of an annulment of general legal norms, and above all of statutes and international treaties, should not be tied to a temporal limitation, determined in the constitution, of, say, three to five years, starting from the point in time at which the norm that is to be annulled comes into force. It is surely questionable in the highest degree to annul as unconstitutional a statute, and even more so an international treaty, if these norms have already been in force for many years without having been contested.

In any case, it is advisable in the interest of legal security not to give any retroactive effect, in principle, to the cassation of general norms. At least in this sense: that all legal acts that have been enacted pursuant to the general norm up to the point of its annulment remain untouched by the cassation. The retroactive effect of the annulling judgment would be completely excluded only if all matters of fact that fall under the general norm, if they came into being before the cassation of the norm, were to be evaluated in accordance with the norm even after its cassation, for the reason that the general norm is invalidated only *pro futuro*, i.e. for those matters of fact that came into being after the cassation. However, there is no absolute need, from the point of view of legal security, to apply the already annulled norm to matters of fact that came into being while the statute (or decree, etc.) had not yet been annulled, but about which no decision was taken, by any public authority, before the cassation. The following will make clear that the limited retroactivity implicit in this exception is even necessary, given a certain design of the procedure of the constitutional court.

If a general norm is annulled under exclusion of retroactivity, or at least under the restriction of retroactivity just discussed, and if, consequently, the legal effects that the general norm has had [**1519**] before its cassation, or at least those legal effects that have found expression in the application of the norm on the part of public authorities, remain untouched by the cassation, then the legal effect that the annulled norm, when it came into force, exercised against the norms that had previously regulated the same subject matter must also remain intact: the legal effect of the invalidation of conflicting norms in accordance with the principle *lex posterior derogat priori*. This means that it is not at all the case that the legal situation which existed before the annulled statute entered into force automatically comes to life again with the cassation of a statute on the part of the constitutional court. The statute that was replaced by the annulled statute, as it had regulated the same subject matter, is not resurrected by the cassation. This implies that the cassation gives rise, so to speak, to a legal vacuum. A matter that was previously regulated by general norms is now unregulated; where there was hitherto legal obligation, there is now legal freedom. This may, under certain circumstances, have very undesirable consequences. Especially if a statute was annulled not by virtue of its content, but only due to procedural defects of one form or another that occurred during its enactment; and even more so if the enactment of a new statute that will regulate the matter at hand requires a long time. In order to deal with this problem, it is advisable to provide for the possibility to let the annulling judgment come into force a certain period of time after its promulgation. However, apart from this possibility, which is yet to be discussed later on, there is another means available to solve the problem: the constitutional court is authorized to proclaim, in its judgment that annuls a general norm, that, as soon as the cassation comes into force, the general norms that were in place up to the point in time at which the annulled norm came into force will once again acquire validity. It is advisable to leave it to the discretion of the constitutional court to decide in which cases it wants to make use of this authorization to resurrect the old legal situation. It would be problematic if the constitution was to bindingly prescribe, as a general rule, the resurrection of the old legal situation in case of the annulment of a general norm. The cassation of a statute the content of which consists in nothing more than in the annulment of another statute previously in force might perhaps constitute an exception. The cassation of such a statute on the part of the constitutional court would have no point, after all, if the only legal effect of the statute that is to be annulled, the annulment of the older statute, was not annulled. The annulment, in that case, would have to amount to the reinstatement of the older statute. As for the rest of cases, a general rule of the aforementioned kind could only be taken into consideration on the presupposition that the constitution will permit the annulment of a general norm – and especially of a statute or of an international treaty – only within a limited period of time, as discussed above, from the time the norm that is to be annulled came into force. This would prevent legal norms that have long been obsolete and that are incompatible with the circumstances of the times from coming into force once again. Such a competence positively to validate general norms would, however, [**1520**] endow the function of the constitutional court with a legislative character to an even higher degree than the power to invalidate general norms through an annulling judgment – even if this competence applied only to norms that have been enacted by the ordinary legislator once before, but then lost their validity.

It will make a difference for the formulation of the judgment of the constitutional court whether the latter refers to a legal act, and in particular to a general norm, that still enjoys full legal force at the moment of judgment – that is the normal case – or whether the norm in question has already been annulled at this point, but is still to be applied to older matters of fact. In the latter case, the judgment of the constitutional court – as has already been mentioned – only has to invalidate a remnant of legal force; it nevertheless has constitutive-annulling character. The formula, in such a case, could be expressed as follows: instead of 'the statute is annulled' the court could use 'the statute was unconstitutional'. The effect of the judgment is that the application of the statute declared to be unconstitutional to older matters of fact is thereby excluded as well. It cannot make a difference whether the norm that is reviewed by the constitutional court is younger or older than the constitution with which it stands in conflict. The judgment, in both cases, will pronounce the cassation of the unconstitutional norm.

It must be emphasized, before we move on, that a cassation need not necessarily invalidate a statute as a whole, or a decree as a whole. It can restrict itself to individual provisions. Provided, of course, that the rest of the statute or of the decree can still be applied without the annulled provision, and provided that it does not change its meaning in an unexpected way. It must be left to the discretion of the constitutional court to decide whether it should annul only a part or rather – for the reasons mentioned – the whole of the statute.

5 *The procedure of the constitutional court*

Finally, we still have to discuss the basic principles of the procedure of a constitutional court.

Of the greatest importance is the question: in what way can proceedings in the constitutional court be initiated? The extent to which the constitutional court will be able to fulfil its task as a guarantor of the constitution depends primarily on the regulation of this question. The strongest guarantee would, without a doubt, be provided by the admission of an *actio popularis*: the constitutional court is obliged to initiate proceedings for the review of the legality of the acts subject to its judicature – and thus, in particular, of statutes and decrees – whenever anyone requests that it do so. That the legal-political interest in the removal of legally defective acts would, in this way, be satisfied in the most radical way cannot be doubted. Such a solution of the problem, nevertheless, cannot be recommended. The opportunity [**1521**] to mount frivolous challenges and the danger of an intolerable overburdening of the constitutional court would be too large. There is a wealth of other possibilities that should be considered here. Let me emphasize the following: all law-applying public authorities have the right and the duty, in case they are to apply a norm subject to the control of the constitutional court and harbour doubt as to the legality of the same, to interrupt their own proceedings concerning the concrete individual case at hand and to make a reasoned request to the constitutional court to review and, if necessary, to annul the norm in question. This competence could be restricted to higher or to highest public authorities – administrative institutions and courts, ministers and highest courts, etc., – it could also be restricted to the courts alone (though the exclusion of administrative institutions is no longer fully justifiable, given that their procedures have come to resemble those of courts more and more). If the constitutional court annuls the challenged norm, then, and only then, the authority that initiated the challenge will no longer have to apply the norm to the concrete case that gave rise to the challenge. Rather, it now has to decide the case, a case that in fact arose while the annulled norm was still in force, as though the annulled norm – which is normally annulled only *pro futuro* – had not been in force for this case. Such retroactivity of the cassation is technically necessary, since the law-applying authorities would otherwise have no immediate and therefore perhaps no sufficiently weighty interest to put the constitutional court in motion. If the latter is exclusively or even only for the most part dependent on the references of the law-applying public authorities, then these references must be given an incentive, in the form of the reward of – limited – retroactivity.

A very useful extension of the possibility to challenge unconstitutional acts that points in the direction of an *actio popularis* consists in providing the parties to a judicial or administrative proceeding with the opportunity to challenge acts of public authorities – judicial decisions or administrative acts – for the reason that these acts, while immediately legal, execute a norm that is itself legally defective and that is subject to the control of the constitutional court; in case, in other words, we are faced with the execution, in itself legal, of an unconstitutional statute or of a decree that fails to conform to statutory requirements. However, a challenge to an act that is thus open to indirect challenge by the party should be permitted only if the court or administrative tribunal that is called upon to decide, in the judicial or administrative proceeding, joins the legal opinion of the party, and thus interrupts its proceedings, in order to request a review of the statute or of the decree by the constitutional court.

The initiation of proceedings in the constitutional court may take a further, special form in a federal state, in that a right to challenge legal acts that originate from the union may be accorded to the governments of the *Länder* or constituent states, while a similar right is given to the union with regard to legal acts originating from a *Land* or one of the federation's constituent states. Constitutional review may be needed here, above all, with respect to the determination of the content of the general legal norms, characteristic for the constitution of a federal state, [**1522**] which provide the delimitation of the competences of the union and the *Länder* or constituent states.

An altogether novel institution, but one that is worthy of the most serious consideration, would be the appointment of an advocate of the constitution (constitutional advocate) at the constitutional court, who – in analogy to the public attorney in the criminal process – would be officially charged with the task to initiate proceedings for the review of those of the acts subject to the control of the constitutional court that he, the constitutional advocate, considers to be legally defective. It is to be understood, of course, that the office of such an advocate of the constitution would have to be endowed with all imaginable guarantees of independence both from the government and from parliament.

As far as the contestation of statutes, in particular, is concerned, it would be of the greatest importance to provide that opportunity also to a minority – however qualified – of the parliament that enacted the unconstitutional statute. This all the more for the reason that constitutional adjudication in parliamentary democracies – as will have to be established later on – must necessarily put itself into the service of the protection of minorities.

Finally, we have to take into account the possibility that the constitutional court may initiate a review of a general norm that is subject to its control *ex officio*, because it has to apply this norm in some case or other, but harbours doubts as to its legality. The constitutional court can end up in such a situation not only when it is called upon to review the conformity with statute of a decree, and then discovers the unconstitutionality of the statute with which the decree is said to conflict, but in particular when it is competent as well to decide on the legality of certain individual legal acts, where the immediate question is only of their conformity to statute, decree, or treaty and where the constitutionality of those acts is therefore in question only indirectly. In such cases, the constitutional court will, just like the public authorities that are competent to refer challenges to it, interrupt the proceedings concerning the concrete case and – this time *ex officio* – enter into the review of the norm which it would have had to apply to the concrete case. If it comes to the cassation of that norm, the constitutional court – just as, in the analogous case, the public authorities that refer challenges to the constitutional court – will have to decide the concrete legal issue it was dealing with, once ordinary proceedings resume, as though the annulled norm had not been in force.

In case the constitutional court is also competent to decide on the legality of individual acts of state, and in particular if it is competent to decide on the legality of acts of administrative authorities, it must, of course, be possible for those persons who were harmed by a legally defective act, in their legally protected interests, to make appeal to the court. If there is a possibility to challenge an individual legal act in the constitutional court because of the alleged legal defectiveness of the general norm in whose – immediately legal – execution the act took place, then private parties will have an even stronger opportunity indirectly to contest general norms – in particular statutes and decrees – in the constitutional court than they enjoy by virtue of the possibility to bring a challenge in the context of administrative proceedings. [**1523**]

The principle of publicity and the use of oral arguments are in general recommended for the proceedings in the constitutional court, despite the fact that what is at issue, for the most part, are pure questions of law, and despite the fact that the legal arguments in the written briefs that the parties to the trial may submit to the court, or may perhaps even be required to submit in order to help it prepare its decision, must be given the greater weight. The public interest in the issues that occupy the constitutional court is so great that the publicity of the trial, which can only be guaranteed fully by public hearings in front of the court, must not be excluded in principle. It might even be worth considering whether to let the judges' deliberations on the judgment take place in public.

The following are to be summoned to the trial as parties: the public authority whose act is being challenged, in order to give it the opportunity to defend the legality of its act, as well as the institution that initiated the challenge; possibly also the private party whose legal case, pending with a court or an administrative agency, provided the occasion for the proceedings in constitutional court, or, if applicable, the private party that is legitimated to appeal directly to the constitutional court. The public authority is represented by its chief, chairman, or by one of its civil servants who may be knowledgeable about the legal issues at hand. It is advisable, due to the eminently juristic nature of constitutional adjudication, to make it compulsory for private parties to appoint an attorney.

The cassation of the challenged act – assuming the challenge has been upheld – is to be pronounced in the judgment of the constitutional court in such a way that the annulment appears as brought about by the judgment itself. In the case of a cassation of norms whose validity requires promulgation, the act of annulment – here the judgment of the constitutional court – must likewise be promulgated, and in the same way as the annulled norm. Although one cannot reject out of hand the possibility of providing the constitutional court with its own organ for the independent publication of its annulling judgments, it is nevertheless advisable to publish the cassation of the norm in the same organ in which it was originally published and thereby put into force. It follows from this that the public authority responsible for the promulgation of a statute, a decree, or an international treaty must also be put under an obligation to promulgate the judgment of the constitutional court that annuls the norm in question. Hence, the judgment of the constitutional court has to pronounce this obligation, while designating precisely the public authority that is responsible for the promulgation. The annulment will then become effective only once it is promulgated. Especially in the case of statutes (and probably also in the case of international treaties), the constitutional court should have the power to let the annulment take effect only after the expiry of a certain period of time after the promulgation, if only to give parliament an opportunity to enact a constitutional law in place of the unconstitutional, so that the matter regulated by the annulled law does not remain without regulation for an extended period of time, i.e. so as to avoid the existence of the legal vacuum already mentioned earlier on. If the challenge to the statute originated from a law-applying public authority [**1524**] – a court or an administrative agency – in the course of the authority's attempt to apply the statute to a concrete case, then a certain difficulty arises with respect to the question of retroactivity. If the challenged statute is to lose its legal force only after a certain time from the promulgation of the annulment in the public gazette, if it is therefore still to be applied, up to that point, by public authorities, one cannot well release the authority that brought the challenge from its duty to apply the statute to the concrete case at hand that occasioned the challenge. This means that the interest of the law-applying public authorities to bring challenges to unconstitutional laws in constitutional court is once again somewhat diminished. This makes more attractive the possibility – discussed above – of coupling the instant annulment of the statute with a resurrection of the legal situation that was in place before the annulled law came into force. Under this modality, the retroactive effect of the annulling judgment on the case that occasioned the challenge, required for reasons of procedural technique, can take place without giving rise to further problems, and the legislative organ will, at the same time, have the necessary leisure to prepare a new statute that conforms to the requirements of the constitution.

V The juristic and political significance of constitutional adjudication

As long as a constitution lacks the guarantee, presented in the foregoing, of the annullability of unconstitutional acts it also lacks the character of full legal bindingness in the technical sense. A constitution according to which unconstitutional acts, and in particular unconstitutional statutes, must remain valid because they cannot be annulled on the ground of their unconstitutionality amounts to little more, from a legal-technical point of view, than a non-binding wish; though one is in general unaware of this fact, for the reason that a politically motivated jurisprudential theory prevents the growth of that awareness. Any statute whatsoever, any simple decree – yes, even any general legal transaction of private parties – surpasses such a constitution in legal force, surpasses it though the constitution stands above them all, though all lower levels of legal order draw their validity from it. Legal order, after all, takes care that every act which puts itself in contradiction with any norm of a level lower than the constitutional can be annulled.

And this lesser degree of real legal force stands in a stark disproportion to the appearance of rigidity, bordering on inflexibility, that one confers on the constitution through the enactment of conditions of amendment that are very difficult to meet. Why take such precautions if the norms of the constitution, though more or less un-amendable, are almost non-obligatory? To be sure, even a constitution that does not provide for a constitutional court or a comparable institution for the annulment of unconstitutional acts is not altogether irrelevant legally. Its [**1525**] violation can, at least where the institution of ministerial responsibility exists, lead to some kind of reaction against certain organs who were involved in the enactment of unconstitutional acts, on the assumption that the behaviour of these organs was culpable. But apart from the fact that this guarantee – as has already been stressed – is in itself not very effective, since it leaves the validity of the unconstitutional statute untouched, we will not be in a position to assume, in the absence of proper guarantees of constitutionality, that it is the meaning of the norms that determine the procedure of legislation and the permissible content of statutes or, in other words, that it is the meaning of the constitution to indicate a unique procedure of legislation as the only possible way to legislate and to provide a real direction to the content of legislation. Admittedly, the constitution says, given its wording and given its subjective meaning, that statutes are to be enacted in such and such a way, and only in such and such a way, and that they may or may not have this or that content. But its objective meaning is: statutes are to be regarded as valid even if they come into being in some other way and even if their content violates the directives of the constitution. One is forced to interpret the constitution in this way if unconstitutional statutes, despite their legal defects, are to be regarded as valid; since even such statutes must be able – as valid statutes – to base themselves on some constitution, they must draw their validity from somewhere, and hence from the constitution; they must somehow, since they are valid, also be constitutional. But this means that the procedure of legislation explicitly laid down in the constitution, and the guidelines contained in it, do not, contrary to appearances, constitute an unambiguous determination. They must be understood, rather, in the sense of an alternative:* either in this way or, if not in this way, then in other ways, almost without limit. That constitutions which lack the guarantee of the annullability of unconstitutional acts are not understood in this way is, ironically, the result of the theory – it has already been mentioned here several times – that conceals the true state of affairs for political reasons, reasons which are at odds with the political interests that are expressed in the constitutions in question. A constitution, whose prescriptions regarding legislation may be violated, without a consequent annulment of the unconstitutional statutes, has no more legal force, vis-à-vis the lower levels of the legal order internal to the state, than international law vis-à-vis the legal order of the individual state. If the latter puts itself in contradiction with international law, with any one of its acts, from the constitution down to the last administrative act, the validity of the acts in question will remain unaffected. Of course, the state that is affected by the violation of international law may, as a last resort, go to war against the state that violated international law. This, however, is only a penal sanction, not an annulment of the legally defective act. In just the same way, a constitution that lacks constitutional adjudication can react to its violation only with a penal sanction made available by the institution of ministerial responsibility. It is this reduced legal force of international law that leads some authors – though mistakenly – to deny its legal character altogether.* And the interests that oppose the institution of an international court endowed with a competence to annul, as well as the legal-technical strengthening of international law that could be brought about in this way, are very similar to those [**1526**] that work against the increase in the legal force of the constitution that goes along with the function of a constitutional court.

One needs to keep all this in mind, in order to appreciate the significance of the question of constitutional adjudication that we are discussing here.

Apart from this general significance that it has for every constitution, the question may also enjoy a particular significance, depending on the specific structure of the constitution. This applies, above all, to a democratic republic. Institutions of control belong to the conditions of existence of the latter. The best way to defend this form of state against the many criticisms, some of them justified, to which it has been subjected in recent times is to put in place all the guarantees that can be given for the legality of the functions of the state. The control of the functions of the state must be strengthened to the same degree as democratization progresses. This is the point of view from which constitutional adjudication is to be evaluated here. Insofar as it makes sure that statutes come into existence in conformity with the constitution, and in particular also that their content is constitutional, constitutional adjudication serves the function of an effective protection of the minority against assaults on the part of the majority, whose rule becomes tolerable only by virtue of the fact that it is exercised in legal form. The specific form of constitution, which typically consists in the fact that a constitutional amendment is tied to the requirement of a heightened majority, ensures that certain fundamental questions can only be resolved with the participation of the minority. The simple majority does not have the right – at least when it comes to certain issues – to impose its will on the minority. It is only through a statute that is unconstitutional, because it has been enacted by a simple majority, that the majority can interfere with the minority's constitutionally protected sphere of interest against the latter's will. The constitutionality of statutes is therefore a pre-eminent interest of the minority; regardless of what type of minority it is, be it class-based, national, or religious, whose interests are protected by the constitution in some way.

This applies in particular to the case of a shift in the proportion between majority and minority, when a majority turns into a minority, but still remains strong enough to prevent the qualified decision that is necessary to bring about a lawful change of the constitution. If one does not take the essence of democracy to consist in unfettered majority rule, but rather in the continuing compromise between the different parts of the people that are represented in parliament by the majority and the minority, then one should acknowledge that constitutional adjudication is a particularly suitable means to realize that idea. The mere threat of making appeal to the constitutional court may well turn out to be a sufficient instrument in the hands of the minority to prevent unconstitutional violations of its interests on the part of the majority, and thus, in effect, to prevent a dictatorship of the majority that is no less dangerous to social peace than the dictatorship of a minority.

Constitutional adjudication attains its greatest importance, however, in a federal state.* One does not go too far in making the claim that this political idea, [**1527**] from a legal point of view, cannot reach its completion without the institution of a constitutional court. The essence of a federal state – assuming one regards the issue not as a problem of the metaphysics of the state but rather, from a realistic perspective, as a problem of organizational technique – consists in the fact that the legislative and executive activity of a legal community that is regarded as a state are divided between one central organ, an organ referred to as 'union' or '*Reich*', etc., with competence for the state as a whole and all of its territory, and several local organs with competence only for parts of the territory or for some limbs of the state, which are referred to as 'constituent states', '*Länder*', 'cantons', etc., but in such a way that elected representatives of the constituent parts, who may be appointed indirectly (through election by local parliaments or designation by local governments) or directly (by the people of a constituent state), participate in central legislation, and perhaps also in central administration. The federal state represents a specific case of decentralization. The legal regulation of this decentralization forms the essential content of the constitution of the whole. The latter will determine, above all, which matters are to be regulated by statutes of the union and which are to be governed by local statutes of the constituent states; and it will also divide the responsibility for executing the law between the central and the constituent states. This division of competences is the political core of the idea of a federal state. From a legal-technical point of view, the constitution does not only, as in the case of a unitary state, determine the procedure of legislation and provide certain guidelines for the content of statutes. It also delimits the material sphere of the validity of *Reich* as well as of *Länder* statutes. Every violation of these boundaries, as drawn by the constitution, is a violation of the fundamental law of the federal state, and the preservation of the boundaries of competence that the constitution draws between the union and the constituent states is a political question of life and death. Of course, it is also perceived as such in a federal state, a state that is invariably a stage of the most passionate in-fighting about competence. If it exists anywhere, then the need for an objective authority that can mediate these fights in a peaceful way, for a forum in which these quarrels can be raised as questions of law, and be decided as such, exists here. The institution required here, needless to say, is none other than a constitutional court. After all, every violation of the competence of the union by a constituent state, or of that of a constituent state by the union, is a violation of the constitution; a violation of the common constitution which integrates the union and the *Länder*, the *Reich* and the constituent states, into one whole. This common constitution, whose most essential element is the division of competences, must not be confused with the special constitution of the union (*Reich*), which stands below it, and which, just like the constitutions of the constituent states (*Länder*), is only the constitution of a part of the whole community, even where one and the same organ is competent to change the constitution of the whole and to change the constitution of union (*Reich*).

When it comes to judicial or administrative acts that violate the distribution of competences, the possibility of making appeal within the judicial or administrative hierarchy of the union or the constituent states provides an initial opportunity to annul such acts on the ground of their failure to conform to statute. Whether this guarantee suffices effectively to prevent acts [**1528**] of union administration interfering with the competences of the constituent states, or acts of the administration of the latter interfering with the competences of the union, must remain open to doubt, especially if the union and its constituent states lack a common supreme administrative court. Such a court would, if it had to control acts for their conformity with the distribution of competences, i.e. for their constitutionality, already function as a constitutional court – at least indirectly. The question of the competences that are to be allocated to the constitutional court must here be answered in a slightly different way from that of a centralist and unitary state, due to the opposition of the interests of the central and the constituent states that is a characteristic of federal states, and due to the strong need that prevails here for an objective institution that can, as an organ of the overarching community, play the role of a referee between the fundamentally co-ordinate legal communities of the union and the constituent states. It appears, at the least, to be debatable whether a federal constitutional court should also be tasked with the legal control of individual administrative acts – but only with regard to their conformity to the distribution of competences. The demand, at any rate, should be uncontroversial that statutes and decrees of union as well as of the constituent states be open to challenge in a constitutional court that can guarantee sufficient objectivity due to its composition, which should give equal representation to both levels of government, and that is competent – as an organ of the constitution of the whole, and not as a one-sided organ of the union or of the constituent states – to annul such statutes and decrees for the reason that they violate the constitution of the whole, and in particular, hence, for the reason that they disturb the constitutional distribution of competences.

It is one of the paradoxes of the theory of the federal state that it advocates the principle: the law of the *Reich* takes precedence over the law of the *Land** as a principle that allegedly conforms to the essence of a federal state. With this alone, it has already obscured the necessity of a constitutional court in a federal state. It is easy to show that nothing can be as much in conflict with the idea of a federal state as this principle, which makes the political and legal existence of the constituent states depend on the discretion of the union, and thus on the discretion of a mere part of the federal state as a whole, by allowing the union to interfere with the competences of the constituent states by means of ordinary statute, or even through simple decrees, in a way that conflicts with the constitution of the whole, and to usurp the competences of the constituent states in an unconstitutional manner. If the idea of a federal state, as it has found expression in the constitution of the whole, is to be preserved, the law of the *Reich* must not be allowed to violate the law of constituent states any more than the law of constituent states must be allowed to violate the law of the *Reich*. Rather, one as much as the other is, both are, to be evaluated in the same way, in their respective relationship to one another, according to the constitution of the whole which delimits their spheres of validity against one another. A legal act of the union that steps over the boundary drawn for it by the constitution of the whole, and that penetrates into the sphere of competence of the constituent states, has, from a legal point of view, no more right to exist than the legal act of a constituent state that interferes with the competence of the union. This principle alone comports with the essence of the federal state, and it cannot be realized in any other form than by way of a constitutional court. It would, finally, have to belong to the natural competence of the constitutional court, according to the idea of a federal state, [**1529**] to decide on all violations of duty of which both the constituent states as well as the union can make themselves guilty if their relevant organs, in the pursuit of their office, violate the constitution of the whole. What is usually called the federal execution of the constitution,* and poses such a difficult problem for the theory and practice of the federal state, should be permissible – irrespective of whether it takes place through the primitive form of a strict and collective liability of the community as such, or in the technically more advanced form of an individual criminal liability of the responsible organ – only as the implementation of a judgment issued by the constitutional court, a judgment in which the court has determined some behaviour, be it on the part of the union or of a constituent state, to have been unconstitutional.

The tasks that are to be discharged by a constitutional court in the framework of a federal state put into stark relief the affinity between constitutional adjudication and an international adjudication that serves the purpose of the preservation of international law, not least with respect to the mutual proximity of the levels of legal order that are to be guaranteed. And just as the one aims to make war between peoples superfluous, the other proves its worth – and serves its most fundamental purpose – as a guarantee of political peace within the individual state.

*Guidelines of the co-rapporteur**

1. *Adjudication in matters of state is constitutional adjudication; as such it is a limb of the system of measures whose purpose it is to ensure the legality of the state's functions.*
2. *Constitutional adjudication aims, in principle, to guarantee the legality of legal acts (norms) immediate to the constitution – statutes, decrees that take the place of statutes and are therefore immediate to the constitution, etc. – and thus to guarantee the constitution itself.*

3. *The guarantees of legality are:*
   (a) *preventative or repressive;*
   (b) *personal or material.*

   Constitutional adjudication is a guarantee that is mainly repressive and material in character.

   Among the material-repressive guarantees that have to be considered are: nullity of the legally defective act, its annulment (cassation), and perhaps its replacement with a legal act (reformation).

   Constitutional adjudication, for the most part, aims at the annulment of the legally defective act.
4. *The annulment of the legally defective act can – if the norm that is to be annulled is general – remove the validity of the legally defective norm:* [**1530**]
   (a) *only for a particular case or for all cases to which the general norm is to be applied;*
   (b) *only for matters of fact that occur after the annulment or also for all or some that occurred before the annulment (i.e. with or without or with limited retroactivity);*
   (c) *the annulment of the legally defective act may be performed by the organ that enacted the act or by some other organ.*

   Constitutional adjudication is the cassation of the legally defective norm with or without restriction to a concrete case, with or without retroactive effect, by an organ other than that which enacted the legally defective act; and by a court, i.e. by an institution that is independent in a specific way.
5. *With regard to the composition of the constitutional court, which is formed as a collegial organ, one has to take care, above all, to eliminate party-political influence and to attract legal expertise, in particular in constitutional law.*
6. *The object of the judicature of the constitutional court is to consist in:*

   Above all, statutes (union statutes and statutes of the Länder*) and decrees that replace statutes and are thus immediate to the constitution. It is also advisable to subject all other decrees that execute statutes – with consideration to the inner affinity that exists between statute and decree as general legal norms – to the review and decision of the constitutional court.*

   To endow the constitutional court with a right to review international treaties, and to annul them for unconstitutionality, is in general not advisable, for reasons of foreign policy.

Individual legal acts (norms) should, insofar as they are enacted by courts, be excluded from control by the constitutional court. The same holds for individual legal acts that originate from administrative institutions; even if they have the character of acts that are immediate to the constitution. The latter restriction is required by the interest of a purposeful delimitation of constitutional from administrative adjudication.

It is advisable, by contrast, to subject individual legal acts of parliament to the judicature of the constitutional court.

7. *General norms that still enjoy validity at the time of the decision of the constitutional court are not the only general norms that are to be regarded as possible objects of the judicature of the constitutional court. Rather, one must also consider general norms that have already been annulled – not by the constitutional court, but by some other authority – but without retroactive effect, so that they are still to be applied to matters of fact that took place while the annulled norm was still in effect.*

   It is advisable, moreover, to subject the question of the derogation of an older statute (or decree) by the younger constitution to the decision of the constitutional court. [**1531**]
8. *The standard of the judicature of the constitutional court is to be:*
   (a) *The constitution, with regard to acts immediate to the constitution (constitutionality of statutes and of decrees that are immediate to the constitution, etc.).*
   (b) *In exceptional cases the statute: with regard to decrees that execute statutes and are thus mediate to the constitution.*
   (c) *General international law: if its rules (the 'generally recognized rules of international law') are recognized as a part of the state's legal order; as well as particular international law (international treaties), insofar as the constitutional court has been made competent to review the conformity of statutes, decrees, etc. with international treaties.*
   (d) *At any rate, the positive law is the only permissible standard for the review and the decisions of the constitutional court.*
9. *The outcome of the judicature of the constitutional court ought to be: the cassation of the legally defective act, not its reformation.*

   The cassation of general norms (statutes, decrees, etc.) by the constitutional court is a judicial decision that has legislative character. (The court as a negative legislator.)

It is advisable to give the opportunity to the constitutional court, in case of the cassation of a general norm, to determine, under certain circumstances, that the general norm that was valid prior to the annulled norm be made valid once again, for the time being.

Moreover, it is advisable, in general, not to give retroactive force to the cassation by the constitutional court. Exception: in case the proceedings in constitutional court are initiated by a reference made by a law-applying institution, in which case the retroactivity of the cassation is to be limited to the concrete case that provided the occasion for an initiation of proceedings in constitutional court.

10. *Proceedings in constitutional court can be initiated by: an* actio popularis, *a reference from certain institutions or parties, a parliamentary minority,* ex officio *either by the court itself or by a constitutional advocate, etc.*

*The proceedings of the constitutional court, in principle, are supposed to be public and oral. The organs whose acts are to be reviewed for their legality, as well as private parties, as far as is necessary for the protection of their legal interests, are to be admitted as parties to the trial. The judgment of the constitutional court, by which general norms are annulled, is to be promulgated in the official gazette. It is advisable to give the constitutional court the opportunity to determine that the cassation of a general norm will take effect some time after the promulgation of the judgment (*vacatio legis*).*

2

The guardian of the constitution: Schmitt's argument against constitutional review

Translation of Carl Schmitt (1931a) *Der Hüter der Verfassung*, 4th edn (Berlin: Duncker & Humblot, 1996), 12–48, 60–4.

CARL SCHMITT, *THE GUARDIAN OF THE CONSTITUTION*, CH. I.1–3

I The judiciary as guardian of the constitution

1 The general (accessory) so-called material right of judicial review does not constitute a guardian of the constitution in Germany

The trial-deciding courts of civil, criminal, and administrative justice are not guardians of the constitution in the precise meaning of the term. But it is easy to fall into the mistake of referring to them as such where courts exercise a so-called material judicial right of review, i.e. where they review ordinary statutes for their substantive conformity with the provisions of constitutional statutes and deny application to the ordinary statute in case of a collision. As a result the *Reichsgericht*, too, has sometimes been called a guardian of the constitution, after it declared itself to be entitled, in its decision of 4 November 1925,* to review ordinary statutes of the *Reich* for their substantive conformity with the constitution of the *Reich*.[1]

The tendency to portray trial-deciding courts as the highest guarantee of the constitution is probably to be explained mostly as a result of certain widely shared ideas about the Supreme Court of the United States of America. This justly famous court has, it seems, become a

[1] On 'Das Reichsgericht als Hüter der Verfassung', see my paper in *Die Reichsgerichtspraxis im deutschen Rechtsleben. Festgabe der juristischen Fakultäten zum 50jährigen Bestehen des Reichsgerichts*, ed. O. Schreiber (Berlin and Leipzig, 1929), pp. 154–78.

kind of myth for a fair number of German jurists. Strange misconceptions about this court came to the fore during the deliberations of the constitutional committee of the Weimar national assembly, and were documented in the protocols of its constitutional committee. There was talk about a 'court of justice in matters of state for the protection of the constitution' that, allegedly, has been introduced by 'all great democratic states, for example by America', where 'its existence has proven to be useful'.[2] To counter this assessment, I would like to remind the reader, in a few words, of the fact that the Supreme Court of the United States, as has rightly been pointed out, 'possesses a position that is unique in all of world history', and especially in the economic area,[3] [**13**] by virtue of its authoritarian interpretation of concepts like 'property', 'value', and 'freedom', an interpretation that cannot simply be transferred to the socially and politically altogether different situation of a Continental European state. The position of the Supreme Court of the United States developed within the context of a jurisdictional state* of Anglo-Saxon origin. Such a state, as a state without administrative law, stands in the starkest of contrasts to the states of the European Continent. It makes no difference here whether the European state is a republic, like France, or a monarchical administrative state, like nineteenth-century Prussia. The American Supreme Court is anything but a *Staatsgerichtshof* and its jurisdiction is not to be confused with what Germans nowadays tend to refer to as *Staatsgerichtsbarkeit* or constitutional adjudication.* The Supreme Court restricts itself, on the basis of a clear and principled consciousness of its own character as a trial-deciding court, to the decision of particular kinds of disputes (real, actual 'cases' or 'controversies' of 'judiciary nature').[4] It is unwilling, with a view to its 'strictly judicial function', to take any political and legislative position, and it does not even want to be an administrative court.[5] It strictly refuses to issue advisory opinions, either for Congress

[2] *Bericht und Protokolle des achten Ausschusses der verfassunggebenden Deutschen Nationalversammlung über den Entwurf einer Verfassung des Deutschen Reiches* (Berlin, 1920), p. 485; against this view earlier H. Preuß, *ibid.*, pp. 483–4.

[3] '... that court occupies the unique position of the first authoritative faculty of political economy in the world's history': J. R. Commons, *Legal Foundations of Capitalism* (New York, 1924), p. 7.

[4] C. Warren, *The Supreme Court in United States History* (Boston, 1924), vol. I, pp. 52, 108–9; C. E. Hughes, *The Supreme Court of the United States* (New York, 1928), p. 31 (*Muskrat* v. *United States*, 1911, 219 US 346); on the strict limitation to genuine adjudication ('cases of Judiciary Nature') see p. 22.

[5] For evidence see Hughes, *The Supreme Court of the United States*, p. 22.

or the president.[6] As far as the court's practical significance and effectiveness is concerned one must not, given Germany's current abnormal situation, evaluate its activities by looking at times of economic prosperity and domestic security. Rather, one has to take into account critical and insecure times. Here, however, the famous precedents of the epoch of the Civil War – decisions that concerned politically disputed questions like slavery or the devaluation of the currency – show that the authority of the court was severely threatened in these cases and that its opinion as to the issue at hand was by no means always able to prevail.[7] The most important and fundamental peculiarity [**14**] of the Supreme Court, however, probably lies in the fact that it reviews the justice and reasonableness of statutes with the help of general principles and fundamental considerations – principles and considerations that can only be called 'norms' if one is willing to abuse the term – and then treats a statute it deems to conflict with these to be inapplicable.[8] It is capable of that because what it really does is to oppose the state, as the guardian of a social and economic order that is undisputed in principle. The court has, as *R. Gneist* already pointed out quite rightly, a power that transcends that of the state.[9] The common criticism that the court, for years and years, prevented and hindered statutes for the protection of workers as well as other pieces of social legislation by treating them as unconstitutional, including statutes concerning women's and child labour that were utterly uncontroversial to us in Germany, has to be considered from within this context. What concerns us here, as should be clear, is not to offer an apology or to issue an indictment of the American Supreme

[6] The only case so far in which the court gave an advisory opinion took place under president Monroe; see Warren, *The Supreme Court in United States History*, vol. II, p. 56; compare the remark in Hughes, *The Supreme Court of the United States*, p. 31: 'nothing of the sort could happen today'. The solicitor-general, J. M. Beck, has made the proposal, but so far without success, to give congress together with the president a right to ask the Supreme Court for an advisory opinion, in cases where the constitutionality of a proposed bill is in doubt, see F. A. Ogg and P. O. Ray, *Introduction to American Government*, 2nd edn (New York, 1926), p. 422, note 3.

[7] Warren, vol. III, pp. 22–3 (*Dred Scott Case*), p. 244 (*Legal Tender Case*); moreover the *Income Tax Case* of 1895.

[8] This is where concepts like reasonableness and expediency belong. On the combinations and identifications of 'constitution', 'fundamental rights', 'natural equity', 'will of the people', etc. see the interesting remarks in J. Dickinson, *Administrative Justice and the Supremacy of Law in the United States* (Cambridge, 1927), pp. 97 and 101.

[9] R. Gneist, *Gutachten zum 4. deutschen Juristentag über die Frage: 'Soll der Richter über die Frage zu befinden haben, ob ein Gesetz verfassungsmäßig zustande gekommen ist?'* (Berlin, 1863), p. 28. Compare the detailed quotation below p. 154 note 39.

Court, but only to provide a short correction, in order to prevent unthinking transfers and mythologizations. Generally speaking, one can say that a judicial right of review is sufficient on its own to make trial-deciding courts the guardians of the constitution only in a jurisdictional state that subjects all public life to the control of the ordinary courts, and only if we take the term 'constitution' to refer above all to the basic rights implicit in a liberal-bourgeois understanding of the rule of law, to personal freedom and private property, which are to be protected by the ordinary courts against the state, i.e. against legislation, government, and administration. In this way, the practice of the American Supreme Court, on the basis of the Fifth and the Fourteenth Amendments, and by developing the much-discussed formula of 'due process of law',[10] defended the principles of bourgeois social and economic order, and attempted to protect them against the legislator as a kind of higher order and true constitution.

The judicial right of review, by contrast, that is claimed by the German *Reichsgericht*, [**15**] in its famous decision of 4 November 1925[11] and, in analogous fashion, by other highest courts (*Reichsfinanzhof*, *Reichsversorgungsgericht*, *Preußisches Oberverwaltungsgericht*, etc.),* has only a very modest significance in comparison with the right of review exercised by the American Supreme Court. Closer scrutiny of its scope reveals that it keeps within very narrow boundaries. The justification of the decision of 4 November 1925 is based on the following sentence: that the judge is subject to statute (article 102 of the constitution of the *Reich*) 'does not rule out the possibility that a statute of the *Reich* or some of its provisions may be declared to be invalid by a judge if that statute stands in contradiction with other provisions that enjoy precedence and that the judge must take into account as well'.[12] What

[10] Fifth Amendment (directed to the federal government) of 1791: 'No person shall be deprived of life, liberty, or property, without due process of the law; nor shall private property be taken for public use without just compensation.' Fourteenth Amendment (directed to the states) of 1868: 'Nor shall any state deprive any person of life, liberty, or property, without due process of law; nor deny within its jurisdiction the equal protection of the laws.' The critique that is suggested by the oft-repeated saying, 'due process is what the Supreme Court says it is', is exaggerated but revealing.

[11] RGZ. 111, p. 322; see my detailed analysis in the *Festgabe zum 50jährigen Bestehen des Reichsgerichts*, vol. I, pp. 171–2.

[12] For purposes of comparison, let me cite the corresponding sentences of the famous and fundamental decision of the highest court of the United States *Marbury* v. *Madison* (1 Cranch, 137) – Chief Justice John Marshall from the year 1803: 'The powers of the legislature are defined and limited ... It is a proposition too plain to be contested that

this says is that if there are provisions in a constitutional statute that regulate a certain kind of matter of fact, and if we can subsume a case that is to be decided under that regulation, then the regulation contained in the constitutional statute is to be given preference, in the case of collision, over the regulation of the same matter of fact in an ordinary statute. A provision in a constitutional statute, however, can lead to an instance of collision only insofar as its content allows for a calculable and measurable subsumption of the facts of the case that is to be decided. Such a collision, like any real collision, logically presupposes that the colliding provisions are of the same kind. Things are rather different in the case of general principles and foundational values, authorizations, and mere determinations of competence that do not allow for the subsumption of a factual situation under a rule. It is only the possibility of subsumption of the facts of a case under the provisions of the regulation in the constitutional statute that makes it possible for a judge (as the *Reichsgericht* expresses itself) to refuse to apply the ordinary statute (but not to invalidate it) or, to be more precise, [**16**] to decide the case at hand by subsuming it under the provisions of the statute that is to be given priority. This is not really a denial of the validity of the ordinary statute. It is only a non-application of the ordinary statute to the concrete case at hand that occurs by virtue of an application of the constitutional statute. A later sentence in the decision therefore rightly says (pp. 322–3) that the judge is under a compulsion to 'leave aside' the ordinary statute. A closer analysis of the decision of the *Reichsgericht* thus already shows that the subjection of the judge to statute is not contradicted by this kind of right of judicial review. Rather, the subjection of the judge to statute is its basis and its only justification. But this means, at the same time, that only constitutional norms which allow for a clear subsumption of matters of fact under their provisions, but not general principles or

either the constitution controls any legislative act repugnant to it, or that the legislature may alter the constitution by an ordinary act. Between these two alternatives there is no middle ground. The constitution is either a superior paramount law, unchallengeable by ordinary means, or it is on a level with ordinary legislative acts, and, like other acts, is alterable when the legislature is pleased to alter it. If the former part of the alternative be true, then a legislative act contrary to the constitution is not law; if the latter part be true, written constitutions are absurd attempts on the part of the people to limit a power, in its own nature illimitable.' The *Reichsgericht* avoids such disquisitions in constitutional law; it reasons more cautiously, in spite of the brevity of its argumentation, and in a less principled way, and it rests content with the sentence: 'the prescriptions of the constitution of the *Reich* can only be invalidated by a constitution-amending statute that has been enacted in the proper way'.

authorizations, can determine the judge's decision, in a case of collision, in place of the ordinary statute.

The reasons given for the decision of 4 November 1925 emphasize, moreover, that a right of review is claimed only over ordinary statutes of the *Reich*, but not over statutes of the *Reich* that change the constitution, i.e. not over statutes that are enacted under the procedure of article 76 of the constitution of the *Reich.** As soon as a court is faced with a statute that has been enacted under article 76, every further opportunity for judicial review ends, according to the reasoning of the *Reichsgericht*. The important question in constitutional law* of whether there are limits to the power of revision or amendment; the possibility of an obvious abuse of the provisions of article 76; the necessity of drawing a distinction within the power of amendment, which has already been discussed in detail in the jurisprudence of the current constitution and that we cannot possibly dismiss by appeal to a summary absolutism that wants to find an all-powerful sovereign or even a bearer of the constituent power in article 76;[13] all these issues cannot be relevant for the exercise of a judicial right of review that stays within such narrow boundaries. With this, the question of whether there are illicit breaches of the constitution that could not be legalized through the employment of the procedure of article 76, as well as the question of whether this article customarily allows for 'apocryphal acts of sovereignty',* likewise disappears. Moreover, the *Reichsgericht* apparently does not claim a judicial right of review in case the legislature enacts an order or measure, in the form of an ordinary statute, that, in substance, fails to conform to the concept of statute characteristic of the rule-of-law state and that consequently may not, absent an explicit constitutional permission, [**17**] be enacted by way of legislative procedure and that exceeds the legislative competence of the legislator. The procedure of legislation can easily be abused to enact regulations that do not have the structure of genuine legal norms,

[13] On this issue see C. Schmitt, *Verfassungslehre* (Berlin, 1928), p. 102; *Juristische Wochenschrift* (1929), 2314; C. Bilfinger, *Der Reichssparkommissar* (Berlin and Leipzig, 1928), p. 17; moreover *Archiv des öffentlichen Rechts*, 11 (1926), 194 and *Zeitschrift für Politik*, 20 (1930), 81–2; R. Thoma in *Die Grundrechte und Grundpflichten der Reichsverfassung: Kommentar zum zweiten Teil der Reichsverfassung*, ed. H. C. Nipperdey (Berlin, 1929), vol. I, pp. 38–9, as well as in the *Handbuch des deutschen Staatsrechts*, ed. G. Anschütz and R. Thoma (Tübingen, 1930), vol. I, p. 143 and W. Jellinek, *ibid.*, vol. II, p. 154 (restriction at least for breaches of the constitution by way of article 76). Finally, and above all, E. Jacobi, 'Reichsverfassungsänderung' in the *Festgabe der juristischen Fakultäten zum 50jährigen Bestehen des Reichsgerichts*, vol. I, pp. 233–4.

for example for individual orders, dispensations, pardons, breaches of the law, to create privileges, etc. Very often, this practice threatens the independence of the judge, and one should therefore assume the existence of a (defensive) judicial right of review for the preservation of the constitutional position of the judiciary. This would be a form of self-protection of the courts against illicit interferences by other powers of the state. In this way the courts could be the guardians of a part of the constitution, namely of that part which concerns their own basis and position, of the provisions about the independence of the judiciary. The justification offered by the *Reichsgericht* for its aforementioned decision does not note this possibility. As a result, an important distinction within the judicial right of review – between the refusal to apply statutes that collide with constitutional provisions on the one hand and the defence against unconstitutional interferences on the part of other powers within the state on the other hand – fails to receive proper attention.[14] But it is certainly conceivable that the courts could refuse to apply the worst abuses and the most obviously exceptional statutes, by way of article 105 and article 109* of the constitution of the *Reich*. In this case, one would have to take note of the fact that an exercise of the judicial right of review based on an appeal to these articles of the constitution would amount to a different form of guardianship of the constitution than the one that becomes relevant in the cases the *Reichsgericht* had in mind in its decision of 4 November 1925, since the right of review, in these latter cases, is based only on the collision of subsumptions of matters of fact under statutes. The reasoning for the decision of 4 November 1925 strictly confines itself to the problem of the subsumption of matters of fact under statutes, and it does not speak in any way of the right of review that serves as a protection of the independence of the courts, which is different in kind.

Finally, the reasons offered for the decision of 4 November 1925 make clear that the *Reichsgericht* does not want to review the conformity of ordinary statutes of the *Reich* with the general principles of the constitution. It is concerned exclusively with the conformity of ordinary

[14] When the third civil senate, in its decision of 25 January 1924 (RG. 107, p. 319), says that article 105 in connection with article 103 burdens 'the courts with a responsibility to ensure that adjudication is exercised in all those cases in which, according to statute, it is to take place', it likely has this defensive right of review in mind. But compare the subsequent plenary decision of 22 February 1924, *ibid.*, p. 323, according to which article 103 and article 105 do not imply anything with respect to the scope of the adjudication that is to be exercised by the courts. For an example of the reverse case of the self-defence of a legislative body against the judiciary see note 5 on pp. 9–10* above.

statutes with individual constitutional norms that allow for subsumption. It does not claim a general power – exceeding the basis of a subsumption of the matter at hand under a constitutional statute [**18**] to review whether a statute agrees with the spirit of the constitution or whether it respects the general principles – namely basic rights and the separation of powers – which form the part of the constitution concerned with the rule of law. Rather, the argument cautiously, not to say formalistically, focuses on those legal norms contained in the constitution whose character and logical structure makes possible a confrontation with a regulation contained in an ordinary statute. Above all, there is no judicial right of review, according to this decision, of the conformity of a statute with general legal principles like good faith, natural law, reasonableness, expediency, or other such conceptions, which are employed in the practice of the Supreme Court of the United States. In the decision RGZ. 118, pp. 326–7 (*Juristische Wochenschrift* 1928, pp. 102–3) it is even made explicit that the concept of decency (§ 826 BGB.) applies only to relations in private law and cannot be transferred to the relationship in public law between the legislator and the citizen. The president of the *Reichsgericht*, Dr Simons, reported, apparently approvingly, that the senates of the *Reichsgericht* refused to criticize a legal norm enacted in accordance with the constitution from the point of view of natural law and to put themselves above the 'sovereign legislator'.[15] This remark is of particular interest, given that the association of judges had used a judgment of the fifth civil senate of 28 November 1923 (on the principle of revaluation according to equity and good faith from case to case, RGZ. 107, p. 78) to raise the demand that the principle of good faith also be applied to the statutory regulation of revaluation.

The right of judicial review claimed by the *Reichsgericht*, to sum up, is indistinguishable from the judicial right of review pertaining to any court that has to decide a case: it is only 'accessory' and only, as H. Triepel put it, a form of 'occasional adjudication'.[16] It is exercised only incidentally, if such exercise is needed to arrive at a judicial decision of a case, and potentially by every judge, hence diffusely.[17] Its effect is

[15] *Deutsche Juristen-Zeitung* (1924), 243.

[16] 'Wesen und Entwicklung der Staatsgerichtsbarkeit' in *Veröffentlichungen der Vereinigung der deutschen Staatsrechtslehrer*, issue 5 (Berlin and Leipzig, 1929), p. 26.

[17] I would like to propose the word 'diffuse' to designate the contrast with a right of review that is concentrated in the hands of a single authority.

restricted to the force of a precedent set by a highest court, a court, moreover, that has to compete, in Germany, with several other highest courts of the *Reich* and of the *Länder*. The main difference from the right of review claimed by the American judiciary is to be seen in the fact that the latter safeguards general principles and thus makes the court into the guardian and preserver of the existing social and economic order. The German *Reichsgericht*, [**19**] given the limitations of its right of review that we just outlined, is far from trying to lay claim to such a position. The power of review claimed by the *Reichsgericht* thus acknowledges that the process of legislation remains the centre of political decision-making. All adjudication is bound to norms and the possibility of adjudication ends as soon as the content of the norms themselves starts to get unclear and disputed. In a state like the contemporary German *Reich* the judicial right of review is therefore dependent on norms that allow for a clear subsumption of a matter of fact under a legal norm. It is another question to what extent it is conceivable and permissible to provide a certain freedom of movement to the discretion of the judge in matters of private law, on the basis of indeterminate and general conceptions, or by reference to standards of good faith and recognized custom. A relatively stable state of affairs as well as a firm social morality may be able to bring about a sufficient measurability and determinacy here. In the realm of public law, namely in matters of administrative law and in matters concerning the law of police, indeterminate conceptions are possible as well, as long as the situation of normality that is presupposed by any norm* can find a sufficiently clear and secure regulation, even without explicit decisions of the legislature and the government, through the views of the subjects of the law and through established legal practice. In all cases, however, norms that allow for determinate and measurable subsumption must remain the foundation of judicial review and decision. The subjection to such a norm is also the presupposition and the condition of all judicial independence. As soon as a judge leaves the ground on which a subsumption of matters of fact under general norms, and thus a determination of the decision by the content of statute, is actually possible, he can no longer be an independent judge, and no appearance of judicial form can protect him from this conclusion. 'The obligation to apply statute, to which alone the judge is subject, according to article 102, does not merely signify a boundary, but also the real justification for the freedom of decision: all other forms of restriction on judicial activity must be removed in order that the rule of statute can come to be sole determinant of the judge's decision.'[18] The problem of the *Freirechtsbewegung** and of the 'creative' judiciary is therefore, in the first instance, a problem of constitutional law.[19] [**20**]

The judicial right of review of the trial-deciding judge, according to all this, is not based on a superiority of whatever kind of the judge over the statute or the legislator but rather on its opposite. It originates from a kind of emergency situation in which the judge finds himself if he is faced with contradictory statutory provisions, but nevertheless has to take a decision in a trial, despite the fact that he is faced with conflicting obligations.[20] If he chooses one of the colliding statutory provisions as

18 M. Grünhut, 'Die Unabhängigkeit der richterlichen Entscheidung', *Monatsschrift für Kriminalpsychologie*, 3 (1930), 3; Schmitt, *Verfassungslehre*, pp. 274–6.

19 The *Freirechtsbewegung*, in spite of the pointer given by G. Radbruch, 'Rechtswissenschaft als Rechtsschöpfung – Ein Beitrag zum juristischen Methodenstreit', *Archiv für Sozialwissenschaft und Sozialpolitik*, Neue Folge 4 (1906), 355, frequently misunderstood the connections in constitutional law between independence and subjection to statute. Very apt E. Kaufmann's discussion at the *Staatsrechtslehrertag* (1926) (*Veröffentlichungen der Vereinigung der deutschen Staatsrechtslehrer*, issue 3 (Berlin and Leipzig, 1927), p. 19): the judge must stay within the limits of his specifically adjudicatory task, he must not overthrow the order that relates the judge to the legislator, and he must not usurp specifically legislative tasks; he may only criticize the violation of certain outermost limits. Despite all the 'freedom' of the 'creative activity' of the judge, despite the broadness of his discretion and the vagueness of some concepts, this 'subjection to statute' remains as long as one holds on to the bourgeois rule-of-law state. Compare also W. Jellinek, *Verwaltungsrecht* (Berlin, 1928), p. 10: 'The judiciary keeps itself wholly free from all legislation' or H. Triepel, 'Streitigkeiten zwischen Reich und Ländern', in *Festgabe der Berliner juristischen Fakultät für Wilhelm Kahl zum Doktorjubiläum am 19. April 1923* (Tübingen, 1923), p. 52: 'The filling up of statutory gaps through a balancing of interests must always, first and foremost, start out from the valuation of interests that has been provided, in a recognizable form, by the statute itself.' Very good on the boundaries of judicial discretion with respect to the creation of new law is J. Juncker in the 3rd edn of Friedrich Stein's, *Grundriß des Zivilprozeßrechts und des Konkursrechts* (Tübingen, 1928), pp. 23–4; on the point that there is no discretion 'in accordance with duty' but only 'in accordance with statute': U. Scheuner, 'Zur Frage der Nachprüfung des Ermessens durch die Gerichte', *Verwaltungsarchiv*, 33 (1928), 77 (this is undoubtedly correct as far as the courts are concerned; apart from that there remains the problem of the difference between provisions that 'authorize' a 'free' action and norms that bind materially, and that allow for a subsumption under a matter of fact, even if only through a reference to norms such as 'good faith', established commercial custom, etc.).

20 On the constitutional 'emergency situation' of the judge see Radbruch, 'Rechtswissenschaft als Rechtsschöpfung'. The connection with the constitutional question of the separation of powers is recognized in this paper (with reference to J. Hatschek, *Englisches Staatsrecht* (Tübingen, 1905), vol. I, pp. 155, 157–8), but then nevertheless once again misunderstood, under the influence of the critique put forward by the *Freirechtsbewegung*, and perhaps also due to the vacuum of constitutional theory in the pre-war era. The separation of powers is dismissed as 'rationalism' (see also E. Kaufmann, *Auswärtige Gewalt und Kolonialgewalt in den Vereinigten Staaten von Amerika* (Leipzig, 1908), p. 34). Radbruch speaks of the 'ghost of Montesquieu

the basis of his decision in the trial in order to arrive at a judicial decision, the other colliding provision will fail to find application. That is all. It is, as has already been shown, inaccurate to say that the trial-deciding judge 'declares the statute' he refuses to apply 'to be invalid'. The only thing one can correctly speak of here is a 'non-application of the statute' that is restricted to the decision of the concrete trial, a non-application that will, as a precedent, have a more or less calculable influence on the decisions of other courts. Above all, however, the judiciary remains bound to statute, and it does not become the guardian of the constitution by virtue of the fact that it gives precedence to its subjection to a constitutional statute over its subjection to an ordinary statute. [**21**] In a state that is not a pure jurisdictional state the courts cannot perform such functions. Apart from this we must not overlook that the goal of compliance with the general principle of conformity to statute, and consequently of the principle of conformity to constitutional statute, does not constitute a special institution. Otherwise we would have to discover a potential guardian of the constitution in any organ of the state, and finally in any citizen, an idea to which some constitutions have given expression by entrusting the defence of the constitution to the vigilance of all citizens of the state.[21] But this idea only gives rise to a general right to disobedience, and finally to a right to passive or perhaps even to active resistance, which has also been called a 'revolutionary right of necessity'.[22] In systematic treatises of constitutional law the right of resistance therefore appears as the last guarantee of the constitution whose defence and preservation it is supposed to serve.[23] But the function of a guardian of the constitution in constitutional law is precisely to

that still haunts us' (p. 365), but this ghost, whether we like it or not, is the spirit of the bourgeois rule-of-law state itself, and it will disappear only together with the bourgeois rule-of-law state itself. On Montesquieu's views concerning the proper limits of adjudication see also p. 136 below, note 25.

21 Thus the French constitutions of 1791 (final sentence), 1830, and 1848 (on the failed attempt to draw practical conclusions from these provisions compare Schmitt, *Verfassungslehre*, p. 116). More recently the constitution of the Free City of Danzig of 15–17 November 1920/14 June 1922, article 87: 'It is the duty of every citizen of the state to protect the constitution against illegal attacks', or the Greek constitution of 2 June 1927, article 127: 'La garde de la constitution est confiée au patriotisme des Hellènes' (F. R. Dareste and J. Delpech, *Les Constitutions modernes*, 4th edn (Paris, 1928), vol. I, p. 656).

22 Gneist, *Gutachten zum 4. deutschen Juristentag*, p. 31.

23 For example, R. von Mohl, *Die Verantwortlichkeit der Minister* (Tübingen, 1837), pp. 18, 575; F. C. Dahlmann, *Die Politik, auf den Grund und das Maß der gegebenen Zustände zurückgeführt*, 3rd edn (Leipzig, 1847), pp. 197–8; J. C. Bluntschli, *Allgemeines Staatsrecht*, 4th edn (Munich, 1868), vol. II, pp. 552–3; F. Gény as cited in

replace this general and incidental right to disobedience and to resistance and to make it superfluous. A guardian of the constitution in the institutional sense exists only where this replacement has taken place. It is therefore wrong to describe as guardians of the constitution all the many organs and people who can, through their occasional refusal to apply unconstitutional statutes or through their refusal to obey unconstitutional orders, contribute to a situation in which the constitution is respected and no interest protected by constitutional statute is violated. This is the systematic consideration that justifies the decision not to regard the courts as guardians of the constitution, despite the fact that they exercise an accessory and diffuse judicial right of review. Of course, it is perhaps less dangerous for courts, due to the guarantee of judicial independence, to disobey unconstitutional statutes and orders than it is for ordinary people. But it is impermissible to declare a particular category of public institutions to be the guardians of the constitution only because the preservation of the constitution is less risky [**22**] for these institutions than for others. The question of who runs the smallest risk cannot determine who is to be the 'guardian of the constitution'.

2 Material limits of adjudication (criminal justice for political crimes against state and constitution, impeachment)

It is a further, independent question what adjudication could, in principle, do for the protection of the constitution and how far it is possible to organize special institutions in the field of adjudication whose meaning and purpose it is to secure and guarantee a constitution. In the post-war period one did not at first ask this obvious question. Rather, discussion focused almost exclusively on a protection of the constitution through the courts, to be exercised by a *Staatsgerichtshof*, and people took it for granted, without giving the matter much thought, that the guardian of the constitution was to be found in the sphere of the judiciary. There are several reasons for this. The first is a mistaken and abstract conception of the rule of law. It seems natural to identify the decision of all political questions through the employment of judicial procedure with the ideal of the rule of law and to overlook that such an expansion into matters that are not justiciable can only damage adjudication. The consequence, as I have shown several times with respect to questions of constitutional as well as international law,*

Charles Eisenmann, *La Justice constitutionnelle et la Haute Cour Constitutionnelle d'Autriche* (Paris, 1928), pp. 44–5 would not be a juridification of politics but rather a politicization of adjudication. A consistently formalist method, however, stands above such concerns, and is in itself irrefutable, since it works with fictions that have no content and are therefore incapable of falsification. There are no longer any substantial problems or concerns as soon as it becomes permissible to disregard all substantial differences and as soon as the substantial difference between constitution and constitutional statute,* the difference between a statute that conforms to the rule-of-law state's concept of statute and a statute in the formal – that is, the political – sense,* the difference between a statute and a judicial decision, or Triepel's fundamental distinction between legal decision-taking and bargaining[24] may be ignored. As soon as one transforms all law into adjudication, and further formalizes all adjudication by claiming that everything that takes place in a court merits being called adjudication, one can solve the problem of the rule of law rather quickly. It will then be the easiest thing to simply let the *Reichsgericht* determine the general principles of policy according to the standards of good faith, in order to perfect the rule of law in the formal sense.

Such a mixing-up of concepts may explain in part why it seems to be a foregone conclusion to many that we ought to demand a *Staatsgerichtshof* endowed with open-ended competence. This demand, however, does not lead to a concrete institution, and one should avoid appealing to 'the rule of law' in this somewhat naïve way. [**23**] The phrase 'rule of law' alone does not decide anything for our question. It is possible to demand totally different and contradictory institutions on the basis of an appeal to the rule of law. Some renowned authors, for instance, portray the accessory right of judicial review as the only method conformable to the rule of law and put up a lively fight against the institution of a special *Staatsgerichtshof*, since they fear that the latter will inevitably lead to a restriction of the general right of review and concentrate the diffuse control exercised by all judges in one court, thus making it easier to bend it to political aims and to influence it. Hugo Preuß, in this context, even speaks of 'the fox that one appoints to guard the hen-house',[25] and H. Stoll says: 'The full judicial right of review is

[24] 'Streitigkeiten zwischen Reich und Ländern', pp. 19–20.

[25] In the constitutional committee of the Weimar national assembly, *Bericht und Protokolle des achten Ausschusses der verfassunggebenden Deutschen Nationalversammlung*, pp. 483–4: 'Now you want to choose (in the place of the general judicial right of review) a way out that deprives the ordinary courts of the right of review, and that creates,

what crowns the rule of law.' 'Just as independent administrative courts offer review of and protection against the interferences of the administrative state, independent organs must watch over the state as legislator.'[26] In the nineteenth century there were demands for a legal responsibility of ministers, which were often defended with the same phrases about the rule of law. People believed [**24**] this responsibility to be the cornerstone and the crowning achievement of the constitution. Gneist, for example, opined that 'the legal responsibility of the ministers is the final supplement that completes the rule of law'.[27] Or: 'The legal responsibility of ministers is not only the cornerstone of the responsibility of public servants in general, but also of the rule of law as such; it is the highest guarantee of a public state of right: without it, the constitution and the rights that people are to enjoy under the constitution are exposed to every violent abuse, without it the whole public law of a people must remain a *lex imperfecta*.'[28] But as I will show in the following

instead, an exceptional court (!), which can take action at the demand of 100 members of the *Reichstag*. That is a regulation – and I hope the members of the *Reichstag* will forgive me for saying this – that, to a certain extent, makes the fox the guardian of the hen-house . . . That is not an adequate replacement for the legal protection that one takes from every citizen by depriving the ordinary judge of one of his most important tasks.' Very interesting also the subsequent discussion: 'It would be a different thing if one wanted to give to a determinate number of members of the *Reichstag* the opportunity to force a decision on such a question (of the material constitutionality of a statute), but without any provision that excludes review in ordinary courts. One could justify that on the basis of the consideration that such a review of constitutionality, in fact, is likely to take place only infrequently.' This error of Preuß's is to be explained by the fact that he neither foresaw nor wanted the immense expansion of the so-called basic rights. Against the so-called 'Austrian solution' (p. 6 above) and the patronizing attitude towards the *Reichsgericht* that comes to the fore in the present drafts (p. 5 above, note 1) with special emphasis: F. Morstein Marx, *Variationen über richterliche Zuständigkeit zur Prüfung der Rechtmäßigkeit des Gesetzes* (Berlin, 1927), pp. 116–17, 139–40.

[26] *Ihering's Jahrbücher für die Dogmatik des bürgerlichen Rechts*, 76 (1926), 200, 201; *Juristische Wochenschrift* (1926), 1429 (remarks on the judgment of the *Reichsgericht* of 4 November 1925; here, however, *Stoll* argues for the 'Austrian example'), moreover in Nipperdey's collection, *Grundrechte und Grundpflichten der Deutschen*, vol. III, p. 187. Similarly Morstein Marx, *Variationen über richterliche Zuständigkeit*, pp. 151–2: 'The unrestricted judicial right of review, in the ordinary course of the legal process, realizes nothing less than the lawfulness of legislation, its conformity with juristic form. This, and only this, is the perfection of the rule-of-law state.' F. Adler, 'Verfassung und Richteramt', *Zeitschrift für öffentliches Recht*, 10 (1930), 120 takes the general right of review of all courts to be the natural, and the concentration in the hands of a special authority to be an 'artificial', solution.

[27] R. Gneist, *Der Rechtsstaat* (Berlin, 1872), p. 175.

[28] H. Schulze, *Preußisches Staatsrecht auf Grundlage des deutschen Staatsrechts dargestellt*, 2nd edn (Berlin, 1888/90), vol. II, p. 905; concurring with him T. von Pistorius, *Die*

pages, all experience attests that it is precisely the judicial responsibility of ministers that is relatively unimportant and uninteresting in comparison to the political, and that the perfection and completion of the rule of law through such legal formalities becomes problematic to the same degree to which legal formality perfects itself. The lesson to be drawn from these historical experiences, as well as from the ambiguity of the term 'rule of law', in any case, is that it is better to avoid an abstract appeal to the rule of law and to use the concepts and distinctions of a concrete constitutional theory instead.

Apart from the ambiguity and lazy convenience of the phrase 'rule of law', apart, moreover, from the widespread desire to centralize and concentrate the diffuse right of review that is exercised by several of the highest courts in contemporary Germany, there may be one further interesting explanation for contemporary attempts to turn a court that decides on the basis of judicial procedure into the guardian of the constitution. If one demands a guardian, one of course expects a particular kind of protection, and one argues on the basis of a conception of some specific danger that comes from a particular direction. The guardian is not supposed to offer abstract protection against dangers as such; he is to offer protection, rather, against very specific dangers and concrete fears. Whereas the danger to the constitution, throughout the nineteenth century, came from the government, i.e. from the sphere of the executive, present concerns are primarily directed against the legislator. Nowadays, provisions in constitutional statute already in large part serve the purpose of protecting certain matters and interests that would otherwise be the subject of ordinary legislation from this legislator, i.e. from changing parliamentary majorities. The 'anchoring' in a constitutional statute is supposed to secure certain interests, especially minority interests, against the present majority. This constitutes a strange transformation of function and expresses a tendency directed against the democratic majoritarian principle. [**25**] However, according to John Stuart Mill – who provided many of the typically liberal political-theoretical constructions of the nineteenth century, and who even today continues to influence political ideas much more strongly than the proponents of these conceptions tend to realize, due to their lack of

Staatsgerichtshöfe und die Ministerverantwortlichkeit nach heutigem Deutschem Staatsrecht (Tübingen, 1891), p. 209. Von Mohl says in the foreword to *Verantwortlichkeit der Minister*: 'A statute on the responsibility of ministers appears to most to be the cornerstone of the edifice of the constitutional state.'

concrete historical consciousness[29] – 'true' democracy can also be defined as the protection of the minority. A continuing compromise between the majority and minority, then, is supposed to be democracy's real and true essence.[30] This is a good example of how any political conception can be miraculously transformed with the help of the supplements 'true' or 'false'. Even the traditional view that, in a democracy, the majority decides, and that the outvoted minority has made a mistake concerning its own true will,* can thus be turned into its opposite. However that may be, it is of course inevitable that the change in function of the regulation by constitutional statute is followed by a change in the conception of the guardian of the constitution. Whereas the nineteenth century was primarily concerned with the protection against the government, people today often think only of the protection of the constitution against the legislative power of the parliamentary majority. And if the danger to the constitution threatens to arise in the sphere of legislation, the legislator can of course no longer be the guardian of the constitution. One did not look for the guardian in the sphere of the executive, because one was still under the influence of the constitutional battle against the government that had been waged for centuries. If the guardian of the constitution, then, neither belongs to the sphere of

[29] J. S. Mill, *Considerations on Representative Government*, 1st edn (London, 1861), ch. 7: 'Of true and false Democracy': false democracy is exclusively a representation of the majority, while true democracy is the representation of all, including the minorities. Of course, the 'true' democracy is the 'true' democracy. In reality, however, it is a liberalism that tries to protect itself from democracy, as L. von Ottlik, 'Diktatur und Demokratie', *Archiv für Geschichte der Philosophie und Soziologie*, 39 (1930), 223, rightly points out. Such definitions that operate with the distinction of true and false, authentic and inauthentic, are by no means a peculiarity of the German romantics and of Othmar Spann's. Rather, they are reflexes of genuinely political distinctions, and their 'true' or 'false', their 'authentic' or 'inauthentic' is the reflex of an existential distinction between friend and enemy. On the structural conformity of the political ideas of Austrian social democrats with J. S. Mill's liberal construction of the state, compare notes 26 and 27 of my talk on Hugo Preuß (Carl Schmitt, *Hugo Preuß. Sein Staatsbegriff und seine Stellung in der Deutschen Staatslehre*, no. 72 of the book series *Recht und Staat* (Tübingen, 1930), p. 34), see also p. 142 below.*

[30] H. Kelsen, 'Wesen und Entwicklung der Staatsgerichtsbarkeit', p. 81 [ch. 1 above, 1526]. Perhaps there is, besides the 'formal' concept of the monarchist, which has been aptly defined by A. Hensel, *Archiv des öffentlichen Rechts*, Neue Folge 15 (1928), 415 ('a monarchist, then, would be someone whose opinion differs from that of the Vienna School'), also an analogously constructed formal concept of the democrat. Hensel's quip is not merely 'humorous'; its humour hits the essential point, with the clarity of a joke: namely, that it is precisely the formalist approach to public law that can have a specifically political meaning; compare also pp. 75 and 128 below.

the legislative nor to the sphere of the executive, no other plausible candidate apart from the courts appears to remain. Such trains of thought once again show that the doctrine of the division of powers, [**26**] and its customary distinction of the authority of the state into three separate branches, is still very much alive in Germany as well as elsewhere. Here, it tends to go along with the tradition of the medieval jurisdictional state which still exercises a strong influence. As a result, it leads to the 'natural' demand for a sovereign court of law.

Consequently, we must initially ask the following question: how far is it possible at all to constitute the guardian of the constitution within the sphere of adjudication? Is it possible, in principle, for the function of guardianship of the constitution to be performed in adjudicative form? And would such an activity of courts, even if its exercise was surrounded by the appearance of judicial procedure, still be jurisdiction in the substantive sense and the judicial procedure be more than a misleading cloak for different and presumably highly political powers?

To begin with, cases in which a violation of a provision of a constitutional statute leads to a genuine trial in a criminal, civil, or administrative court are clearly of interest if we want to answer this question. In the case of civil and administrative justice, the protection offered by the courts serves the legal interest and the realization of the claims of one of the parties. Only criminal trials for certain kinds of offences aim directly to protect the constitution as such: high treason and other criminal actions where the constitution as a whole (as opposed to particular constitutional statutes) is the object to be protected by the criminal law. The political character of such trials usually results in deviations from the standard order of competence in criminal cases: in a trial for high treason, for example, the *Reichsgericht* is to act as a court of first and last appeal (GVG. § 134). The 'Statute for the Protection of the Republic' of 21 July 1922 (RGBl. I, p. 525), which has since expired, introduced a special *Staatsgerichtshof* as an extraordinary court for politically motivated crimes. In other states, we often find a second chamber of parliament, following the example of the English House of Lords, that functions as a *Staatsgerichtshof*. According to article 9 of the French constitutional statute of 24 February 1875, for example, the second chamber, the senate, can be constituted as a court of justice (*cour de justice*), in order to hold trial over the president of the republic or over ministers as well as to decide on attacks against the security of the state (*attentats commis contre la sûreté de l'État*). Even the states most deeply committed to the rule of law, for reasons of political interest, deviate from the general competence of ordinary criminal courts in such cases.[31] Despite these modifications, however, trials of this kind still intend a punishment after the fact of deeds committed in the past. They are still a form of vindicatory and repressive criminal justice. Such criminal justice is an important and valuable affair, [**27**] and it may be classified as a protection of the constitution in a wide and general sense. Nevertheless, this does not solve the problem of the guardian of the constitution. As a result of the judicial form of the proceedings in court, this protection of the constitution is restricted to past actions that have already been completed. The really interesting cases of constitutional protection therefore remain outside of the sphere of such judicial proceedings. As soon as one takes juridification seriously, and thus designs a full-blown juridical procedure with standing for contending parties, this protection will, for the most part, turn into a mere retrospective correction, since only completed actions are capable of being subsumed under established legal norms.

The fate of the courts for the impeachment of ministers is very instructive in this regard. Benjamin Constant, a liberal proponent of this institution, was still well aware of the peculiarity and abnormality of an accusation against a minister. He notes, in his famous essay on ministerial responsibility (1815), that the statute concerning ministerial responsibility must 'neither be precise nor detailed', despite the fact that the rule of law otherwise requires that criminal law and criminal procedure be characterized by the possibility of clear subsumption. '*C'est une loi politique dont la nature et l'application ont inévitablement quelque chose de discrétionnaire.*' For this reason, such cases, in Constant's view, ought to be tried by a court with special characteristics, namely a chamber of peers who exhibit independence and neutrality. The essential and at the same time general corrective, in this as well as in other contexts, is the publicity of discussion, '*la publicité de la discussion*', the central conception of liberal thought. The minister, according to Constant, cannot legitimately complain of the fact that the safeguards for the protection of the defendant that characterize ordinary criminal trials are not applicable here, since he is said to have made a special contract with the state whose service he entered. If his ambition needs to be satisfied by the high and splendid position of a minister, he ought to be

[31] See on this point Schmitt, *Verfassungslehre*, p. 134; moreover H. Triepel, 'Wesen und Entwicklung der Staatsgerichtsbarkeit', pp. 9–10.

willing to take the risk of such a political trial and to face a court that will decide, in large part, on the basis of free discretion (*arbitraire*). '*Mais cet arbitraire est dans le sens de la chose même.*' It is moderated by the solemnity of form, the publicity of the discussion, the echo in public opinion, the distinction of the judges, and the special character of the punishment.[32] We give a reminder of these arguments of a classical proponent of the liberal ideal of the rule of law because they show a keen sense of the peculiar nature of the procedure and of the problem of political justice in general. They are far from being raw abstractions. But the politically paralyzing effect of judicial form remains inevitable, even if we give the greatest consideration to the special character of political justice. [**28**] The experiences of the nineteenth century have shown as much. One may say that this was the most essential constitutional-historical experience and the core of the whole domestic conflict between German monarchy and German bourgeoisie throughout the nineteenth century. In the German constitutional monarchies the legal responsibility of ministers had the political function of preventing a political responsibility of the minister and thus to render the whole idea of ministerial responsibility as politically harmless as possible.[33] Judicial form was a reliable means of bringing about political ineffectiveness. People comforted themselves by claiming that the *Staatsgerichtshof* had already performed its function 'if its existence leads to the result that it never needs to take action'.[34] By now the institution of the judicial responsibility of ministers has lost its practical significance, and article 59 of the Weimar Constitution, a residual provision harking back to the fights between parliament and monarchy, dissolves the grounds and the content of responsibility into a general unlimitedness, in determining

[32] *De la responsabilité des ministres* (Paris, 1815), pp. 36, 44, 52, and elsewhere. On Constant's great significance for the constitutional theory of a bourgeois rule-of-law state and of the parliamentary system, see below, p. 134.

[33] Schmitt, *Verfassungslehre*, p. 331.

[34] Pistorius, *Der Staatsgerichtshof und die Ministerverantwortlichkeit*, p. 209; compare also Otto Mayer's remark quoted on p. 3 above. Apart from that, even the legal responsibility of ministers, as is well-known, was not realized in Prussia and in the *Reich*. And where it was regulated in a way that made it applicable, as in most of the medium-sized states, it could, without great effort, be made ineffective in consequence of the subordination of these states to the German *Bund*. 'It was precisely the constitution that made ministers responsible in the most effective way, the constitution of *Kurhessen*, that, in the year 1850, collapsed under the blows of the *Bundestag*'; F. Thudichum, 'Die Minister-Anklage nach geltendem deutschen Recht und ihre Unräthlichkeit in Reichssachen', *Annalen des Deutschen Reiches für Gesetzgebung, Verwaltung und Statistik*, ed. G. Hirth and M. von Seydel (Munich, 1885), vol. XVIII, p. 668.

that an action may be brought not only by virtue of a culpable violation of the constitution but even in case of a violation of an ordinary statute of the *Reich*.[35]

In order to attain a clearer grasp of this constitutional-historical experience, let us take a look at the most important and most widely discussed case of a constitutional conflict in the nineteenth century, the Prussian conflict of 1862–6.* Let us try to evaluate it on the basis of the textbook of Anschütz, one of the most famous German constitutional theorists. Anschütz is a particularly determined proponent of the view that a general *Staatsgerichtshof*, i.e. one competent to decide all constitutional disputes, is a demand of the rule of law.[36] But if we apply his statements and positions [**29**] to the interesting case of the constitutional dispute that arose in 1862, we arrive at the following: According to Anschütz, it is 'self-evident' that a constitutional court may only decide legal questions (in contrast to political questions). 'I do not believe', says Anschütz, 'that it is still necessary to say anything more about this point.'[37] However, with respect to the question that was at issue in the Prussian constitutional conflict, namely whether the government was entitled to continue to do its business without a budgetary law, he literally says, in the textbook Meyer-Anschütz, that 'public law ends at this point. The question how to proceed in the case of the absence of a budgetary statute is not a legal question.'[38] What, then, could a Prussian or German *Staatsgerichtshof* have done, according to Anschütz, if it had had to decide on the Prussian constitutional conflict? On the one hand, the *Staatsgerichtshof* is said to be restricted to purely legal questions, and on the other hand, public law is said to run out here. In the face of a case as concrete and important as the Prussian constitutional conflict of 1862, Anschütz's statements imply that there is no possibility of arriving at a judicial decision. And still, the value of such a court of law is supposed to

[35] For criticism of article 59 see above all K. Binding, 'Die staatsrechtliche Verantwortlichkeit' in K. Binding, *Zum Leben und Werden der Staaten. Zehn staatsrechtliche Abhandlungen* (Munich and Leipzig, 1920), p. 408: 'It is clear by itself that no atom of its former nature, which followed from the co-authorship of the pact between the King and the state's people, has been preserved in this new action against ministers.' The force of substantially juristic thought, always to be admired in Binding, proves itself as well in these state-theoretical expositions and immediately gets to the essential point: in the past, the constitution was a contract, while it is no longer a contract today.

[36] Compare p. 5 above, note 1.

[37] *Verhandlungen des Deutschen Juristentags 1926* (Berlin, 1927), p. 13.

[38] G. Meyer, *Lehrbuch des deutschen Staatsrechts*, 7th edn, revised by G. Anschütz (Munich and Leipzig, 1919), p. 906.

consist in the juridification of all constitutional disputes, and in their decision through a court judgment. The possibility of a *non liquet*, which had already been recognized by R. von Mohl, even for the case of an impeachment of a minister, as well as the 'very possible case' that the judge will have to 'declare that the meaning of a statute is ambiguous',[39] is not even taken into account. Consequently, such a view will have to lead to problems and contradictions in the case of any serious constitutional conflict. That is in the nature of things, which makes it extraordinarily difficult to combine genuine adjudication and genuine constitutional conflict. And this problem cannot be solved by declaring that the constitutional court is entitled to determine the ambiguous meaning of a constitutional statute by itself.

For the present, let us illustrate the simple unchanging structure of every political dispute about the presuppositions and the content of powers conferred by constitutional law with the help of another example that leads to a similar conclusion with respect to our question. By way of a decree issued on 18 July 1930 the president of the *Reich* dissolved the *Reichstag** with the following words: 'Since the *Reichstag* has decided today to demand that my decrees of 16 July enacted under article 48 of the constitution of the *Reich* be suspended, I hereby dissolve the *Reichstag* on the basis of article 25 of the constitution of the *Reich*.' After the dissolution, the government of the *Reich* re-enacted most of the provisions whose annulment had been demanded by the dissolved *Reichstag*, in a decree issued on the basis of article 48 on 26 July 1930. [**30**] The one question that ought to be especially important, among the many doubts and disagreements in constitutional law that arise here (and only some zealots of a blind normativism will still demand that they all be decided by the *Staatsgerichtshof* in Leipzig), is the following: whether the application of article 48 contained in the decree of 26 July 1930 constituted an unconstitutional bypassing or removal of the legislative competence of the majority of the *Reichstag*, and, moreover, whether one can rightly claim that the *Reichstag* was no longer capable of forming a majority and thus lacked any capacity to act. The answer to this question, in turn, depends on whether one believes that the government had really done everything possible to try to gain a majority; a question that is much disputed in the papers and in electoral agitation. It is, of course, unnecessary to comment here on the purely instrumental arguments and on the agitation one finds in party propaganda. As an

[39] Von Mohl, *Die Verantwortlichkeit der Minister*, p. 185.

extraordinarily revealing indication of the depth of the problem, however, it may be permissible to cite two contradictory statements from one and the same issue of a social-democratic journal of excellent reputation and high quality. In issue number 8, year 1 (August 1930) of the *Neue Blätter für den Sozialismus* August Rathmann makes the following comment on p. 340, in his essay 'Bourgeois Attack on Parliament and Constitution': 'The actions of the Brüning government would be excusable if it could have believed, in good faith, that it would, in any case, turn out to be impossible to find a stable majority capable of supporting a government. But it made no effort whatsoever to find such a majority on the left, the only place where it could have been won. To the contrary, the government snubbed and destroyed all efforts that were made, with an intensity that almost bordered on self-denial, by the social democrats. It is perfectly clear: the Brüning government wanted either a majority supported by the right or no majority at all. Since the first was unachievable, the government preferred to become a minority government and to stay in power through the tactical abuse of article 48. Hence, there is no possibility of conceding to the government that it believed in good faith that the conditions for a use of article 48 were objectively at hand. We are faced with a simple breach of the constitution and nothing else.' In the same issue, however, we find the following statement by Eduard Heimann on p. 374: 'I believe it is false to claim, as the official social democratic statements do, that a majority on the left was possible. . . . But without the participation of a people's party there was no possibility of any majority. If this is right, Brüning did not have a choice. He had to look for a majority on the right and, in the case of a failure of that option, he had to resort to a dissolution of the *Reichstag* or to the use of article 48.' That such disagreements concerning a recent state of affairs of which everyone is still immediately aware are possible amongst members of the same ideological circle and the same journal makes apparent – and to make this point is the only purpose of the citations – [**31**] that the only thing that, from a juristic point of view, can really be at issue, in all such pronouncements on constitutional disputes, is the *quis iudicabit*,* i.e. the question of who is to decide, and not the pseudo-normativity of a judicial procedure. According to the constitution of the *Reich* it is, depending on the situation, either the government, i.e. the president together with the chancellor who provides a countersignature, or the *Reichstag* that is competent to decide. If the *Reichstag* really is incapable of forming a majority, and thus incapable of making use of its constitutional competences (for example, of the power to withdraw its trust from the chancellor on the basis of an explicit vote of no confidence under article 54, or the power under article 48 paragraph 3 to demand the suspension of decrees enacted under article 48 paragraph 2), a court will not be able to make up for this shortcoming. If one were to install, in the place of the organ competent under the constitution, a constitutional court that is supposed to decide on all doubts and disagreements that may arise, and that may be appealed to by a majority of the *Reichstag* otherwise incapable of taking a decision, or perhaps even by a minority, one would install a political institution alongside the *Reichstag*, the president of the *Reich*, and the government of the *Reich*. This would accomplish nothing but a situation in which acts of government, by appeal to arbitrary 'reasons for decision', would either be taken or be prohibited under an appearance of judicial form. No fiction, however strained, could prevent everyone looking upon and evaluating such a court as a political institution. The problems and contradictions that have to result from any attempt to combine serious constitutional disputes with authentic adjudication would then become all too obvious.

The problematic character of this combination has been analysed by R. Smend (in his book *Verfassung und Verfassungsrecht*) and H. Triepel (in his report for the German *Staatsrechtslehrertag* 1928).[10] But even on the basis of the experiences so far, one can formulate the following simple alternative for any court of justice. It is perfectly evident in the case of a *Staatsgerichtshof* for the impeachment of ministers, and it will always repeat itself in all the different forms of adjudication controlling the legislator or government on matters of state or constitution: either we are dealing with an obvious violation of the constitution that can be ascertained without any doubt, in which case the court will exercise a vindicatory and repressive kind of adjudication and will, in some form or other, pronounce someone guilty for past behaviour; or the case is unclear and doubtful, be it for reasons of fact, or be it by virtue of the necessary incompleteness and vagueness of every written constitution in general, or by virtue of the ambiguous character of the second part of the Weimar Constitution in particular. [**32**] In that case, the question is not a 'purely legal question' and the decision of the court is something other than a judge's decision, i.e. something other than adjudication. The inner

[40] R. Smend, *Verfassung und Verfassungsrecht* (Munich, 1928), p. 135; Triepel in *Veröffentlichungen der Vereinigung deutscher Staatsrechtslehrer*, issue 5 (1929), p. 8: 'the essence of the constitution, *to a certain degree*, stands in conflict with the essence of constitutional adjudication' ('to a certain degree' emphasized in the original).

logic of judicial form, if thought through to the end, inevitably leads to the conclusion that an authentic judicial decision always arrives *post eventum*. If one tries to remedy this disadvantage through temporary injunctions issued by a court, the judge will find himself in a position to take political measures or to prevent them, and to become politically active in a way that will make him into a powerful factor in the domestic and perhaps even the foreign policy of the state. His judicial independence can, in such a case, no longer protect him from political responsibility, if a political responsibility is supposed to continue to exist at all.[41]

[41] On the permissibility of temporary injunctions of the *Staatsgerichtshof* for the German *Reich* under article 19: Fr. Giese, *Deutsche Juristen-Zeitung* (1929), 132. Giese holds that it is 'altogether unproblematic to also regard it as permissible for the court to order or to prohibit sovereign acts of the *Reich* by way of temporary injunction'. Affirmative also Heinsheimer, *Juristische Wochenschrift* (1926), 379 and Lammers, *ibid.*, 376, as well as W. Simons, in the introduction to H. Lammers and W. Simons (eds.), *Die Rechtsprechung des Staatsgerichtshofes für das Deutsche Reich und des Reichsgerichts auf Grund Art. 13 Abs 2 der Reichsverfassung*, vol. II (Berlin, 1930), p. 11. Differently, the president of the *Reichsfinanzhof*, G. Jahn, 'Darf der Staatsgerichtshof einstweilige Verfügungen erlassen?', *Juristische Wochenschrift* (1930), 1160, especially 1162: 'Here, the issue is of tasks that pertain to government, which has to bear the responsibility' and p. 1163 (against the analogy with § 944 ZPO., according to which the presiding judge can, in urgent cases, issue a temporary injunction without the full court): 'This would create a right of a single person to decide arbitrarily, over the heads of the president of the *Reich*, of the ministers, of the *Reichstag*, and of the state parliaments. This does not seem to me to be compatible with the ideological basis of a democratic constitution, as it has been created in Weimar.' For the practice of the *Staatsgerichtshof* for the German *Reich*: Decision of 17 November 1928 (RGZ. 122, Appendix, pp. 18–19; Lammers and Simons (eds.), *Die Rechtsprechung des Staatsgerichtshofes* (Berlin, 1929), vol. I, pp. 156–7): The *Staatsgerichtshof* claims this competence for itself, but one should pay attention to the fact that the dispute at hand was about monetary claims. The permissibility of temporary injunctions, it would appear, has been affirmed explicitly in the decision of 10 October 1925 (RGZ. 111, Appendix, pp. 21–2; Lammers and Simons (eds.), vol. I, p. 212), with consideration for the possibility (and for the protection) of an execution, and with the interesting argument: 'There is nothing to suggest the view that the issuance of temporary injunctions is supposed to be impermissible' (that amounts, on closer inspection, to a mere 'why not?'). On the other hand, there are a number of rejections of appeals for temporary injunctions: Decision of 23 October 1929 (RGZ. 126, Appendix, pp. 1–2; Lammers and Simons (eds.), vol. II, p. 72), here already a principled restriction: 'only with great hesitation and in exceptional cases'; especially important the decision of 13 July 1929 (Lammers and Simons (eds.), vol. II, p. 98): the *Staatsgerichtshof* cannot, by way of temporary injunction, prevent the promulgation of statutes that have been decided upon; and above all the declaration in the decision of 17/18 July 1930 (RGZ. 129, Appendix, p. 31) 'that the *Staatsgerichtshof* will, in the future, as it has in the past, make use of the instrument of a temporary injunction only with the utmost care and hesitation'. In this decision, by the way, it is also stated explicitly that these temporary injunctions are a balancing of interests, not adjudication.

Judicial independence loses its basis in constitutional law [**33**] to the same extent to which it distances itself from the uncontroversial content of the provisions of constitutional statutes. It is simply inevitable that adjudication, as long as it stays adjudication, will always come too late politically, and the more so the more thoroughly and carefully, the more in conformity with the rule of law and with judicial form we design the procedure. In the case of indisputable violations of the constitution, which will not tend to be an everyday occurrence in a civilized state, this will lead, in the best of cases, to a punishment of the guilty party and to a rectification of past injustices. In doubtful cases, however, the mismatch between judicial independence and its presupposition, the strict subjection to statutes whose content binds the judge, will become evident.

This is confirmed not merely by the development of the action of impeachment against ministers, but also by other practical experiences. We will still have to speak, below, of the peculiarities of a constitutional court in the case of a federal organization of the state,* as well as about the *Staatsgerichtshof* for the German *Reich* under article 19 of the constitution of the *Reich* (in the fourth section of this chapter). But the general principle that always prevails, with respect to the relation between the protection of the constitution and the judicial process, is everywhere recognizable in the reality of political life. For this reason, corrections and modifications of judicial procedure become inevitable even in the states most stringently and honestly committed to the rule of law, as soon as a consideration for the constitution makes itself felt. If it has turned out to be necessary even in tax law to determine that, in the interpretation of statutes concerning taxation, 'their purpose, their economic significance, and the development of the economic situation is to be taken into account' (§ 4 of the *Reichsabgabenordnung**), then it is still less possible not to pay attention to the concrete issue in constitutional law. Why is it that every state, when it comes to delicts such as high treason or the attack on the foundations of the state, departs from the competence of the general ordinary criminal courts, and either declares competent a highest court, acting as the first and last instance, or even appoints a special *Staatsgerichtshof*, as an extraordinary court for the protection of the security of the state?[42] With what justification does one restrict or eliminate the right of review of the ordinary courts through a *Staatsgerichtshof* or constitutional court, and with what justification does

[42] Compare p. 26 above.

one reserve the right to initiate proceedings in front of such a *Staatsgerichtshof* or constitutional court to particular political authorities (government, parliament, *et al.*; article 13 paragraph 2 of the constitution of the *Reich* accords the right only to the 'competent' central institution of the *Reich* or the state)?[43] Why is it reasonable and inevitable to give special consideration to questions of practicality, [**34**] as is the practice, for example, in the field of the tax law of the federal state, where one has to delimit the respective competences of the *Reichsfinanzhof* and of the *Reichsrat*?[44] Why did the statute of the *Reich* of 30 August 1924 (so-called Dawes plan*) provide the government of the *Reich* and the *Reichsbahn* corporation with the opportunity to appeal to an arbitrator, against the decisions of the *Reichsbahngericht*, if one of them believed that the execution of the court's decision might endanger the payment of the interest and principal on the reparation-bonds?[45] If such corrections may become necessary, for practical reasons of foreign policy, with regard to the decisions of a special court such as the *Reichsbahngericht*, are they not, then, at least equally necessary with

[43] According to the German draft of 1926 (*Deutsche Juristen-Zeitung* (1926), 842) the *Reichstag*, the *Reichsrat*, and the government of the *Reich* are supposed to be able to appeal to the *Staatsgerichtshof* for a decision. For further examples see Schmitt, *Verfassungslehre*, p. 137. On the purely political meaning of this restriction of the right of appeal, with very remarkable criticism, Morstein Marx, *Variationen über richterliche Zuständigkeit*, pp. 116–18.

[44] § 6 of the statute on the financial adjustment between *Reich*, *Länder*, and local authorities of 27 April 1926 (RGBl. I, p. 203): in the case of differences of opinion between the *Reich's* minister of finances and the government of a state on the question whether a tax regulation in the law of a *Land* is compatible with federal law, the *Reichsfinanzhof* decides, on appeal by the *Reich's* minister of finances or the government of the *Land*. The decision is to be taken by the grand senate of the *Reichsfinanzhof*, in the composition prescribed by § 46 para. 2 sentence 1 of the tax code of the *Reich*. The enactment of more detailed regulations remains reserved to special statutory regulation. By contrast, the decision on the question of whether taxes levied by a *Land* or by a local authority are likely to damage the tax revenue of the *Reich*, and whether preponderant interests of the *Reich* are opposed to the levying of these taxes, is taken by the *Reichsrat*, on appeal by the *Reich's* minister of finances or the government of a *Land*. Furthermore, the *Reich's* minister of finances can submit questions concerning the interpretation of tax statutes to the *Reichsfinanzhof* for an advisory opinion (§ 43 of the tax code of the *Reich*).

[45] § 44 para. 3 of the federal statute on the German *Reichsbahn* corporation (*Reichsbahn* statute) of 30 August 1924, RGBl. II, p. 272: if the government of the *Reich* or the corporation is of the opinion that, in the case of the execution of the judgment of the court, payment of the interest and principal on the reparation bonds is endangered, either of these two parties may, within the period of a month from the promulgation of the decision, appeal to the mediator (§ 45). The federal statute of 13 March 1930 (Young-plan) struck this paragraph out, together with § 45, RGBl. 1930, II, p. 364.

respect to the decisions of a court of justice that has to decide on all constitutional disputes of the German *Reich*? And if they are necessary, does this not imply that we have, once again, already given up on the principle of boundless justiciability?

As long as the difficult problem was treated with a concrete awareness of the problems of constitutional law, authors consistently avoided talking in general terms of 'adjudication in matters of state' or of 'constitutional adjudication'. Sieyès, who is widely recognized as the father of such ideas, spoke only about a *jury constitutionnaire* or a *magistrature constitutionnelle* that was supposed to be employed to protect the constitution against infringements. He said, in this context, that this magistracy was nothing in the sphere of the executive or the government, and also nothing in the legislative sphere; that it was, rather, a constitutional magistracy. He does not explicitly call it a court of justice. Rather, he makes it understood that he takes it to be a part of the constituent power, or at least [**35**] to be an organ involved in the exercise of that power.[46] In the Swiss constitutional plans of the time, which envisage a court of jurors that is to guard over the constitution, the proposal, again, is that of an action against violations of the constitution that have already been committed.[47] Where, as in the Napoleonic constitutions, a *sénat conservateur* is made the guardian of the constitution, the sphere of adjudication is already left behind once again, and a legislative or advisory authority has become competent. The representatives of the liberal ideal of the rule of law, in particular Benjamin Constant and Guizot, remain aware of the natural limits of adjudication, and often express themselves on this issue with epigrammatic precision, Constant in the expositions on the legal responsibility of ministers cited above,[48] Guizot with the sentence, that one cannot repeat often enough in Germany today, that 'politics has nothing to gain and the judiciary all to lose' through such juridifications.[49] The teachers of constitutional theory in nineteenth-century liberal Germany who are committed to

[46] References in A. Blondel, *Le Contrôle juridictionnel de la constitutionnalité des lois* (Paris, 1928), pp. 174–5.

[47] On this point see E. His, *Geschichte des neueren Schweizerischen Staatsrechts* (Basel, 1921), vol. I, pp. 196, 202.

[48] Above p. 27.

[49] *Des Conspirations et de la justice politique* (Brussels, 1846), p. 101. In the context of the conflict between the president of the *Reichsgericht*, Dr Simons, and the government of the *Reich*,* this sentence, unfortunately, has also shown itself to be true in a personal respect.

the rule of law, in particular von Mohl, Bluntschli, and Gneist, take the problem to consist in large and systematic political interconnections; for them, it is either the legislative assembly (as the representation of property and education) or the co-operation of the hereditary monarch and the two chambers that is the most secure guarantee of the constitution.[50] Apart from that, they are mainly interested in the possibility of an impeachment of ministers – which was then the only instrument to enforce the responsibility of ministers and, allegedly, the 'cornerstone of the edifice of the constitutional state'[51] – or in the judicial right to review the monarch's decrees; but even here these authors avoid superficial fictions of absolute justiciability.[52] [**36**] Later, in the security of the

[50] Below pp. 77 and 154, note 39.

[51] Von Mohl, *Verantwortlichkeit der Minister*, preface: 'A statute on the responsibility of ministers appears to most to be the cornerstone of the edifice of the constitutional state.'

[52] Von Mohl, *Verantwortlichkeit der Minister*, for instance p. 15 (criticism of the Saxon solution, which turns the *Staatsgerichtshof* into a referee and an interpreter), p. 187 (of the excuse by virtue of a state of emergency) etc.; moreover in the remarks on the French constitution of 1848 in R. von Mohl, *Staatsrecht, Völkerrecht und Politik. Monographien* (Tübingen, 1860), vol. I, pp. 561–4, at p. 562: 'However a state court of justice might be organized, and however the responsibilities may be determined, this much is clear in any case, that the law, after a victory over a treasonous attack has been achieved, can concede no more than a firm and just treatment.' Bluntschli, *Allgemeines Staatsrecht*, vol. II, pp. 550–1; compare also the quotation on p. 77 below. Gneist, *Gutachten zum 4. deutschen Juristentag*, p. 23: no review of violations against general principles of the constitution; Gneist's misleadingly formulated sentence: 'For every article of the constitution, jurisdiction takes the place of interpretation' (*Der Rechtsstaat* (1876), p. 175), is meant to refer only to administrative jurisdiction. Apart from that, Gneist put little trust in a state court of justice or constitutional court staffed with professional public servants; compare his utterance in the session of the Prussian *Abgeordnetenhaus* on 9 February 1866 (*Stenographische Berichte*, p. 130): 'As far as I am acquainted with history, the public service has not yet met the test even a single time, in cases where one wanted to put the whole question of the constitutionality of a government standing in full power onto the shoulders of a few trusted men! Even in England, the judiciary, resplendent in its quasi-ministerial position, and surrounded by its colleagues of the splendid, independent, and public-spirited bar, has not passed such a contest of power, as is supposed to take place here on any given day, even a single time. And, in the poor condition of our own public service, ... seven such men are honestly supposed to give an impartial judgment on this question, that stands between the ministers and those who accuse them?! I never doubted that the whole grand college of the superior tribunal, with its six or seven senates, would hardly be strong enough – if we had to enact statutes – to form a *Staatsgerichtshof* out of its permanent members.' – What Thudichum has to say on the 'inadvisability' of the action against ministers ('Die Minister-Anklage', pp. 637–8) is already born of a different spirit. A. Haenel, *Deutsches Staatsrecht* (Leipzig, 1892), vol. I, pp. 562–4, addresses the federal jurisdiction over cases of constitutional conflicts within the constituent states in the systematic context of the external relations between states and not in the context of the rule of law state.

pre-war years, one could afford to endorse a cheap formalism that simply denied the substantive problems. As soon, however, as concrete political conflicts once again broke out, the consciousness of the fact that all judicial form is confined to narrow limits immediately awoke from its slumber, and when the attempt was made, in the year 1919, to decide the question of the culpability for the war by way of such means, Erich Kaufmann reminded us, with an impressive treatise, of the boundaries that the rule of law imposes on legitimate adjudication.[53]

3 The authoritative determination of the content of a constitutional law that is doubtful in its content is in substance constitutional legislation, not adjudication

In order to answer the fundamental constitutional-theoretical question, we have to repeat once again that there is no rule of law in the liberal-bourgeois sense without independent courts, that there are no independent courts without subjection to the content of statute, and that there can be no subjection to the content of statute without a distinction in kind between statute and court judgment. The bourgeois rule-of-law state, after all, rests on a material distinction between different powers. One can reject the separation of powers [**37**] on the basis of absolutist tendencies, as was customary in the public law theory of German constitutional monarchy. One can also leave a certain freedom to the judge, but one cannot give him the power of political decision, which pertains to the legislator, without changing a judge's constitutional position. The fundamental distinction between legislation and adjudication cannot be refuted by stretching the literal meaning of imprecise terms (separation of powers, division of powers), or by pointing out that there are difficulties of separation in particular cases, as well as an overlap of boundaries, and so on, or by remarking, finally, that, apart from the usual tripartite division (legislature, executive, judiciary), there are other classifications and distinctions that are equally conceivable. Larnaude is right to say[54] that there are as many separations of powers as there are states. But this diversity does not prove that there is no distinction at all, or that we are entitled to disregard all differences between legislation and

53 E. Kaufmann, *Untersuchungsausschuß und Staatsgerichtshof* (Berlin, 1920), pp. 83–4, on the concept of judicial process.

54 F. Larnaude, 'L'Inconstitutionnalité des lois et le droit public français', *Revue politique et parlementaire*, 126 (1926), 186.

adjudication. It remains a valid principle of the bourgeois rule of law that a state without a material distinction between legislation, execution (government and administration), and adjudication is a state that does not have a constitution in the liberal sense of the term.[55]

In a bourgeois rule-of-law state, adjudication exists only as a court judgment that is based on a statute. The formula 'on the basis of a statute', which was employed by all German constitutions since the nineteenth century in a typical way, is of central importance for the organization of a bourgeois rule-of-law state. I made this point repeatedly throughout the last few years and explained the systematic context of this idea.[56] The formula has no lesser (even though a slightly different) significance for the sphere of all German constitutions than the formula of 'due process of law' in Anglo-Saxon constitutional law. This latter formula likewise implies that we have to distinguish between statute and court judgment, and therefore also between legislator and judge. However diverse the institutionalization of the separation of powers may turn out to be in different states, the point of the differentiation of powers in the rule-of-law state always remains the same. The organizational distribution of the state's functions is supposed to correspond, at least as far as the ordinary distribution of competences is concerned, to a material difference in the activity. A statute is not a court judgment, and a court judgment is not a statute, but rather the decision of a 'case' on the 'basis of a statute'. The special position of the judge in the rule-of-law state, [**38**] his objectivity, his position above the parties, his independence as well as the fact that he cannot be removed, all this rests only on the fact that he decides on the basis of a statute and that his decision is derived, in a measurable and calculable way, from the content of another decision that is already contained in the statute. If the legislative organs, in exceptional cases, perform functions other than that of legislation, by the use of legislative procedure, then one can designate that as 'formal legislation', just as it is possible, in an analogous fashion, to introduce a formal conception of adjudication, namely if a judicial organ that has been formally authorized to do so takes decisions, by way of judicial procedure, outside of the material sphere of adjudication. But this does

[55] Schmitt, *Verfassungslehre*, p. 127.

[56] *Ibid.*, p. 157. Carl Schmitt, *Unabhängigkeit der Richter, Gleichheit vor dem Gesetz und Gewährleistung des Privateigentums nach der Weimarer Verfassung* (Berlin, 1926), pp. 17–18; *Juristische Wochenschrift* (1926), 2271 (misunderstood in R. Grau, 'Der Vorrang der Bundeskompetenz', *Festschrift Ernst Heinitz zu seinem 50jährigen Dienstjubiläum* (Berlin, 1926), p. 103).

not yet license the inversion of an empty formalism that simply turns things upside down, and now begins to call everything that is handled by the legislative organs through legislative procedure a statute, and that considers everything that is done by a court to be adjudication. This kind of logic, while constantly mixing things up, proceeds in the following manner: adjudication is what is done by a judge, hence everything that is done by a judge has to be adjudication; the judge is independent, hence, everyone who is independent has to be a judge; everything that is done by an independent organ, under the protection of its independence, is therefore adjudication; consequently one only has to see to it that all constitutional disputes and differences of opinion are decided by independent judges, and one will have 'constitutional adjudication'. If one uses formal concepts of this kind, it is possible to put everything under any label. Anything can become adjudication, just as anything may be called a 'norm' and, at the same time, be described as the enactment of norm, or finally even turn out to be a part of the constitution.[57] The constitutional organization turns into a world of treacherous fictions and legal science into the training ground of a mode of thought that Hofacker has referred to as 'goose-leg logic'.[58] [**39**]

[57] 'Through the mediation of the idea of constitutional form', as Kelsen expresses himself ('Wesen und Entwicklung der Staatsgerichtsbarkeit', p. 38, [ch. 1 above, 1491]).

[58] After the syllogism Schopenhauer makes fun of: a human being has two legs, everything that has two legs, therefore, is a human being, therefore, the goose is a human being, etc.; *Der Gerichtssaal*, 94 (1927), 213–14; W. Hofacker, 'Die Erneuerung des Rechtsbetriebs durch die Rechtsphilosophie', *Archiv für Rechts- und Wirtschaftsphilosophie*, 21 (1927–8), 18–19; *Reichsverwaltungsblatt* (1930), 34. On the devastations which this kind of logic has wrought in the theory of the concept of statute, compare Schmitt, *Verfassungslehre*, pp. 143–4. With regard to the general legal-theoretical problem, I would like to add the following: according to its true nature, there is no adjudication other than adjudication bound to statute. Therefore, one has to hold on to the material difference between legislation and adjudication, and it is impossible to construct a 'continuous hierarchy' from the constitution to the judge's decision, as Kelsen tries to do ('Wesen und Entwicklung der Staatsgerichtsbarkeit', pp. 31–2, 42 [ch. 1 above, 1486–7, 1494–5']). What the judge does on the basis of a statute is determined, in its content, by the statute, and is therefore something essentially different from legislation 'on the basis of the (constitutional-) statute'. The phrase 'on the basis of statute' loses its specific meaning for the rule of law if it is transferred in such a way to relations not determined by content and thus made 'continuous'. One can say, by exploiting an imprecision of language, that the legislator, too, enacts his statutes 'on the basis of' the provisions in constitutional statutes that make him the legislator; that the *Reichstag*, for example, legislates 'on the basis of' article 68 of the constitution of the *Reich*. One can claim that the chancellor of the *Reich* determines the basic guidelines of policy 'on the basis of' article 56 of the constitution of the *Reich* and that the president of the *Reich*

The complete erroneousness of this kind of logic, which plays itself out in a strange mixture of empty abstractions and fantastic metaphors, becomes fully apparent once we turn to the problem of the guardian or guarantor of the constitution. [**40**] A statute cannot be the guardian of another statute. The weaker statute, of course, cannot protect or

takes dictatorial measures 'on the basis of' article 48 of the constitution of the *Reich*. It is impossible, however, to derive the content of the concrete act of state from such regulations of competence and 'authorizations', which is what is meant when we talk of the application of a statute on the part of a judge or of a decision 'on the basis of' a statute. If a judge condemns the defendant to prison on the basis of a provision in a criminal statute, the sentence of imprisonment is derived from the content of the statute, with the help of a subsumption of the facts of the case at hand under a norm which allows for such a subsumption of the facts of the case and which, within a certain frame (punishment by imprisonment), already determines the content of the judgment in advance. If the chancellor of the *Reich* brings about an alliance with Russia, 'on the basis of' article 56 of the constitution of the *Reich*, or if the president of the *Reich* orders economic help for eastern Germany, 'on the basis of' article 48, then the Russian alliance or the help for the east is not derived, in its content, by way of a subsumption of a matter of fact, from the provisions of the constitutional statutes in article 56 or 48, in the way that the prison sentence is derived from the norm of criminal law. It is an abuse to blur the distinction between regulations of competence and material norms and to let them fade into each other, to designate the most different judgments, commands, regulations, authorizations, and decisions with the word 'norm', and, where adjudication is at issue, to not even distinguish anymore between justiciable and non-justiciable 'norms'. It is of the essence of the judicial decision that its content be derivable from the norm upon which it is based, that the norm that purportedly binds the judge is really binding, in a measurable and calculable way, instead of merely authorizing the judge. A certain range of conceptual vagueness can remain; but if the 'norm' becomes so wide and devoid of content that it is no longer possible to subsume matters of fact under it, if the norm does no more than to allocate a competence, then the basis for the possibility of legitimate adjudication falls away, to the same extent, together with the justiciable norm. If the guidelines of policy were to be determined by the *Reichsgericht*, instead of the *Reichskanzler*, under the protection of its judicial independence, this would nevertheless fail to amount to adjudication, even if one declared all provisions of the code of civil or criminal procedure to be applicable 'by analogy', even if one enacted the 'strict norm' that the *Reichsgericht* is only allowed to enact correct guidelines, and even if the decision was then taken 'on the basis of' this 'norm' and 'on the basis of' the pleas of parties and counsellors after a hearing in court; even if, in short, one was to put on a parody reproducing every single detail of a judicial proceeding.

Like every other problem in constitutional theory, the problem of 'constitutional adjudication' can be solved very easily with the help of 'formal' concepts. But as soon as one keeps in mind the material difference of legislation and adjudication, as well as the difference between justiciable and non-justiciable norms, it turns out that this simple and easy solution represents nothing more than a game of equivocations. When Kelsen, for example, speaks of a continuous 'hierarchical construction of legal order' and builds his whole argument on this conception, then this is possible only as long as the different significations of the ambiguous word 'constitution' – basic norm, general political decision, the 'contingent content of written paragraphs of the constitution' guarantee the stronger statute. What about the other way around? Is the statute that is more difficult to change supposed to guard the weaker statute? This would turn everything into its opposite, since we are concerned with the protection and the defence of the constitutional statute, not with that of the ordinary statute. The problem, after all, is how to protect the statute that is more difficult to change from changes introduced by ordinary statute. This problem would not arise if a norm could normatively protect itself. A norm is valid, to a stronger, a lesser, or

(R. Smend), allocation of competence through constitutional statute, material legal regulation by a particular constitutional statute – as well as the many kinds of 'norms' are not distinguished, but rather perpetually confused with one another. In A. Caspary's, 'Versuch über den Begriff des Staatszweckrechts', *Zeitschrift für die gesamten Staatswissenschaften*, 83 (1927), 238 the author fittingly remarks: if the constitution becomes positive law, then it is 'no more and no less law than, for instance, the code of civil law, which is also not at all valid "on the basis of" the constitution'. The theory of 'legal hierarchy' with its 'continuity' of the norm, then, might perhaps be interesting for an abstract theory of law, but not for constitutional theory. It misses the specific problem, because it merely provides an empty legal-theoretical schema of a 'legal order' and a continuous 'stepwise construction' of a 'hierarchy' of 'norms', instead of a foundation in constitutional theory. This alone explains the rather peculiar idea that, in the case of constitutional adjudication, we are faced with an adjudication of norms over norms, that the constitutionality of statutes 'does not differ, from a legal-theoretical and legal-technical point of view, from the demand that jurisdiction and administration be conformable to statute' ('Wesen und Entwicklung der Staatsgerichtsbarkeit', p. 53 [ch. 1 above, 1504]), and that a statute as such can become the object of a trial instead of the basis of the judicial decision. Since there are statutes with a stronger and with a weaker force of validity, and since a constitutional statute is changeable only under the more onerous conditions laid down in article 76 of the constitution of the *Reich*, whereas an ordinary statute may be changed or abrogated by a later ordinary law, one may, with a certain justification, speak of stronger or weaker, or of 'higher' and 'lower', norms. The expression is useful, and not liable to be misunderstood, as long as it is used merely to designate the different degrees of difficulty in changing or abrogating a statute. But it turns into a metaphor full of fantasy if one then proceeds to speak of a general 'hierarchy of norms', and if one mixes together, in this picture, three or four different kinds of superiority and subordination – the 'superiority' of the constitution over all the life of the state, the 'superiority' of the stronger statute over the weaker, the 'superiority' of the statute over the court judgment and other acts of the application of statute, the superiority of the superior over the subordinate. Strictly speaking, there is only the hierarchy of concretely existing beings, the superiority and subordination of concrete authorities. A 'hierarchy of norms' is an uncritical and un-methodological anthropomorphization of the 'norm' and an improvised allegory. If one norm is more difficult to change than some other, then this is in every conceivable respect – logically, juristically, sociologically – something other than a hierarchy; the relation of an allocation of competence to the acts issued by the institution which it makes competent is not comparable to the relation of a superior to an inferior administrative authority (for the reason that a norm is not an authority), and the ordinary statute, *a fortiori*, is not the subordinate of the statute that is more difficult to change.

an equal degree than some other norm; [**41**] it is possible for there to be contradictions and collisions between norms that must be dealt with somehow; a norm can repeat the content of another norm; it can also give it a new and strengthened validity (for example, if an ordinary statute is repeated as a constitutional statute); a norm may introduce new legal consequences, threats of punishment, etc. (strengthened 'sanction'); it is possible to create ever stronger norms, norms ever more difficult to change. But as long as things proceed normatively, we can achieve a protection and guarantee of a norm only through another, even stronger norm. But this is no longer possible with respect to a constitutional statute, at least if we regard it as a conceptual truth that the constitutional statute is a highest and strongest norm. The problem of the guardian of the constitution is the problem of the protection of the strongest norm against a weaker norm. This problem does not even exist for a normativist and formalist logic because, in its view, the stronger validity cannot be threatened or endangered by a weaker validity. Formalist constitutional law, here as everywhere else, stops where the real problem begins.

If constitutional adjudication were an adjudication exercised by the constitutional statute over the ordinary statute, it would be adjudication of a norm as such over another norm as such. But there can be no adjudication of a norm over another norm, at least not as long as the concept of a 'norm' retains a certain precision, and the word is not simply turned into a mere catchphrase with dozens of side- and back-doors, thus becoming a vehicle for boundless ambiguity, an abuse to which it is, however, particularly suited. Otto Mayer issued a strong warning against the abuse and confusion surrounding the word 'norm' years ago.[59] Unfortunately in vain. Otherwise, the idea of constitutional adjudication as an adjudication of a norm over a norm would probably not have been possible. If we use the word 'constitutional adjudication' to designate a form of adjudication that is determined only by the kind of statute used as a basis for decision, then every civil trial that is decided on the basis of article 131 or article 153 of the constitution* will have to count as constitutional adjudication. Or are we supposed to think of the constitution (or more precisely: the constitutional statute) as the subject matter of the trial? A statute that serves as the basis of a decision, however, is not the subject matter of a trial, but rather what grounds the decision. Or are we supposed to personify the constitutional statute

[59] O. Mayer, *Deutsches Verwaltungsrecht*, 3rd edn (Berlin, 1924), vol. I, p. 84, note.

into a judge and think of the ordinary statute as a party to the trial? In this case, the specific character of 'constitutional adjudication' would consist in the fact that a norm is judge, as well as party, basis of the decision, and finally even tenor of the decision. This would be a strange trial, the conceivability of which only proves that one can do anything with the word 'norm' once the abstractions turn into metaphors, and once the 'continuity' of the concepts no longer consists in anything more than the fact that empty and meaningless abstractions can be confounded without limit, [**42**] just as the shadow of one figure in a play of shadows can be made to traverse through that of any other.

The application of a norm to another norm is qualitatively different from the application of a norm to a matter of fact, and the subsumption of a statute under another statute (if it is at all conceivable) is essentially different from the subsumption of a regulated matter of fact under its regulation. If it is determined that there is a contradiction between an ordinary statute and a constitutional statute, and if the ordinary statute is declared invalid, this cannot be called an application of the constitutional statute to the ordinary statute, at least not in the sense in which we talk about the judicial application of a statute to a particular case. In the first case, we compare norms, and in the case of collisions or contradictions, which are possible for a number of very different reasons, one of the norms invalidates the other. In the second case, the case of the judicial application of a statute to a particular state of affairs, we subsume a singular case under general concepts (and thus under the statutory regulation). If a constitutional statute determined that 'the theological faculties are to be preserved' (article 149 paragraph 3 of the constitution of the *Reich*) and if an ordinary statute determined, to the contrary, that 'the theological faculties are to be abolished', it would be an application of the constitutional statute to preserve the theological faculties and an application of the ordinary statute to abolish them. That can hardly be denied. In both cases we have an application of a statute to a state of affairs and the decision, in both cases, is equally based on a subsumption of the state of affairs under the determination contained in the statute. If, on the other hand, we confront the content of the one statute with that of the other, determine that there is a collision or contradiction, and raise the question of which of the two contradictory statutes is to be considered valid, we compare general rules with one another, but without subsuming them under each other or 'applying' them to each other. The decision that one or the other of the two general rules is to be considered valid is not the result of a subsumption of one rule under another. What is supposed to be subsumable in such a case? If one statute orders something that is contrary to what another statute orders, and if the contradiction is decided by invalidating one and validating the other of the two contradictory orders, we do not subsume the invalid statute under the valid or the valid statute under the invalid. In our example, the state of affairs to which the two contradictory statutes are to be applied is precisely the same in both cases: the existence of theological faculties. One cannot, therefore, say that the theological faculties of the constitutional statute are subsumed under the theological faculties of the ordinary statute. Neither does the solution of the contradiction rest on a subsumption of one of the contradictory orders under the other or on an application of one to the other. It would be nonsensical to claim that 'being abolished' is subsumed under 'being preserved' or the other way around. This clearest case of a collision of norms [**43**] thus shows that the typical juridical procedure of arriving at a decision, namely the judge's subsumption of a state of affairs under a statute, is in no way applicable here. No subsumption is taking place at all. We merely declare the existence of a contradiction, and then go on to decide which of the contradictory norms is supposed to be valid and which is to be 'refused application'.[60]

[60] Compare p. 16 above. The 'contradiction' of the one norm with the other is also something other than the 'contradiction' with a norm that is determined to exist in case a judge declares a defendant to be guilty. If the norm determines: you ought not to kill, and if the judge determines: X has killed, then the contradiction that is hereby determined to exist is a contradiction that differs in kind from the contradiction between two norms that contradict each other: you ought not to kill and you ought to kill. The determination: what X has done here is a killing, and the other determination: the one norm determines the opposite of the other norm, cannot logically or juristically be brought under a common and 'continuous' category. It is possible that the normativist approach wanted to apply the method of fictional doublings here, which is in general characteristic of it, because it does not speak of the thing, but only of its formalized shadows. Just as normativism leads us to undergird the validity of a concrete contract with the validity of the general norm that contracts are binding (compare Schmitt, *Verfassungslehre*, pp. 69–70), so we can, as normativists, add to the validity of any statute the validity of the general norm that valid statutes are valid, just as every prohibition may be supplemented by a further prohibition of disregarding valid prohibitions, etc., etc. With the help of such empty additions one might say that there is, apart from the constitutional statute and the ordinary statute, a provision in constitutional law according to which it is forbidden to enact ordinary statutes that contradict a constitutional statute; and if the creator of the ordinary statute violated this provision, the violation would then have to be ascertained by the judge. But even this would not be a hierarchy of norms and no constitutional adjudication. If a judge, here, was to decide that the legislator did act against this prohibition, this would, in substance, be repressive criminal

If one keeps to this simplest case of an obvious contradiction between a constitutional statute and an ordinary statute, one is not likely to be tempted to speak of an adjudication of the constitutional statute over the ordinary statute. The only form of adjudication that is possible, in such a case, is the vindicatory criminal justice against a person, but not against a norm. The practical interest in a decision of a collision of statutes, however, is usually not directed towards such cases of obvious contradiction, and neither towards a retrospective correction of violations that took place in the past. Such cases will, in normal times, not be very frequent. That interest centres, rather, on the very different question of who is to decide doubts and disagreements [**44**] as to whether and to what extent there is a contradiction or not. The interest in this question is very large, in the context of the Weimar Constitution. Especially in the second main part of the constitution we find a most perplexing juxtaposition of a large diversity of basic principles, individual material provisions, programmes, guidelines, and dilatory compromises* that defer a decision.[61] The word 'norm' would lose any value and usefulness if one decided to designate all these different propositions as 'norms'. In the most difficult and practically most important cases the ambiguity or contradiction arises from within the constitutional provisions themselves, because they are in themselves unclear or contradictory, due to the fact that they are based on conflicting principles which stand side by side without having any real connection. The possibility of working with the fiction of a hierarchy of norms obviously comes to an end at this point, and if one provision of a constitutional statute determines something in a way that conflicts with another provision of the same constitutional statute (as for example paragraph 1 and paragraph 2 of article 146*) it is impossible to find a solution for the collision with the help of the metaphor of a 'hierarchy' of norms. But even in less extreme cases of doubt or disagreement over the question of whether there is any contradiction between a constitutional statute and an ordinary statute we do not perform subsumptions of matters of fact in the manner of true adjudication, because the doubt

justice and not constitutional adjudication. Apart from that, nothing is to be gained by the addition of the constitutional prohibition against enacting ordinary statutes that conflict with constitutional statutes; the determination that there is a contradiction between a command and the opposite command thereby still does not turn into a subsumption of a matter of fact of the kind that is characteristic of the judicial application of statute.

61 Schmitt, *Verfassungslehre*, pp. 31–2.

always concerns the content of a constitutional statute. If the constitutional statute determines 'the theological faculties are to be preserved', and an ordinary statute determines 'the theological academies are to be abolished', it may be doubtful whether the theological academies are theological faculties and whether the state of affairs regulated by the ordinary statute also falls under the constitutional statute. Taking a closer look, this scenario, likewise, is not a subsumption of the ordinary statute under the constitutional statute, not a subsumption of the same kind as a judge's subsumption of a concrete matter of fact under a statute. The question is, rather, whether the state of affairs falling under the ordinary statute also falls under the constitutional statute. One and the same state of affairs is being subsumed under both statutes. The subsumption of the same state of affairs under the constitutional statute is similar to its subsumption under the ordinary statute. The question is merely under which of the two contradictory statutes the concrete state of affairs ought to be subsumed, and it is only the concrete state of affairs, not the ordinary statute, that is subsumed. This is clear proof that the questions and doubts exclusively concern the content of the constitutional statute, but not the subsumption of an ordinary statute under a constitutional statute. The question of whether the matter of fact regulated by the ordinary statute (theological academies) falls under the matter regulated by the constitutional statute (theological faculties) concerns the possibility of subsuming a narrower concept under a wider concept, not the possibility of subsuming an existing state of affairs under a normative rule. [**45**] Only in a psychological and unspecific sense can we say that this is a subsumption (and this we could not even say in a psychological sense in case of an obvious contradiction between two norms). But this kind of subsumption is not specifically that of adjudication; it is only that of all human judgment and thought in general. If we accept this meaning of subsumption, then it will also be 'adjudication' and 'enactment of a norm' if someone says that a horse is not a donkey. In the case of a decision of doubts and disagreements over whether there is a contradiction between two norms, we do not apply one norm to the other. We rather – because the doubts and disagreements always arise with respect to the content of the constitutional statute – authentically determine and put beyond doubt the contestable content of a norm. This is, in substance, a removal of an ambiguity in the content of the constitutional statute and thus a determination of the content of that statute. Hence, it is legislation, or even constitutional legislation, and not adjudication.

We always arrive at the same clear alternative: either there is an obvious and indubitable violation of the provisions of a constitutional statute, and in this case a court will punish the violation, by explicitly ascertaining it in all due form and by exercising vindicatory criminal justice; or the doubt concerning the content of the norm is so well-founded, and the content of the norm itself so unclear, that it is impossible to speak of a violation, even if the court is of a different opinion from the legislator or the government whose acts are said to stand in contradiction with the ambiguous constitutional statute. It is clear that, in this latter case, the decision of the court can have no other meaning than that of an authentic interpretation. The Saxon constitution of 1831 therefore said quite fittingly, in its § 153 paragraph 3, that the opinion given by the *Staatsgerichtshof*, if doubts arise as to the interpretation of particular points of the constitutional charter that cannot be removed through agreement between the government and the estates, ought 'to be regarded as an authentic interpretation and to be followed'. This corresponds to the nature of things and it applies to all cases in which some organ determines the authentic content of a norm in this fashion. It does not matter here whether this organ is organized like a court or in some other way, and it does not matter either whether it decides through the use of a judicial procedure or in some other manner. Every organ that authentically puts the disputed content of a statute beyond doubt in fact acts as a legislator. And if it puts beyond doubt the ambiguous content of a constitutional statute it acts as a constitutional legislator.

The ultimate legal-theoretical reason for this ever-recurring alternative is the following: every decision, even that of a trial-deciding court that subsumes a concrete matter of fact, contains a moment of pure decision that cannot be derived from the content of the norm.[62] **[46]** I refer to this as 'decisionism'.* This decisionist element is recognizable even where a court is exercising an accessory right of review only. If one is willing to make the effort, for instance, to read *Warren's* history of the Supreme Court of the United States, one will find that all important decisions of this court were characterized by vacillating arguments and by strong minorities of outvoted or dissenting judges. So-called 'five against four' or 'one man decisions' do occur and are criticized, perhaps too severely.[63] This observation ought to

[62] C. Schmitt, *Gesetz und Urteil* (Berlin, 1912); *Politische Theologie* (Munich and Leipzig, 1922); moreover H. Isay, *Rechtsnorm und Entscheidung* (Berlin, 1929).

[63] On this point see, for instance, Ogg and Ray, *Introduction to American Government*, p. 428.

put to rest the naïve faith that holds that the arguments in these decisions have no other purpose than to transform a hitherto doubtful unconstitutionality into an unconstitutionality that is now evident for all the world. The point is not overwhelming argumentation, but rather decision, through the authoritative removal of doubt. The decisionist character of every judgment of an organ whose specific function it is to decide insecurities and disagreements, needless to say, is even stronger and more thoroughgoing. Here, the decisionist element is not merely a part of the decision, a part that has to supplement the norm in order to make a *res judicata* possible in the first place. Rather, the decision as such is the point and purpose of the sentence, and its value does not consist in an overwhelming argumentation, but in the authoritative removal of the doubt that arises from the many different and contradictory possible argumentations. It is an old experience, unfortunately not made obsolete by the progress of our critical thought, that logical sophistication, far from ending doubts, can easily produce ever new questions. This, by the way, also puts to rest the view – a view that often shows up in the plans for a constitutional court or that at least unconsciously contributes to such plans – that such a court will remove doubts and disagreements in its capacity as the best expert on legal matters, that it would function as a kind of supreme legal-scientific referee. Such arguments usually overlook that the effectiveness of an advisory opinion is essentially based on its argumentative convincingness, and that an advisory opinion therefore constitutes the opposite pole vis-à-vis the pure decision. A judge is not a legal advisor, and the connection between advising and judging is of itself liable to lead to confusion, because the activity of an advisor is not a judicial activity or adjudication, but, in substance, an administrative activity.[64] If one endows

[64] The advisory opinions of the *Reichsgericht* under § 4 of the *Einführungs-Gesetz zum GVG*. and of the *Kartellgericht* under § 20 of the decree against the abuse of positions of economic power from 2 November 1923, RGBl. I, p. 1067, likewise belong in this context. On the advisory opinions of the *Reichsfinanzhof* under § 43 of the tax code of the *Reich*: J. Popitz, in *Steuer und Wirtschaft*, 8 (October 1928), 985 and A. Hensel, *ibid.*, 1130 ('an interesting indication of the functional change of the institutions of the state'). An especially odd connection is contained in § 106 of the *Arbeitsgerichtsgesetz*: 'Insofar as the parties can enter into a contract providing for the mediation of labour disputes in accordance with § 91 they can agree, even without excluding the possibility of an appeal to the courts of labour law, that questions of fact that are relevant for the decision of the legal dispute are to be decided through a mediatory opinion (contract providing for a mediatory opinion). The agreement has the effect that questions of fact which are to be decided by the mediatory opinion are withdrawn from further material scrutiny and evidential assessment during the trial in the labour court, and that the labour court is bound to the mediatory opinion.' On the attempt to construct a neutral state of experts compare p. 103 below.*

an advisory opinion with binding force, [**47**] then it is decision and no longer counsel.[65] If this is true of every judge it has to be true to an infinitely heightened degree of an organ that is appointed to remove, authentically and finally, doubts and disagreements of opinion.

This point, in addition, has immediate practical relevance for a constitution of the kind of the Weimar Constitution, due to a special reason. Every constitution contains lots of 'reservations'. But the creators of this constitution, to make matters worse, disregarded the old experience all too much that one must not write too many things into a constitution.[66] The party politicians, rather, scribbled an awful lot into the second main part of the constitution, quite contrary to the spirit of Preuß's original drafts. Given the state of constitutional theory at the time, this seemed perfectly reasonable and legitimate. If the constitution is equated with the particular constitutional statute in a formalistic fashion, and if a constitutional statute is defined, once again in purely formal terms, [**48**] as 'nothing but a statute that is more difficult to amend', then everyone does well to make use of the occasion and to try to protect everything that he holds dear by making it more difficult to change. What is more, the colourful diversity of the declarations of principle and of the particular provisions of constitutional statutes contained in the second part of the constitution, a diversity that has given rise to a particularly large number of doubts and disagreements, often does not contain any real decision at all, not even a compromise, but only ambiguous formulas that defer the

[65] A. Bertram, *Zeitschrift für Zivilprozeß*, 53 (1928), 428: 'With the quasi-authentic interpretation by way of advisory opinion, the *Reichsgericht* would, *de facto*, become a court of law for the binding interpretation of statute; all that has rightly been put forward against the plan for such a court of law (compare H. Reichel, *Gesetz und Richterspruch* (Zürich, 1915), p. 111, and the authors cited there) also speaks against the introduction of such a duty of the *Reichsgericht* to issue advisory opinions. A *Reichsgericht* that was to amend doubts and gaps in the statute, would perform a trespass into the sphere of the legislator, and would rob itself, at the same time, of the impartiality that is required for judicial activity.' 'To issue advisory opinions is not part of judicial activity, it is an administrative activity, and it must therefore be restricted (namely because of § 4 of the *Einführungs-Gesetz zum GVG*) to that aspect of administrative activity which can be transferred to the courts, namely to business having to do with the administration of justice.'

[66] On the problem of reservations: C. Bilfinger, 'Betrachtungen über politisches Recht', *Zeitschrift für ausländisches öffentlisches Recht und Völkerrecht*, 1 (1929), 63; for 'adjudication in matters of state' see F. W. Jerusalem, *Die Staatsgerichtsbarkeit* (Tübingen, 1930), pp. 97–8. Apart from these, compare B. Constant, *Réflexions sur les Constitutions* (Paris, 1814), ch. 9: 'De la nécessité de ne pas étendre les constitutions à trop d'objets'.

decision and that attempt to cater to fundamentally different and often even contradictory points of view. The compromises concerning the question of the church and the question of education provide illuminating examples of this. In the case of such 'dilatory compromises',[67] the decision over 'doubts and disagreements' is, in truth, tantamount to the enactment of the deferred regulation itself. If some institution had decided on the constitutionality of the hotly debated draft of a federal educational statute in 1927, it would, for the first time, have provided article 146 with its missing content, and it would have decided the question of education authoritatively. If a court judges in a case like this, it obviously acts as a constitutional legislator and exercises a highly political function.

. . .

4(c) *State- and constitutional adjudication as an expression of the tendency to transform the constitution into a constitutional contract (compromise)*

To focus on the constitutional law of a federal state is not the only possible way to view the constitution as a contract. Apart from this, there is one further and essentially different possibility for treating the constitution as a contract, and thus to turn it into the basis of an adjudication in matters of state or of constitutional adjudication. Namely, if the state is not considered as a unity closed in itself (be that unity brought about by the rule of a monarch or of a ruling group, or by the homogeneity of a people at one with itself), then it is grounded, dualistically or even pluralistically, on the contract and compromise of several parties. The kind and form of its political existence, in that case, are determined by contracts and agreements.[68] The medieval corporate state, for instance, **[61]** was based on contracts of many

[67] Schmitt, *Verfassungslehre*, pp. 31–2; compare p. 44 above.

[68] The distinction of contract and agreement* may be left aside here; but it needs to be noted, at the least, that it is a remarkable if not a disturbing symptom that this distinction, which was developed by Binding and Triepel for relations between states (in international law and the law of a federation), and which has only recently been called 'incontestable' by E. A. Korowin, *Das Völkerrecht der Übergangszeit. Grundlagen der völkerrechtlichen Beziehungen der Union der Sowjetrepubliken* (Berlin-Grunewald, 1929), p. 25, is transferred to domestic relationships and agreements in Germany today, for instance H. Liermann, 'Über die rechtliche Natur der Vereinbarungen politischer Parteien untereinander', *Archiv des öffentlichen Rechts*, Neue Folge 11 (1926), 411; on the notion of 'agreement' in the literature in labour law that deals with the doctrine of

different kinds, on agreements, reciprocal promises, capitulations, compromises, recesses, *stabilimenta*, understandings; in short, on a system of mutual contracts, with rightfully acquired contractual rights and with typical existential reservations – including, if necessary, a right of resistance – which, for better or worse, belong to this kind of contract. According to a widespread German view of the nineteenth century, moreover, a view that was more or less dominant for decades, the constitution was to be seen as a contract, and more specifically as a written contract, whose partners were the sovereign and the people, the king and the chambers of parliament, the government and the representative assembly of the people. This conception gave rise, as a particularly important practical conclusion, to an unambiguous conception of a constitutional dispute, a conception that was, as one rooted in historical tradition, for the most part undisputed in Germany before the year 1919: only quarrels between the government and parliament, concerning their reciprocal rights under the constitutional compact, were seen to qualify as constitutional disputes. Another consequence, extremely important from a political point of view, consisted in the fact that a change of the constitution, as a result, was to be regarded as a further contract between the parties to the constitutional contract. With respect to the issues that interest us here, however, what counts, above all, is that disagreements, differences, and quarrels over the content of the written constitution were supposed to be resolved by way of mutual agreement. That is how the famous *Verfassungsverständnis* of the year 1843* came about in Bavaria. Although this agreement was not regarded as an authentic interpretation of the constitution, but only as an 'instrument of exegesis', it nevertheless served, with reservation of the points of contention that had not been resolved, as the basis for the exercise of the right of the estates to approve the budget.[69] The consequence was drawn openly and

collective agreement see E. Jacobi, *Grundlehren des Arbeitsrechts* (Leipzig, 1927), pp. 260–1; moreover A. Hueck and H.C. Nipperdey, *Lehrbuch des Arbeitsrechts* (Mannheim, 1930), vol. II, p. 116 where the distinction is portrayed as having no value for labour law, as well as the literature referenced there.

69 M. von Seydel, *Bayerisches Staatsrecht*, 2nd edn (Tübingen, 1896), vol. II, pp. 565–6. Von Seydel declares the *Verfassungsverständnis* to be a valuable instrument of exegesis, whose political significance was to be seen in the fact that it gave expression to concurrent legal convictions of the crown and the chambers (p. 571). The *Verfassungsverständnis* is printed in F. Stoerk and F.W. von Rauchhaupt (eds.), *Handbuch der deutschen Verfassungen. Die Verfassungsgesetze des deutschen Reiches und seiner Bundesstaates nach dem gegenwärtigen Gesetzesstande*, 2nd edn (Munich, 1913), p. 109. Especially clear on the connection between the concept of constitution and constitutional interpretation: von Mohl, *Verantwortlichkeit der Minister*, pp. 173–4: 'If,

explicitly in § 153 of the Constitution of Saxony of 1831: [**62**] the *Staatsgerichtshof* decides only once doubts arise as to the interpretation of particular points of the constitutional charter, and once these cannot be removed by way of agreement between the government and the estates. The close relationship of some phenomena in constitutional law with those of the law of peoples, which has been emphasized by Carl Bilfinger,[70] becomes recognizable with particular clarity wherever the idea of a constitutional contract or of a constitutional compromise appears. The typical expression of this is that the doubtful or contested issue first becomes the object of negotiations and that the competence of the court is grounded in the voluntary subjection of the parties.

The current constitution of the *Reich*, however, holds fast to the democratic idea of the homogeneous, indivisible unity of the German people as a whole, which has given this constitution to itself, by virtue of its constituent power, through a positive political decision, and thus through a unilateral act. With this, all interpretations or applications of the Weimar Constitution that aim to turn it into a contract, a compromise, or something similar, are solemnly rejected as violations of the spirit of the constitution. A contractual element, however, was reintroduced into the Weimar Constitution insofar as the latter preserves a federal organization. Even though the federative basis was given up, a federalist element, and thus one that unavoidably contains relationships of a contractual character, was recognized as constitutional. This forms the basis for the kind of *Staatsgerichtshof*, focused on the constitutional law of a federal state, that we discussed in the previous section.* In addition, however, a different, pluralistic element, one that is akin to the contractual element or that, at least, leads towards it, also appears in the reality of our contemporary constitutional situation. The development of some social groups, political parties, interest groups, and other organizations tends towards a situation in which a plurality of firmly organized complexes, each with its own bureaucracy and with a whole system of institutions that aid and support it, spread to the whole

however, the law that is to be interpreted has not yet been determined in such a sufficient way, the following principles are to be applied: 1. A constitutional charter is the constitutional instrument concerning the basic principles of government that have been laid down by the prince and the people in mutual agreement', etc.

70 C. Bilfinger 'Betrachtungen über politisches Recht', 63; also Jerusalem, *Die Staatsgerichtsbarkeit*, pp. 97–8. The 'analogy to international disputes' is already pointed out in Thudichum, op. cit., p. 681 and von Mohl, *Verantwortlichkeit der Minister*, p. 209; compare also p. 17 note 66 above, on the analogy with labour law see the note on p. 144 below.*

German *Reich*, crossing the boundaries of the *Länder*, and take control of the will-formation of the state as well as of positions of public power in the *Reich*, the *Länder*, and in the institutions of local self-government. A number of different social powers and organizations may come to be the bearers of this pluralism, about which we will have to say more below: firmly organized political parties, interest groups (industrial associations, the *Landbund*,* labour unions), [**63**] religious associations. They exist and act as the possessors of a relatively secure, firm, and calculable plenitude of social power. Their significance differs within different issue-areas (foreign policy, economy, culture, ideology), and it is correctly ascertainable only if attention is paid to their systematic co-operation. But the pluralistic division of the state is visible clearly enough as a tendency. One effect, above all, that is of importance for the problem of the constitution as a contract, is ascertainable here: the constitution itself, as well as the will-formation of the state that takes place within its framework, appears as a compromise of the different bearers of pluralism within the state. The changing coalitions of social organizations of power, which depend on the issue-area of the compromise – foreign policy, economic policy, social policy, cultural policy – transform the state itself into a pluralistic entity with their methods of negotiation. In the theoretical literature, one has already proclaimed the thesis, with great carelessness, that the parliamentary state as such is, in its essence, nothing but a compromise.[71] With this, it is said openly, even if perhaps without a consciousness of all the consequences for constitutional law, that today's state, together with its constitution, is nothing but the object of the compromise of the social powers that participate in the contract of compromise.

[71] H. Kelsen, *Allgemeine Staatslehre* (Berlin, 1925), p. 324 (with the typical liberal confusion of liberalism and democracy); *Wesen und Wert der Demokratie*, 2nd edn (Tübingen, 1929), p. 57; especially characteristic also 'Wesen und Entwicklung der Staatsgerichtsbarkeit', p. 81 [ch. 1 above, 1526–7], where the compromise character of the modern democratic state is associated with constitutional adjudication in a federal state. The whole report assumes that constitution equals constitutional statute, and that constitutional statute equals norm. The ambiguous concept of norm once again proves, in this context, to be the ideal vehicle to bring about conceptual shifts: since all kinds of things count as norms, even the fundamental difference in the understanding of the concept of constitution, a difference that stands in the centre, theoretically and practically, of any discussion in constitutional law can disappear by a sleight of hand. Is the constitution a political decision of a united people, homogenous within itself? Is it a statute, and if so, of what legislator? Is it a contract or a compromise, and if so, who are the parties to the contract? All these differences between a decision, a statute, and a contract can be covered up with the one word 'norm'.

The Weimar Constitution, too, is often considered to be and defined as a compromise, and this either as a whole – in that one sees it as a 'peace among classes' or a 'peace among religions', or perhaps only as a mere 'ceasefire' between the German working class and the German bourgeoisie, Catholics and Protestants, Christians and Atheists, etc.[72] – or else with respect to important particular sections and provisions, for instance those concerning church and education, where the designation 'school-compromise', in particular, is very common and not without importance. In all such cases of a pluralistic [**64**] splintering into pieces of the unity of the state and of the constitution, the parties that carry the pluralism lay claim to the constitution itself, i.e. to the power of the state and to its exercise. The constitution becomes their constitution, because they are the ones who made it. They claim rights to the power of the state itself, since they can appeal to the fact that they are the bearers of the compromise, i.e. that they are the parties to the contract through which the constitution as well as the other will-formation of the state comes about. Their differences come to resemble conflicts under international law more and more, and are therefore resolved, at first, through mutual negotiations or through mediation, and, eventually also through judicial decision, on the condition that the parties have voluntarily decided to subject themselves to it, and to the extent that the issue is arbitrable or justiciable. The contemporary German doctrine of the state and constitutional theory lacks a systematic consciousness of these conditions. The interests behind this pluralism, moreover, do not, for the most part, want to see their practices carried into the light of a systematic clarification. They do not even have an interest in carrying the practical conclusions of their behaviour to their end, because they try, if possible, to avoid the risk of the political, if for no other reason than out of consideration for their supporters and voters. A lot, thus, comes together in order to veil reality with the help of a so-called formalism, and to keep it in an inscrutable half-light, by the use of an unclear antithesis of the 'legal' and the 'political' that serves to bolster all kinds of evasions and prevarications.

[72] See Schmitt, *Hugo Preuß. Sein Staatsbegriff und seine Stellung in der deutschen Staatslehre*, pp. 31–2.

3

The guardian of the constitution: Schmitt on pluralism and the president as the guardian of the constitution

Translation of Carl Schmitt (1931a) *Der Hüter der Verfassung*, 4th edn (Berlin: Duncker & Humblot, 1996), 73–91, 129–40, and 149–59.

II.1(a) The development of parliament into the arena of a pluralistic system

The constitutional situation of the present is characterized by the fact, first of all, that many institutions and norms of the nineteenth century have been preserved without change, even while today's situation is completely different from that of the past. The German constitutions of the nineteenth century belong to an epoch whose basic structure was captured, by the impressive German doctrine of the state of that time, in a clear and useful basic formula: the distinction of state and society. It is a secondary question that is of no interest to us here how one evaluates both state and society, whether one attributes superiority to one over the other or not, and whether, and if so how, the one is dependent on the other, etc. All this does not cancel the distinction. We need to keep in mind, moreover, that 'society' was mainly a polemical concept, and that it had in view, as an opposing conception, the concrete monarchical military and administrative state that existed at the time. It was by contrast to this state that that which did not belong to it was called 'society'. The state, back then, was distinguishable from society. It was strong enough, on its own, to face up to all other social forces and thereby to determine their arrangement by itself, so that all the many differences within the 'state-free' society – confessional, cultural, and economic antagonisms – were relativized by the state, if necessary through the common antagonism to it, and thus did not hinder the integration into a 'society'. On the other hand, the state remained in a posture of extensive neutrality and non-intervention towards religion and the economy, and it respected the autonomy of these spheres of life and activity to a large extent; hence, it was not absolute in the sense of reducing everything outside of the state to insignificance; it was not that strong. In this way, an equilibrium and a dualism was possible; in particular, one could assume that a state without religion and ideology, and even a completely agnostic state, was possible, and one could construct an economy free of the state and a state free of the economy. The state, however, remained the decisive point of reference, as it stood before everyone's eyes in its concrete clarity and distinctness. Even today, the ambiguous word 'society', insofar as it is of interest to us, is still supposed to refer, in the first place, to something that is not state, and occasionally also to something that is not church.[1] [**74**] The distinction is the foundation and presupposition of all important institutions and norms of public law that developed in Germany in the course of the nineteenth century and that still make up a large part of our public law. The fact that one tended, in general, to construct the state of the German constitutional monarchy, with its oppositions of prince and people, crown and chamber, government and representative assembly of the people, in a 'dualistic' fashion is only an expression of the more general and more fundamental dualism of state and society. The representative assembly of the people, the parliament, the legislative body, was thought of as the

[1] The simplest and clearest summary of the often incredibly ambiguous ideas of 'society' is to be found in E. Spranger, 'Das Wesen der deutschen Universität' in M. Doeberl and A. Bienengräber (eds.), *Das Akademische Deutschland* (Berlin, 1930), vol. III, p. 9: 'In German sociological terminology, it is common to designate as "society", without any further differentiation, the whole infinite plenitude of free and organized, grown and created, fleeting and permanent forms of human connectedness that are not state and not church. The entity is as nebulous as the "milieu".' This remark of Spranger's captures the negative character of the idea of 'society'; but it does not, it seems to me, do justice to the further historical fact that 'society', in the concrete situation of the nineteenth century, did not merely have a negative sense. Beyond that negative sense, the word also had a polemical significance, by virtue of which it ceased to be 'nebulous' and gained the concrete precision that a political concept receives from the concept that is its concrete opposite. As a result of this fact, all the concepts that are formed with the help of the word '*societas*', as soon as they acquire historical significance, typically have an oppositional sense, not just 'socialism' but also 'sociology', which, as Carl Brinkmann says, came into being as an 'oppositional science' (*Versuch einer Gesellschaftswissenschaft* (Munich and Leipzig, 1919)). Mr stud. jur. G. Wiebeck (Berlin) draws my attention to a passage of the book of L. von Hasner, *Filosofie des Rechts und seiner Geschichte in Grundlinien* (Prague, 1851), p. 82, which contains the following turn of phrase that is interesting for the subsequent explications in the text above, namely for the situation of a society that finds itself in 'self-organization': 'Society, however, as a swirling, unorganized mass is not an ethical but only a transitory, historical appearance. Once it is organized, it is an ethical entity, but in that case it is the state itself, if the latter is to be more than an *abstractum*.'

stage on which society appeared and faced the state. Here, it was supposed to integrate itself into the state (or the state into society).[2]

This dualist basic structure expresses itself in all important conceptual constructions. The constitution is regarded as a contract between prince and people. The essential content of a statute enacted by the state is seen in the fact that it interferes with 'the freedom and property of the citizens'. A legal decree [**75**] addresses itself, in contrast to an administrative ordinance that is issued only to administrative organs and civil servants, to all citizens of the state. The right of budgetary approval is based on the idea that an agreement on the budget should, as a rule, be reached among the two partners, and in the last edition of the textbook *Meyer-Anschütz* (1919, pp. 890, 897), the statute containing the budget is still called an 'agreement on the budget'. If one demands a so-called formal statute for an act of administration, like the decision on the state's budget, then what becomes visible in this formalization is nothing other than the politicization of the concept: the political power of parliament is large enough to make sure, on the one hand, that a norm counts as a statute only if it is enacted with the participation of parliament, and at the same time, on the other hand, to conquer a formal concept of statute that no longer looks to the material content of the process; this formalization, hence, simply expresses the political success of the assembly representing the people against the government, the success of society against the monarchical administrative state. Local self-government likewise presupposes, in all its institutions, the distinction of state and society; self-government is a part of the society that is opposed to the state and to its civil service; its concepts and institutions developed and were formulated, in the nineteenth century, on this basic presupposition.

A 'dualist' state of this sort is a balancing of two different kinds of state: it is a governmental state and a legislative state at the same time. It developed the more into a legislative state, the more parliament, as the legislative body, showed itself to be superior to government, i.e. the more the society of the time showed itself to be superior to the state that existed then. One can classify all states according to the sphere of state action in which they find the centre of their activity. Accordingly, there are

[2] In place of many others see, for instance, L. von Stein, *Geschichte der sozialen Bewegung in Frankreich von 1789 bis auf unsere Tage*, ed. Gottfried Salomon (Munich, 1921), vol. II, p. 41: the chamber is the organ 'by which society rules over the state', or the remark, rich in content, of R. Gneist, *Die nationale Rechtsidee von den Ständen* (Berlin, 1894), p. 269: the general demand for a secret ballot is 'the infallible sign of the flooding of the state by society'.

justice – or better – jurisdictional states, there are states that are essentially governmental and executive states, and finally there are legislative states. The medieval state, and to a large extent also the Anglo-Saxon doctrine of the state, up to the present, assumes that the core of the state's authority is to be found in adjudicative institutions. The authority of the state and jurisdiction are here equated. This view conforms to the way in which the *Codex Juris Canonici* still expresses itself today (see, for example, can. 196, 218), though one must here take note of the fact that the determinative description of the authority of the Roman Catholic church and of its highest offices expresses itself not in the picture of the judge, but rather in the picture of the shepherd who watches over his flock. The absolute state that won its form from the sixteenth century onwards originated precisely from the breakdown and the dissolution of the medieval, pluralistic, feudal, and estate-based rule-of-law state and its jurisdiction, and it based itself on the military and a professional civil service. It is therefore essentially a state of the executive and of government. Its *ratio*, the *ratio status*, the oft-misinterpreted reason of state, does not consist in the content of its norms, but rather in the efficiency with which it [**76**] creates a situation in which norms can be valid in the first place, because the state puts a stop to the cause of all disorder and civil war, to the fight about what is normatively correct. This state 'produces public security and order'. Only after this had been achieved could the legislative state of the bourgeois constitution committed to the rule of law intrude into it. The respective centre of the state openly comes to light in a so-called 'state of exception'.* Here, the jurisdictional state employs martial law (or, more precisely, courts of martial law), i.e. a summary justice; the state as executive relies, above all, on the concentration of executive power, which is coupled, if necessary, with a suspension of basic rights; the legislative state, finally, uses decrees to govern the emergency or state of exception, i.e. it relies on a summary procedure of legislation.[3]

When it comes to such divisions or classifications of forms of state, one must never lose sight of the fact that there can be no pure legislative state, just as there can be no pure jurisdictional state or a state that is

[3] For more on the state of exception see below, pp. 115–16.* The connection between a jurisdictional state and martial law is noted in the work of L. Waldecker, 'Die Grundlagen des militärischen Verordnungsrechts in Zivilsachen während des Kriegszustandes', *Archiv des öffentlichen Rechts*, 36 (1917), 389–90, but the way in which the further development follows from that connection is not recognized.

nothing other than government and administration, without more. Hence, every state is a combination and mixture of these forms, a *status mixtus*. But keeping in mind this proviso, it is possible to gain a useful characterization of states on the basis of the central sphere of state activity. It is therefore justifiable, and especially illuminating for the problem of the guardian of the constitution, to characterize the bourgeois constitutional state committed to the rule of law, as it developed in the nineteenth century, as a legislative state. It belongs, as Richard Thoma aptly pointed out, to the 'tendencies determining the form of the modern state to leave' the decision, 'over the reasonableness and justice of which one can always quarrel, to the legislator, and to take it away from the judge'.[4] A jurisdictional state is possible as long as norms that are determinate in their content can be assumed to exist, even without conscious and written norm-enactment by an organized central authority, and as long as these norms are indisputably recognized. In a legislative state, by contrast, there can be no constitutional adjudication or adjudication in matters of state that plays the role of the real guardian of the constitution. This is the ultimate reason that the judiciary, in such a state, does not decide disputed constitutional or legislative questions on its own initiative. In this context, an utterance of Bluntschli's deserves to be cited at some length, [77] because it can claim to be a classical passage of the nineteenth century's doctrine of the state, due to its clarity about the issue at hand and due to the wisdom of its concrete knowledge. Bluntschli concedes that the constitution, of course, also binds the legislator, and that it is by no means the case that the latter has the right to do what the constitution explicitly prohibits. He knows to accord due respect to the reasons for and the advantages of the American practice of judicial review of legislation. But then he continues: 'However, if one takes into account that the legislator is typically convinced of the constitutionality of the statute, and wants his statutes to be constitutional, and that, nevertheless, it is very easy for differing

[4] 'Grundrechte und Polizeigewalt' in H. Triepel (ed.), *Verwaltungsrechtliche Abhandlungen. Festgabe zur Feier des fünfzigjährigen Bestehens des Preußischen Oberverwaltungsgerichts, 1875-1925* (Berlin, 1925), p. 223; not precisely in the same way in the debate at the *Staatsrechtslehrertag* in Vienna, 1928, *Veröffentlichungen der Vereinigung der deutschen Staatsrechtslehrer*, issue 5 (Berlin and Leipzig, 1929), p. 109; moreover in the Festschrift for the *Reichsgericht* (R. Thoma, 'Die Staatsgerichtsbarkeit des Deutschen Reiches' in O. Schreiber (ed.), *Die Reichsgerichtspraxis im deutschen Rechtsleben. Festgabe der juristischen Fakultäten zum 50jährigen Bestehen des Reichsgerichts* (Berlin, 1929), vol. I, pp. 179–200), at p. 200 and in G. Anschütz and R. Thoma (eds.), *Handbuch des deutschen Staatsrechts* (Tübingen, 1932), vol. II, pp. 109, 136–7.

opinions on this question to arise, so that, if the legislature's pronouncement can become the object of a dispute, the court will perhaps have a different opinion on the matter than the legislator; and if one keeps in mind that, in this case, the higher authority of the legislator would have to make way, in case of success of the constitutional challenge, though not in principle, to the lower authority of the courts and that the representative of the nation as a whole, in case of a conflict with an individual organ of the body of the state, would have to stand back behind the latter; if one considers the disturbance and division that would, in such a way, be brought into the unified progress of the life of the state and if one remembers that courts, according to their contemporary design, are appointed primarily to judge norms and legal relations of private law, and have a prevailing tendency to put emphasis on formal-logical aspects, while we are here often dealing with the most important public interests and with the general welfare, the recognition and the promotion of which is the task of the legislator: then one will nonetheless give preference to the European system, although the latter does not protect against all evils and has its share in the imperfections of the human condition. Normally, there are no external remedies either against unjust judgments of the highest courts. The legislative body, however, contains in the mode of its appointment the most important guarantee that it will not exercise its power in an unconstitutional spirit.'[5] The last sentence is decisive. It shows that, in the view of the nineteenth century, parliament, due to its nature and essence, carried the most important guarantee of the constitution within itself. That belongs to the faith in parliament, and it is the precondition for the legislative body to be the pillar of the state, and for the state itself to be a legislative state.

However, this position of the legislative body was possible only in a specific situation. It is always presupposed, in all this, that parliament, the legislative assembly, as the representative of the people [**78**] or of society – both, people and society, can be identified for as long as both are still put up against the government and the state – stands face to face

[5] J. C. Bluntschli, *Allgemeines Staatsrecht*, 4th edn (Munich, 1868), vol. I, pp. 561–2. It is especially instructive to compare these sentences of Bluntschli's with the argument of R. Gneist: the latter takes the guarantee to consist in the co-operation in the legislative process, which involves the participation of the hereditary monarchy, the permanent first chamber, and of the elected second chamber; see R. Gneist, *Gutachten zum 4. deutschen Juristentag über die Frage: 'Soll der Richter über die Frage zu befinden haben, ob ein Gesetz verfassungsmäßig zustande gekommen ist?'* (Berlin, 1863), p. 23.

against a strong, monarchical administrative state that is independent of it, that can serve as its partner in the constitutional pact. Parliament, insofar as it is a representative of the people, here turns into the true guardian and guarantee of the constitution, since the other party to the contract, government, has entered into the contract only unwillingly. The government therefore deserves distrust; it demands spending and taxes; it is thought of as spendthrift, and the representative assembly of the people as frugal and opposed to expense, which could indeed be the case, and, on the whole, was in fact the case. The tendency of the nineteenth century, after all, went into the direction of trying to restrict the state to a minimum, and above all to stop it from intervening in and from interfering with the economy, and in general to neutralize it, as far as possible, in its relation to society and its conflicts of interest, so that society and economy can take the decisions necessary for their sphere in accordance with their own immanent principles. In the free play of opinion, based on free advertisement, parties come into being, whose discussions, through a struggle between different opinions, form a public opinion and thus determine the content of the will of the state; the freedom of contract and of economic activity governs the free play of social and economic forces, as a result of which the highest possible degree of economic prosperity appears assured, because the automatic mechanism of the free economy and the free market steers and regulates itself according to economic laws (through supply and demand, the exchange of services, and the setting of prices and of incomes in the national economy). The basic rights and freedoms of the bourgeois – in particular, personal liberty, the freedom of the expression of opinion, the freedom of contract, the freedom of economic activity, and the freedom to enter into any profession, private property, or, in other words, the real guiding principles of the practice of the Supreme Court of the United States that has been discussed above – all presuppose such a neutral state, a state that does not intervene, as a matter of principle, unless it is for the purpose of restoring the disturbed conditions of free competition.

This state, which was neutral in principle towards society and economy, in the liberal, non-interventionist sense, remained the presupposition of the constitution even where exceptions were made in the field of social and cultural politics. But it changed from the ground up, to the same extent that the dualistic construction of state and society, government and people, lost its tension and the legislative state came to completion. Now, the state becomes the 'self-organization of society'. The distinction between state and society, between government and the people, which had hitherto always been presupposed, disappears as a result, as already noted. Consequently, all the concepts and institutions built on this presupposition (statute, budget, local self-government) turn into new problems. But something even more momentous and profound happens at this point. If society organizes itself into a state, if society and state are supposed to be identical, [79] then all social and economic problems immediately turn into problems that concern the state, and it is no longer possible to distinguish between issues that are political, and as such concern the state, and issues that are social and thus non-political. All the hitherto prevailing contrasts, since they rested on the presupposition of a neutral state and had appeared as a result of the distinction between state and society, and were nothing but applications and re-descriptions of this distinction, cease to be relevant. Antithetical separations such as state and society, state and culture, state and education – moreover, politics and economy, politics and school, politics and religion, state and law, politics and law, which make sense if they correspond to materially separate, concrete quantities or social spheres – lose their meaning and become empty. The society that has turned into the state becomes an economic state, a cultural state, a caring state, a welfare state, a providing state; while the state that has turned into the self-organization of society, and that is consequently no longer materially separable from it, comes to encompass everything social, i.e. everything that concerns the collective life of human beings. Within it, there is no longer any sphere towards which the state could maintain unconditional neutrality in the sense of non-intervention. The parties, in which the different social interests and tendencies organize themselves, are the society itself that has become a party state, and because there are parties that are determined economically, denominationally, culturally, it is no longer possible for the state to remain neutral towards the economical, the denominational, or the cultural. In a state that has become the self-organization of society, there simply isn't anything that is not at least potentially political and of concern to the state. This new state takes a hold of all spheres, just as the concept of potential armament that has been invented by French jurists and soldiers encompasses everything, not merely what is military or technical in a narrow sense, but also the industrial and economic preparation of war, and even the intellectual and moral education and preparation of the citizens. An outstanding representative of the German front-line soldier, Ernst Jünger, introduced a very succinct formula for this astonishing development: total mobilization. Even without considering the content and the correctness that we can accord to these formulas of potential armament or total mobilization in particular cases, we will have to pay heed to the very important insight that is contained in them, and we will have to make use of it. They express something that is all-encompassing, and they signal a great and deep transformation: the society that organizes itself in the state is well on its way to changing the liberal and neutral state of the nineteenth century into a potentially total state. This enormous turn can be reconstructed as part of a dialectical development that proceeds through three phases: from the absolute state of the seventeenth and eighteenth century via the neutral state of the liberal nineteenth century to the total state characterized by an identity of state and society. [**80**]

The turn comes to the fore most conspicuously in the sphere of the economy. It is safe to assume, as a recognized and undisputed matter of fact, that public finance, both in comparison to its former dimension in the pre-war years and in its present relation to the free and private, i.e. the non-public sector of the economy, has taken on such a magnitude that we are faced not just with a quantitative increase but also with a qualitative change, with a 'structural transformation' that affects all areas of public life, and not only matters immediately financial or economical. We do not have to put particular numbers on the change here and answer the question, for instance, whether the oft-cited claim, calculated for the year 1928, that 53 per cent of the German people's income is controlled by the public sector,[6] is statistically correct or not. The overall phenomenon cannot be and is not denied by anyone. An expert on the issue of the highest authority, secretary of state Professor Johannes Popitz, assumes, in a summarizing speech on the financial adjustment,[7] that the self-regulating mechanism of a free economy and a free market is indeed switched off for the distribution of the larger part of the German people's income, and that 'the decisive influence of a will that is in principle non-economical, namely of the will of the state' has taken its place. Another financial expert of the highest rank, the *Reich's*

[6] This figure is calculated in the *Vierteljahreshefte für Konjunkturforschung*, 5:2 (1930), 72; it is employed and taken to be accurate for instance by J. Popitz (see the following note), and by G. Müller-Oerlinghausen, in his presentation on the economic crisis on 4 November 1930, *Mitteilungen des Langnamvereins*, Neue Folge 19 (1930), 409; compare Otto Pfleiderer, *Die Staatswirtschaft und das Sozialprodukt* (Jena, 1930) and Manuel Saitzew, *Die öffentliche Unternehmung der Gegenwart* (Tübingen, 1930), pp. 6–7.

[7] *Der Finanzausgleich und seine Bedeutung für die Finanzlage des Reichs, der Länder und Gemeinden* (*Veröffentlichungen des Reichsverbands der deutschen Industrie*) (Berlin, 1930), p. 6; moreover: 'Der öffentliche Finanzbedarf und der Reichssparkommissar', *Bankarchiv* 30:2 (15 October 1930), 21.

commissioner for savings, Minister of State Saemisch, says that the management of public finance influences the political situation in Germany decisively.[8] An exceptionally incisive formulation of the contrast of the previous system with the contemporary has been put forward by a representative of the science of economics: from a system of shares (in which the state is entitled only to a share of the income of the people, a kind of dividend on the net profit) to a system of control, through which the state, as a result of the strong relations between public finance and the national economy, as a result of the strong enlargement both of the financial needs of the state and of the state's income, [**81**] decisively co-determines the national economy, as a shareholder in and re-distributor of the social income – as a producer, consumer, and employer. This formula, which has been put forward by Fritz Karl Mann in an interesting and significant monograph, *Die Staatswirtschaft in unserer Zeit* (Jena, 1930), is also to be used here only as a formula , without being subjected to any further critique from the point of view of the science of national economics. What is decisive here for constitutional theory and the theory of the state is that the relation of the state to the economy is the real issue behind all contemporary problems in domestic politics, and that the accustomed formulas of the old state, which was based on the distinction between state and society, serve only to conceal this fact.

The relationship of the state to the economy forms the real object, in every modern state, of the immediately pressing questions of domestic politics. These can no longer be answered with the old liberal principle of unconditional non-interference, of absolute non-intervention. Bar a few exceptions, this also seems to be generally recognized. In today's state, and the more so the more it is a modern industrial state, economic questions make up the main part of the domestic political difficulties, and both domestic and foreign policy are, to a large extent, economic policy, and not only as customs policy, trade policy, or social policy. If the state enacts a statute 'against the abuse of positions of economic power' (such as the German decree on cartels of 2 November 1923), then the concept and the existence of an 'economic power' is officially recognized with this formulation by the state and the law. The contemporary state has an extensive labour law and law of collective bargaining, and it engages in the public arbitration of labour disputes, through which it decisively influences wage levels. It provides enormous subsidies to the different branches of industry; it is a welfare state and a caring state, and

[8] *Deutsche Juristen-Zeitung* (1 January 1931), 17; also in *Der Reichssparkommissar und seine Aufgabe* (*Finanzrechtliche Zeitfragen*, vol. 2) (Berlin, 1930), p. 12.

consequently at the same time, to an enormous extent, a taxation state. In the case of Germany we have to add that the state is also a reparations state that is forced to raise billions in tributes to foreign states. In such a situation, the demand for non-intervention turns into a Utopia, and even into a self-contradiction. To adopt a policy of non-intervention would mean to give free rein, in the social and economic antagonisms and conflicts of today's world, which are by no means always fought out with purely economic means, to the different power groups in society. Under such circumstances, non-intervention is nothing more than an intervention in favour of the party that is stronger and more ruthless, whichever it may be, and the simple truth of the seemingly paradoxical sentence that Talleyrand uttered for the field of foreign policy shows itself once again: non-intervention is a difficult concept; it means roughly the same as intervention.

The turn towards the economic state is the most visible change away from the nineteenth century's conception of the state. [**82**] But the turn can also be observed elsewhere, though it is often perceived, for now, to be less pressing in other areas, due to the crushing weight of economic difficulties and problems. It is not surprising that the defence against such an expansion of the state appears at first as a defence against that activity of the state's which determines, in such a moment, the form of the state, and that it consequently appears as a defence against the legislative state. For this reason, one first clamours for protections against the legislator. This is likely to be what explains the initial and rather unclear attempts to provide a remedy that we discussed in the first part of this book, and that clung to adjudication in order to gain a counterweight against the legislator who grows ever more powerful and encompassing. They had to end in empty superficialities, since they did not originate from a concrete insight into the overall situation of constitutional law, but only from a reflexive reaction. Their fundamental error was that they could oppose the power of the modern legislator with nothing but a judiciary that was either materially bound to determinate norms issued by that very same legislator or else unable to confront the legislator with anything but indeterminate and controversial principles that could not possibly help to ground an authority superior to the legislator's. While the turn towards the economic and the welfare state certainly marked a critical moment for the traditional legislative state, it did not therefore by itself have to supply new force and political energy to the courts, and in fact it has not yet done so. In a situation thus changed, and in the face of such an expansion of the tasks and the problems of the state, a government may perhaps be able to provide a remedy, but certainly not the judiciary. Today, the judiciary, in most countries on the European Continent, appears to lack all material norms that might enable it to master the completely new situation on its own initiative.

Parliament, the legislative body, which carries the legislative state and forms its centre, at the very moment when its victory seemed complete, turned into an entity divided within itself and began to disown its own presuppositions and those of its victory. Its previous position and superiority, its urge to expand its powers against the government, its claim to represent the people; all that presupposes a distinction between state and society that did not continue to exist, at least not in the same form, after the victory of parliament. Its unity, even its identity with itself, had thus far been determined by its adversary in domestic politics, by the old monarchical military state and its administrative apparatus. When the latter disintegrated, parliament, so to speak, broke apart itself. The state is now, it is said, the self-organization of society. But this raises the question of how a society that organizes itself arrives at its unity, and whether that unity really comes about as a result of the 'self-organization' of society. 'Self-organization', after all, initially signifies no more than a postulate and a procedure that is characterized, in a purely negative and polemical fashion, by its opposition to older methods of the formation of the will and of the unity of the state that no longer exist today. [**83**] The identity that is implied by the word 'self' and that is linguistically attached to the word 'organization' does not have to come about in every case and with absolute certainty, neither as a unity of society itself, nor as a unity of the state. There are organizations, as we have experienced often enough, that lack success or fail to achieve results.

At first, the political parties were taken to be the agents of self-organization. It soon turned out, however, that they had, for the most part, changed rather drastically. It is an essential characteristic of the party, in the sense which the term had been given in the liberal constitutional state, to be an entity based on free advertisement, and thus not to be something solid, not to be something that has turned into a continuous, permanent, and highly organized social complex. The notions of 'freedom' as well as of 'advertisement' forbid, at least according to the idea, every form of social or economic pressure. The only motivation they permit is the free conviction of people who are socially and economically free, spiritually and intellectually independent, and thus capable of arriving at their own judgement. This conception of a political party is still presupposed by the constitutions of contemporary states which are committed to the bourgeois rule of law, and it is the foundation of the provisions of the current constitution of the *Reich*. It has often been emphasized that the constitution of the *Reich* does not know the 'party', and that it uses the word only at one point, in article 130 paragraph 2,* and there only in a negative and unsympathetic way. The great distance of this provision from the reality of the conditions of today's domestic politics has often been described. One should add to this that the constitution of the *Reich*, when it ignores the political party, is doing that, and can do that, only because it wants to continue to maintain that a political party, from a sociological point of view, is so far from being a solid – so far from being a formed – entity, that it is an entity so fluid or even airy, that it may be treated as non-existent. The only region where a party is supposed to exist at all, as Hugo Preuß stated consistently and emphatically, is in the sphere of public opinion, which he considers – in conformity with the whole tradition relating to this concept – to be an unorganized, 'indefinable fluid'. By contrast, most of the larger political parties of today are either solid and thoroughly organized entities or they stand within a thoroughly organized social complex, with influential bureaucracies, a standing army of paid functionaries, and a whole system of organizations of help and support that bind together an intellectually, socially, and economically captive clientele. The extension to all spheres of human existence, the abolition of the liberal separations and neutralizations of different spheres like religion, economy, and education – in a word, what we previously referred to as the turn towards the 'total'– has already been realized, to some extent, for a part of the citizenry by several organizational complexes in society. While we do not yet have a total state, we do, as a result, have several social party complexes that aspire to totality, and that take a complete hold of their members from their youth onwards. [**84**] Every one of these organizations, as Eduard Spranger points out, has a 'whole cultural programme', and the co-existence of these groups forms and carries the pluralist state. The fact that there is a plurality of such organizational complexes which compete with one another and keep each other within certain bounds, i.e. the fact that there is a pluralist party state, prevents the trend towards the total state from making itself felt with the same momentum that it has already attained in the so-called one-party states, in Soviet Russia and in Italy. However, the turn towards the total is not reversed by the development of pluralism. Rather, it is only parcelled out, so to speak, in that every organized social power-complex, from the choir and the sports club to the association for armed self-defence, aims to realize totality, as far as possible, within itself and for itself. That it was at all possible to introduce an expression like 'one-party state' as the designation of non-pluralist states, and that the expression was immediately received into the common usage of language, is probably the most decisive proof of the extent to which the word 'party' has ceased to refer to a non-organized entity based on free advertisement. The clear and unfailingly liberal critic of this development, M. J. Bonn, has characterized this change as the transition to a new feudal and estate-based state; a teacher of public law of Triepel's authority has shown* that the system of firmly organized parties contradicts the provisions and the presuppositions of the constitution; a voluminous literature on the transformation in form and structure of the German party system shows that science has long recognized the turn that hides itself behind the formula of the 'self-organization of society through the party' as a novel problem.

The concept of party presupposed in the constitution nevertheless appears to fade away with unconscious naturalness. As far as I can see, it does not make a sustained impression, outside of the boundaries of the aforementioned specialized scientific literature, and it does not elicit more than a few nostalgic complaints, when a scholar like Max Weber holds on to the definition of the party as an entity that is essentially 'based on free advertisement'.* The *Staatsgerichtshof* for the German *Reich*, for example, put forward a contrary definition which makes the deep transformation of the concept of the party, and thus of our state as a whole, impressively evident, precisely by virtue of its seemingly unproblematic matter-of-factness. The *Staatsgerichtshof* says in its judgment of 7 July 1928: 'For the purposes of a trial in front of the *Staatsgerichtshof* an association of persons can be recognized as a political party only if there is a possibility that its activity will be of relevance to the outcome of an election. Groups that are undoubtedly incapable of winning admission to the representative assembly of the people, whose opportunities for political action are therefore not at all affected by the structure of electoral law, are not parties in the parliamentary sense'. If only political advertising that stands a chance of success (as evidenced by previous electoral successes) is permitted to enjoy legal equality, [**85**] the formerly determinative principle of absolutely free advertisement, that every political opinion and every political party should enjoy an absolutely equal opportunity to advertise its views, has clearly been abandoned.[9] The *Staatsgerichtshof* imposes a number of requirements as criteria for

[9] The sentence quoted in the text can be found in the reasons for the decision of the *Staatsgerichtshof* from 7 July 1928, and concerns the Independent Social Democratic Party of Saxony (RGZ. 121, Appendix p. 8, H. Lammers and W. Simons (eds.), *Die Rechtsprechung des*

recognition as a party in the parliamentary sense. In the first place, the number of members must not be too small; the Independent Social Democratic Party of Saxony was not recognized as a party on the ground that, in the course of the elections to the *Reichstag* on 20 May 1928, it received only 2,953 votes in the three constituencies of Saxony, and therefore does not possess even the smallest chance to win a seat in the elections for the parliament of the *Land* of Saxony. Moreover, the court recognizes only firmly organized parties but not 'loose groups', on the ground that an election based on the principle of proportional representation would otherwise be impossible. The former are discernible by the following characteristics: a programme; a relatively comprehensive organizational basis; newspapers that are at the disposal of the party. In short, parties must be entities that 'cannot be denied a certain solidity' and 'in respect of which one can expect a sufficient duration'. 'A party presupposes the firm unification of a larger number of citizens for the attainment of political goals.'[10] A party, a fraternity, an order are treated as one and the same thing.

On closer inspection, the *Staatsgerichtshof's* definition of party is an indication that it is not only the concept of party but also the concept of election that has changed fundamentally. The concern for the implementation of an electoral system of proportional representation plays a decisive role in the reasons that the *Staatsgerichtshof* gives for its decision, a role which still stands in need of closer scrutiny. It is not only the new concept of party that is justified with reference to the necessities of an electoral system of proportional representation. Even departures from the principle of electoral equality are defended on the ground that a system of proportional representation allegedly makes such restrictions of electoral equality necessary, since electoral equality is not to be regarded, in the court's view, as a logical-mathematical, but rather as a legal concept, and for the further reason that the prevention of a splintering of parties is a political goal that ought to be recognized. The *Staatsgerichtshof* passes in silence over the point that the two things it negates – the 'mathematical' and the splintering of parties – have only

Staatsgerichtshofes für das Deutsche Reich und des Reichsgerichts auf Grund Art. 13 Abs 2 der Reichsverfassung (Berlin, 1929), vol. I, pp. 309–10). The following sentence in the decision of 17 December 1927 concerning the People's Right Party in the Land of Hamburg (Lammers and Simons, vol. I, p. 348) does not fully conform to this treatment of 'incapability': 'It is therefore not appropriate to subject hopeless electoral proposals … to conditions different from those that apply to the more promising ones.'

10 Decisions of 17 December 1927, Lammers and Simons, vol. I, p. 346; of 12 May 1928, Lammers and Simons, vol. I, p. 414; and of 7 July 1928 (Independent Social Democratic Party of Saxony), RGZ. 121, Appendix p. 8 and Lammers and Simons, vol. I, p. 311.

come into our party-system, in their present intensity, [**86**] as a result of the electoral system of proportional representation, and that these two considerations therefore speak for a restriction of the system of proportional representation rather than for a restriction of electoral equality and the immediacy of elections. It is the case, after all, that the electoral system of proportional representation and the solidly organized party are most intimately connected with each other. However, the current constitutional conditions would likely be characterized by a solid organization of political parties even absent an electoral system of proportional representation. The common, often very sharp critique of the electoral system of proportional representation should not overlook this, in particular when it poses the question of whether reforms are possible and when it asks what would be achieved by an 'abolition' of the system of proportional representation. But the most important point that should be noted in this context, and that most clearly shows the complete transformation of the traditional concepts, is the following: in the reality of today's electoral practice, it is not only the equality of the election and not only the immediacy of the election that are restricted and partially undermined by the preponderance of the system of proportional representation. The process that is referred to as 'election' has itself acquired a completely novel content. The superiority of the old parliament over constitutional monarchy rested on the fact that its members had been personally elected. The old parliament faced the king and his government, in the name of the people, as a corporation elected by the whole people. The election expressed an immediate connection between the voter and the representative. That the outvoted minority did not receive its own organized representation was consistently democratic; one destroys the basic presupposition of any democracy once one abandons the axiom that the outvoted minority only wanted the result of the election (and not its own particular will), and that it has therefore given its assent to the will of the majority as its own will. Now, if one organizes a representation of minorities, through a system of proportional representation, in order to prevent the outvoting of minorities, one must, to be consistent, also permit a large number of smaller parties. If one fights against the splintering of parties, then one fights against an unavoidable effect of a system that no longer grasps the basic democratic axiom of the identity of the will of all citizens. If one goes on to restrict the equality and the immediacy of elections, to make the system of proportional representation work, one thereby expresses the view that a procedure of election which is governed by the electoral system of proportional representation, and that collides with the two fundamental characteristics of an equal and immediate democratic electoral law, takes precedence over these fundamental characteristics and is to be regarded as more important than the democratic election itself. In its last consequence, the electoral law of proportional representation, with its system of party lists, leads to the result that the mass of those entitled to cast a vote no longer elect a representative at all. What happens, rather, is this: from out of the dark of the secret deliberations of uncontrollable committees, a number of party lists with a long row of names is presented to the mass of voters; the latter then divide up into groups, when votes are cast, that support one or another of the party lists. [**87**] There is no longer any talk of the individual voter immediately determining an individual representative; the only thing that remains is a statistical grouping and division of the mass of voters in accordance with a plurality of party lists. This procedure, insofar as the voter is a socially bound member of a firm party organization as well as of the social power groups allied with the party, amounts to nothing more than a roll call of the standing party armies. To the extent that the mass of the rest of the citizens, who are not yet in the grip of such organizations, and who are often contemptuously referred to as 'driftwood' or 'drifting sand', participate in the election, they fluctuate back and forth between these firm organizations and thereby usually determine the outcome. That, as well, cannot be called an election, although it does not contradict the ideal of democracy to the same degree as the pluralism of firmly organized complexes. It is no longer an election in the sense of the traditional conception of a choice of delegates or representatives. It is, in reality, a process akin to a plebiscite. The process of a contemporary federal or provincial parliamentary election, which is still misleadingly called an 'election', thus breaks up into two different sides: on the one side the merely statistical determination of the pluralistic division of the state into several firmly organized social complexes and, on the other side, a bit of plebiscite.

The democratic state has often been referred to or even been defined as a party state. The parliamentary democratic state is, in a special sense, even more of a party state. One can perhaps call every state a party state, in one sense or another. But this proves no more than that such a designation is empty and meaningless as long as one does not add a more specific description of the kind, organization, structure, and number of the parties. In order that a parliamentary democratic legislative state, and a state that is a party state in this special sense, is able to execute its constitutionally regulated functions in accordance with the presuppositions of the constitution, the parties must conform to the concept of party that is presupposed by the constitution, and that is, as we saw, the liberal concept of party that understands the party exclusively as a free entity. It is the purpose of all institutions and methods that conform to the constitution of a parliamentary democracy – and it belongs, in particular, also to the parliamentary system of the Weimar Constitution – that a continuous process of transition and ascent lead from egoistical interests and opinions, by way of the will of the parties, to a unified will of the state. The solidification of the party, hence, must not be too strong, since it would, in that case, put up too much resistance to this transformation and reconfiguration. The parties are meant to be an instrument of the will-formation of the state, and their permission and recognition, of course, does not imply that they are supposed to use their participation in the formation of the will of the state as the object of compromise-oriented deal-making with other parties, or even as a means of blackmail. Parliament, rather, is supposed to be the scene of a process of transformation, [**88**] through which the manifold of social, economic, cultural, and confessional conflicts, interests, and opinions is shaped into the unity of a political will. It is an old, albeit more of a liberal than a democratic belief, that it is precisely the parliamentary method that is best suited to use the parties in such a way as agents of transformation, and that it is parliament, more than any other institution, that is the place where the egoism of party, by virtue of the cunning of the idea or the cunning of the institution, becomes a means for the formation of a neutral state-political will that transcends factional egoism. In particular, a party is said to be forced, once it comes to form the government, to take into account considerations that are wider and more elevated than the narrow motives that stem from its nature as a party. But as a result of the character, composition, and number of parties – as a result, moreover, of the transformation that we just discussed of the parties into solidly organized groups with a firm administrative apparatus and a firmly bound clientele – and, finally, by virtue of the great number of parties and parliamentary parties that are necessary to reach a majority, the ascent from the egoistic will of the party to a responsible will of the state is prevented again and again. Only such governments then come into existence, in defiance of the presuppositions of the constitutional regulation, as are too weak and too restrained to govern, since they are bound by compromises between parliamentary parties, but that, on the other hand, still have enough of a will to keep power and to maintain possession to prevent others from governing. The aforementioned 'cunning' of the idea or the institution, then, simply does not work anymore, and instead of a will of the state, the system only produces an arbitrary addition of fleeting and special interests that tries to strike bargains on all sides to remain in power. The current condition of the parliamentary system in Germany is characterized by the fact that the formation of the will of the state must rely on unstable parliamentary majorities that change from case to case and that are made up of a large number of parties that are heterogeneous in every respect. The majority is never more than the majority of a coalition, and its composition is altogether different depending on the different areas of political struggle – foreign policy, economic policy, social policy, cultural policy. This parliamentary, democratic, party state is, in short, an unstable coalition party state. The deficiencies and shortcomings of such a situation have been portrayed and criticized often enough: incalculable majorities; governments that are incapable of governing and that fail to assume political responsibility, since they are bound by compromises of all sorts; incessant compromises between parties and parliamentary groups that come about at the cost of the interests of a third party or of the state as a whole, and that require a pay-off to every party involved in exchange for its participation; the distribution of positions and sinecures in the state as well as in communal or other public institutions among the followers of parties, in accordance with some formula derived from the strength of parliamentary parties or from the tactical situation. Even those parties that, with an honest public spirit, want to put the interest of the whole above the goals of the party are forced, in part by the necessity of giving consideration to their clientele and voters, but even more by the immanent pluralism of such a system, [**89**] either to take part in the continuous trading of compromises or to stand aside as irrelevant. At the end, they find themselves in the position of the dog, known from La Fontaine's fable, that guards the roast of his master with the best of intentions, but that, when he sees the other dogs devour it, eventually decides to participate in the feast.

The difference between a parliamentary party state with free parties – that is, with parties that are not firmly organized – and a pluralistic party state with firmly organized entities that control the will-formation of the state, can be larger than the difference between a monarchy and a republic or some other form of state. The solid social associations, which now carry the pluralistic state, turn parliament, where their representatives appear as members of parliamentary parties, into a mere image of the pluralistic division of the state itself. Where, given this situation, is the unity supposed to come from that takes up the hard loyalties to party and factional interest and melts them into one? A discussion no longer takes place; and the mere fact that I mentioned this normative principle of the parliamentary system prompted Richard Thoma to refer to it as a 'completely mouldy' basis.* Some so-called 'lateral connections' that run through the different political parties (agrarian interests and the interests of workers, public servants, and in some cases women) may, admittedly, bring about a majority in a certain area of policy. But since contemporary pluralism is more than a pluralism of parties or parliamentary parties, and since, moreover, such lateral connections may themselves be factors that give rise to pluralistic groupings, they do represent a complication, but not a reversal or cancellation, of the pluralist condition, which they are more likely to confirm and to intensify. The famous '*solidarité parlementaire*' – that is, the shared egotistic and private interests of members of parliament, of the professional politicians in the true sense of the term, which run across the boundaries between parties – may turn out to be a strong motive and a useful spur to unity. For understandable reasons, though, these interests no longer suffice to create unity, in a situation as difficult as that of today's Germany, and given the strong solidification of party organizations. Thus, parliament turns from the scene of a free deliberation of free representatives of the people that can give rise to unity, from a transformer of partial interests into a will above the parties, into a scene of the pluralistic division of organized social powers. The consequence of this is that it either becomes incapable of reaching a majority and of acting due to its immanent pluralism, or that the momentary majority employs all legal possibilities as instruments and means of the protection of its own hold on power, that it abuses the time during which it possesses the power in the state in all directions, and, above all, that it attempts to restrict as far as possible the chance* of its most powerful and dangerous opponent to do the same. It would perhaps be naïve to explain this solely as a result of human malignity, or even as the result of a special baseness that has become possible only today. [**90**] The history of the state and constitutional history in Germany know of analogous events in earlier centuries that occurred in disquieting number and with disquieting frequency. What the emperor and the princes did to secure the power of their own house, in the process of the dissolution of the old Roman Empire of the German Nation, repeats itself today in numerous parallels.

In this respect, too, the change from the situation of the nineteenth century is fundamental. Here, as well, that change is concealed by the veil of words and formulas that continue to be used in the same way, by old ways of thinking and speaking, as well as by a formalism that stands in the service of these residues. But one must not be deceived about the fact that the effect on the spirit of loyalty to the state and to the constitution, as well as the immediate effect on the state and the constitution itself, is exceptionally large. It consists, for the most part, in a process by which the loyalty to the state and to the constitution is replaced, to the same degree as the state transforms itself into a pluralistic entity, by the loyalty to the social organization, to the entity that carries the pluralism of the state; the more so, as has already been pointed out, since the social complex often exhibits a tendency to become absolute – that is, to bind to itself completely, both economically and ideologically, the citizens whom it has in its grasp. This eventually gives rise to a pluralism of moral obligations and duties of loyalty, to a 'plurality of loyalties',* that stabilizes the pluralistic division more and more, and which increasingly endangers the formation of a unified state. The logical result of this pluralism is that a public service loyal to the state thereby becomes impossible, since this kind of public service likewise presupposes a state that is distinguishable from the organized social complexes. And in addition we see the rise of a pluralism of concepts of legality that destroys any respect for the constitution and turns the ground of the constitution into an insecure terrain contested from several directions, whereas it is the point of any constitution to express a political decision which puts the shared basis of the unity of the state that is constituted by the constitution beyond doubt.* The group or coalition that is presently ruling, with the very best conscience, refers to the employment of all legal opportunities and to the protection of its own position of power, to the utilization of all its public and constitutional competences in legislation, administration, appointment, disciplinary action, and communal self-government, as legality, from which it follows by itself that it perceives all serious critique or even endangerment of its position as illegality, as a coup, and as a violation of the spirit of the constitution; while every opposing organization that is affected by such methods of government appeals to the idea that the restriction of the equal chance guaranteed by the constitution signifies the worst violation against the spirit and the foundations of a democratic constitution, and thus returns the charge of illegality and unconstitutionality, again with the very best conscience. [**91**] The constitution itself is pulverized between these two reciprocal negations that function almost automatically in a situation where the state has turned pluralist.

This glance at the concrete constitutional situation is supposed to highlight a reality that many prefer not to face, for motives of different kinds and on the basis of all sorts of excuses, the clear appreciation of which is nevertheless altogether indispensable for an inquiry into constitutional law that occupies itself with the problem of the preservation and the protection of the current constitution of the *Reich*. It is by no means sufficient to talk in general terms about a 'crisis', or to brush off the reflection just offered by relegating it to the 'literature of crisis'. If today's state is supposed to be a legislative state, and if, moreover, there comes about such an extension of the spheres of the life and of the activity of the state that one can already speak of a turn towards the total state, but if, at the same time, the legislative assembly then becomes the stage for and the centre of the pluralistic division of the unity of the state into a manifold of firmly organized social complexes, then it will not help us much to speak of the 'sovereignty of parliament', using formulas and counter-formulas that were coined for the situation of the constitutional monarchy of the nineteenth century, in order to answer the most difficult question of contemporary constitutional law.

. . .

II.2(d)4

The real basis of all concerns against decrees that replace a financial statute* is likely to be sought less in formal legal considerations than in constitutional-historical memories and in the after effects of earlier constitutional conflicts. These stem from past situations with a constitutional law that was different in kind from today's. They are what sociologists refer to as a '*résidu*'. It is therefore necessary to keep in mind that the situation of the constitutional monarchy of the nineteenth century, with its distinctions of state and society, politics and economy, no longer obtains. This is of immediate importance for constitutional law. The legal-scientific interpretation of the constitution cannot proceed without a critical historical consciousness, if it is not to end up in a thoughtless formalism and empty disputes about words. Most of all, it is the concept of a statute in the formal sense, and within this concept, in turn, the concept of a formal financial statute, that stands in need of clarification. It is bound to a determinate situation in constitutional law, and it is characterized by the most intimate connection with a particular constitutional structure, a connection that also affects the norm's content in positive law. The concept, precisely in its 'formal' character, is thoroughly determined by political considerations, and the formalization, in this case, as already pointed out (p. 75 above), signifies the very opposite of a de-politicization. It is the expression of a purely political expansion of power and competence that calls itself 'formal' because it wants to free itself, in its opposition to a specific adversary, from a material concept of statute that restricts its power: a statute in the formal sense, such as, for instance, certain administrative acts in fiscal law, is supposed to be a statute not by virtue of its material content, but merely by virtue of the authority that enacts it or participates in its enactment; the 'formal' character developed by the public law theory of constitutional monarchy (which was not explicitly expressed in the wording of the written constitutions) does not imply anything other than that the authority or competence to perform certain actions, or to participate in them, pertains to parliament, regardless of the character of these actions and notwithstanding any other regulation of competence. With this simple clarification, we do not intend to claim that the formal concept of statute is unjust or wrong. It turns out to be that only if one tries to avoid its critical correction and to turn it into an absolute, by transferring it to situations that are legally and constitutionally heterogeneous. The concept of the unconditionally formal statute is meaningful and comprehensible as a weapon of the bourgeoisie in its fight with constitutional monarchy, and given the presupposition of a separation of state and society. The formalization, here, has the exclusive sense of a politicization; it is supposed to extend parliament's sphere of power, [**129**] against a non-parliamentary government, to important processes and actions in fiscal law. The proviso of the formal statute, hence, is polemically directed against a very specific political opponent, namely against the monarchic government of the German constitutional monarchy that is independent of the representative assembly of the people; and the proviso of the formal statute expresses, in the German constitutions of the nineteenth century, that certain areas and affairs are exempted from the power of the monarch, a power that is otherwise restricted only by exceptions that are explicitly listed in the constitution, and that these areas are reserved to the legislator – that is, that they require the participation of parliament. The budgetary statute, throughout, is referred to as an agreement between the monarchic government and the representative assembly of the people (so still Meyer-Anschütz, *Staatsrecht*, pp. 890, 897; see also p. 75 above), a fact that exactly corresponds to the dualistic construction of such a state, as well as to the view that the constitution is a contract between the prince and the representative assembly of the people. The concept of an unconditionally 'formal' statute fits into no other constitutional structure than this.[11] The formal statute of budgetary law developed in the fight against a monarchic government that was independent of parliament, and the fight against the monarch's right to issue decrees was a fight against a power of the monarch's that was still presumed to be unlimited; it was not a fight against a right to issue decrees that was delegated by constitutional law or by statute. In democratic states, consequently, the proviso of fiscal law is not at all considered to be an absolute and unconditionally formal proviso.[12] [**130**]

Wherever there is a proviso of an unconditionally formal fiscal statute, it is therefore always presupposed that a parliament, as the representative assembly of the people, is facing a government that is independent of it, and that can in no way ground its authority on the people; the right of the crown, likewise, to dissolve parliament, did not, in German constitutional monarchy, have the constitutional meaning of an appeal to the people; it was only supposed to secure the dualistic structure and the balance between state and society. The constitutional situation of today's German *Reich*, as determined by the Weimar Constitution, is fundamentally different. First, today's state is not based on a contract between the representative assembly of the people and the government, and the budgetary statute is not an 'agreement' between parliament and government; secondly, the government is no longer a power that is independent

[11] As soon as this 'formal' concept leads to a restriction of the power and competence of the representative assembly of the people – for instance, in the application to the pre-constitutional statutory law, that would, formally, not be statute in the constitutional sense, and that would, therefore, according to a stringently executed understanding of the formal concept of statute, still belong to the sphere of power of the kingly government – it is of course dropped immediately and one again recurs to a material concept of statute (statute = interference with freedom and property). R. Thoma has portrayed this process with exemplary clarity in his paper on 'Der Vorbehalt des Gesetzes im preußischen Verfassungsrecht' in the *Festgabe für Otto Mayer: zum siebzigsten Geburtstag dargebracht von Freunden, Verehrern und Schülern* (Tübingen, 1916), pp. 165–222.

[12] For example, the French statute of 14 December 1879, which forms the basis of the regulation in French public law that is currently in force. According to this statute, bonds may be issued, in certain cases, by way of decree (*par décret*) even if parliament is in session. For the occasions that parliament is not in session, the possibilities under budgetary law to proceed by decree are regulated in great detail. The principle of the proviso of a formal financial statute, then, is by no means absolute and without exception. The French theoretician of budgetary law, G. Jèze – who is known both as a legal authority in the field of finance as well as a good, democratic republican – expresses himself as follows (*Allgemeine Theorie des Budgetrechts* (Tübingen, 1927), p. 191) on the basic question of principle: 'Whichever way one chooses to pursue (namely regulating pressing and unforeseen expenditures by the government), this much is clear: the government will not hesitate, in serious times of crisis – for example, if there is a threat of the danger of war – to commit to expenditures without parliamentary authorization . . . *Salus populi suprema lex*.'

of parliament. Rather, the means of influence and control at the disposal of parliament are so strong, as long as there is a parliament that is capable of forming a majority and thus of acting, that one cannot, for this reason alone, transfer considerations that were meaningful in the context of the opposition to the kingly government of a German monarchy to this new constitutional context; thirdly, the president of the *Reich* is elected by the German people as a whole, so that he, as well, is a representative of the people, with the result that the monopoly of the representation of the people that, in the norms and concepts of monarchic constitutional law, is presupposed to inhere in parliament, is cancelled; fourthly, and finally, the Weimar Constitution is a democratic constitution and is grounded in a balance of parliamentary and plebiscitary elements; its structure is essentially determined by the fact that the people, as the higher third, decide (through new elections, plebiscites, or other votes), against parliament as well as against the government and the president. A constitutional conflict in the manner of the nineteenth century, therefore, is just as impossible and unthinkable today, as the arguments and concepts of such a conflict are non-transferable to the contemporary situation.

If the peculiar character of the current constitution of the *Reich* is emphasized here, to ward off the aftereffects of and the transfers from monarchic constitutional law, and if the permissibility of the right to issue decrees that replace fiscal statutes is affirmed, this does not imply anything like a boundless and uncontrolled power and competence of the president of the *Reich*. In making these points, one also, at the same time, makes it clear that the presuppositions, the content, and the boundaries of the president's extraordinary competences, as long as they are not specifically regulated by an implementing statute, must be developed from the norms and principles of the constitution that is now in force. Here, one must pay attention to what Hugo Preuß already insistently emphasized in the constitutional committee (*Protokolle*, p. 277) as the decisive point, which is developed in more detail in my presentation on the 'Diktatur des Reichspräsidenten' (*Staatsrechtslehrertagung*, 1924, p. 103; *Die Diktatur*, 2nd edition, p. 254): [**131**] namely that the real boundary of the extraordinary competences of the president of the *Reich* and the real protection against an abuse of his power is provided by the *Reichstag's* powers of control, not by normativisms or restraints in judicial form. A *Reichstag* that is capable of forming a majority and of acting will have no great difficulty to make its opinion count, against the president of the *Reich* and the government of the *Reich*, through the demand for a suspension of the dictatorial measures or, if necessary, through an explicit vote of no confidence. The current constitution of the *Reich* provides a *Reichstag* that is capable of forming a majority and of acting with all the rights and opportunities that a parliament may need to establish itself as the decisive factor in the formation of the will of the state. If a parliament that has become a stage for the pluralistic system is no longer able to do this, then it does not have the right to demand that all other responsible authorities become equally incapable of action. It would not only be historically impossible and morally unbearable, but also juristically wrong, today, to ground such a right to a general incapability of action on arguments with which a nineteenth-century liberal parliament of bourgeois dignitaries attempted to incapacitate its monarchical opponent. The fact that it is precisely a practice of the economic and financial state of exception, together with a right to issue decrees that replace statutes, that has formed in the contemporary constitutional situation of Germany is not the result of arbitrary exercises of power or of mere chance, and neither is it 'dictatorship' in the sense of the vulgar, party-political slogan. Rather, it is an expression of a deep and immanently regular constellation of factors. It corresponds to the turn that the legislative state takes towards the economic state, and that can no longer be followed by a pluralistically divided parliament. The state of exception, as was pointed out above (p. 76), unveils the core of the state in its concrete specificity; the jurisdictional state develops martial law, a summary judicial procedure, and the military and police-state the transfer of executive power, as their typical means of dealing with a state of exception. The right to issue decrees that replace statutes, to deal with economic and financial problems, as it is implicit in today's practice of article 48, analogously remains in conformity with the existing order, as it seeks to rescue the constitutional legislative state, whose legislative assembly is pluralistically divided, from an unconstitutional pluralism. The fact that this strongest attempt at a remedy and a countermovement to pluralism may be undertaken, constitutionally and legally, only by the president of the *Reich* at the same time makes apparent that the president of the *Reich* is to be regarded as the guardian of the constitutional order as a whole. [**132**]

III The president of the *Reich* as guardian of the constitution

1 *The state-theoretical doctrine of the 'neutral power'* (pouvoir neutre)

Differences of opinion and conflicts between those who exercise rights of political decision and of influence cannot in general be decided in judicial form, except where open violations of the constitution are to be punished. They are either resolved, from above, by a stronger political force, that is by a higher third that stands above the differing opinions – such a power, however, would not be a guardian of the constitution, but rather a sovereign ruler of the state – or they are arbitrated or settled by an authority that is not superior to but that stands alongside the conflicting parties, and hence by a neutral third. That is the purpose of a neutral power, of a *pouvoir neutre et intermédiaire*, which is placed at the side and not above the other constitutional powers, but which is endowed with peculiar competences and opportunities of influence. If this is not to be a merely accessory side effect of other activities of the state – that is, if a special institution or authority is to be organized whose task it is to secure the constitutional functioning of the different powers and to preserve the constitution – then it is only logical, in a rule-of-law state characterized by a separation of powers, not to confer this power on one of the existing authorities, to be exercised on the side, because the authority in question would, thereby, only gain a preponderance over the other powers and acquire the ability to shield itself from control. It would, thus, become a ruler of the constitution. Hence, it is necessary to appoint a special neutral power in addition to the other powers, and to connect and balance it with those others by endowing it with specific competences.

In the constitutional history of the nineteenth century, a special doctrine of the *pouvoir neutre*, *intermédiaire* and *régulateur* appears in Benjamin Constant,[13] **[133]** in the course of the struggle of the French bourgeoisie for a liberal constitution and against Bonapartism and the

[13] First in the *Réflexions sur les constitutions et les garanties*, published on 24 May 1814, printed in the *Collection complète des ouvrages publiés sur le gouvernement représentatif et la constitution actuelle de France* (Paris, 1818), vol. I, pp. 14–15; see also the *Cours de politique constitutionnelle* (edition of 1818), vol. I, pp. 13–14, in É. Laboulaye's edition of the *Cours de politique constitutionnelle* (Paris, 1872), vol. I, pp. 18–19; *Oeuvres politiques de Benjamin Constant*, ed. C. Louandre (Paris, 1874), p. 18. A monographical treatment of this important question is so far missing. As far as France is concerned, this can be explained as a result of the political fate of the French monarchy and of the head of state. With regard to the development in Germany up to now, the explanation is to be seen in the absence of a constitutional theory. Constant himself refers, without providing more specific information as to the time and place of publication, to the constitutional ideas of Clermont-Tonnerre (p. 14, footnote), but rests content to point out that one will there find 'the germs' of his doctrine ('*on en trouve les germes*' etc.). That was apparently the only basis for the reference to Clermont-Tonnerre in G. Jellinek's *Allgemeine Staatslehre*, 2nd edn (Berlin, 1905), p. 590, since the historical connection of the doctrine of a *pouvoir neutre* with the constitutional constructions of Clermont-Tonnerre has not, so far, been more closely investigated. Constant's doctrine undoubtedly conforms to the

restoration of monarchy. This doctrine essentially belongs to the constitutional theory of the bourgeois rule-of-law state, and it has had an effect on more than just the two constitutions into which it has been incorporated more or less verbatim.[14] The catalogue of prerogatives and competences of the head of state (monarch or president of state) that is typical of all nineteenth-century constitutions, moreover, can be traced back to it. [**133**] All of these prerogatives and competences are conceived of as means and opportunities of influence that pertain to such a *pouvoir neutre*: the inviolability or at least the privileged position of the head of state, the power to issue and promulgate statutes, the right of pardon, the power to appoint ministers and civil servants, the right to dissolve the elected chamber. This construction is ascertainable, in one way or another, in the constitutions of almost all larger states, insofar as they conform to the type of the bourgeois rule-of-law state, be they monarchies or republics, and regardless of whether the political situation allows

moderate liberal theory of a monarchy based on a separation of powers, as one can find it already in Mounier and Clermont-Tonnerre; Clermont-Tonnerre, moreover, characterizes the position of the king as that of a *pouvoir régulateur* (*Oeuvres complètes de Stanislas de Clermont-Tonnerre* (Paris, an III), vol. IV, p. 316), but I have not yet been able to determine, in detail, in what way Constant was influenced by Clermont-Tonnerre, and whether the latter did already use the important and characteristic formula '*pouvoir neutre*'. As far as the biographical connections are concerned, no reference to Clermont-Tonnerre is to be found either in G. Rudler's book *La Jeunesse de Benjamin Constant (1767–94)* (Paris, 1909), or in his comprehensive *Bibliographie critique des oeuvres de Benjamin Constant* (Paris, 1909). The two biographies by P. L. Léon and L. Dumont-Wilden that appeared in the year 1930 likewise contain no further information concerning this question.

[14] Brazilian Constitution of 25 March 1824, art. 98: 'Le pouvoir modérateur est la clef de toute l'organisation politique, il est délégué exclusivement à l'empereur comme chef suprême de la nation et de son premier représentant, pour qu'il veille incessament sur la conservation de l'indépendance, de l'équilibre et de l'harmonie des autres pouvoirs politiques.' Similarly, the Portuguese Constitution of 29 April 1826, art. 71: 'Le pouvoir modérateur est la clef de toute l'organisation politique et appartient exclusivement au Roi', etc. The influence of Constant's doctrine was also very strong in Italy and Spain, as I was able to find out in conversations with Italian and Spanish colleagues; but here, as well, a monographical investigation is missing. In the draft of a new Spanish constitution, which the government that was then in power published in July 1929, a *Consejo del Reino* is described as: 'instrumento del Poder armónico; garantia de la independencia judicial; moderator de la Cámera legislativa; *salva guarda de la constitucion*, frente al Gobierno o a las Cortes; possible organo de soberanía en circunstancias culminantes; clave y ornamento de todo el organismo politico, al cual presta estabilidad y decoro'. That is an interesting attempt to connect the monarch (whose essential task is defined in art. 43 as *funcion moderadora*) with the party-politically neutral authority of a council of state or of the crown. The phrases that interest us here are not yet used in the older Spanish constitutions (of 1812, 1837, 1845, 1869, and 1876).

for its actual employment or not. From the point of view of constitutional theory and of the theory of the state the doctrine of the *pouvoir neutre* is therefore of the greatest interest. It is based on a political intuition that clearly grasps the position of the monarch or of the president in a constitutional state and that expresses it in a fitting formula. It clearly belongs to the classical conception of the bourgeois rule-of-law state; and what Lorenz von Stein said about the time from 1789 to 1848, a time that was decisive not only for France but for Continental European constitutional history as a whole, refers, among other things, to the doctrine of a neutral power: 'Nowhere does the world know a more profound and inexhaustible source of greater truths about constitution and society.'[15] The originator of this doctrine quite deserves the praise that Georg Jellinek accorded to him, when he lauded Constant's 'gaze that was free of doctrinaire prejudice', and when he attributed to him the undeniable accomplishment of having been 'the first who pointed the way, for the continental development, towards the correct constitutional position of the ministers'.[16] Barthélemy admires the clarity of his line of thought ('*l'admirable lucidité du raisonnement*') and rightly says that Constant was the true pioneer of liberal parliamentarianism who educated the French bourgeoisie in the ways of parliamentarianism.[17] It is a remarkable sign that his name, after a long period of oblivion, is once again mentioned in Germany as well, and is highlighted repeatedly in a German state-theoretical document as important as H. Triepel's presentation to the fifth *Staatsrechtslehrertag*.[18]

[15] *Geschichte der sozialen Bewegung in Frankreich von 1789 bis auf unsere Tage*, I: *Der Begriff der Gesellschaft und die soziale Geschichte der Französischen Revolution bis zum Jahre 1830*, ed. G. Salomon (Munich, 1921), p. 502; Stein mentions Constant's doctrine of a neutral power explicitly *ibid.*, vol. II, p. 51, and says that this neutral power appeared in France with the July monarchy, which, in his view, represents the classical form of true constitutionalism.

[16] 'Entwicklung des Ministeriums in der konstitutionellen Monarchie', *Grünhuts Zeitschrift für das private und öffentliche Recht*, 10 (1883), 340, 342. Compare also Jellinek, *Allgemeine Staatslehre*, p. 590. The judgment that G. Jellinek, on this occasion, passes on Sieyès I hold to be unjust, and to be a misrepresentation of this astonishing constitutional architect.

[17] *L'Introduction du régime parlementaire en France* (Paris, 1904), pp. 184–5. Also correct H. Michel, *L'Idée de l'état* (Paris, 1896), p. 304: 'On n'a jamais mieux défini, avec plus de délicatesse et de sûreté dans l'expression, le rôle d'un roi constitutionnel.'

[18] 'Wesen und Entwicklung der Staatsgerichtsbarkeit', in *Veröffentlichungen der Vereinigung deutscher Staatsrechtslehrer*, issue 5 (Berlin and Leipzig, 1929), pp. 10 and 19: 'As we see, Benjamin Constant turns out to have been right: it is not as important to punish the minister as to render him harmless.'

For the history of state-theoretical concepts, [**135**] it seems to me to be of particular interest that the duality of *auctoritas* and *potestas*,* which I hold to be a fundamental distinction of the European theory of the state, is also recognizable in this doctrine of Constant's.[19]

The practical value of this doctrine of a neutral, arbitrating, regulating, and preserving position of the head of state consists, in the first place, in the fact that one can now answer the question of what the significance, if any, of a head of state is supposed to be in a bourgeois rule-of-law state, be it a constitutional monarchy or a constitutional democracy, and what purpose one can assign to his competences, given that the power of legislation is altogether in the hands of the chambers, that the ministers appointed by the head of state are altogether dependent on the trust of the legislative assemblies, that the head of state himself is bound in all things to the countersignature of the ministers, and that one can consequently say of the head of state: *il règne et ne gouverne pas.*[20] The distinction of *règner* and *gouverner* was not understood in Germany, neither theoretically, because the distinction between *auctoritas* and *potestas* had long been forgotten; nor practically, because the monarch of a German-style constitutional monarchy really did rule and govern. According to F. J. Stahl's well-known distinction, this was the basis of the contrast between a constitutional (i.e. a truly governing) and a parliamentary monarchy, an antithesis that cleverly combines an adaptation to the demands and forms of expression of the time with an attempt to render them harmless, and that becomes comprehensible only once it is understood to be a distinction for a political purpose.[21] The nineteenth-century German doctrine of the state claimed, from the beginning, against the construction of the French liberals, that the king must also act and really execute, since he would otherwise be a mere

19 Compare note 25 on p. 136 below.

20 Thiers's sentence of the year 1829 is phrased as follows: 'Le roi règne, les ministres gouvernent, les chambres jugent' (where *jugent*, of course, is not meant to refer to adjudication). On the genesis of this famous formula see G. Jellinek, 'Entwicklung des Ministeriums', p. 343, A. Esmein and H. Nezard, *Éléments du droit constitutionnel Français et comparé*, 7th edn (Paris, 1921), vol. I, p. 231.

21 *Rechts- und Staatsphilosophie*, 2nd edn, §§ 97–80;* for an explication of the contrast between 'constitutional' and 'parliamentary' see C. Schmitt, *Verfassungslehre* (Berlin, 1928), p. 289. The insoluble difficulties show themselves in Binding's paper on ministerial responsibility (above, p. 28 note 35). Ministerial responsibility remains incomprehensible and cannot be constructed without the doctrine of the neutral position of the head of state.

shadow.[22] Max von Seydel found a striking argument for this view: the monarch must, in all cases, really govern and have real power, since nothing would, after all, remain of the *régner* if one subtracted the *gouverner*.[23] Authors often cited a rather uncouth saying of Napoleon's,[24] [**136**] and they were right insofar as the German constitutional monarchy, up to 1918, was indeed a higher and stronger power that justified the distinction between state and society, and not merely a 'nothing but neutral' third party. But this does not solve either the problem of the general theory of the state that is implicit in the distinction of *auctoritas* and *potestas*, or the problem of the party-political neutrality of the state, or the problem, in constitutional theory, of the role of the head of state in a parliamentary constitutional state, or, finally, the special problem of the position of the president of the *Reich* in the current, the Weimar Constitution. In general, von Seydel's question, the question of what remains if one subtracts the *gouverner* from the *régner*, can be answered by saying that the head of state, in such a constitution, beyond exercising the competences allocated to him, represents the continuity and permanence of the unity of the state and of its unified functioning, and that the head of state must, for reasons of continuity, of moral prestige, and of general trust, possess a special form of authority that belongs to the life of each state, as much as the daily exercise of the state's power and right to command.[25] This is of

[22] So already, for example, C. von Rotteck, *Lehrbuch des Vernunftrechts und der Staatswissenschaften*, 2nd edn (Stuttgart, 1840), vol. II, p. 219: without a sphere of authority of his own, without the power to act and to execute, the king would be a 'mere shadow'.

[23] M. von Seydel, 'Über konstitutionelle und parlamentarische Regierung' (1887), in M. von Seydel, *Staatsrechtliche und politische Abhandlungen* (Freiburg and Leipzig, 1893), p. 140; moreover, for example, A. Samuely, *Das Prinzip der Ministerverantwortlichkeit* (Berlin, 1869), p. 15; H. Frisch, *Die Verantwortlichkeit der Monarchen und der höchsten Magistrate* (Berlin, 1894), p. 186; against this view correctly L. C. Dolmatowsky, 'Der Parlamentarismus in der Lehre B. Constants', *Zeitschrift für die gesamten Staatswissenschaften*, 63 (1907), 608.

[24] According to which such a human being is nothing more than a 'cochon engraissé', cited, for example, in Bluntschli, *Allgemeine Staatslehre*, vol. I, p. 483; Jellinek, 'Entwicklung des Ministeriums', p. 341.

[25] On the contrast between *potestas* and *auctoritas*: Schmitt, *Verfassungslehre*, p. 75, note. On the difficult construction of the position of the head of state in conformity with the social and political reality of a parliamentary state characterized by a separation of powers: von Stein, *Geschichte der sozialen Bewegung in Frankreich*, vol. I, p. 498, moreover (on Constant's doctrine) vol. II, p. 51. It is remarkable, in this context, that B. Constant, in his discussion of the *pouvoir neutre*, also mentions the *auctoritas* of the Roman senate as an example (*Oeuvres politiques*, vol. I, pp. 17–18). On this senate as a guardian of the constitution compare p. 9 above. That one speaks of a *pouvoir neutre* and

special interest for the doctrine of a neutral power, [**137**] for the reason that the peculiar function of the neutral third does not consist in a continuously commanding and rule-making activity, but rather, initially, in arbitration, preservation, and regulation. The neutral power is active only in a state of emergency, since it is not to compete with the other powers with a view to expanding its own influence, and since it must normally, according to the nature of its business, be discreet and unobtrusive. Nevertheless, the neutral power is present and indispensable, at least in the system of a rule-of-law state with a separation of powers. Here it is, as Constant already knew, even though this aspect of his doctrine failed to attract attention, a *pouvoir préservateur*, a 'preserving power'. Of course, such a position of authority requires tactfulness, just as its discovery and formulation required the intuition of a Benjamin Constant. Constant, with this doctrine, succeeded in characterizing the position of a head of state as such, and keeping alive

a neutral power finds its explanation in the fact that the distinction between *auctoritas* and *potestas* has disappeared from state-theoretic consciousness and that *pouvoir* has turned into a colourless concept. Constant himself, in the decisive passage, speaks of *autorité* and not of *pouvoir*: 'Le roi est au milieu de ces trois pouvoirs (législatif, exécutif, judiciaire) autorité neutre et intermédiaire' (*Cours de politique constitutionnelle*, vol. I., p. 15). Apart from that, his terminology is not always perfectly consistent, which need not occasion surprise, because the distinction had already become almost unknown in the eighteenth century. In the sentence of Hobbes's that I have cited repeatedly: *autoritas, non veritas facit legem* (*Leviathan*, Latin edn, ch. 26), one can still distinguish *autoritas* from *potestas*, but Hobbes himself grounds this *autoritas* exclusively in the *summa potestas*. That Montesquieu, in a much-discussed saying, can declare the *puissance de juger* to be '*en quelque façon nulle*' (*Esprit des lois*, XI, 6), likewise stands in a material connection with the distinction, since the judge has *auctoritas* more than *potestas*; but Montesquieu is no longer aware of this point. The tradition, for a long time, connected a senate with the specific concept of *auctoritas*, so that the contrast that interests us here frequently shades over into the opposition of *deliberare* and *agere*. Several different forms of authority can be connected with the idea of a senate: the authority of old age, of experience and wisdom, of an expertise that merely gives counsel. Bodinus, *Six livres de la République*, 2nd edn (Lyon, 1580), III, ch. 7, pp. 365–6, still knows the difference very well: 'et quoy qu'on dit de la puissance du Sénat Romain, ce n'estoit que dignité, authorité, conseil et pas puissance'; for him, the contrast transforms itself into that of *conseil* and *commandement*. I have been able to find examples for a loss of every sense of the material difference only from the French Revolution onwards; especially characteristic is an utterance of P. N. Gautier in the *Dictionnaire de la constitution et du gouvernement Français* (2nd edn, Paris, 1792) under the heading: *Autorité*: '*Ce mot signifie pouvoir, puissance, empire.*' Here we see the beginning of the lazy alternatives in which the forgetfulness of tradition of the modern theory of the state unveils itself: authority and freedom, authority and democracy etc., until, finally, even authority and dictatorship, or autocracy and authority, are no longer distinguished in the brawl of party political slogans.

an old wisdom grounded in the tradition of the structure of the Roman state. Most of the significant heads of state of the nineteenth and twentieth century knew how to step behind their ministers without thereby losing any authority. A constitutional statute, needless to say, cannot prescribe or enforce the personal qualities of character that are necessary in order perfectly to fill the role of a *pouvoir neutre*, just as it cannot prescribe that a prime minister must be a great political leader who really determines the guiding principles of policy by himself. But neither the practical nor the theoretical significance of the concept stands refuted by this fact.

The position of the president of the *Reich*, elected by the people as a whole, under the positive law of the Weimar Constitution can only be constructed with the help of a further development of the doctrine of a neutral, arbitrating, regulating, and preserving power. The president of the *Reich* is endowed with competences that make him independent of the legislative authorities, [**138**] despite the fact that he is, at the same time, bound to the countersignature of ministers who are dependent on the trust of parliament. The competences that are allocated to him by the constitution (the appointment of public servants according to article 46, the right of pardon according to article 49, the promulgation of statutes according to article 70) conform to the typical catalogue of competences of a head of state as it was already put forward by B. Constant.[26] The peculiar, much-discussed balancing of the plebiscitary with the parliamentary element of the constitution, the connection between an independence from the *Reichstag* grounded in self-standing competences and a dependence grounded in the general requirement of ministerial countersignature (article 50 RV), the federal execution, i.e. the protection of the constitution of the *Reich* against the *Länder*, and finally the protection of the constitution (as opposed to the protection of the individual constitutional statute) according to article 48; all that would be a contradictory and meaningless mixture of irreconcilable provisions if it did not become comprehensible through the doctrine of the neutral power. The creators of the Weimar Constitution, to the extent that they undertook their task with a systematic consciousness, were well aware of that. Hugo Preuß pointed out, in the constitutional committee (*Protokolle*, p. 277), that it is 'only one of the functions of the president of the *Reich* to form a counterweight to the *Reichstag*'. 'Aside from that, there is the more important one: to form a kind of centre in the

[26] *Oeuvres politiques*, vol. I, p. 18.

constitution, a pole that is at rest.' Preuß adds to this sentence the following further remark, a remark that anticipates the splintering and the dissolutions of a pluralistic system and the necessity of an effective remedy: 'The more committees you are going to have that are supposed to work together, the more votes there will be, to be taken by the masses through referenda, by the *Reichsrat*, or by workers councils, the greater will be the need to have, besides all this, a firm point in which, at least ideally, all the threads run together.' F. Naumann declared in reply (*Protokolle*, pp. 277–8) that he would like to 'express himself in a similar manner on the question of the president'. He foresees, even more clearly than Preuß, the pluralistic coalition party state, and then says, in these precise words: 'The electoral law of proportional representation that governs the elections to the *Reichstag*, and the plurality of parties that must result from this, lead to the conclusion that the prime minister will be a coalition-minister. Precisely for this reason, the need for a personality who has the whole in view will make itself felt especially strongly.' In this context, we find both the characterization of the president of the *Reich* as a 'mediating authority', as a *pouvoir intermédiaire*, as well as a pointer to the possibility, which has by now become real, of a *Reichstag* that is no longer able to form a majority: 'The reason why I believe that we need a president, is grounded above all in the fact that we, in Germany, cannot attain a complete unity without the president, given the multitude of portfolios. We also have to have someone who fulfils representative duties, who entertains relations to all parts of the country as well as to all parties and (!) to foreign states, [**139**] and who can function as a mediating authority between parliament and government. There is a possibility that no majority is to be found in the *Reichstag*, and that, as a result, it is not possible, at least not without great difficulty, to form a government. At this point, the president must be able to take action ... The whole question of the presidency is not a question of party, but rather a question of political technique and harmony.'

These claims have, to a large extent, been confirmed by the practical reality of the life of the state. A large part of the activity of President of the *Reich* Ebert, who referred to himself as a guardian of the constitution in a politically important moment, as well as of the current incumbent, President of the *Reich* Hindenburg, can be characterized as a neutral and arbitrating mediation of conflicts, and one will have to acknowledge that these two presidents of the *Reich*, both in their own way, have discharged their difficult task better than many a head of state who could not grasp what might remain of the *régner* once the *gouverner* is subtracted. I will allow myself to add to the discussion in my *Verfassungslehre* (pp. 351–2) that it was also justifiable, from this point of view, for the former President of the *Reichsgericht* Simons to turn to the president of the *Reich* during his conflict with the government of the *Reich** in December 1928. The president of the *Reich*, to be sure, was not 'competent' to receive and to decide formal 'complaints' of the president of the *Staatsgerichtshof* about the government of the *Reich*. And he was, if one wants to judge here according to the standards of a keeper of a land registry, not allowed to give any response, other than to point out that neither the complaint as such, nor the appeal to the president, was permissible. One occasionally hears that the president of the *Reich* ought to have referred the complainant to the 'proper channels', via the *Reich's* minister of justice or the *Reich's* minister of the interior, and to have alerted him to the unconstitutionality of his proceedings. Even in newspapers that otherwise showed a great deal of understanding for the personality and the aims of the President of the *Reichsgericht* Simons one finds the remark that 'the appeal to the president of the *Reich* by the president of the *Reichsgericht* simply does not conform to the constitution'.[27] [**140**] If the president of the *Reich* instead, in his answer,

[27] A. Feiler, *Frankfurter Zeitung* (10 January 1929), no. 24. Giese is right to say, against this, in *Deutsche Juristen-Zeitung*, 34 (1929), 134, that one will 'hardly be able to deny to the president of the *Staatsgerichtshof*, as a highest organ of the *Reich*, the right to issue formless complaints against real or alleged violations of the constitution' – but why are these complaints to be directed to the president of the *Reich*, if the latter is not supposed to be the 'guardian of the constitution'? The former President of the *Reichsgericht* Simons himself has taken a stand on the question, in the introduction to the second volume of the collection *Die Rechtsprechung des Staatsgerichtshofes für das Deutsche Reich* (pp. 9 and 11), which he edits together with H. H. Lammers. His statements culminate in the following exceedingly apt sentence: 'The position of the president of the *Reich* is not circumscribed so narrowly and precisely, by the constitution, that the mediatory activity that he was asked to perform could be regarded as being prohibited to him by a legal norm; on the contrary, it would, given article 42 and 48 of the constitution of the *Reich*, according to which the president of the *Reich* is the highest guardian of its law and of its constitution, have conformed rather well to the purpose and meaning of the position of this organ.' With this, and with the above remarks in the text, the objections made by F. Glum, 'Staatsrechtliche Bemerkungen zu dem "Konflikt" zwischen dem Staatsgerichtshof für das deutsche Reich und der Reichsregierung', *Zeitschrift für ausländisches öffentliches Recht und Völkerrecht*, 1 (1929), 466, ought to be regarded as refuted. Glum himself, by the way, refers to the president of the *Reich* as the 'guardian of the constitution' in his paper: 'Parlamentskrise und Verfassungslücke', *Deutsche Juristen-Zeitung* (15 November 1930), 1417–18, and draws such far-reaching practical conclusions from this claim that the legitimacy of the mediatory activity that the president of the *Reich* exercised in December 1928 would, in comparison, have to be regarded as an almost anodyne matter of fact.

apart from declaring that he 'does not regard himself to be competent, for reasons of constitutional law, to give a formal decision on the complaint', nevertheless does take a position on the question at issue and affirms his agreement with the government of the *Reich*, while at the same time answering the president of the *Reichsgerichtshof* in a personally accommodating manner, then his actions conform to a correct conception of a neutral, arbitrating, regulating, and preserving position of the head of state and are to be understood, and to be justified, on the basis of this doctrine.[28] This also invalidates the criticism of the fact that the president has, on occasion, exercised influence over processes of negotiation, through personal letters, which had not been countersigned by the chancellor of the *Reich*, or through other pronouncements. In a state with an organization as complicated as that of the German *Reich*, and given today's concrete constitutional situation – the German *Reich* is not only a federal, but at the same time a pluralistic and polycratic entity* – the arbitrating and regulating function of the *pouvoir neutre* acquires a central significance, a significance that one cannot do justice either through a subaltern formalism, or through arguments adapted from the monarchic era before the war.[29]

. . .

[28] H. Pohl, in G. Anschütz and R. Thoma (eds.), *Handbuch des deutschen Staatsrechts* (Tübingen, 1930), vol. I, p. 502. As an example from *Ebert's* presidency compare the letter to the Bavarian government of 27 July 1922 (conflict between the *Reich* and Bavaria in the summer of 1922); here, the president of the *Reich* states of himself: 'My task as the guardian of the constitution of the *Reich* and of the idea of the *Reich* therefore gives rise to a duty on my part to work for the invalidation of the Bavarian decree, in accordance with article 48 of the constitution of the *Reich*.' (This letter as well as the reply of the Bavarian prime minister are printed in R. Joeckle, *Bayern und die große politische Krise in Deutschland im Sommer 1922: Dokumente und Dokumentarisches zur politischen Auswirkung der Ermordung des Reichsaußenministers Dr. Walther Rathenau* (*Politische Zeitfragen*, vol. 7/11) (Munich, 1922), p. 237.) Here, as well, it is characteristic for a formalism trapped in a logical dead-end to claim that the president of the *Reich* either ought to have judged Bavaria to be in the wrong or, if he did hold the Bavarian actions* to be permissible, to have refrained from writing such a letter.

[29] Article 50 of the constitution of the *Reich* (countersignature of the chancellor of the *Reich* or of the competent minister of the *Reich*) is not usually applied, naturally, in the exercise of the *pouvoir intermédiaire*, because that exercise does not consist in 'directives and regulations' issued by the president of the *Reich* but rather in personal influence, suggestions, and mediation; compare F. Freiherr Marschall von Bieberstein, in *Handbuch des deutschen Staatsrechts*, vol. I, p. 531. To draw the conclusion, from article 50, that the president is permitted to issue only such statements as can be regarded as 'directives and regulations' would be illogical. Compare H. Pohl, *ibid.* p. 484 and (unclear) R. Thoma, *ibid.*, p. 508.

III.3 The public service and the different possibilities of an 'independence' from the pluralistic party state

The fact that the state's public service appears at a decisive point, in the discussion of the powers which are, though ambiguously, referred to as 'neutral', as well as in relation to the question of the unity of the state – because the mediators as well as the judges in our courts of labour law and in our system of collective bargaining are, in general, drawn from the professional civil service – reveals a large functional change that inevitably also occurs in this area. The traditional, static opposition of state, i.e. of a monarchy administrated by a professional public service, on the one hand and of society, i.e. of a 'free' sphere of life that is in principle distinct from the state, on the other is dissolving. The public service no longer stands above a 'society' that is separated from it; it is no longer supposed to have a position that transcends society, as in the monarchic state. Nevertheless, it is consciously preserved as an impartial power. According to the constitution, the public service is not supposed to stand below society either. The constitution of the *Reich*, in articles 129–30, contains an institutional guarantee* of the professional public service, and thus a constitutional element of stability and permanence that is not supposed to be swallowed by the methods of 'functional integration' mentioned above. Public servants are 'servants of the whole', but their neutrality is not that of a mere 'civil service' in the British sense or of a technical functionary. Rather, it is intended to continue the great tradition of the German professional public service* in the democratic state.[30]

[30] On the 'new mission of the public service' in Germany: A. Köttgen, *Das deutsche Berufsbeamtentum und die parlamentarische Demokratie* (Berlin, 1928), p. 243; *Sächsische Schulzeitung*, 96 (Dresden, Nov. 1929), 757–8 and 825–6 (against the dissolution of the tenure of civil servants into a contractual labour relationship secured by social policy, as advocated by H. Potthof); and *Handbuch des deutschen Staatsrechts*, vol. II, p. 15; moreover E. Zweigert, 'Der Beamte im neuen Deutschland' in B. Harms (ed.), *Volk und Reich der Deutschen* (Berlin, 1929), vol. II, p. 467: 'Our professional ethos has not been reduced by the constitution of Weimar. To the contrary, it is deepened and ennobled by the idea of a commitment to the whole.' In this passage, Zweigert also speaks of an 'inner connection with the whole, that does not merely stand above the connection to any political party, but that is also ethically superior to the previous connection to the person of the monarch', and that remains untouched by the subordination of the public servant to 'changing political powers'. H. Leisegang, 'Die Ethik des Berufsbeamtentums' (in the lecture series: *Berufsbeamtentum, Volksstaat, und Ethik* (Leipzig, 1931), p. 32) even states that this ethos of the professional public service is 'the only ethical substance that holds this state together, this state in which everything else that binds people to one another, in particular ideological orientation and religion, has become a private affair'. The two lectures of W. Kaskel, *Beamtenrecht und Arbeitsrecht*

That is possible only on a new basis, [**149**] after the monarchic basis and the separation of state and society have become obsolete. That new basis is discernible in the fact that it is the president of the *Reich* who, in accordance with article 46 of the constitution of the *Reich*, appoints and dismisses the public servants of the *Reich*. These two constitutional provisions – article 130 and article 46* – thus belong together. It is, practically speaking, at least a remarkable restraint against party-political methods of appointment that it is not the party-comrade turned minister himself, but rather a head of state independent of parliament, and therefore of any political party, who appoints public servants. But even more important than this practical advantage is the systematic connection between a state based on a professional public service and a president of the *Reich* who stands on a plebiscitary basis, and who controls the plebiscitary element of the constitution of the *Reich*.

This connection, to be more precise, provides the only way to create an independent authority in a democratic constitution, without which there can be no guardian of the constitution. 'Independence' is the fundamental presupposition, and all proposals for a guardian of the constitution are based on the view that one must create an independent and neutral authority. In most cases, however, it does not become perspicuous and not systematically clear enough how many different forms of 'independence' there are in the life of today's state, [**151**] and why ever more institutions have to be made exempt from the party-political business of the pluralistic system. There are, after all, very different kinds of independence: an independence of the judge, an independence, different

(Berlin, 1926), and of Fr. Giese, *Das Berufsbeamtentum im deutschen Volksstaat* (Berlin, 1929) (both have been published by the *Verlagsanstalt des Deutschen Beamtenbundes*) are particularly noteworthy in this context. The discussion in E. Michel, 'Das Beamtenproblem', *Deutsche Republik*, 3 (August 1929), 1501–2 is also of the greatest interest, for the reason that Michel recognizes and pays attention to the turn towards the 'self-organization of society' that has been discussed above (p. 79), and for the reason that he does not harbour any illusions concerning the fact that we now live in a 'societal state that is politicized through and through'. Within this, as I would prefer to put it: 'total state' he takes the public service to be called to the task of 'performing the gigantic work, through its daily responsible collaboration, of *calming down* social conflicts in the small, and to become an organ of peace that, in the midst of the revolutionary changes of society, stands *above* the economic, social, and political struggles' (my emphases). I intend to deal explicitly, in a future publication, with the question of whether the German public servants are today representatives of the state, which has been raised, with new arguments very worthy of consideration, by A. Köttgen, in his review of G. Leibholz, 'Der Begriff der Repräsentation', *Archiv des öffentlichen Rechts*, 19 (1930), 307. For now, I hold on to the view that public servants are servants, as the constitution says. Compare Schmitt, *Verfassungslehre*, p. 213.

from the first, of the professional public servant, and an independence, composed of the first two, of the judge who is a professional public servant; besides, there is an independence of the president and of the members of the audit office for the German *Reich*.[31] There is, moreover, the independence of the member of parliament, according to article 21 of the constitution of the *Reich*,[32] as well as the independence and freedom, a freedom that is again special in kind, of the academic teacher who is guaranteed the freedom of instruction in article 142 of the constitution of the *Reich*.[33] Additionally, there is the independence of the expert witness or advisor that follows from the nature of the latter's task.[34] The tendencies towards neutralization discussed above (pp. 100–1*),

[31] §§ 118, 119 of the tax code of the German *Reich*.

[32] On this issue see Schmitt, *Verfassungslehre*, p. 255.

[33] K. Rothenbücher, in his report for the German *Staatsrechtslehrertag* in Munich 1927, in *Veröffentlichungen der Vereinigung deutscher Staatsrechtslehrer*, issue 4 (Berlin and Leipzig, 1928), pp. 32–3; R. Smend, *ibid.*, pp. 56–7; W. A. E. Schmidt, *Die Freiheit der Wissenschaft*, third in the series *Abhandlungen zur Reichsverfassung*, ed. W. Jellinek (Berlin, 1929), pp. 126–7; F. Freiherr Marschall von Bieberstein, 'Die Gefährdung der deutschen Universität', *Die Tatwelt*, (July–September 1929), 92–3. Very instructive for the problem of the religiously and ideologically neutral state, and of its relationship to education and the school, is the essay of G. Giese, 'Staat, Staatsgedanke und Staatserziehung', *Die Erziehung*, 5 (1929), in particular at 153; the different kinds of impartiality, supra-partiality, and neutrality, however, would have to be more precisely distinguished in this context (see above pp. 111–15*). The *ratio* of academic freedom is especially well-expressed in Spranger, 'Das Wesen der deutschen Universität', p. 5: 'Put more precisely, academic freedom is not an individualistic basic right, as for example the right to free expression of opinion. It is, rather, a collective right that imposes obligations on the individual academic, and that is grounded in the supra-individual objectivity of the search for truth.' The guarantee of the freedom of academic instruction in article 142 of the constitution of the *Reich* is an institutional guarantee (Schmitt, *Verfassungslehre*, p. 172; approvingly G. Anschütz, *Die Verfassung des Deutschen Reiches vom 11. August 1919. Ein Kommentar für Wissenschaft und Praxis* (Berlin, 1929), p. 572; F. Giese, *Die Verfassung des Deutschen Reiches vom 11. August 1919* (Berlin, 1931), p. 299; A. Köttgen, *Mitteilungen des Verbandes der Deutschen Hochschulen*, January 1931). On the connection of this freedom of academic instruction with the principle of free discussion and with the privilege of *Kolleggeld** see the interesting discussion in L. von Stein, *Lehrfreiheit, Wissenschaft und Kolleggeld* (Vienna, 1875) (freedom of teaching as freedom of discussion, *Kolleggeld* as a guarantee of independence and freedom).

[34] A. Bertram, *Zeitschrift für Zivilprozeß*, 53 (1928), 421: 'In the sphere of administration in general it is the advisory opinion, in particular, that occupies a special position, insofar as the advisory opinion, conceptually, does not tolerate a directive. To be sure, a superior authority may direct an authority that is inferior to it to provide an assessment on more or less general or on precisely determined questions; but it cannot, without turning the requested statement into something other than an advisory opinion, direct it to arrive at a particular result. The content of an advisory opinion, therefore, is always based on the expert's own activity, uninfluenced by directive.'

[**152**] as well as the creation of autonomous entities split apart from the authority of the state, like the *Reichsbank* or the *Reichsbahn* corporation, also resulted in peculiar forms and protections of independence, of which one ought to mention, above all, apart from incompatibilities and other special provisions, the appointment to the general council of the *Reichsbahn* through co-optation as well as decisions in respect of conflicts between the government of the *Reich* and the *Reichsbahn* corporation by a special *Reichsbahn* court. There is, finally, the independence of a head of state, be it that of a monarch in a constitutional monarchy, whose independence is based on the heritability of the succession to the throne and on the inviolability of his person, or be it the independence of a state's president in a constitutional democracy, that is secured, in the Weimar Constitution, through the election of the president by the whole German people (article 41 of the constitution of the *Reich*), the seven-year term of office (article 43 paragraph 1 of the constitution of the *Reich*), and through the severe obstacles to a recall (article 43 paragraph 2 of the constitution of the *Reich*).

The independence of a judge, thus, is only one special case of independence, and not to be confused with independence as such; it is, moreover, as we pointed out, a composite form of independence. When thinking of judicial independence, one normally has in mind the independence of the professional judge who is also a public servant. Through the guarantee of his legally protected position, the professional public servant, who is appointed for life or for a long period of time, and who cannot be deposed or be dismissed without due cause, is taken out of the quarrel of the economic and social opposites. He becomes 'independent' and therefore capable of being neutral and impartial, as article 130 of the constitution demands of him. The independence of the judges in today's state is grounded, in its specificity, in the fact that these general legal guarantees of the public service are strengthened even further, in that article 104 of the constitution of the *Reich* prescribes that the judges of the ordinary judiciary are to be appointed for life, and that they can be deprived of their office, against their will, temporarily or permanently, or be transferred to a different position or into retirement, only by virtue of a judicial decision, pursuant to the reasons and under the procedures determined by the law. The judicial independence guaranteed by the Weimar Constitution thus connects two kinds of independence with one another; on the one hand, the specifically judicial independence, in the exercise of the judicial office, from directives and commands issued by superiors (article 102), which independence is also enjoyed by judges who are not professional public servants (lay assessors, jurymen, or lay judges), and, secondly, the strengthened independence of the judicial public servant. The independence of the judicial public servant who is appointed for life, and who can be stripped of his position only by a formal procedure in front of his peers, is not to be understood merely as a guarantee of the first of the two forms of judicial independence. It does not apply to judges who are not professional public servants (assessors, jurymen, lay judges, commercial judges, etc.), [**153**] and its effect, in substance, is simply to strengthen the guarantees of articles 129–30 of the constitution of the *Reich*, which are to be enjoyed by all public servants, including those who are not judges. This part of judicial independence is only a qualified case of the general independence of the public servant. Nobody would consider a court of law composed of party politicians to be independent and neutral, even if its members were 'not bound to directives and commands in the exercise of their judicial activity'; everyone would remember the fate of the independence of the member of parliament according to article 21 of the constitution of the *Reich*, and would suspect that such a court of law – in its composition as well as in its activity – would have to turn into an arena of the pluralistic system in just the same way as has parliament, as well as every office that depends on the 'trust of parliament'.

A college of professional judges who cannot be deposed, and who are endowed with the special guarantees of judicial independence, appears to a very high degree to be an independent, neutral, and objective authority, and it is therefore only too understandable that one may believe one has depoliticized all constitutional conflicts once they are left to the decision of a college of judges who are also public servants. But those who, for such reasons, demand a *Staatsgerichtshof* or a constitutional court for all constitutional conflicts usually forget that judicial independence is only the flip side of a judge's subjection to statute and that the constitution, in general, cannot bind judges in the same way.[35] One also usually overlooks the experiences of the last decade in the area of labour disputes that have led to a clear distinction between the judge and the mediator. In truth, what the advocates of a constitutional court aim for is not so much a judicial, but rather an independent and neutral authority. One simply wants to instrumentalize the judicial character, as it is the clearest and most secure form of an

[35] Compare pp. 47–8 above.

independence guaranteed by constitutional law. Most proposals, for this reason, do not, by any means, conceive of judicial independence in the narrowest way, i.e. as an independence from directives issued by another authority that concern the exercise of judicial activity. What they have in mind, rather, is the independence of the professional judge who is also a public servant, which is strengthened by the general guarantees of the independence of the professional public service. One is therefore usually concerned, in such proposals, to strengthen the guarantees of the professional judicial public service even more. A *Staatsgerichtshof* or constitutional court would, for instance, have to be protected against a change, by way of an ordinary statute, of the number or composition of the judges on the court or of its procedure, in order not to allow for court-packing or similar forms of influencing, as they tend to occur, according to our experience, in politically important cases, and as they are well known, in particular, to the history of the Supreme Court of the United States.[36] Finally, it would certainly [**154**] be consistent to demand that appointment to such a court take place only on the basis of proposals made by its president or by the college as a whole,[37] or that it take place only by way of co-optation.[38] The demand for ever stronger protections simply goes to show that adjudication and judicial form, when it comes to proposals for a *Staatsgerichtshof* or a constitutional court, really only serve the aim of creating a neutral and independent authority and to secure a certain

[36] So the Dred-Scott case decided during the time of the struggle over the abolition of slavery (C. Warren, *The Supreme Court in the United States* (Boston, 1824), vol. III, pp. 22–3), or the Legal Tender Cases decided at a time of inflation during the war of secession (*ibid.*, p. 244); compare p. 13 above; Gneist's judgment on public servants is also remarkable in this context (p. 35 above, note 52).

[37] As in the case of the right of proposal of the president of the audit office for the German *Reich*; *Reichshaushaltsordnung* § 119 paragraph 2. G. Lassar has recommended a similar right of proposal for the planned administrative court of the *Reich* (draft of a statute on the federal administrative court from 26 August 1930, *Reichsratdrucksache*, no. 155), in *Das Reichsverwaltungsgericht, eine Kritik des Regierungsentwurfs* (Berlin, 1930), p. 14. The right of proposal of faculties in the appointment to academic positions is a residue of an autonomy that presupposes the independence of science.

[38] Thus Kelsen in 'Wesen und Entwicklung der Staatsgerichtsbarkeit' in *Veröffentlichungen der Vereinigung der deutschen Staatsrechtslehrer*, issue 5 (Berlin and Leipzig, 1929), p. 56 [ch. 1 above, 1506]. So far, one has been able to push through this kind of co-optation, in the German *Reich*, only for the general council of the central bank of the *Reich* and only under the external pressure of the creditor states. On another (failed) attempt to introduce co-optation that was undertaken in France, see note 40 below.

'permanence',[39] i.e. a certain stability, in the midst of the ongoing party-political hustle and bustle.[40] [**155**]

The guardian of the constitution must indeed be independent and party-politically neutral. But it is an abuse of the concepts of judicial form and of adjudication, as well as of the institutional guarantee of the German professional public service, immediately to demand the introduction of a court staffed by professional jurists who are public servants, and of a judicial procedure, in all cases where an independence or neutrality appears to be useful or necessary for practical reasons. The judiciary as well as the professional public service are burdened in an unacceptable way if all political tasks and decisions whose discharge requires independence and party-political neutrality are heaped upon them. What is more, the installation of such a guardian of the constitution would be directly opposed to the political implications of the democratic principle. The judicial right of review could be politically successful in the nineteenth century, against the monarch's right to issue decrees, in France as well as in the German constitutional

39 An expression used by Gneist in his *Gutachten zum 1. deutschen Juristentag*, p. 23. Gneist rejects the judicial scrutiny of statutes for their reasonableness and justice (i.e. their rationability), as it is practised in the United States of America, for the following reason, which is especially interesting in connection with the discussion in the text above: 'Since the factors of legislation, in the United States of America, lack the necessary permanence, in order to provide a guarantee against overly hasty decisions of the legislative bodies, or against decisions that are determined by changing interests, one has attempted to preserve certain advantages of hereditary monarchy by superimposing the courts as guardians of certain boundaries defined by the social contract. But this transcendental authority of a highest court surely does not fit into the constitution of the German judicial process. The sought-after guarantee, rather, is more securely provided by a hereditary monarchy, by a second (permanent) and by a third (elected) body, as well as by their co-operation in the process of legislation; at least it is provided therein as far as human institutions are at all capable of providing such a guarantee.'

40 The safest way to achieve this goal would be to introduce a second (or first) chamber organized on the basis of heredity. But since it would hardly be possible, in today's democratic state, to introduce a chamber of peers modelled on the English example, one could only repeat the attempt of a wholly or partially irremovable senate that recruits its members by co-optation. That attempt failed in republican France. According to the constitutional law of 24 February 1875, 75 of 300 senators were first appointed for life by the national assembly, who were then to refill their positions through co-optation, while the majority of the senate, apart from the co-opted members, was appointed by election. However, a constitutional law of 9 December 1884 eliminated this restriction of the democratic principle of election. The members appointed for life still remained in their irremovable position, but they were no longer replaced through co-optation. The last of these irremovable senators died only a few years ago.

monarchies.[41] Today, however, the judiciary would no longer be required to set itself against a monarch but rather against a parliament. That would signify a far-reaching change of the function of judicial independence. Here, as well, the old separation of state and society has become obsolete, and one must not simply transfer the formulas and arguments of the nineteenth century to the situation of the twentieth century, which is altogether different, politically as well as socially. The necessity of stabilizing institutions and of a counterweight to parliament is a problem, in today's Germany, altogether different in kind from the old problem of the control of the monarch. That applies as much to the general, diffuse right of judicial review as to the control that is concentrated with a single authority. The concentration of all constitutional disputes in a single court of justice, formed of professional civil servants who cannot be removed, and who are independent on that ground, would create a second chamber whose members would be professional civil servants. No amount of judicial procedure could veil the fact that such a *Staatsgerichtshof* or constitutional court would be a highly political authority endowed with a competence of constitutional legislation. [**156**] From a democratic point of view, it will hardly be possible to transfer such powers to an aristocracy of the robe.

4 *The democratic basis of the authority of the president of the* Reich

The purpose of judicial independence in today's state, in any case, is not at all to create an agency of correct political will-formation, but rather to carve out and to protect a sphere, within a well-ordered state, of adjudication bound to statute. Other forms of independence have other functions, among these in particular also that of making possible a strong political will-formation that is independent of the state-dissolving methods of the pluralistic party state, as has been shown above (p. 114*). This is often overlooked, as a consequence of the confusion of neutralization, de-party-politicization, and de-politicization.[42] But it is immediately

41 For France compare the exceptionally apt remark in M. Leroy, *Les Transformations de la puissance publique* (Paris, 1907), p. 97: the French courts took the place of the *Sénat conservateur* that had become vacant in 1829; for Germany see Gneist's *Gutachten zum 4. deutschen Juristentag* that has already been cited repeatedly, in particular also the passage to which we just drew attention on p. 154, note 39.

42 It is in particular L. Wittmayer's treatise *Reichsverfassung und Politik* (Tübingen, 1923) (*Recht und Staat*, vol. XXIV) that suffers from an infelicitous identification of 'de-politicization' and 'de-party-politicization'; on this identification see p. 108 above.* It is a mistake, moreover, for

recognizable once one pays attention to the fact that the different forms of independence correspond to different non-removabilities, immunities, and – there seems, admittedly, to be little understanding of this point in Germany and little inclination to take it seriously – incompatibilities, even though these institutional safeguards are not always systematically thought through and put into practice.[43] Most notably, in German public law, at any rate, the office of the president of the *Reich* is incompatible with that of a member of the *Reichstag* (article 44). Its political meaning is to give expression to the independence of the plebiscitary system that was introduced by the constitution from the parliamentary system. It thus points towards an independence from political parties, but not towards a non-political independence.[44] The incompatibility introduced for the members of the audit office (§118 of the *Reichshaushaltsordnung*), by contrast, intends a de-politicization. What is to be achieved in other cases of incompatibility that we have already discussed is an exemption from the sphere of party politics, as in the case of the *Reichsbank* and the *Reichsbahn*. While a number of further incompatibilities that attach to the status of a public servant are accepted more or less as a matter of fact in other democracies, such incompatibilities are little known in Germany. [**157**] But it deserves to be mentioned that a general incompatibility with parliamentary office has recently been proposed, from a well-respected quarter, for judges who are public servants.[45] The very strictest of incompatibilities, of course,

Wittmayer to believe that 'entrenchments' in the constitution are 'de-politicizations'; these can, to the contrary, lead to a new kind of party-political action; on this point see J. Popitz, 'Verfassungsrecht und Steuervereinheitlichungsgesetz', *Deutsche Juristen-Zeitung* (1929), 20. Politics and party politics, after all, are not the same thing.

43 What mainly matters in this context are parliamentary incompatibilities that have been discussed by W. Weber, *Archiv des öffentlichen Rechts*, Neue Folge 19 (1930), 161–254.

44 W. Weber, *ibid.*, p. 205 note 116 is very good: 'It is likely that the idea of the separation of powers and the tendency towards neutralization are equally influential in Germany, with respect to the justification of presidential incompatibilities; but the two points do not face each other in isolation. They condition and reinforce each other.'

45 E. Schiffer, *Entwurf eines Gesetzes zur Neuordnung des deutschen Rechtswesens, nebst Begründung* (Berlin, 1928), p. 1 (§ 16): 'Judges are neither eligible to be elected to the *Reichstag* nor to be elected to the parliament of a *Land*. They must not be members of any political organization, and they may not engage in political activity in a way that is publicly visible'; compare this with the justification on p. 29, which is based on the exemption of the office of a judge from the political sphere. Also compare A. Köttgen, *Das deutsche Berufsbeamtentum und die parlamentarische Demokratie* (Berlin, 1928), pp. 105–6 and *Handbuch des deutschen Staatsrechts*, vol. II, pp. 17–18. More literature in W. Weber, op. cit., pp. 208–9.

are put into effect for the members of a constitutional court even where a sense for clear distinctions is otherwise not very developed.[46]

With regard to the different cases of 'independence', one therefore has to pay attention, in the first place, to the question of whether the independence is merely to provide a negative and defensive protection against political will-formation, or whether it is intended, by contrast, to secure an autonomous, positive share in the determination of, or in the influence on, the political will. The independence of judges is merely the other side of the judicial subjection to statute, and is therefore non-political.[47] It is of great significance, moreover, that both the independence of the professional public servant and the independence of a member of parliament, and finally also the position of the head of state, protected by the difficulty of a recall and by other special privileges, are most intimately connected with the idea of the whole of the political unity. The Weimar Constitution says: 'The public servants are servants of the whole, not of a party' (article 130). 'The members of parliament are representatives of the whole people' (article 21). 'The president of the *Reich* [**158**] is elected by the whole German people' (article 41) and represents the *Reich* to the outside (article 45). The reference to the whole of the political unity always contains a contrast with the pluralistic groupings of economic and social life, and it is supposed to establish a superiority over such groupings. Where that is not the case, the external

[46] § 4 para. 2 of the federal statute on the *Staatsgerichtshof* of 9 April 1921, RGBl.: 'Eligible are Germans who have completed their 30th year. Members of the government of the *Reich*, of the *Reichsrat*, of the economic council of the *Reich*, of a state government, or a state parliament, or of a state council may not act as assessors.' See moreover § 61 of the constitution of Baden, § 67 of the constitution of Mecklenburg-Schwerin, and the Czechoslovakian statute of 9 March 1921, concerning the constitutional court § 1 para. 6: 'Members of the constitutional court as well as their replacements must be persons who are versed in the law and eligible to the senate, and who are not members of one of the aforementioned legislative bodies' (L. Epstein, *Studien-Ausgabe der Verfassungsgesetze der Tschechoslowakischen Republik* (Reichenberg, 1923), p. 21); art. 147 para. 4 of the Austrian federal constitutional statute in the version of 7 December 1929 (Bundesgesetzbl. 1929, p. 1323). Differently, § 70 of the Bavarian constitution and § 2 no. 3 of the statute of 11 June 1920.

[47] It nevertheless goes too far, in my view, for R. Smend, *Verfassung und Verfassungsrecht* (Munich, 1928), pp. 69–70, to say that the activity of the judge, by contrast to the activity of other public authorities, does not stand in the service of the integration of the political community as a whole, but rather, in the first place, in the service of the integration of a special, legal community. That, as well, would lead to a pluralistic dissolution of the state. The many particular branches and areas of material law that would, in turn, correspond to countless special judicial authorities, would then come to represent as many different communities.

adoption of such forms of constitutional law either turns into an empty fiction, or it merely expresses the objectivity of an impartial assessor; as in the case of the members of the preliminary council of the *Reich* for the economy, with respect to whom article 5 of the decree of 4 May 1920 similarly determines that they are 'representatives of the economic interests of the whole people'.[48]

The proper position of the president of the *Reich*, according to the Weimar Constitution, becomes recognizable only once such provisions are put into a comparative perspective. The president of the *Reich* stands in the centre of a whole system of party-political neutrality and independence that is built on a plebiscitary basis. The good order of the state of the current German *Reich* depends on him, to the same extent to which the tendencies of the pluralistic system make a normal functioning of the legislative state difficult or even impossible. We should remember this positive content of the Weimar Constitution, and of its system of constitutional laws, before we install a court of justice as the guardian of the constitution, in order to decide highly political questions and conflicts, and before we burden the judiciary with, and endanger it by, such politicizations. According to the available content of the Weimar Constitution, a guardian of the constitution already exists, namely the president of *Reich*. Both the relatively static and permanent aspects of the presidency (election for seven years, difficulty of recall, independence from changing parliamentary majorities) as well as the character of the president's competences (the powers under article 45 and 46 of the constitution of the *Reich*, the dissolution of the *Reichstag* under article 25 and the initiation of a popular referendum under article 73 of the constitution of the *Reich*, the preparation and promulgation of statutes under article 70, federal execution and protection of the constitution in accordance with article 48) have the purpose of creating an authority that is party-politically neutral, by virtue of its immediate connection with the whole of the state, an authority that is the appointed preserver and guardian of a situation that conforms to the constitution

[48] In contrast to F. Glum, *Der deutsche und der französische Reichswirtschaftsrat* (*Beiträge zum öffentlichen Recht und Völkerrecht*, vol. XII) (Berlin, 1929), pp. 25–6, I do not consider this to be a case of genuine representation, and I do not hold economic interests to be 'representable' in the specific meaning of the word. Compare also the note on p. 98 above.* On the federal economic council as an organ that merely provides expertise and counselling (by contrast to an economic parliament) see W. Haubold, 'Die Stellung des Reichswirtschaftsrates in der Organisation des Reiches', Dissertation at the Berliner Handels-Hochschule (1931).

and of the constitutional functioning of the highest institutions of the *Reich*, and that is equipped, in the case of necessity, with effective competences for the active protection of the constitution. [**159**] The oath that the president of the *Reich* has to swear according to article 42 explicitly states that the president of the *Reich* is going to 'preserve the constitution'. The political oath on the constitution belongs, according to the German tradition of constitutional law, to the 'guarantees of the constitution', and the written text of the regulation of the president's powers in current constitutional law, with sufficient clarity, refers to the president of the *Reich* as the preserver of the constitution. One cannot ignore this authentic word of the constitution, regardless of how one evaluates the significance of a political oath.

The view that the president of the *Reich* is the guardian of the constitution, moreover, alone conforms to the democratic principle on which the constitution is based. The president of the *Reich* is elected by the whole German people, and his political competences as against the legislative institutions (in particular the dissolution of the *Reichstag* and the initiation of a popular referendum) are, in substance, nothing but an 'appeal to the people'. By making the president of the *Reich* the focal point of a system of plebiscitary institutions and competences that are party-politically neutral, the current constitution of the *Reich* aims, precisely on the basis of democratic principles, to form a counterweight against the pluralism of social and economic power-groups and to preserve the unity of the people as a political whole. One may perhaps doubt whether it is going to be possible, in the long run, to withdraw the position of the president of the *Reich* from the business of party politics, and to keep it in a realm of impartial objectivity and neutrality determined by a concern for the state as a whole; one may perhaps fear that the fate of the head of state in a republican Europe is going to follow the fate of the monarch, and that the fate of the plebiscitary president of the *Reich* will follow the fate of the popular referendum triggered by popular initiative,* which, at least so far, has also been rendered toothless. The Weimar Constitution, at any rate, undertakes its effort to provide for a guardian of the constitution very consciously, and with specifically democratic means. It presupposes the whole German people as a unity that is immediately capable of action, and not merely by virtue of the mediation of the organizations of different social groups, a unity that is capable of expressing its will, and that is supposed to come together across the pluralistic divisions, in the decisive moment, and make itself prevail. The constitution, in particular, seeks to give to the authority of the president of the *Reich* the opportunity to connect itself immediately with this unified political will of the German people and to act, on that basis, as the guardian and the preserver of the constitutional unity and wholeness of the German people. The existence and permanence of today's German state depends on whether this effort will succeed.

4

Who ought to be the guardian of the constitution? Kelsen's reply to Schmitt

Translation of Hans Kelsen (1931) 'Wer soll der Hüter der Verfassung sein?' in Hans R. Klecatsky, René Marcic, and Herbert Schambeck (eds.), *Die Wiener rechtstheoretische Schule. Schriften von Hans Kelsen, Adolf Merkl, Alfred Verdross*, 2 vols. (Vienna: Verlag Österreich, 2010), II, 1533–73.

HANS KELSEN, 'WHO OUGHT TO BE THE GUARDIAN OF THE CONSTITUTION'?

I

'Guardian of the constitution': in its original sense, this term refers to an organ whose function it is to protect the constitution against violation. Therefore, one can also speak, and usually does speak, of a guarantee of the constitution. Since the constitution is an order and a complex of norms with determinate content, to violate the constitution is to create a fact contrary to those norms, either through an action or through an omission. The latter, however, can only amount to a violation in the case of the non-performance of a duty, not if an organ fails to claim a right conferred upon it by the constitution. The constitution, like any other norm, can be violated only by those who are to execute it. This can take place either in an immediate or in a mediate way. The violation of a statute that was enacted on the basis of the constitution, for example, is a mediate violation of the constitution, even if the constitution itself explicitly demands that the execution of statutes take place in accordance with statute. If one talks about institutions that are to protect the constitution, one is, of course, talking about protection against immediate violations of the constitution only. The organs whose actions can constitute such violations are organs that are immediate to the constitution; it is they who are subject to 'constitutional control'.

The legal-political demand for guarantees of the constitution, for institutions, in other words, that control the behaviour of certain organs immediate to the constitution, such as parliament or government, with respect to its conformity to the constitution, conforms to a principle specific to the rule-of-law state, namely that the exercise of the state's functions be as lawful as possible. One can – from different political points of view and in relation to different constitutions – disagree deeply about the usefulness of this demand. In particular, there may be situations that make it unfeasible to realize the constitution, [**1534**] either at all or at least in important respects. In such circumstances constitutional guarantees may lose all meaning because they necessarily have to remain ineffective. The legal-technical question as to the best design for guarantees of the constitution is also open to very different answers, depending on the peculiarities of the constitution and on how it distributes political power. Serious discussion is possible about questions such as the following: whether to prefer repressive or preventative guarantees, whether to put emphasis on the elimination of the act that is in violation of the constitution or on the personal responsibility of the organ violating the constitution, etc. Only one thing seems to have been universally agreed upon so far, and seems to have been considered an insight of such a primitive and self-explanatory nature that no one even bothered to explicitly emphasize it within the careful discussion about the problem of the guarantee of the constitution that has taken place in recent years: namely, that if an institution is to be created at all that will control the constitutionality of certain acts of state immediate to the constitution, in particular those of parliament and government, this power of control must not be conferred upon one of the organs whose acts are to be subjected to control. The political function of the constitution is to impose legal limits on the exercise of power. To give a guarantee of the constitution is to create an assurance that these legal limits will not be overstepped. That no institution is less suitable to perform this task than the one upon which the constitution confers the exercise, in whole or in part, of the power to be controlled, and which therefore has the best legal chance as well as the strongest political motive to violate the constitution, would seem to be certain if anything is. No legal-technical principle commands a more universal assent than the demand that no person ought to be judge in his own cause.

When the proponents of the so-called 'monarchical principle' in the constitutional theory of the nineteenth century put forward the thesis that the monarch ought to be regarded as the ordinary 'guardian of the constitution' they were peddling – who would nowadays still doubt it? – a mere ideology that it was all too easy to see through. It was one of the many ideologies that formed the so-called constitutionalist doctrine and by means of which this interpretation of the constitution attempted to veil its basic tendency: to compensate for the loss of power that the head of state had experienced by virtue of the transition from absolute to constitutional monarchy.[1] The real aim, motivated by reasons the political value of which is of no concern to us here, was to prevent an effective guarantee of the constitution, at least against violations on the part of the organ that posed the greatest danger to the constitution, namely on the part of the monarch, or, to be more precise, since the monarch could no longer act on his own, on the part of the government, i.e. on the part of the monarch in company with the ministers countersigning his acts. This, as well, was a part of the method of constitutionalist [**1535**] ideology: to talk only of the monarch despite the fact that the real actor was a collegiate organ of which the monarch formed no more than a non-independent part. Since one could not openly declare the real political goal of avoiding an effective guarantee of the constitution, constitutionalist doctrine concealed it behind the claim that the guarantee of the constitution was the task of the monarch.

The constitution of a constitutional monarchy has a strongly dualistic character. It distributes political power amongst two factors, parliament and government, but in such a way that the latter can claim a certain preponderance over the former, not only *de facto* but also *de jure*. It is impossible to doubt that the government, and in particular the monarch forming its apex, is, in political reality as well as constitutionally, an organ exercising the power of the state, just as the parliament – if not more so. That the power conferred upon the government is in constant competition with the power of the parliament is equally indubitable. It is therefore necessary to conceal the true character of the function of government, in order to make possible the conception that it is government, and only government, which ought to be regarded as the natural 'guardian of the constitution'. Hence the well-known doctrine that the monarch is – exclusively or at least in part – an objective third party located above the competition of the two mutually opposed powers purposely installed by the constitution, and possessor of a neutral power. The view that the power to control exercises of political power,

[1] In my *Allgemeine Staatslehre* (Berlin, 1925) I established this tendency of constitutional doctrine with regard to several of its theses.

so as to ensure their constitutionality, pertains to the monarch, and only to the monarch, can be justified only on the basis of this assumption. This is a fiction of remarkable boldness, especially if one keeps in mind that the following teachings are equally paraded around in the arsenal of the constitutionalist doctrine: that the monarch is the highest and therefore really the sole organ of the exercise of the state's power; that the monarch is the true possessor, in particular, of legislative power; that the command of the law proceeds from him and not from the parliament, since the representatives of the people are only entitled to participate in the determination of the content of the laws. The monarch, then, is the possessor of a large part or even of the whole of the power of the state, but he is nevertheless supposed to be neutral with respect to its execution and therefore the only authority called upon to control its exercise for its constitutionality. The complaint that this is an unbearable contradiction would be wholly out of place here. Such a criticism would apply the criteria of scientific rationality (of the science of the law and state) to something that can be understood only as an ideology. The law of non-contradiction has no place in a system of thought whose deep affinity with theology* can no longer be overlooked by anyone today. It is irrelevant whether the claims of such a constitutional theory are true or not. All that matters is whether they perform their political function. And this they have done to the highest degree. In the political atmosphere of monarchy, the doctrine of the monarch as guardian of the constitution served as an effective counter to the demand for a constitutional court that already began to be voiced from time to time.[2] [**1536**]

II

Given the political situation in which the democratic and parliamentary constitution of the German *Reich* – inevitably – finds itself, given that this constitution has – for its protection, as its friends hope – now retreated into just one of its articles, article 48, a legal space that is obviously too narrow to escape the danger of being blown apart by this manoeuvre; given such a state of affairs it would certainly be

[2] It is, of course, the same ideology, only in the service of the democratic principle, if the parliament is proclaimed to be the guardian of the constitution, because, as Bluntschli says: 'The legislative body, however, carries in the mode of its appointment the most important guarantee that it will not exercise its power in an unconstitutional spirit' (J. C. Bluntschli, *Allgemeines Staatsrecht*, 4th edn (Munich, 1868), vol. I, pp. 561–2).

understandable if the discussion of guarantees of the constitution were to cease for the time being. It is therefore quite surprising that a new series of monographs in public law, the *Beiträge zum öffentlichen Recht der Gegenwart*,[3] starts off with a text, entitled *Der Hüter der Verfassung*, which is devoted to the problem of the guarantee of the constitution. Even more surprising, however, is that this work retrieves the dustiest prop from the store room of the constitutional theatre – namely the view that it is the head of state, and no other organ, that is to be regarded as the natural guardian of the constitution – in order to put this rather dated stage prop to renewed use for the democratic republic in general and the Weimar Constitution in particular. But the most surprising thing is that this work, which mainly attempts to renew a doctrine of one of the oldest and most well-tried ideologists of constitutional monarchy, Benjamin Constant's theory of the monarch's *pouvoir neutre*, and to transfer it without any restriction to the republican head of state, was authored by Carl Schmitt, professor at the *Handelshochschule** in Berlin. It is his own declared ambition to show 'how many traditional forms and concepts are so wholly dependent on past situations, that they are not even old bottles for new wine anymore, but only outdated and mistaken labels'.[4] He tirelessly reminds us 'that the situation of the constitutional monarchy of the nineteenth century, with its distinctions of state and society, politics and economy, no longer obtains'[5] and that the categories of constitutionalist constitutional theory therefore cannot be applied to the constitution of a parliamentary and plebiscitary democracy like contemporary Germany. From this observation, for example, he draws the conclusion that the formal concept of statute that derives from nineteenth-century constitutionalist doctrine, and that was supposed to guarantee the right of budgetary approval of the parliamentary legislator against the monarch, can no longer have its original meaning and that, notwithstanding the explicit prescription of article 85 and 87,* [**1537**] legislative form is therefore not at all 'absolutely and unconditionally' required in order to approve of the budget, to authorize loans, or to take over sureties. Rather, the form of a presidential decree under article 48 paragraph 2 is said to be sufficient (pp. 128–9). Of course, constitutionalist doctrine had made similar attempts to dissolve or to weaken the constitution's requirement of a parliamentary approval

[3] Published by J. C. B. Mohr (Paul Siebeck), Tübingen, 1931.

[4] Carl Schmitt, *Verfassungslehre* (Berlin, 1928), p. 9.

[5] Schmitt, *Der Hüter der Verfassung*, p. 128, see also p. 117.

of the budget. The 'formal concept of statute' did not hinder the latter from making the claim that the monarch had the power to approve a budget and to authorize loans by way of emergency decree, as shown, for example, by the practice of the infamous paragraph 14 in Austria.* But the 'historical-critical consciousness' which saves us from the 'thoughtless formalism' of interpreting the provision of the *Reich's* constitution that 'the budget is to be determined by a statute' and that 'such an appropriation as well as the offering of sureties by the *Reich* may take place only on the basis of a statute of the *Reich*' as making the claim that the budget must be determined by a statute, and that the taking of loans or the offering of sureties may take place only on the basis of a statute, this 'historical-critical consciousness', according to C.S., must not prevent us from adopting an ideology of the constitutionalist doctrine that, more than any other, clearly wears its indebtedness to a particular historical-political situation on its sleeve: the doctrine of the *pouvoir neutre* of the head of state! C.S. even turns this formula of Constant's into the main instrument of his interpretation of the Weimar Constitution. It is only with its help that he can arrive at the conclusion that the 'guardian of the constitution' is not, as one should expect on the basis of article 19, the *Staatsgerichtshof* or some other court, but only the president of the *Reich*; and this according to the constitution now in force, not according to a constitutional reform that is yet to take place.

Benjamin Constant's claim that the monarch is to be regarded as the bearer of a 'neutral' power is mainly based on the assumption that the executive divides into two distinct powers, an active and a passive one, and that only the passive power is in the monarch's hands. Only as a passive power is executive power 'neutral'. The fictitious nature of the attempt to portray the power of a monarch to whom the constitution grants the representation of the country in the international sphere, in particular the power to enter into treaties, the power to veto laws, the supreme command of army and fleet, the appointment of officials and judges, as well as some other powers as a merely 'passive' power, and to oppose it to the rest of the executive understood as an active power, cannot be overlooked.[6] The attempt to transfer Constant's **[1538]**

[6] B. Constant, originally a moderate republican, turns into a monarchist after the revolution, and after the fall of Napoleon comes to support the legitimate dynasties in his book *De l'esprit de la conquête et de l'usurpation*. With this writing, he also becomes one of the founders of the legitimist ideology. He nonetheless participates in the attempt to put Bernadotte on the throne. Since this attempt fails, he joins the side of the Bourbons.

ideology of the *pouvoir neutre* to the head of state of a democratic republic has to become especially dubious if it occurs together with the tendency to enlarge the powers of this organ even beyond the normal sphere of competence of a constitutional monarch. Admittedly, C.S., in order to portray the president as a suitable 'guardian of the constitution', characterizes the *pouvoir neutre* of the head of state as a power that does not 'stand above the other bearers of political rights of decision and influence'. He does not conceive of the president as a 'higher third' or as a 'sovereign ruler of the state' but rather as a co-ordinated office, as a power 'which is put alongside and not above the other constitutional powers' (p. 132). But at the same time, he tries to extend the competence of the president, through a more than extensive interpretation of article 48, to such a degree that the latter necessarily turns into a sovereign ruler of the state and acquires a position of power which is not diminished in any way by C.S.'s refusal to call it a 'dictatorship' and which, in the light of the statements just cited, is at any rate incompatible with the function of a guardian of the constitution.

That C.S. believes himself to be entitled to transfer the ideological thesis of the *pouvoir neutre* of the constitutional monarch, more or less directly, to the elected head of state of a democratic republic is rather puzzling, as he occasionally seems to appreciate the real facts that unmask the ideological character of the constitutionalist doctrine of the monarch as the guardian of the constitution clearly enough. He says, for example, that the danger of a violation of the constitution, in a constitutional monarchy, emanated from the government, i.e. from the sphere of the 'executive', a fact that ought to destroy once and for all the idea of the 'neutral' power of a monarch who is the head of the government and of the executive, as well as the idea that he is particularly suited to function as a guardian of the constitution! But C.S. concedes the danger that emanated from the monarchical government throughout the nineteenth century only in order to make the claim that nowadays, in

Against Napoleon, returning from Elba, he writes in the *Journal des Débats* that Napoleon is an Attila and Genghis Khan. But after a few weeks, he is a member of the council of state and, under the instructions of Napoleon, draws up the amendment to the constitutions of the Empire. After the second restoration, Constant is once again a follower of the *Charte* and of the Bourbons. In 1820, in the chamber of deputies, he claims, for instance: 'Les Bourbons avec la charte sont un immense avantage, parce que c'est un immense avantage qu'une famille antique [serait] sur un trône incontesté.' After the ousting of Charles X, we meet him again as an industrious defender of the legitimacy of Louis Philippe. See A. M. Dolmatowsky, 'Der Parlamentarismus in der Lehre Benjamin Constants', *Zeitschrift für die gesamten Staatswissenschaften*, 63 (1907), 602.

the twentieth century and in a democratic republic, we mainly ought to be concerned about possible violations of the constitution by the legislator, i.e. by parliament, and not by the presidential government (p. 24). As if the fate of the Weimar Constitution, in today's Germany, did not depend on the question of the constitutionality of the functioning, based on article 48, of a government of president and ministers! If there is no possibility of a violation of the constitution by the government it sounds rather harmless, unsurprisingly, to declare [**1539**] that the head of state is the 'guardian of the constitution', and it becomes superfluous to object to the lack of precision of this formula, a formula that does not just – as one might think at first glance – claim the function of guaranteeing the constitution for the person of the president alone, but rather for a collective body* consisting of him and his countersigning ministers. One is well advised not to lose sight of the fact that this argumentation is nothing but a political theory of the 'as if'.*

III

In order to support his thesis that the president is the guardian of the constitution, C.S. has to turn against the institution of a constitutional judicature that has often been demanded and has already been realized in some states. He has to turn against the idea, in other words, that the function of the guarantee of the constitution ought to be assigned to an independent court. Such a court functions as a central constitutional court insofar as it has to decide, in an adversarial trial, on the constitutionality of disputed acts of parliament (in particular of statutes) but also of acts of government (of decrees and executive orders), to invalidate these acts in the event of their unconstitutionality, and perhaps to pass judgment on the responsibility of certain organs, if such claims of responsibility are raised by the accusation. It is certainly possible to disagree about the usefulness of such an institution. No one will claim that it is an absolutely effective guarantee under all conceivable circumstances. However, of all the many points of view from which one can debate the legal-political problem of a central constitutional court, and weigh its pros and its cons, one is utterly irrelevant: namely the question of whether this organ would be a genuine 'court' and whether its function would be real 'adjudication'. This may be a very important legal-theoretical question of classification. But nothing at all could follow from the answer to that question – be it affirmative or negative – that would speak either for or against transferring the said function to a collegial organ whose members, however they are to be appointed, are fully independent – an independence from government and parliament that is called 'judicial' because modern constitutions tend to grant it to courts (though not only to courts). To infer, from some arbitrarily defined concept of adjudication, that the institution that is here referred to as a 'constitutional court' is impossible or illegitimate would be a typical example of the kind of 'conceptual jurisprudence'* that can surely be regarded as obsolete today.

One suspects that C.S. does not intend to offer an argumentation of this kind. But he invites the charge by putting the strongest emphasis, in his fight against constitutional adjudication, and in a publication that is thoroughly legal-political, on the legal-theoretical question whether constitutional adjudication is genuine adjudication, and by going so far as to regard the question of whether a judicial institution [**1540**] could function as the guardian of the constitution as the decisive problem. It seems strange that he feels compelled to show, at the expense of disproportionate effort, that the German civil, criminal, and administrative courts that exercise a material right of review with respect to the statutes that they are to apply are 'in the precise meaning of the term' not 'guardians of the constitution' (p. 12). For reasons that do not seem to be very plausible he does not, however, deny this title to the Supreme Court of the United States, despite the fact that this court, for the most part, is not doing anything different from German courts that make use of their material right of review, namely: not to apply statutes that are judged unconstitutional to the concrete case at hand. The ordinary courts, when exercising their right of review, differ from a central constitutional court with a power to invalidate statutes – an institution that C.S. will, I trust, not refuse to subsume under the concept 'guardian of the constitution', even while he insists that it is not a 'court' – only quantitatively, only in that they annul the unconstitutional statute only for a concrete case and not, like the latter, for all cases. So what is the point of making the claim that the constitutional function of a guardian of the constitution is 'to replace this general and incidental right to disobedience and to resistance' that is actualized by exercises of the material right of review 'and to make it superfluous'? 'A guardian of the constitution in the institutional sense exists only where this replacement has taken place' (p. 21). This idea is truly insufficient to allow us to gain a 'precise meaning' of the concept 'guardian of the constitution'. It suffices only to arrive at the conclusion that the courts, despite the fact that they exercise a right of review, are 'not to be regarded as guardians of the constitution'. But this is a purely terminological claim. C.S. can hardly deny that a court that refuses to apply an unconstitutional statute, and thus invalidates it with respect to the concrete case, in substance functions as a guarantee of the constitution, even if one refuses to confer upon it the awe-inspiring title of a 'guardian of the constitution', i.e. if one abstains from phraseology, as one should, in any case, if one wants to guard against the ideological tendencies that go along with such bathos. What matters is whether it is useful to assign the function of guaranteeing the constitution to courts in this way, and, if not, whether it would be better to take away their right of review. One will look in vain for a clear answer to this question in C.S.'s writings.

But one will find, as I already mentioned, a plethora of arguments that again and again – though in a very unsystematic fashion – attempt to prove that the decision on the constitutionality of statutes as well as the annulment of unconstitutional statutes by an organized body of independent men after an adversarial trial is no adjudication (Schmitt does not pay any attention to the possibility of a judicial control of other acts immediate to the constitution). But these arguments not only fail to prove anything for the decisive legal-political question; they are also unserviceable from a legal-theoretical point of view. ⌊**1541**⌋

IV

They rest on the erroneous assumption that there is an essential difference between the function of adjudication and 'political' functions, and in particular on the assumption that the decision on the constitutionality of a statute and the annulment of an unconstitutional statute are 'political' acts, from which it is inferred that such activities are no longer adjudicative. If one wanted to attribute a reasonably fixed meaning to the ambiguous and abused word 'political', one would have to assume that, in this context, where we are talking about an opposition between politics and adjudication, the word is supposed to express something like an exercise of power in contrast to an execution of law. The function of the legislator is 'political', then, insofar as he subjects people to his will and exercises a power that forces people's pursuit of their own interests into the limits drawn by his norms. The legislator, thus, decides existing conflicts of interest, whereas the judge, not as bearer of this power but only as its instrument, merely applies the order created by the legislator. This conception, however, is mistaken because it presupposes that the process of the exercise of power ends with the legislative decision. This view overlooks or wants to overlook that the exercise of power necessarily continues in the courts, no less than it does in the other, administrative arm of the executive. Under some circumstances the exercise of power even has its real beginning in the courts. If one conceives of 'the political' as the authoritative resolution of conflicts of interest, i.e. if one conceives of it, to use C.S.'s terminology, as 'the decision', then one should admit that every court judgment contains, to a higher or lesser degree, an element of decision, an element of an exercise of power. The political character of adjudication is the stronger, the larger the sphere of free discretion that legislation, which is in its essence general, necessarily has to leave to adjudication. The view that only legislation is political, and that 'real' adjudication is not, is just as wrong as the belief that legislation alone is productive creation and adjudication nothing but reproductive application of the law. At bottom, these are only two variants of one and the same mistake. In authorizing the judge, within certain limits, to weigh conflicting interests against each other, and to decide conflicts in favour of one or the other interest, the legislator confers upon the judge a power to create law and hence a power that endows the judicial function with the same 'political' character that inheres, though to a higher degree, in legislation. There is only a quantitative but no qualitative difference between the political character of legislation and adjudication. If to be non-political really was an essential feature of adjudication, international adjudication would be impossible. To be more precise, the deciding of conflicts between states on the basis of international law, conflicts that differ from domestic conflicts only in that their character as conflicts of power is more readily apparent, would have to be given another name. It is true that the theory of international law is used to distinguish between arbitrable and non-arbitrable conflicts, [**1542**] between conflicts of law and conflicts of interest or power, between legal and political disputes. But what does this mean? After all, every conflict of right is also a conflict of interest or power, every legal dispute therefore a political dispute. Every conflict that is described as a conflict of interest, power, or politics can be decided as a legal dispute, provided it is reduced to the question of whether the claim that the one state makes against the other and that the other refuses to fulfil – and this is the structure of every conflict – has a basis in international law or not. It is always possible to decide this question on the basis of international law and thus juristically. And the question is decided on the basis of international law even if the answer of the court is not affirmative but negative, even if the court dismisses the claim instead of granting it.

Tertium non datur. A conflict, to be sure, may turn out to be 'non-arbitrable' or political, but not because it is in its nature not a legal conflict and therefore incapable of being decided by a 'court', but rather because one of the parties or both, for whatever reason, are unwilling to have it decided by an objective authority. The theory of international law, and its distinction between 'arbitrable' and 'non-arbitrable' disputes, supplies the ideology that is needed to cover up such unwillingness and to justify the tendencies directed against the development of international adjudication that stem from it. In distinguishing – like so many other theorists of public law – between justiciable and non-justiciable matters, and in warning against an extension of adjudication to the latter, while claiming that 'such an extension into matters that are not justiciable can only damage adjudication' (p. 22), C.S. merely transfers this ideology to the sphere of domestic law. According to C.S., all 'political' questions are non-justiciable. All that one can say from the standpoint of a theoretically oriented perspective, however, is that the function of a constitutional court is political in character to a much higher degree than the function of other courts. Those who advocate the institution of a constitutional court have never failed to note or to acknowledge the eminently political meaning of the decisions of a constitutional court. But legal theory does not show that it is therefore not a 'court' or its function not an 'adjudication'; least of all does it show that this function therefore must not be assigned to an organ that enjoys judicial independence. To make this claim would be tantamount to attempting to deduce demands concerning the design of a state's institutional organization from some arbitrarily defined concept, for instance of 'adjudication'.

V

Given that C.S. puts such strong emphasis on an attempt to prove that so-called constitutional adjudication is not adjudication we are entitled to expect from him a clear and precise determination of this concept. However, this expectation is severely disappointed. What C.S. has to contribute to the question of the essential character of adjudication is more than meagre and, for the most part, boils down to a relapse into views that have long been recognized as erroneous. [**1543**]

If one tries to sum up C.S.'s scattered remarks that deal with the subject in question, one arrives at something like the following thesis: adjudication is essentially bound to norms, more particularly to norms that 'allow for a clear subsumption of a matter of fact' that is to be adjudicated and the content of which, moreover, is not 'doubtful' or contested (pp. 19, 36–7). Since the decision on the constitutionality of a statute is never a mere 'subsumption of a concrete matter of fact under a statute', since it is usually an 'authentic determination of the content of a constitutional statute', the decision on the constitutionality of a statute does not qualify as adjudication. Starting with the second of the qualities that are used here to characterize 'adjudication' I can only confess that I am bewildered by the fact that C.S. appears to believe that civil, criminal, or administrative courts, whose claim to be engaged in genuine adjudication he does not seem to question, never do anything more than to apply norms whose content is not doubtful nor disputed, and that the cases to be decided by these courts always hinge on the question of fact and never on the question of right, which latter question can only arise, after all, if the content of the norm that is to be applied is doubtful and therefore contested. As an example of a case in which there is no 'obvious contradiction' between the constitutional statute and the ordinary statute, and that consequently gives rise to 'doubts and disagreements' as to 'whether and to what extent there is a contradiction or not', we get the following: 'If the constitutional statute determines: "the theological faculties are to be preserved" and an ordinary statute determines: "the theological academies are to be abolished"' (p. 44). It is evident that the content of the constitutional statute is doubtful because it is unclear whether 'theological academies' count as 'theological faculties'. Every single word that served to prove that, in countless cases, the jurisdiction of ordinary courts – the adjudicative character of which has never been and could never be questioned – amounts to the determination of the content of a statute whose content is doubtful in just the same way would be superfluous here. When C.S. talks about 'the fundamental difference between a judicial decision and a decision of doubts and disagreements concerning the content of a constitutional provision' (p. 4) one can only reply that most decisions of trials in court are decisions of doubts and disagreements concerning the content of a statutory provision. I doubt that anyone has ever before come up with a statement about adjudication that misrepresents its character as thoroughly as the following: 'All adjudication is bound to norms and the possibility of adjudication ends as soon as the content of the norms themselves starts to get unclear and disputed' (p. 19). Only a complete reversal of this sentence leads us back to the simple and evident truth that adjudication usually begins where the content of norms starts to get doubtful and contested.

Otherwise, there simply would be no disputes concerning 'questions of right' but only disputes about questions of fact. One may doubt that it is useful to assign the power to determine the content of a constitutional statute whose content is in doubt to an independent court, and one may prefer, for whatever reason, to have this function performed by government or by parliament. [**1544**] But it makes no sense to argue that the function of a constitutional court is not adjudicative as soon as the content of the norm it is supposed to apply turns out to be doubtful and its decision therefore turns out to be a determination of the content of the norm. One cannot possibly claim that the doubtfulness of the content of the norm in the case of a constitutional statute is any different from that of a statute that does not have the character of a constitutional statute.

The other criterion – that the norms to be applied by the courts have to allow for the subsumption of a matter of fact under a legal rule – is not mistaken. But it is all the more erroneous to claim that the decision on the constitutionality of a statute must fail to amount to such a subsumption. Unfortunately, C.S. omits to explain in detail what he takes to be the meaning of the word 'matter of fact'. But one is perhaps entitled to assume that he would think of a case in which a criminal court has to decide on a criminal accusation as the simplest and clearest example of the process of the subsumption of a matter of fact under a statute. If a criminal court determines that a defendant's behaviour is identical to the matter of fact that some statute describes as a delict, i.e. as the condition of the application of a certain sanction, it performs the same basic operation that takes place when a constitutional court declares a statute whose validity is disputed by some party to be unconstitutional. At first glance, it seems that the unconstitutionality of a statute may consist not only in the fact that it was not enacted in accordance with the procedure determined by the constitution, but also in the fact that it has a content that, according to the constitution, it must not have. This second form of unconstitutionality can arise wherever the constitution does not just regulate the procedure of legislation but also restricts the content of future statutes in some way, for example by enacting guidelines, principles, etc. But constitutional adjudication with respect to statutes is possible only if material constitutional norms also appear in a special constitutional form, i.e. as qualified statutes protected against amendment through ordinary legislative procedure. Otherwise, a materially constitutional statute would simply be annulled or amended by any ordinary statute contradicting it, and procedurally valid yet unconstitutional ordinary statutes would be impossible. Hence, the scrutiny of the constitutionality of a statute by a constitutional court is always reduced to the question of whether the statute was enacted in accordance with the procedures determined by the constitution. To say that a statute is unconstitutional because it contains a provision that is unconstitutional is the same as saying that it is unconstitutional because it was not enacted as a constitutional amendment. And even where a constitution categorically prohibits a certain legislative provision, with the result that there is no constitutional way to enact a statute with this provision – as for instance in the case of a statute enacted by a constituent state that interferes with the competences of the union and that violates the federal constitution even if it is enacted as a constitutional law of the constituent state – the unconstitutionality of the statute consists in how it was brought about; not in the fact that it was not enacted in the proper way, but rather in the fact that it was enacted at all. The 'matter of fact' that is to be subsumed under the constitutional norm in the case of a decision on the constitutionality of a statute [**1545**] is not a norm – fact and norm are two different concepts – but rather the creation of the norm. And the creation of a norm is a genuine 'matter of fact', namely the matter of fact regulated by the constitutional norm. Because and insofar as it is regulated by the constitution, it can be 'subsumed' under the constitution in just the same way as any other matter of fact can be subsumed under any other norm. One can 'subsume' a matter of fact under a norm only insofar as the norm regulates it, i.e. if it treats it as a legal condition or a legal consequence. Whether a civil court determines the validity of a testament or of a contract, whether it declares a decree to be unconstitutional and refuses to apply it to the case at hand, or whether a constitutional court qualifies a statute as unconstitutional: in all these cases it is the matter of fact of the creation of a norm which is 'subsumed' under the norm that regulates it, and which is thus recognized as conforming to the norm or as failing to conform to it. The constitutional court, moreover, reacts to the recognition of the unconstitutionality of a statute with an act that corresponds, as an *actus contrarius*, to the unconstitutional enactment of the norm: namely with an annulment of the unconstitutional norm, be it individually for the concrete case or – generally – for all cases.

C.S.'s characterization of the review of the constitutionality of a law – 'we confront the content of the one statute with that of the other' and 'determine that there is a collision or contradiction', and 'we compare general rules with one another, but without subsuming them under each other or applying them to each other' (p. 42) – blocks any insight into the true nature of this matter. The reason for this is that he fails to see the difference between the statute as norm and the creation of the statute as a matter of fact. He is simply the victim of an equivocation. And for this reason, his argument, in all its constantly recurring variants – that there can be no 'adjudication exercised by the constitutional statute over the ordinary statute', 'no adjudication of a norm over another norm' (p. 41), that 'a statute cannot be the guardian of another statute' (p. 40) – altogether misses the mark. Contrary to what C.S. imputes to the 'normative theory' analysing this function, it is not the point of constitutional adjudication that 'a norm is supposed to normatively protect itself' or that a stronger statute is to be protected by a weaker or a weaker statute by a stronger. The point is simply that a norm is to be annulled, for the individual case or generally, because its creation stands in contradiction to a higher norm that is higher precisely because it regulates its creation.

VI

In order not to have to recognize constitutional adjudication as 'adjudication', and in order to be able to characterize it as 'legislation', C.S. clings to a picture of the relationship between these two functions that I hitherto felt entitled to assume had long been rejected. It is the idea that the judicial [**1546**] decision is already fully contained in the statute and that all that a judge has to do is to 'derive' it from the statute by way of a logical operation: judges as legal automata! C.S. claims, in all seriousness, that a judge's 'decision is derived, in a measurable and calculable way, from the content of another decision that is already contained in the statute' (p. 38). This doctrine, as well, stems from the ideological arsenal of constitutional monarchy. The judge, who had just gained independence from the monarch, was not supposed to develop an awareness of the power that statutory law concedes to him or, more precisely, must concede to him, given that it is always general in character. The judge was supposed to believe, rather, that he is nothing but an automaton, that he does not create law but only 'finds' already existing law, in the form of a decision already contained in the legislative norm. This fiction was unmasked long ago.[7] It is therefore not all too surprising that C.S. does not bother to hold on to this theory of judicial automata –

[7] See my *Allgemeine Staatslehre*, pp. 231–3, 301.

after it has served him to fundamentally distinguish adjudication as mere application of the law from legislation as creation of the law, after, that is, it has provided him with the main theoretical argument that he uses in his fight against constitutional adjudication: 'a statute is not a court judgment, and a court judgment is not a statute' (p. 37). C.S., rather, declares with great determination: 'Every decision, even that of a trial-deciding court that subsumes a concrete matter of fact, contains a moment of pure decision that cannot be derived from the content of the norm' (pp. 45–6). Precisely this insight implies, of course, that there is no qualitative difference between legislation and judicial decision, that the latter is creation of law as much as the former, that the judgment of a constitutional court does not cease to be an act of adjudication and of application of the law because it is an act of legislation, i.e. of creation of the law. Last but not least, the insight implies that the function of adjudication must have a 'political' character, as much as the function of legislation, since the element of 'decision' is not at all confined to the latter, but also, and necessarily, contained in the function of adjudication. This implication undercuts the whole argument according to which constitutional adjudication is not authentic adjudication because it is political in character. The only remaining question is why an author of such extraordinary intelligence as C.S. entangles himself in such manifest contradictions, only in order to defend the thesis that constitutional adjudication is not adjudication but legislation, and notwithstanding the fact that his own insight implies that it can and must be both at the same time. No other explanation seems possible than this: the claim that constitutional adjudication is not a real form of 'adjudication' is taken to be crucially important, and it is defended even in the face of one's own conflicting theoretical insights, because it is considered to be indispensable for a legal-political demand – namely, if a decision on the constitutionality of a statute and the annulment of an unconstitutional statute through a judicial procedure are not 'adjudication', this function must not be assigned to a body of independent judges but rather to some other organ. [**1547**] C.S.'s distinction of states, on the basis of their most important function, into jurisdictional states and legislative states (p. 75) is only another way to put the same claim. The same goes for the inference he wants to draw from this classification, namely that a state which is, like the contemporary German *Reich*, a legislative state cannot have a constitutional court: 'In a legislative state, by contrast, there can be no constitutional adjudication or adjudication in matters of state that plays the role of the real guardian of the constitution' (p. 76). He also claims: 'In a state that is not a pure jurisdictional state the courts cannot perform such functions' (p. 21). But it would perhaps be more appropriate to say that a state whose constitution provides for a constitutional court therefore ceases to be a 'legislative state', rather than to claim that such a state 'cannot' have a constitutional court because it would then fail to fit into the theoretical framework of the legislative state. Again and again, C.S. tries to infer a desired institutional design from some presupposed legal concept, and thus commits the typical mistake of failing to distinguish between legal theory and legal politics.[8] [**1548**]

[8] Strangely enough, the view that there is an essential difference between statute and judicial decision, a view that nobody contradicts as emphatically as C.S., with his claim that both are essentially the same since they are both a 'decision', forms the basis, for this very same author, of a polemic against the theory of legal hierarchy defended by myself. This theory, since it recognizes the essential similarity of legislation and adjudication, looks for a quantitative difference between the two. Since the theory of legal hierarchy views both legislation as well as adjudication as forms of norm-creation, it proceeds in the same way, with regard to its method, as C.S. himself when he recognizes 'the element of decision' in both. This may explain the intensity of his polemic, which works less with reasoned arguments than with rather affect-laden value judgements, like 'empty abstractions', 'metaphors full of fantasy', 'goose-leg logic'. The hierarchy of norms, as the result of the theory of legal hierarchy, a theory that I constructed on the basis of a radical critique of method and through the most uncompromising struggle against all anthropomorphism in legal theory, is casually dismissed, in a footnote, as 'an uncritical and un-methodological anthropomorphization' and an 'improvised allegory' (pp. 38–40). It would make little sense to debate a theory that does nothing more than offer a structural analysis of the law in the context of a publication that is primarily concerned with legal politics. I will therefore restrict myself to pointing out that the doctrine against which C.S. directs his polemic has almost nothing to do with the theory that I propose. This is a case of crude misunderstanding. C.S. believes that he is refuting this theory of legal hierarchy when he writes: 'If one norm is more difficult to change than some other, then this is in every conceivable respect – logically, juristically, sociologically – something other than a hierarchy; an allocation of competence in a constitutional statute does not stand in the relation of a superior public authority to the acts issued by the competent authority (for the reason that a norm is not an authority), and the ordinary statute, *a fortiori*, is not the subordinate of the statute that is more difficult to change.' If I did claim that the constitution stands above the ordinary statute only because it is harder to amend, then my theory would indeed be as nonsensical as it is portrayed to be by C.S. Alas, this presentation overlooks the tiny little fact that I distinguish, with the utmost emphasis, between the constitution in the material and the constitution in the formal sense, and that I ground the superiority of the level of the constitution over the level of ordinary statute not in the merely accidental and unessential constitutional form, but rather in the constitution's content. The constitution can be regarded as a norm superior to ordinary legislation for the reason that it determines the procedure of legislation and, to a certain extent, also the content of the statutes that are created in accordance with the constitution; just as legislation stands above the so-called execution (adjudication and administration) insofar as it regulates the enactment and – to a very large extent – also the content of executive acts. The question of how easy or

A legal-scientific inquiry concerned with the possibility of constitutional adjudication, finally, ought not to leave aside the fact that there already is one state – namely Austria – in which a fully developed, centralized form of constitutional adjudication has been functioning for more than a decade. To analyse the factual efficiency of the latter would likely be more fruitful than to ask for its compatibility with the concept of the legislative state. C.S. is content to put the 'Austrian solution' in scare quotes and to remark that one 'hardly inquired into the material significance of such an extension of adjudication, in the fatigue of the first decade after the breakdown, and was willing to make do with abstract normativisms and formalisms' (p. 6). In case the talk of 'normativisms and formalisms' is supposed to refer to the Vienna School* – well, the latter has not been prevented by its 'abstraction' from accomplishing a good deal of concrete creative legal work; among other things, it helped establish the Austrian constitutional court; whereas C.S. refuses to climb down from the height of his own abstractions to discuss the 'material significance' of that institution.

The theoretical impossibility of this method, its inner contradiction, manifests itself towards the end of the essay. Here, C.S. starts to deduce the desired legal-political result from his legal-theoretical premisses. He says: 'before we install a court of justice as the guardian of the constitution, in order to decide highly political questions and conflicts, and before we burden and endanger the judiciary by such politicizations' (p. 158) we ought to remind ourselves of the positive content of the Weimar Constitution which, according to C.S., makes the president the guardian of the constitution. This means nothing more and nothing less than: we are not supposed to install a court as guardian of the constitution, to deal with highly political questions and conflicts, because such an activity of a court would politicize and thus strain and endanger the judiciary. But how can this be? How could the judiciary be endangered and put under strains by constitutional adjudication, if constitutional adjudication, as C.S. goes to great length to argue, has nothing to do with jurisdiction?

difficult it is to amend a norm does not play any role whatsoever for the relationship between the level of legislation and the level of execution. Even if C.S. had only read, of all my writings, my report on 'Wesen und Entwicklung der Staatsgerichtsbarkeit' in *Veröffentlichungen der Vereinigung der Deutschen Staatsrechtslehrer*, issue 5 (Berlin and Leipzig, 1928), and even if he had read only p. 36 [ch. 1 above, 1490] of this report, he should know that.

This is not meant to deny that the question raised by C.S. concerning the 'limits' of adjudication in general, and of constitutional adjudication in particular, is quite legitimate. It is only that, in the present context, the question must not be understood as a conceptual question asking for the essential characteristics of adjudication, but rather as a pragmatic question that concerns the most useful way of organizing the function of adjudication. It is important to distinguish clearly between these two questions. If one wishes to restrict the power of the courts and thus to rein in the political character of their function – a tendency that is especially characteristic of constitutional monarchies, but that is also observable in a democratic republic – one has to make sure that the sphere of free discretion that the statutes leave to those who apply them is narrowed down as far as possible. The norms to be applied by a constitutional court, especially those which determine the content of future statutes, like the provisions concerning the basic rights, must not be formulated too broadly and must not operate with vague slogans [**1549**] like 'freedom', 'equality', 'justice', and so forth. Otherwise there is a danger of a politically highly inappropriate shift of power, not intended by the constitution, from the parliament to some other institution external to it 'that may turn into the exponent of political forces completely different from those that express themselves in parliament'.[9] But this problem is not specific to [**1550**] constitutional adjudication. It is just as relevant in the context of the relation of statute to statute-applying civil, criminal, and administrative courts. It is the old platonic dilemma: *politeia* or *nomoi*, kingly judges or royal legislator. From a theoretical point of view, the difference between a constitutional court empowered to invalidate statutes and a normal civil, criminal, or administrative court is that the latter, though it is applying as well as creating law, just like the former, only creates individual norms, whereas a constitutional court, by applying the constitution to a fact of norm-creation, arrives at an annulment of unconstitutional statutes. A constitutional court does not enact statutes, but it destroys them by setting the *actus contrarius*

[9] Kelsen, 'Wesen und Entwicklung der Staatsgerichtsbarkeit', p. 70 [ch. 1 above, 1517]. These sentences stand in the context of a discussion that I will reproduce here in its entirety, in order to show to those who have read only C.S.'s text how one of the 'zealots of a blind normativism' (p. 30) argues, and to show how his 'normativist and formalist logic' (p. 41) as well as what the 'devastations' look like 'which this kind of logic has wrought in the theory of the concept of statute' (p. 38): 'One occasionally encounters the claim . . . [Editorial comment: For the full text of this quotation see ch. 1 above 1516–17] . . . it must make sure to determine them as precisely as possible'.

that corresponds to the creation of law. It functions, as I have put the point, as a 'negative legislator'.[10] But there is no hard-and-fast distinction between the function of a constitutional court [**1551**] and that of an ordinary court, for the reason that the latter's right to review statutes and decrees constitutes a very important intermediary form of constitutional control. An ordinary court that refuses to apply a statute or a decree to the concrete case, for reasons of unconstitutionality, also destroys a general norm and thus functions as a 'negative legislator' (in the material sense of the word 'statute'). The only difference is that the annulment of the norm is restricted to one case, and thus does not, as in the case of a decision by the constitutional court, take place in total, i.e. for all possible cases.

VII

It is a legal-political question whether one ought to design the procedure by which an organ endowed with judicial independence reviews the constitutionality of a statute to be essentially the same as in a criminal, civil, or administrative trial, in particular whether one ought to design it as an adversarial trial, i.e. in such a way that the arguments for and against the constitutionality of the statute are publicly debated. This procedure is not restricted to matters of adjudication; administrative proceedings can likewise be organized in an adversarial way. The reason why we associate this device [**1552**] in particular with 'the form of adjudication' is simply that, historically, it first appeared in the procedures of 'courts', where it still occurs most frequently today. In ancient Athens even legislative procedure was, for some time, organized in this form: if an old statute was to be replaced with a new one it had to be put to trial in front of the *nomothetes*. And Athens was certainly anything but a 'jurisdictional state' in C.S.'s sense. The dialectical procedure of the modern parliament is, at bottom, something quite similar to the 'judicial form' of a trial in court. Its purpose is to bring to light everything that speaks for and against some project. Experience shows that this aim is best achieved by assigning attack and defence to two distinct parties. It is

[10] See Kelsen, 'Wesen und Entwicklung der Staatsgerichtsbarkeit', p. 54 [ch. 1 above, 1504–5]. In anticipation of the main argument against constitutional adjudication, the separation of adjudication and legislation, I wrote: 'Things do not look so very different . . . [Editorial comment: For the full text of this quotation see ch. 1 above 1504–5] . . . are to be controlled by the constitutional court'.

easily possible to do so if there are two distinct interest groups with different goals that have a stake in the matter at hand. When it comes to the question of the constitutionality of a statute, that is undoubtedly the case. We only have to think of differences of interest based on nationality, religion, the economy, or of differences between groups that favour centralization or decentralization, and so on. The task of the order of procedure of a constitutional court is to express such interests in a way that is correct from the point of view of procedural technique. The adversarial structure that gives the procedure its so-called 'judicial form' is quite appropriate even in cases that deal with the application of a constitutional norm that concedes a wide sphere of free discretion. In that case, the dispute is not – or to be more precise, not exclusively – one about the constitutionality but also one about the usefulness of the challenged act. It is, in other words, also a dispute about how best to fill the framework outlined by the constitution through the creation of individual or general legal norms. Assume we deal with the question of whether some ordinary statute violates the constitution, and assume that the relevant constitutional text does not have a fixed meaning, with the result that the judgment of the constitutional court will inevitably bring about a development of the constitution in a certain direction: it is in this situation, in particular, that the existing conflicts of interest are of the greatest importance. And particularly in such cases, it makes rather a lot of sense to let the will-formation of the state that manifests itself in the form of the judgment of the constitutional court take place according to a procedure that expresses the existing differences of interest. The 'dispute', in all civil cases, to the extent that the civil statute leaves the judge with a degree of discretion, is always also one about the usefulness of the decision. Judicial form is helpful here precisely with respect to this creative and 'political' activity of the court, and especially insofar as the judgment aims to perform a 'balancing of interests'. We need not even speak here of administrative procedure, whose judicial form is not at all at odds with the comparatively wide freedom of discretion that is usually granted to administrative organs. Even if one wanted to speak, in consideration of the free discretion granted to those who apply the law, of more or less 'justiciable' norms, in a legal-political as opposed to a legal-theoretical sense, it would still be fundamentally wrong to claim (p. 39) that 'the basis for the possibility of legitimate adjudication falls away, to the same extent, together with the justiciable norm'. [**1553**]

One will inevitably fail to appreciate the real purpose of what is called 'judicial form', as well as its suitability for the procedure of an organ that functions as a 'guardian of the constitution', if one does not recognize the basic sociological fact behind the institution of an adversarial procedure: the fact that opposed interests with opposing goals participate in the decisions of a court, and in particular in the decisions of a 'guardian of the constitution', in much the same way they generally participate in the creation of law that concerns them. Every 'decision' decides a conflict of interest, either in favour of one or another of the parties, or by mediating between them. An adversarial trial at least makes sure, even if it does nothing else, that the actual constellation of interests is clearly exposed. But one cannot see all this as long as the actual conflict of interest is veiled by the fiction of a general interest or of a unity of interest, a unity that is supposed to be essentially different from and essentially more than what, at best, it can be, namely a compromise of interests. This is the typical fiction employed by those who want to operate with the idea of the 'unity' of the 'will' of the state, or with the idea of a 'totality' of the collective, in a more than merely formal sense, so as to justify a particular substantive design of the order of the state. The discussions through which C.S. develops the category of the 'total state', and opposes it to the system of 'pluralism', end up presenting a point of view of this sort.

VIII

Both concepts are introduced to characterize the concrete constitutional situation of today's German *Reich*. (The concepts of 'polycraty' and 'federalism', which are also employed by C.S., play a relatively insignificant role compared to 'pluralism'.) By 'pluralism' C.S. understands 'a multitude of firmly organized social complexes of power, that penetrate the state, i.e. the different spheres of the life of the state, as well as the territorial boundaries of the *Länder* and of the autonomous territorial corporations, and that, as such, take control of the will-formation of the state without ceasing to be merely social (non-public) entities' (p. 71). In talking about 'social complexes of power', C.S. refers, first and foremost, to the political parties; and the factual situation that C.S. characterizes with the word 'pluralism' consists above all in the condition that one hitherto referred to with the expression 'party state'. As the determination of the concept implies, the existence in social reality of an antagonism of state and society is a decisive presupposition of a political structure that is to be designated as 'pluralistic'. Pluralism, after all, is said to consist above all in the fact that complexes of power that are 'merely social' and that are explicitly characterized as 'non-public', take control of the will-formation of the state. In order for it to be possible at all to talk of 'pluralism', there must, therefore, be a sphere of social life that is free from the interference of the state, [**1554**] and from out of which there proceed, from different sides, attempts to influence the will-formation of the state. By contrast, the 'turn to the total state' consists in the fact, according to C.S., that the antagonism between state and society disappears: 'The society that has turned into the state becomes an economic state, a cultural state, a caring state, a welfare state, a providing state; while the state that has turned into the self-organization of society and that is, consequently, no longer materially separable from it, comes to encompass everything social, i.e. everything that concerns the collective life of human beings. Within it, there is no longer any sphere towards which the state could observe unconditional neutrality in the sense of non-intervention' (p. 79). C.S. views the decisive characteristic of the modern 'legislative state', a type of state exemplified, in his view, by today's German *Reich*, in this 'enormous turn' to the 'total state', in this overcoming of the liberal, non-interventionist state that was restricted to only a few social functions, that gave the greatest amount of leeway to a society that was free of its interference, and that was therefore the real presupposition of the conceptual antagonism of state and society. It is without any further significance that no new insight whatsoever into sociological facts appears in the concept of the 'total state', as it has been determined thus far, but only a new word for what one would, up to now, have referred to as the expansive purpose of the state in contrast to the limited purpose of the state. It is equally without significance that the total state of the twentieth century is by no means a new phenomenon, and does not stand above older states in any dialectical progression, as C.S. seems to believe. The state of antiquity, and similarly the 'absolutist state' – that is, the police state of the eighteenth century – already was a total state, and the liberal state of the nineteenth century was thus a reaction against a total state. To give new names to facts that have long been well known is nowadays a very popular and widely practised method of political literature. What is more remarkable, though, is the attempt to describe the concrete constitutional situation of the German *Reich* with two characteristics that exclude one another. How can this situation, at one and the same time, represent, so to speak, the apogee of 'pluralism' and a 'turn to the total state', if pluralism is only possible insofar as the will-formation of the state is influenced by a social, non-public sphere, in whose elimination and integration into the state the 'turn to the total state' is supposed to consist? This contradiction causes considerable difficulties, even to C.S. Of the political parties, which continue to exist in the total state, C.S. says: 'The parties, in which the different social interests and tendencies organize themselves, are the society itself that has become a party state . . .' (p. 79). Since there is no longer a society in the total state, C.S. has to let society, in the parties, become the state. In other words, he must regard the parties as belonging to the state, and deny them the status of social entities. As a result, however, his category of pluralism is no longer applicable. And it is little more than a makeshift attempt to conceal this contradiction for C.S. finally to explain: 'The fact that there is a plurality of such organizational complexes which compete with one another and keep each other within certain bounds, i.e. the fact that there is a pluralist party state, [**1555**] prevents the trend towards the total state from making itself felt with the same momentum that it has already attained in the so-called one-party states, in Soviet Russia and in Italy' (p. 84). According to the initial determination of the concept, the pluralistic state differs from the total state specifically in the fact that the latter absorbs the social sphere, but the former does not. Hence, the following renewed attempt on C.S.'s part to extricate himself from the contradiction is likewise doomed to fail: 'However, the turn towards the total is not reversed by the development of pluralism. Rather, it is only divided up, so to speak, in that every organized social power-complex, from the choir and the sports club to the association for armed self-defence, aims to realize totality, as far as possible, within itself and for itself' (p. 84). This divided-up totality is simply a *contradictio in adjecto*.

The deeper cause of this contradiction is that C.S. connects with each other two pairs of opposites, in his use of the terms 'pluralism' and 'total state', that have nothing to do with one another: the antagonism of state and society as well as that of an autocratic-centralistic and a democratic-de-centralistic mode of will-formation. In C.S.'s use of the concepts of 'pluralism' and 'total state', it is sometimes the one and sometimes the other of these two opposites that takes centre stage. The total state, as a state that fully absorbs society and that takes control of all social functions, is equally possible as a democracy in which the process of public will-formation takes place through the competition of political parties, and as an autocracy in which the formation of political parties is altogether excluded. The 'total state', for this reason, may, at the same time, be a 'pluralistic party state', since an expansion of the purposes of the state, however far it may go, is compatible with a very far-reaching division of the people into different political parties. Far-reaching decentralization would also be compatible with the 'total state', so understood. But it would not be compatible with a total state understood as a community with centralized, 'unified', and therefore 'powerful' will-formation. The 'momentum' of the latter is indeed broken down by a democratic party state. But why does C.S. burden his determination of the concept of 'pluralism' with the antagonism of state and society, given that – as C.S.'s pluralistic total state, his divided-up totality, shows – it is altogether irrelevant for the matter of fact that is to be captured by the concept of pluralism and merely gives rise to contradictions? And above all, why is the antagonism between state and society altogether excluded from the concept of the 'total state', though this evidently stands in contradiction with the social reality that is to be captured by this concept? One does not have to be a follower of the materialist conception of history in order to recognize that a state whose legal order guarantees private property in the means of production treats economic production, as well as the distribution of products, in principle as a non-public function. It delegates the performance of this task, arguably the most important, to a sphere that can be distinguished from the state only as a sphere of 'society', and thus cannot be a 'total state' in the sense of C.S.'s determination of the concept, i.e. it cannot be a state that takes control of everything 'social'. In this sense, in the sense of a coercive order that totally absorbs society, only the socialist state can be a 'total state'. If one claims that the capitalist state of today is already [**1556**] a 'total state', without being able to justify this claim by pointing out that its order has already taken the decisive turn towards state-socialism – and this is indeed impossible, and C.S. does not even attempt to do it – then one will hardly be able to defend oneself against the objection that talk of the 'turn towards the total state' is nothing more than a bourgeois ideology that is meant to veil the antagonism in which the proletariat, or at least a large part of the same, finds itself towards the contemporary legislative state, just like the bourgeoisie used to be in an antagonistic position, at the beginning of the nineteenth century, towards the 'total' police state of absolute monarchy. It is an ideology that proclaims a unity of state and society that does not in fact exist, because the class struggle takes place not as a struggle between different organs of state, but rather as a struggle of one part of society that is not integrated into the state, as it does not identify with the state, against another part of society that 'is' the state, because and insofar as the order of the state guarantees the interests of that part of society. The antagonism of state and society is supposed to have lost its significance with the 'turn to the total state'. But, from the point of view of the proletariat and of a proletarian social theory, the antagonism has much the same meaning as it previously had from the point of view of the bourgeoisie and of a bourgeois theory of state and society. It is therefore as relevant today as it has ever been.[11] **[1557]**

The concepts of pluralism and of the total state, hence, do not hold up against a sociological critique. Their significance reveals itself fully only once one pays attention to the strong emphasis on questions of value with which they appear. Pluralism – that is, the condition in which 'society' pushes back the state, the condition where tendencies hostile to the state threaten the state in its unity and therefore in its existence – signifies 'the power of several social organizations over the will-formation of the state' (p. 71), 'the dissolution of the concept of the state' (p. 69), 'the pluralistic division of the state' (p. 63), 'a pluralistic splintering into pieces of the unity of the state and the constitution'

[11] If the nature of 'pluralism' – as C.S. emphasizes on p. 71 – is characterized by 'an opposition against a closed and homogeneous unity of the state', and if the dualism of state and society recedes into the background in a pluralist society – as it should according to the modified determination of the concept of pluralism on p. 79, since the parties that fight each other constitute a pluralistic element even while they have become public entities – then a federal organization of the state can only be regarded as a pluralistic splintering of the unity of the state. And the same will have to hold for a division of the state through a constitution based on membership in corporatist groups. C.S. in fact admits of the demand for an economic constitution 'of a state based on estates, trade unions, or workers councils': 'Its fulfilment would not strengthen the unity of the will of the state but only endanger it. The economic and social antagonisms would not be solved and taken away; they would, rather, come to the fore more openly and ruthlessly, because the fighting groups would no longer be forced to make the detour through general elections of the people and a representative assembly of the people' (pp. 99–100). This presumably means that the corporatist system is rejected as pluralistic. But the attitude towards the federalism of the federal state is altogether different. Here, C.S. merely concedes the possibility that pluralism and federalism – which, according to the modified determination of the concept of pluralism, is in truth only a special case of pluralism and moreover one that can turn out to be especially dangerous – will form an alliance. But C.S. lets this possibility recede completely into the background, and claims that federalism can 'nevertheless still be a particularly strong counterweight against the pervasive pluralistic complexes of power and the methods of their party politics' (pp. 95–6). In another context, C.S. points out that 'the constitution preserves the character of the *Länder* as states' and that 'federalism can be a reservoir of political forces supportive of the state' (p. 108). It is therefore not surprising that federalism is justified precisely as an 'antidote against the methods of a party-political pluralism' (p. 96). Here, 'pluralism' once again means something completely different; while this justification of federalism of course ignores that the multiplication of parliamentary systems that goes along with a federalist constitution also brings about a multiplication of pluralisms, which implies that everything but federalism is more suitable to function as a counterweight to pluralism!

(p. 63). The 'turn to the total state' is a development in the opposite direction; it is the victory of the state over a society hostile to it, it is the condition of a secured unity of the state. C.S. is looking for 'remedies' (pp. 96–131) against the pluralistic powers hostile to the state, which threaten its unity, and he raises the question of whether it is 'justified to carry this development towards pluralism even further, for instance by appeal to the authentically German principle of association' (p. 108)? And C.S. denies this question in the most decisive way. His value judgement openly appears when he says that 'the pluralistic system, with its constant agreements between parties and parliamentary groups, transforms the state into a series of compromises and treaties, through which the parties that participate in the business of a coalition divide up offices, incomes, and advantages among themselves, according to the law of the quota, and perhaps even experience the parity which they observe therein as a kind of justice' (p. 110). Finally, pluralism is even declared to be 'unconstitutional' (p. 131). And in this way, the category of pluralism can serve to push aside that solution to the problem of guaranteeing the constitution which consists in the establishment of a constitutional court, while the 'total state' serves to provide a foundation for another solution, which is shown to be the right one through the claim that it guarantees the unity of the state, a unity allegedly threatened or even destroyed by the specifically pluralist antagonism of state and society.

IX

According to Carl Schmitt, the pluralistic character of constitutional adjudication consists in the fact that it takes place in the form of a trial in which one can lay claim to 'subjective rights' grounded in the constitution or to a certain exercise of the public power of the state (p. 67). It is wholly unjustified, however, to interpret this as a 'dissolution of the concept of the state'. If the constitution of a federal state legitimizes the union as well as the constituent states to challenge state or federal statutes that violate the distribution of competences, if it authorizes the courts and other organs of public administration to declare the norms that they are expected to apply to be unconstitutional, and even if it concedes an *actio popularis*, in order to radically annihilate unconstitutional acts, it does not thereby create 'subjective rights' in the sense in which they indeed exhibit a tendency that is hostile to the state because it is directed against the objectivity of law; namely in the sense of natural rights possessed by birth, rights that are independent of the objective

[**1558**] order of the state and the law, that are to be respected by that order because they are not conferred by it and are consequently not abrogable by it. The 'subjective' right, however, that consists in nothing but the legitimate standing to go to trial, in the opportunity to initiate a legal procedure with a central public institution, a procedure that aims for the annulment of an unconstitutional act, the removal of a legally defective state of affairs, is nothing other than a technical means for the preservation of the order of the state, and thus precisely the opposite of a right that could be described as a 'pluralistic dissolution of the state' (p. 68). One might just as well speak of a 'pluralistic splintering' of the unity of the state into the attorney's office and the court, for the reason that the state divides itself, in a criminal trial, into the prosecutor and the judge.

The 'turn to the total state' is opposed to constitutional adjudication, first of all, insofar as the call for constitutional adjudication is interpreted as an attempt to impede this 'turn', and with it the process of the solidification and consolidation of the state, its victory over society. 'It is not surprising that the defence against such an expansion of the state' – this refers to the 'turn to the economic state' which is said to constitute the decisive phase in the turn towards the total state – 'appears at first as a defence against that activity of the state's which determines, in such a moment, the form of the state, and that it consequently appears as a defence against the legislative state. For this reason, one first clamours for protections against the legislator. This is likely to be what explains the initial and rather unclear attempts to provide a remedy, . . . that clung to adjudication in order to gain a counterweight against the legislator who grows ever more powerful and encompassing. They had to end in empty superficialities, since they did not originate from a concrete insight into the overall situation of constitutional law, but only from a reflexive reaction. Their fundamental error was that they could oppose to the power of the modern legislator nothing but a judiciary that was either materially bound to determinate norms issued by that very same legislator or else unable to confront the legislator with anything but indeterminate and controversial principles that could not possibly help to ground an authority superior to that of the legislator' (p. 82). But who, in the whole world, ever expected that a constitutional court would oppose itself to an extension of the competence of the legislator? Must an expansion of the legislative power always take place in the form of violations of the constitution? It is almost impossible to think of a more profound misinterpretation of constitutional adjudication. And if, in preparation of his demand to make the government, and not a court, the guardian of the constitution, C.S. continues with 'In a situation thus changed, and in the face of such an expansion of the tasks and the problems of the state, a government may perhaps be able to provide a remedy, but certainly not the judiciary', then one cannot close one's eyes, in particular in this context, to the fact that the legislative expansion also takes place, to a large extent, through the decree-enacting activity of the government. This trend is especially pronounced where the right of the government to issue decrees takes the place of the parliament's right to legislate, on the basis of an interpretation of article 48 paragraph 2 enthusiastically supported by C.S. in particular. A constitutional court is indeed a wholly useless instrument to prevent the turn towards the total state. [**1559**] But how can one discredit an institution by attributing to it a purpose that is completely alien to its nature, to then go on to observe that it is not capable of achieving that purpose?

A further significant effect of the doctrine of the 'total state' consists in the fact that it greatly reduces the value of a major argument that speaks for the conferral of control to an independent court, and against attributing this function to the government. Since the constitution distributes power, for the most part, among two factors – parliament and government (here we have to understand by 'government' in particular the organ which is composed of the head of state and of the ministers that countersign his acts) – there must, for this reason alone, be a continuing antagonism between parliament and government. And the danger of a violation of the constitution must, first and foremost, result from attempts, on the part of one of these two factors, to step across the boundaries that the constitution has imposed on it. Since parliament and government tend to be parties to disputes concerning the most important cases of violations of the constitution, it is advisable to appoint a third institution in order to resolve the dispute, one that stands outside of this antagonism and that does not itself participate in any way in the exercise of the power which the constitution divides, for the most part, among parliament and government. It is unavoidable that this institution, as a result, will itself receive a certain power. But it makes an enormous difference whether one confers on an organ no other power than that which is contained in the function of constitutional control, or whether one strengthens the power of one of the two main bearers of power even further, by transferring the power of constitutional control to it. That remains the main advantage of the constitutional court: that it does not stand in a necessary antagonism to parliament or to government, since it does not participate in the exercise of power from the beginning. According to the doctrine of the 'total state', however, there is no antagonism between parliament and government. And it follows from this, though this does not have to be pointed out expressly, and is not pointed out expressly by C.S., that, where the government – that is, the head of state in connection with the ministers – assumes the role of a guardian of the constitution, in order to protect the constitution against unconstitutional statutes, constitutional control, despite appearances, is not in the hands of an institution that can be regarded as a party to constitutional disputes.

This dissolution of the antagonism of government and parliament, an antagonism that is decisive for the solution of the problem of constitutional guarantees, results from the fact that C.S. interprets it as a mere consequence or variant of the dualism of state and society that allegedly disappears with the turn towards the 'total state'. 'The distinction is the foundation and presupposition of all important institutions and norms of public law that developed in Germany in the course of the nineteenth century and that still make up a large part of our public law. The fact that one tended, in general, to construct the state of the German constitutional monarchy, with its oppositions of prince and people, crown and chamber, government and representative assembly of the people, in a "dualistic" fashion, is only an [**1560**] expression of the more general and more fundamental dualism of state and society. The representative assembly of the people, the parliament, the legislative body, was thought of as the stage on which society appeared and faced the state' (p. 74). 'This state, which was neutral in principle towards society and economy, in the liberal, non-interventionist sense, remained the presupposition of the constitution even where exceptions were made in the field of social and cultural politics. But it changed from the ground up, to the same extent that the dualistic construction of state and society, government and people, lost its tension and the legislative state came to completion. Now, the state becomes the "self-organization of society". The distinction between state and society, between government and the people, which had hitherto always been presupposed, disappears as a result, as already noted. Consequently, all the concepts and institutions built on this presupposition (statute, budget, local self-government) turn into new problems' (p. 78). In the total state that takes control of everything social there can, in particular, be no antagonism between government and parliament, since this antagonism must disappear together with that of state and society. However, C.S.

himself does not explicitly draw this conclusion. All he claims, *expressis verbis*, is that the distinction of state and society and thus that of 'government and people' becomes irrelevant with the turn towards the total state. In his characterization of the total state, C.S. does not speak about the antagonism between government and parliament, which he portrays as a mere expression of the dualism of state and society in his analysis of the constitutional monarchy of the nineteenth century. He leaves it to the reader to continue the thought in this direction. But he nevertheless says, clearly enough: 'All the hitherto prevailing contrasts, since they rested on the presupposition of a neutral state and had appeared as a result of the distinction between state and society, and were nothing but applications and re-descriptions of this distinction, cease to be relevant. Antithetical separations such as state and society, state and culture, . . . state and law, politics and law, . . . lose their meaning and become empty' (p. 79). The antagonism of government and parliament, according to his earlier remarks, clearly must belong to these 'antithetical separations'.

No special acumen is needed to show that the antagonism of government and parliament, just like the dualism of state and society to which it is not at all identical, has not disappeared in the contemporary state. It has not lost its meaning either, but only changed it. It no longer expresses the conflict between the parts of the people represented by the majority of members of parliament and the interest groups supported by the monarch and his government. Rather, it now expresses the conflict that exists between the parliamentary minority and the majority on whose trust the government depends. This, what is more, is by no means the only sense in which an antagonism between parliament and government is possible today. It can take a different meaning if there is a minority government, or if the affairs of government are directed by a head of state elected only by a minority of the people, and especially if a government, since it is not backed up by a parliamentary majority, governs without parliament, in violation of the constitution. [**1561**] At a time when the government of the *Reich* feels it is forced to threaten its resignation in case parliament, or even only a committee of parliament, should convene, in accordance with the wish of the majority of parliament, it is difficult to accept the last consequences of the doctrine of the 'total state' and to regard the antagonism of 'government and parliament' as an 'antithetical separation' that has lost its meaning and become empty with the turn towards the legislative state.

X

The ways, moreover, that lead from the 'total state' to the head of state as the guardian of the constitution are not easy to make out even for a very diligent reader. It seems that the real unity of the 'total state' functions as some kind of sociological foundation for another 'unity', namely for the unity that is said to be presupposed by the preamble of the Weimar Constitution. If this unity is to be more than the juridical unity of the citizen body, a unity that is founded by any constitution, it is only another expression of the same ideology. 'The current constitution of the *Reich*, however, holds fast to the democratic idea of the homogeneous, indivisible unity of the German people as a whole, which has given this constitution to itself, by virtue of its constituent power, through a positive political decision, and thus through a unilateral act. With this, all interpretations or applications of the Weimar Constitution that aim to turn it into a contract, a compromise, or something similar, are solemnly rejected as violations of the spirit of the constitution' (p. 62). The inner connection between the construction of the 'total state' and the 'homogeneous, indivisible unity of the German people as a whole' – a connection that C.S. himself never makes explicit – is apparent from the claim that 'pluralism' is as opposed to the latter unity as it is to the unity of the 'total state'. Pluralism is explicitly characterized as the 'opposition against a closed and homogeneous unity of the state' (p. 71). The pluralistic element that we find in the 'reality of our contemporary constitutional situation' endangers the 'homogeneous, indivisible unity' presupposed by the Weimar Constitution (p. 62), just as the contrast between state and society expressed by pluralism restrains the 'momentum' of the total state and carves up its totality. C.S.'s interpretation of the constitution is mainly based on this unity. It is not just an ethical-political postulate of the kind that is often proclaimed by constitutional preambles. Rather, it is a social reality, at least if the pluralistic tension between the state and the society that endangers it is actually overcome, if the 'total state' that eliminates this contrast has become a reality. At times, social reality itself is characterized by C.S. as having lapsed into pluralistic fragmentation. But this does not stop him from accusing 'the interests behind this pluralism' (as well the theoreticians who support them?) of 'endorsing a cheap formalism that simply denies the substantive problems' (p. 36). [**1562**]

The 'homogeneous, indivisible unity of the German people' invoked by the preamble of the constitution is the most important piece of support for the claim that the president ought to be regarded as the guardian of the constitution. From the idea that the 'Weimar Constitution is a political decision of the unified German people as the bearer of the constituent power' – in truth, the constitution is a decision of a parliament whose identity with the German people can be claimed only on the basis of the fiction of representation – C.S. wants to infer that 'the question of the guardian of the constitution can be answered in a way other than through fictitious judicial forms' (p. 70). To be specific, this is done by claiming that the president is the guardian of the constitution because he is elected by the people as a whole (p. 149) and therefore called upon 'to form a counterweight against the pluralism of social and economic power groups and to preserve the unity of the people as a political whole' and to act as a 'guardian and the preserver of the constitutional unity and wholeness of the German people' on the basis of his power 'to connect immediately with this unified political will of the German people' by initiating a referendum (p. 159). We will come back to the point that this description of the president as a 'guardian of the constitution' is based on a sense of the term that cannot be applied to a constitutional court as a guardian of the constitution and that has never been used by anyone who argued for a constitutional court. To oppose the president to a constitutional court on the basis of this usage is just as meaningless as to claim that we do not need any hospitals because the army is the best protection of the state. Let us only note here that if the constitution installs a constitutional court we are not dealing with a 'fictitious judicial form' but rather with the creation of a real institution. If there is anything here that can be described as 'fictitious' it has to be the 'unity of the people' that C.S. 'presupposes' as a piece of social reality – as, allegedly, does the constitution – while he claims, at the same time, that it has already been dissolved by the reality of the pluralist system; all this in order to declare that the head of state is the only organ that can offer a remedy against this situation and to endow it with the power to reconstitute the people's unity.

To represent the unity of the state in an externally visible form is undoubtedly the function that a head of state is supposed to perform according to all those constitutions which provide for such an office. It is certainly correct for C.S. to say that 'the position of the head of state' is 'most intimately connected with the idea of the whole of the political unity' (p. 157). But for a realistic legal theory free of all ideology this means nothing more than that it belongs to the function of the head of state to symbolically express the indispensable demand for a more than formal, material unity of the state. One can even regard this as the main function of the organ that different constitutions appoint to the position of head of state. This function does not so much depend on the actual competences pertaining to this organ – competences which it does not exercise on its own but only in collaboration with the ministers, i.e. as a dependent part of a complex organ that is, moreover, not the supreme organ of the state but only one amongst several highest organs. Rather, the function depends on the fact that the organ in question is designated as the 'head of state' [**1563**] – as 'emperor', 'king', 'president'– and on the privileges of honour conceded to it. The political significance of this symbolic function is not to be underestimated. But to see in the institution of the head of state more than a symbol of the ethical-political postulate of the state's unity, to interpret it, as C.S. tries to do, by relying on the doctrine of constitutional monarchy, as a product or producer of a unity based on an effective solidarity of interests, is to confuse ideology with reality. The real function of the doctrine of the *pouvoir neutre* of the monarch, which C.S. transfers to the republican head of state, is to veil the actually existing, radical conflict of interest that expresses itself in the existence of political parties and in the even more important underlying fact of class struggle. The formula behind this fiction, in its pseudo-democratic variant, can be expressed as follows: the people that form the state are a unified homogeneous collective and therefore have a unified collective interest that is expressed by a unified collective will. This collective will – it is the 'true' will of the state – transcends all conflicts of interest and stands above all political parties. Hence, it cannot be created by a parliament, since parliament is the scene of the clash of contrary interests, of party-political – C.S. would say of 'pluralistic' – fragmentation. The producer and the instrument of the true will of the state, rather, is the head of state. The ideological character of this interpretation is obvious. To begin with, it flatly contradicts the fact that the constitution binds the acts of the head of state to the collaboration of ministers who are responsible to parliament. But even if the constitution allowed for independent acts of the head of state it would still remain a mystery how a harmony of interests that exists nowhere else, an 'objective' interest of the state that is not the interest of one or another partial group, could be realized in these acts. Even a referendum initiated by the president will at best give us the will of the majority, a will that we can identify with the 'unified political will of the people' only on the basis of the typically democratic fiction of representation.

It is trivially true that any head of state, to the degree that he is independent of interest groups inimical to each other, will seek for a middle line, a line of compromise, in exercising his powers. This strategy, after all, usually serves to secure his own position. But according to C.S. the 'neutral' power is supposed to be something more than this possibility of forging a compromise between competing interests. And even this possibility is already severely restricted by the aforementioned fact that the head of state cannot take action without his ministers, ministers who are responsible to the parliamentary majority.

If one conceives of the 'neutrality' of the head of state realistically and without any ideological bias, as his chance to influence the formation of the will of the state towards some compromise, a chance secured by his independence of the political parties, one has to admit that the presuppositions for exercising this kind of influence are present to a higher degree in the case of a hereditary monarch than in the case of an elected and re-electable president. A presidential election that, inevitably, takes place under the high pressure of party-political actions [**1564**] may be a democratic method of appointing a head of state, but it hardly seems to offer special guarantees of independence. To infer from the fact that the head of state is 'elected by the people as a whole' – which really means that he is elected by a majority of the people or perhaps only by a minority fighting other groups – that he will express the general will of the unified people is questionable not only because such a general will does not exist. It is questionable for the further reason that an election is especially unsuited to guarantee that the head of state will think of his function as that of mediating conflicts of interest. If elected presidents typically perform this function in fact, they do so in spite of this method of appointment. To regard election as a guarantee of independence, as C.S. does (p. 152), is possible only if one closes one's eyes to reality. It would also be wrong to overestimate the effectiveness of the usual means that democratic constitutions employ to preserve the independence of the head of state, such as long terms of office and special protection against impeachment. Such devices are at least partially paralysed by the possibility of re-election provided by the constitution. The determination of incompatibilities, a device on which C.S. puts much emphasis, does not carry a great deal of weight either. This is especially true where the law only forbids membership of the legislative body but not of a political party, a prohibition that would, in any case, not have a great deal of practical significance. In particular, there are no sufficient reasons to believe that the independence of a head of state is stronger or better protected than that of a judge or a public servant. One cannot devalue the neutrality of professional judges in favour of the neutrality of the head of state on the basis of this argument: 'The real possessors of political power can easily exercise the necessary influence on the appointment of judges and experts. If they succeed in doing this, any attempt to handle the matter judicially or to submit it to a panel of experts will turn into a convenient political means, and this is the opposite of the original intention of neutralizing an issue' (p. 109). Judges are usually appointed by the head of state. Is the head of state not a 'real' possessor of political power? And if it is true that the political parties are the only real possessors of political power, would the destruction of judicial independence not presuppose the destruction of the neutrality of the organ that appoints the judges? C.S. believes that 'it is, practically speaking, at least a remarkable restraint against party-political methods of appointment that it is not the party-comrade turned minister himself, but rather a head of state independent of parliament, and therefore of any political party, who appoints public servants' (p. 150). But where is the guarantee that a 'party-comrade' will not be elected president? And since when do political parties lack the power to control officials that have been elected by them or with their help outside of parliament as much as in it? If the neutrality guaranteed by 'independence' really is the crucial requirement for the exercise of the function of a guardian of the constitution, the head of state is at least in no better position than an independent court. [**1565**] And this assessment still fails to take into account one factor that, while it should not be overestimated, may very well be able to justify a certain superiority of the court: namely, that a judge is automatically driven towards neutrality by the ethos of his profession.

Since C.S. is unable to prove that the head of state is more independent and neutral than the judiciary and the public service he finally declares: 'The judiciary as well as the professional public service are burdened in an unacceptable way if all political tasks and decisions whose discharge requires independence and party-political neutrality are heaped upon them' (p. 155). But this turn from quality to quantity is completely illicit and fails to prove anything at all. One cannot compare the judiciary as a whole to a camel whose back would break if one imposed upon it the additional burden of constitutional adjudication. It is not the judiciary as such that is in question, but only one particular court. The tasks of this court do not burden the judiciary as such. The judiciary does not exist as a quantity or an abstract entity that can be burdened as such. The tasks we are talking about fall on one concrete court only, a court that, as C.S. claims to have shown, is not even a judicial organ to begin with. The only question that matters here is the question of who is more independent and neutral: a constitutional court or the head of state. With the inappropriate image of an overloaded judiciary C.S. tries, but in vain, to avoid the acknowledgement that he has failed to defend his thesis that the head of state is the guardian of the constitution. C.S. does not show that the head of state, because he possesses the quality of independence, and hence the quality of neutrality, to a higher degree than a court, is more capable than a court of defending the constitution. Even the formula that C.S. himself employs to determine the essence of the 'neutrality' that is supposed to be a prerequisite for the office of a guardian of the constitution would seem to be tailor-made for a court and to speak directly against the head of state. He says that 'it is only logical, in a rule-of-law state characterized by a separation of powers, not to confer this power on one of the existing authorities, to be exercised on the side, because the authority in question would, thereby, only gain a preponderance over the other powers and acquire the ability to shield itself from control. It would, thus, become a ruler of the constitution. Hence, it is necessary to appoint a special neutral power in addition to the other powers, and to connect and balance it with those others by endowing it with specific competences' (p. 132). Is the head of state not one of the 'existing authorities', especially in a constitution that combines the parliamentary principle with a plebiscitary element and that divides the political power between the parliament and the president (acting in collaboration with the ministers)? Shouldn't this be acknowledged all the more by a constitutional interpretation that tries, by all means possible, to push the centre of gravity of political power towards the president? Is it a court appointed for no other function than to exercise constitutional control or a head of state of which we should say that it is created 'in addition to the other powers' as a special neutral power? Is it such a court or a head of state of which we have to say that it would acquire an additional power of constitutional control – if we chose to appoint it to the function of guardian of the constitution – [**1566**] and that it would gain a 'preponderance' over the other powers authorized by the constitution, by being able 'to shield itself from control'? Even Benjamin Constant's ideology of the *pouvoir neutre* of the monarch cannot cloud this question strongly enough to cast any serious doubt on the answer.

XI

C.S.'s essay confirms rather than refutes the view that the head of state is not the organ most suited to the function of constitutional control, in the context of a constitution of the kind of the Weimar Constitution, and in particular that the head of state is in no way preferable to a constitutional court in terms of independence and neutrality. But C.S. does not merely claim that the head of state is the most suitable guardian of a constitution. He also argues that, according to the constitution presently in force, the president and only the president already is its guardian (p. 158). That the president is one guardian of the constitution among others, that he functions as a guarantor of the constitution – together with the *Staatsgerichtshof* constituted by article 19 and the other court mentioned there, and alongside the civil, criminal, and administrative courts that exercise a material right of review over legislation – insofar as he has the task, in collaboration with these other organs, to secure the constitutionality of statutes and other acts, is something no one will deny. He performs this function when he refuses, in accordance with article 70, to sign into law a legislative decision that came about unconstitutionally, or when he compels a *Land* that violates the constitution to fulfil its duties, with the help of armed force under article 48 paragraph 1; provided he does not merely execute the judgment of a court that has already determined, in an objective trial, that a violation of the constitution has occurred. In this latter case the president would merely act as the executive organ of a guardian of the constitution (as for example the Austrian president under article 146 of the Austrian federal constitution).[12] But to declare that the president is the only guardian of the constitution contradicts the clearest provisions of the constitution of the *Reich*. C.S. states at one point: 'The fact that the German constitutions of the nineteenth century provide for a special *Staatsgerichtshof* for the "judicial protection of the constitution", alongside other guarantees, expresses the simple truth that the judicial protection of the constitution can only form a part of the institutions for the protection and the guarantee of the constitution. It would be a summary superficiality to overlook the very narrow boundaries of legitimate adjudication and to fail to take notice of the many other forms and methods of constitutional guarantee' (p. 11). But since no one has ever made the claim that the constitutional court is the only guardian of the constitution one can say with better justification: the fact that the Weimar Constitution provides for the president as one among other guarantees of the constitution merely **[1567]** expresses the simple truth that this guarantee of the constitution can only be a part of the institutions for the protection of

[12] See for this point H. Kelsen, 'Die Bundesexekution. Ein Beitrag zur Theorie und Praxis des Bundesstaates, unter besonderer Berücksichtigung der deutschen Reichs- und der österreichischen Bundesverfassung' in Z. Giacometti and D. Schindler (eds.), *Festgabe für Fritz Fleiner zum 60. Geburtstag* (Tübingen, 1927), pp. 167–9.

the constitution and that it would be a summary superficiality to forget the narrow boundaries of this kind of guarantee, as well as the many other forms and methods of protecting the constitution, by focusing on the president alone!

The thesis of the president as the only guardian of the constitution can acquire a semblance of plausibility only if the concept of a 'guardian of the constitution', i.e. of the organ which is supposed to secure the constitutionality of certain acts of state by reacting in some way against violations of the constitution, is given a meaning that no one ever connected with the term, and that must not be connected with the term, if it is to be possible to oppose the president as guardian of the constitution to a constitutional court, if it is to be possible for C.S. to say: 'Before we install a court of justice as the guardian of the constitution, in order to decide highly political questions and conflicts, and before we burden and endanger the judiciary by such politicizations' we ought to remind ourselves of 'the available content of the Weimar Constitution' according to which 'a guardian of the constitution already exists, namely the president of *Reich*' (p. 158). It is noteworthy that C.S. lists among the competences of the president that allegedly express his role as a guardian of the constitution also some that have nothing whatsoever to do with a guarantee of the constitution. C.S. detects the function of a guardian of the constitution more or less in all of the competences the constitution assigns to the president: the competence under articles 45–6 of the constitution of the *Reich*, i.e. the diplomatic representation of the *Reich*, the declaration of war and the signing of peace treaties, the appointment of public servants, the command over the armed forces, the dissolution of parliament under article 25, the initiation of a referendum under article 73, and in particular everything that the president, together with the ministers, is authorized to do under article 48 (and not just under its first paragraph). If it were right to say that the president 'guards' the constitution with all these functions assigned to him by the constitution, then a 'guardian of the constitution' would be the same thing as an executor of the constitution. But in this case, the *Reichstag* as well as all other organs immediate to the constitution would be 'guardians of the constitution' as much as the president of the *Reich* himself, and it would be possible to call all courts and administrative agencies 'guardians of the statutes'. Unsurprisingly, C.S. believes he has detected the function of a guardian of the constitution in the formula of the president's oath in article 42. He declares the president the guardian of the constitution because the president vows to 'preserve the constitution'. However, the text of the oath is not, as cited by Schmitt, 'to preserve the constitution' (p. 159) but rather: 'to preserve the constitution and the statutes of the *Reich*', which means nothing but: to execute the constitution and the laws or to exercise one's function constitutionally and in conformity with statute. In this sense, the president is a 'guardian' of the constitution as much as he is a guardian of statute. And indeed, C.S.'s argument ultimately boils down to an attempt to distinguish the function of one of the organs that the constitution creates for its immediate execution, the position [**1568**] of one of the pillars of the constitution – i.e. the constitutional function of the president, or, to be more precise, the function of the government composed of the president and the ministers – from the constitutional functions of all other organs immediate to the constitution, and in particular from that of the *Reichstag*, by describing this function in particular, to the exclusion of all others, as that of a 'guardian of the constitution'. This is not just a mystification of this function. It also creates the impression that a control of the constitutionality of the function of this organ – and such control is very well possible as long as its function is not itself that of control – is at the very least unnecessary. To be 'a guardian of the constitution' means, in the original sense of the word, to be a guarantor of the constitution. To guard the 'guardian' would admittedly be nothing but the first step in a legally and politically meaningless infinite regress. It is only that C.S.'s concept of the guardian of the constitution captures functions very different from that of constitutional control; it even puts the main emphasis on these very different functions.

The real meaning of the concept of a 'guardian of the constitution' that C.S. introduces into the debate about the guarantee of the constitution, the meaning of the term he is primarily concerned to advocate, appears in the strongest and clearest form in the passage of his essay that he believes to deliver the death blow to the idea of constitutional adjudication, namely the passage in which he accuses this institution of being undemocratic. He points out: 'it is an abuse of the concepts of judicial form and of adjudication, as well as of the institutional guarantee of the German professional public service, immediately to demand the introduction of a court staffed by professional jurists who are public servants, and of a judicial procedure, in all cases where an independence or neutrality appears to be useful or necessary for practical reasons' (pp. 155–6). And after having made the claim we refuted in an earlier context, namely that this would put an intolerable burden on the judiciary, he readies himself for the main strike that one can deliver to the legal-political demand for the creation of a constitutional court, on the basis of the democratic principle accepted by C.S.: 'What is more, the installation of such a guardian of the constitution would be directly opposed to the political implications of the democratic principle.' Note that a constitutional court would also be a 'guardian of the constitution', even though one much less suited than the president. Throughout his essay, C.S. uses the concept of a 'guardian of the constitution' not just in the special sense he gives it, but also in the sense in which it can be applied to a court! But why should a constitutional court be an undemocratic guardian of the constitution, or a less democratic guardian than the head of state? The democratic character of a constitutional court, just as the democratic character of a head of state, can only depend on its legal position and on the method of appointment that is used. There is no obstacle to have judges elected by the people, just like the head of state, if one wants to design the constitutional court in democratic fashion. Moreover, it is perfectly possible to put the members of the court in the same constitutional position as the president and not to make them professional public servants, even though it remains an open question whether this is the most useful way, with respect to the function of this organ, of creating and structuring it. [**1569**] But such questions also arise with respect to the head of state, and it is in any case impossible to deny that a court can be created as democratically as any other organ. C.S.'s objection that 'from a democratic point of view, it will hardly be possible to transfer such powers to an aristocracy of the robe' can easily be answered by pointing out that a constitutional court elected by the people or even a constitutional court elected by parliament, for example after the fashion of the Austrian constitutional court according to the constitution of 1920,* is anything but an 'aristocracy of the robe'. However, a constitutional court appears to be undemocratic, according to C.S.'s portrayal of this institution, not just because it allegedly has to be organized in a bureaucratic and aristocratic manner, but also for a further reason. C.S. does not explicitly mention this reason in support of the claim that a constitutional court is an undemocratic institution. But he at least implies that it should be considered, since the argument in question follows immediately after the claim that the creation of a constitutional court contradicts the democratic principle. Within the framework of a parliamentary and plebiscitary democracy of the twentieth century, C.S. points out, a constitutional court would no longer be directed 'against a monarch', as in the constitutional monarchy of the nineteenth century, 'but rather against parliament'. It was possible for the judiciary to be successful against a monarch. It will not be able to function, however, as 'a counterweight to parliament'. 'The necessity of stabilizing institutions and of a counterweight to parliament is a problem, in today's Germany, altogether different in kind from the old problem of the control of the monarch. That applies as much to the general, diffuse right of judicial review as to the control that is concentrated with a single authority.' This has to be one of the most surprising thoughts in a book that is not exactly suffering from a scarcity of logical surprises. That a constitutional court would find itself in opposition only to the parliament but not also to the government is a claim that directly contradicts the facts. If C.S. had bothered to take a closer look at what he ironically calls the 'Austrian solution', he would know that this court, as a result of its judicature, got into a conflict with the government, not with parliament, that threatened its very existence.* A tendency to ignore the possibility of a violation of the constitution by the head of state and the government permeates all of C.S.'s essay. But this possibility is especially relevant in the context of a constitution that numbers among its most important provisions an article 48. By making the unproven and improvable assertion that a constitutional court would find itself in opposition only to parliament, C.S. reinterprets the function of a 'guardian of a constitution' from that of control over the constitutionality of acts of state, in particular of statutes (including those promulgated by the head of state), to that of a 'counterweight to parliament'. But this, of course, is just the role the Weimar Constitution confers on the president, or, to be more precise, it is a plausible political evaluation of the constitutional position of the president under the Weimar Constitution. However, to be such a counterweight is not the function of a constitutional court. This implies, to be sure, that one can never make the claim that **[1570]** a constitutional court, according to the intention of the constitution authorizing it, should function as a guardian of the constitution in this sense, as a political counterweight to a parliament. But we obviously cannot infer anything against the institution of a constitutional court from the fact that it cannot perform this function, a function that is not assignable to it and that no one ever assigned to it. Rather, we should conclude that a constitutional court can exist alongside a head of state who functions as a 'counterweight to parliament' precisely because it has a different function. It will even be doubly necessary in a system in which such a 'counterweight' exists.

XII

It is clear by now what C.S. really understands by a 'guardian of the constitution'. Nothing, nothing at all, that would entitle us to set up the president as a 'guardian of the constitution' in opposition to a constitutional court that, among other things, controls this 'guardian', and nothing that would entitle us to claim that a court cannot also be a 'guardian of the constitution' as well as to declare that this task pertains to the president of the *Reich* – as though we were talking about the same function in both cases and only looked for and found a more suitable bearer of the same function in the head of state. This is what C.S. does when he formulates the result of his inquiry as follows: before we authorize a court to act as the guardian of the constitution, a function it is not suitable for, we ought to remember that the constitution already appoints the president to this function (p. 158). If the constitution intends the president to play the role of a 'counterweight to parliament', which we certainly don't need to deny, it is impermissible to refer to this function as that of 'constitutional guardianship', at least if the guarantee of the constitution by a constitutional court is given the same name. This is not a mere terminological correction, since C.S. derives one of his main arguments against the institution of a constitutional court from this illicit equivocation. And this argumentation also allows him to not just overvalue the competences and functions of the president as one of the two main pillars of the constitution, but also to undervalue those of the other pillar, i.e. those of parliament. It may well be true that parliament is, to borrow C.S.'s terminology, the 'stage of the pluralistic system' (p. 105), since it is the ground on which the actually existing conflicts of interest express themselves as such, in the fight between organized party-political interest groups for influence on the formation of the will of the state. But this process, despite all the dangers for a beneficial formation of the will of the state that may go along with it, cannot be declared unconstitutional. It is the Weimar Constitution itself that does not just appoint the president 'elected by the whole people' but also, and in the first place, a *Reichstag* elected by the very same people. It is the constitution itself that put in place the political system that C.S. calls 'pluralistic'. The constitution authorizes the president to act as a 'counterweight' to the *Reichstag* only because it acknowledges parliament, as well as the 'pluralistic system' that necessarily goes along with it, as another legitimate 'weight' in the play of political powers. [**1571**]

This system may appear to be ruinous from the point of view of some political ideal. But to declare it unconstitutional for this reason, and only for this reason, is a natural lawyer's abuse of a category that is meaningful only as a category of positive law. The system in question would not even be unconstitutional if parliament was incapable of doing its work, due to the lack of a firm majority or due to the obstruction of a minority; especially if the constitution appoints the president as a substitute in this case, as it supposedly does, according to C.S.'s interpretation of the Weimar Constitution. This situation therefore does not amount to a violation of the constitution, just as it is not a violation of the constitution of a constitutional monarchy for a constitutional monarch to lose his ability to perform his duties (for example Ludwig II of Bavaria). The organ which, in that case, steps in for the monarch does not thereby become a guardian of the constitution. But it is precisely this sense that the concept of a 'guardian of the constitution' takes on in C.S. And since the president and only the president – and not the second (or, better, the first) pillar of the constitution, parliament – is declared the guardian of the constitution, and since he is declared to be a guardian with respect to the totality of the competences conferred upon him by the constitution, in particular with respect to his right to act in lieu of a parliament that is incapable of acting, the function of parliament, which forms the 'stage of the pluralistic system', must appear as purely 'centrifugal' (p. 149) and as essentially opposed to the centripetal function of the president. Parliament's function, as a result, is conceived to be directed against the preservation of the constitution and in the final resort must seem to be unconstitutional *per se*. The 'pluralistic system', introduced as a value-neutral sociological category, quickly turns into the 'state-dissolving methods of the pluralistic party state' (p. 156), into the 'constitution-destroying methods of the pluralistic system' (p. 116), and finally into the 'unconstitutional pluralism' (p. 131) from which the state must supposedly be saved by the president of the *Reich*. The constitution, it turns out, is not to be identified with norms that regulate the organs and the procedures of legislation as well as the position and competence of the highest organs of execution. The constitution is not made up of norms or 'statutes' at all. 'Constitution', rather, is a status, the condition of the 'unity' of the German people. C.S. does not provide any further determination of what this 'unity', which has a material and not merely a formal character, consists in. But what could it be, other than some social condition that is judged to be desirable from a certain political point of view? A natural law ideal of 'unity' based on wishful thinking takes the place of the constitution as a piece of positive law. With the help of this ideal it becomes possible to interpret the pluralistic system with its parliamentary stage, and hence the function of this pillar of the constitution, as a violation of the constitution, for the reason that it threatens the 'unity' that has replaced the constitution. At the same time, one can interpret the function of the head of state as that of guarding the constitution, because he supposedly defends and recreates that 'unity'. This interpretation of the constitution cannot stop itself from culminating in an apotheosis of article 48. It leads to the probably unintended but all the more paradoxical conclusion that the pluralistic system or, in plain German, parliament is that which 'severely threatens or disturbs the public security and order in the German Reich'. The true function of parliament, given that it is an essentially pluralistic institution, seems to consist in the permanent fulfilment of the conditions [**1572**] that the Weimar Constitution requires for a use of article 48 paragraph 2.[13]

[13] That the parliamentary system has by no means failed everywhere is shown by a glance at Austria, France, England, the Nordic states. Nevertheless, C.S. believes that he is entitled to pronounce the death sentence for the parliamentary system as such, without any restriction. The method that he uses in doing so is that of an almost mystical dialectic: 'Parliament, the legislative body, which carries the legislative state and forms its centre, at the very moment when its victory seemed complete, turned into an entity divided within itself and began to disown its own presuppositions and those of its victory. Its previous position and superiority, its urge to expand its powers against the government, its claim to represent the people, all that presupposes a distinction between state and society that did not continue to exist, at least not in the same form, after the victory of parliament. Its unity, even its identity with itself, had thus far been determined by its adversary in domestic politics, by the old monarchical military state and its administrative apparatus. When the latter disintegrated, parliament, so to speak, broke apart itself' (p. 82). If one identifies parliament with a society that is opposed to the state, and if the 'total state' signifies the dissolution of this antagonism, then there is no place for parliament in the total state, according to the logic of this social philosophy. But if one were to hit upon the thought that the dissolution of the dualism of state and society, and thus the 'total state', might perhaps also be brought about by a parliament expanding its competences, one that maintains 'its unity, even its identity with itself' by virtue of establishing itself as the highest public organ that concentrates all power in itself, it would be objected: 'The state is now, it is said, the self-organization of society. But this raises the question of how a society that organizes itself arrives at its unity, and whether that unity really comes about as a result of the "self-organization" of society. "Self-organization", after all, initially signifies no more than a postulate and a procedure that is characterized, in a purely negative and polemical fashion, by its opposition to older methods of the formation of the will and of the unity of the state that no longer exist today. The identity that is implied by the word "self" and that is linguistically attached to the word "organization" does not have to come about in every case and with absolute certainty, neither as a unity of society itself, nor as a unity of the state. There are organizations, as we have experienced often enough, that lack success or fail to achieve

The two pillars of the state's authority created by the constitution are turned into an enemy and a friend of the state; one of which attempts to destroy the state, i.e. its 'unity', and another that defends the state against this destruction: the violator and the guardian of the constitution. All this no longer has anything to do with an interpretation of the constitution based on positive right. It is nothing but the mythology of *Ormuzd* and *Ahriman*,* dressed up in a jurisprudential garb.

Of course, this critical analysis cannot and is not supposed to question the political value, in the current circumstances, of the demand for the largest possible extension of the power of the president, i.e. of the government, as well as of the rejection of constitutional adjudication that must go along with it. [**1573**] Here, I am not concerned to criticize C.S.'s essay insofar as it serves this purpose, a purpose that I do not want to denigrate as 'party-political' in the present context. I criticized C.S.'s arguments only insofar as they make use of certain methods, in order to further this political purpose, that make a claim to be sociological analysis and state-theoretical constitutional interpretation, methods that, in short, purport to offer a 'scientific treatment' of the subject. The criticisms offered here aim to show, by focusing on an especially instructive example that is highly symptomatic of the contemporary state of our theory of the state and of public law, how important it is to insist on the strictest separation of scientific inquiry from political value judgement. The careless mixing of science and politics that is so popular nowadays is the typical modern method of forming ideologies. It has to be rejected from a scientific point of view even when it takes place unconsciously, as it certainly does in the present case as well as many others. Given the acute critical consciousness of our times, this method will not serve politics well in the long run. It is all too simple for the political opponent to unmask it or to use it to construct an equally dubious justification for his own contrary goals. While it doesn't serve politics, it can harm science all the more. The whole value of science,

results' (pp. 82, 83). The 'unity' of the total state, then, simply cannot be brought about by parliament but only by the head of state! A Marxist critic will have no great diffulty in recognizing such an argumentation as an ideology that proceeds from the opposite political point of view. This parliament that, in mysterious ways, breaks apart in the moment of its victory, and that turns into an institution denying its own presuppositions, for the sole reason that it no longer has to share its power with a monarch: might such talk simply be an expression of the fact that the bourgeoisie will change its political ideal and desert democracy for dictatorship wherever parliament, as a result of the continuing struggle of the classes, has ceased to be a useful instrument of class domination?

which is the reason why politics tries – again and again, driven by the best ethical motives and in the interest of causes honestly held to be good – to link itself to science, this value, *sui generis* and altogether distinct from ethical-political value, stands and falls with science's willingness to remain strong enough, in this almost tragic conflict, to resist the temptation to mix with politics.

5

Prussia contra *Reich*: Schmitt's closing statement in Leipzig

Translation of Carl Schmitt (1932d) 'Schlußrede vor dem Staatsgerichtshof in Leipzig in dem Prozeß Preußen contra Reich' in Carl Schmitt, *Positionen und Begriffe im Kampf mit Weimar - Genf - Versailles 1923–1939*, 3rd edn (Berlin: Duncker & Humblot, 1994), 205–10.

CLOSING STATEMENT BEFORE THE *STAATSGERICHTSHOF* IN LEIPZIG

The 'formalities' that are talked about here are not mere formalities, in a trial in front of the *Staatsgerichtshof*, but rather very real, political issues. The questions of who is the *Land* of Prussia, who represents the *Land* of Prussia, and where is Prussia today are real and highly political questions. This trial, therefore, arrived at what is truly its core problem in particular when dealing with questions of standing, with the competence to bring suit, and with active legitimation.* For this reason, it was not the result of an evil will or of something like that, but rather, so to speak, of the nature of the thing that the intensity and suddenness of disagreement repeatedly turned out to be strongest especially with regard to the question of the so-called formalities.

According to article 19* of the constitution of the *Reich* there is, among the three permissible kinds of trials in front of the *Staatsgerichtshof* that are mentioned there, only one in which the Reich appears; that is the trial of a *Land* against the *Reich*. A *Land* brings suit against the *Reich*, or the *Reich* brings suit against a *Land* – two 'states', as my colleague Mr Nawiasky said quite correctly. But it does not follow from this, that, as he went on to say, the *Staatsgerichtshof* is an 'international court'. He even spoke of the so-called world court, a somewhat exaggerated designation for the well-known institution in The Hague. This permanent international court always puts special emphasis on a point that is recognized in its statute, and is made explicit in a series of judgments, namely that only states as such can appear in front of it. However, even [**206**] parliamentary parties of the *Land* legislatures appear here, arm in arm with the *Land* of Bavaria and the *Land* of Baden* (von Jan: How awful!). This alone makes for a great confusion and inconsistency.

The most important question of the trial, of course, concerns the *Land* of Prussia. The *Land* of Prussia did not disappear; it still exists; it is still there; it also has a government, a commissarial government, appointed by the president of the *Reich*, on the basis of his constitutional competence, which has the right to represent the *Land* of Prussia. If this is a constitutionally appointed state government, then the question of who has the right to represent Prussia is thereby answered. The view expressed by my colleague Mr Jacobi is precise and juristic, correct and indisputable: it is only on the basis of a fiction, a fiction that is conceivable and permissible only for reasons of procedural technique, that the ministers who have already been removed from their offices can nevertheless appear here; they appear on the basis of a fictitious right to represent that is *ad hoc* and for this case only. My colleague Mr Bilfinger objected to the fact – rightly so, in my opinion, and I also share the affect that propelled him – that the opposing side, in its briefs and in oral argument, constantly attempted to draw conclusions concerning the main question from this fiction and to say: if you concede that what we are doing here is to conduct a trial, then you also recognize that we have the right to represent the *Land* of Prussia; that, moreover, we still belong to the *Reichsrat*, and that, in general, we still have all manner of other competences. This alone was criticized by my colleague Mr Bilfinger. The real question, by contrast, is simply: was the commissarial government of the state appointed constitutionally by the president, on the basis of article 48 of the constitution of the *Reich*, or not? If it was, then any right to represent that was connected with the former offices of the deposed ministers thereby ceased to exist. We do not want to enter, here, into a deeper discussion of the question of what the former acting ministers can still be said to be, after they have been stripped of their right to act as ministers of the state. Neither do we want to discuss the even more difficult question by what title one is to address such a former acting minister from whom one has taken the right to act as a minister. The *Reich* emphasized from the beginning that the action it has taken is nothing but a temporary suspension of an acting state government. And in this context one always has to keep in mind: of an acting government of a highly peculiar kind, since this acting Prussian government owes its very existence to the notorious and devious trick* of a change of the Prussian parliament's rules of procedure on 12 April. That makes the juristic construction of this highly peculiar entity, as which the Prussian state government that was removed from its office by the president of the *Reich* on 20 July 1932 presents itself now, even more difficult. But the question simply remains this: is it constitutionally permissible for the *Reich* to provide a *Land* with a commissarial state government? [**207**]

Accusations have been raised here against the government of the *Reich*, and there was talk of that government 'hiding itself', 'shirking', 'taking cover', and the like. I do not want to take this up, and I stick to the question: can a *Land* government of the form of the Prussian acting government, having been stripped of its office, appeal, against the constitutional powers of interference that lie with the *Reich*, to the autonomy of the *Land* of Prussia? This so-called *Land* government no longer is the *Land* of Prussia. The president of the *Reich* has certain opportunities for interference, by virtue of the constitution of the *Reich*, to which article 17, as an independent norm of competence,* is not opposed after a transfer of executive power has taken place – as has now also been expressly confirmed by Walter Jellinek.* The executive power of the *Land* also includes an organizational power, previously the king's, now in the hands of the ministry of state. Now, if the appointment, on the part of the *Reich*, of a substitute organ, of a commissarial state government that runs the business of government, is permissible, by virtue of opportunities for interference that stem from the constitution of the *Reich*, then, assuming the constitutional requirements are otherwise met, this organ, and no one else, is the acting state government. It has the right to represent, and it is no argument at all, in this context, to invoke the autonomy of the *Land*, which, by the way, has never been put into question. If someone is 'taking cover' here, then it is the former acting government, now stripped of its office, that identifies itself with the *Land* of Prussia – with what inner justification I need not discuss here – and that now continuously brings up the autonomy of the *Land* of Prussia, the inalienable and intangible rights of the *Land*, and suchlike.

The following important point seems to me to have been overlooked in the discussions of the pertinent issues in the law of federalism: the president of the *Reich*, who has several different competences by virtue of article 48, can and must, if necessary, also exercise these competences in the interest of the autonomy of the *Land*. It is perfectly possible to think of a case where the autonomy of a *Land* cannot be rescued at all in any other way than this. One of the biggest and most serious dangers for our system of federalism, and for the autonomy of the *Länder*, after all, consists in the fact that tightly organized and centralized political parties that cross the boundaries of the several *Länder* may attempt to occupy a *Land* and to put its agents and servants into the government of a *Land* (Professor Heller: This is outrageous!) and thus come to endanger the autonomy of the *Land*. One might even argue that a very specific danger of continuous disturbances of function, of continuous endangerment of public security and order, and also of a failure on the part of a *Land* to perform its duties towards the *Reich* threatens from this side, the side of the parties. Now, if such a case occurs – I [**208**] am speaking altogether in the abstract – and if the president of the *Reich* sees himself forced to take action, then this is not at all in conflict with the autonomy of the *Land*. (Objection.) I believe my colleague Mr Nawiasky will concede to me that there are now parties that do signify a threat for the autonomy of a state. The Bavarian People's Party, here, is in the altogether unique position that it signifies the very opposite of a threat to the autonomy of Bavaria. But there are also other parties. (von Jan: But we would be well able to deal with these parties ourselves!) That is your advantage over other parties, your peculiarity, and we want to hope that you do not come into a situation, one day, to thank God for the fact that there are opportunities under article 48 for the president of the *Reich* to interfere.

Hence, the only question is: can there be interference with the affairs of a state, from the side of the *Reich*, in the way that took place?

The contrast between a centralized and a federal state must not at all be connected with other contrasts by way of sloganeering. What seems to me to be decisive is this: if the president of the *Reich* has made use of his constitutional competence against a *Land*, if he has appointed such a commissarial *Land* government, and has suspended the other *Land* government, then the question of the right to represent has been answered, then one knows who is the active caretaker government of the *Land*. To invoke the autonomy of the *Land* as such, in this context, is a manifest confusion. Here in this trial, pictures and similes of an original kind have occasionally been used. I may perhaps be permitted myself, for a change, to become graphic, and to make the following statement, not with reference to this particular case, but in general, in order to clarify what seems to me to be the simple fact of the matter. If the fox has indeed been made the guardian of the henhouse, and if the question is how to get rid of it, then one may try to invoke all kinds of considerations, but surely not the autonomy and independence of the garden! That is the case of a *Land* government that has been suspended by the president of the *Reich*. It cannot invoke the autonomy of the *Land* as such. A commissarial government appointed by the *Reich*, of course, is not a normal government, but neither is an acting government a normal government, or even an acting government like the Prussian government that was deposed from its office, tainted as it is by the odium of 12 April.

Two slogans or key words I would still like to deal with quickly. In the first place, the phrase 'guardian of the constitution' was uttered here. To be more precise, my colleague Mr Nawiasky said, with special emphasis, and perhaps also with a polemical twist: the *Staatsgerichtshof* is the guardian of the constitution. No one disputes that; it is the guardian of the constitution. But it is and it remains a court of justice, and it is consequently dependent on [**209**] the peculiarities of legal and adjudicative form, as they have been explicated very penetratingly and, it seems to me, convincingly by my colleague Mr Jacobi. The *Staatsgerichtshof* only has the judicial and legal protection of the constitution. Since a constitution is a political entity, there is a need, in addition, for essentially political decisions, and in this respect it is, I believe, the president of the *Reich* who is the guardian of the constitution, and his competences under article 48, in particular, have the purpose, above all, of constituting a genuinely political guardian of the constitution, for the parts of the constitution that deal with federalism as well as for all others. If he appoints a commissarial *Land* government, in this capacity, then he likewise acts as guardian of the constitution, on the basis of the essentially political decision which is left to his political discretion, within certain boundaries that we pointed out here. But the decision which is at issue here remains *his political decision*. With this, the question that is important for article 19 of the constitution of the *Reich*, namely who is to represent the *Land* in such a case, is answered at the same time. The representation of the *Land* of Prussia that is exercised, on the basis of such an act of the president of the *Reich*, by the commissarial government, has its good and solid legal basis in the constitution of the *Reich* as well as in the constitution of the *Land* which it supplements.

The second slogan that frequently recurred here was that of the 'honour and dignity' of Prussia that is implied by Prussia's statehood. I would like to say the following about this issue: Mr Ministerial Director Brecht thought it a good thing to remind us, in his closing summary this morning, that Mr President of the *Reich*, in the year 1866, took the field as a Prussian officer. What was going on in 1866? A federal execution of the German *Bund* against Prussia.* And Mr President of the *Reich*, as a Prussian officer, stood on the Prussian side and defended Prussia against this federal execution. If the same man who, back then, defended Prussia against an execution must now resolve to order a federal execution against the same Prussia, then this is a significant, astonishing event. One should become aware of this at least for a moment, since it shows that something has changed. The execution, now, does not have the goal of eliminating the *Land* and destroying its existence, but, to the contrary, protecting Prussia against dangers that threatened this state and this *Land* in particular. Given that there is so much talk here about the statehood, the dignity, and the honour of Prussia, then I must be permitted to put the question to myself, eventually – I do not put it to anyone else, but I do put it to myself, and in full view of the public: where is all that, the dignity and honour of Prussia, in better hands? With the acting ministers who have been removed from their offices on 20 July, and who continued to be acting ministers only due to the devious trick of 12 April (Objection: Situational jurisprudence!), [**210**] or with President of the *Reich* Hindenburg? This question is not difficult for me to answer. It is true, Prussia has its honour and its dignity, but the trustee and guardian of this honour, today, is the *Reich*.

6

Kelsen on the judgment of the *Staatsgerichtshof* of 25 October 1932

Translation of Hans Kelsen (1932a) 'Das Urteil des Staatsgerichtshofs vom 25. Oktober 1932', *Die Justiz*, 8 (1932), 65–91.

THE JUDGMENT OF THE *STAATSGERICHTSHOF* OF 25 OCTOBER 1932

BY HANS KELSEN, COLOGNE

I

The object of the judgment of the *Staatsgerichtshof* of 25 October 1932, a judgment that will turn out to be of great importance in the history of the German Republic, is the decree of the president of the *Reich* of 20 July 1932 (RGBl. I, p. 377). This decree characterizes itself, in its title, as having been enacted for the 'restoration of public security and order in the territory of the *Land* of Prussia'. In its introduction, however, the decree does not only appeal for support to article 48 paragraph 2, as this self-characterization would lead one to expect, but also to article 48 paragraph 1 of the constitution of the *Reich*. The decree, hence, also presents itself as an act of federal execution against Prussia, i.e. as an action whose purpose, according to the constitution, consists in forcing Prussia, with the help of armed force, to fulfil certain duties that are incumbent upon it according to the constitution or according to federal statutes and that it failed to fulfil. The decree does not say, however, which duties were not fulfilled by Prussia. The decree merely authorizes the chancellor of the *Reich* to remove the members of the Prussian ministry from their offices, to exercise by himself all of the competences of the Prussian prime minister, to appoint other persons to lead the several departments of the Prussian government, and to transfer to these persons all competences [**66**] which the ministers of the Prussian government exercise within their respective portfolios. There is no talk, however, of a takeover of all the duties of the ministers of the Prussian government. In particular, there is no provision for the transfer of the political and constitutional responsibilities that are laid down in articles 57 and 58 of the Prussian Constitution.* The closing sentence of § 1 of the decree is formulated as follows: 'The chancellor of the *Reich* and the persons that he appointed to lead the Prussian ministries exercise the competences of the Prussian government.' Insofar as he executes the functions that have in this way been transferred to him, the chancellor of the *Reich* is referred to as the 'federal commissioner for the *Land* of Prussia' and the persons that he appointed to lead the Prussian ministries are designated as 'commissioners of the Reich'.

In execution of the decree of the president of the *Reich*, the Prussian prime minister and the Prussian minister of the interior were, each by order of the chancellor of the *Reich* of 20 July 1932, 'removed from their offices'. The remaining ministers of the Prussian government, each by order of the chancellor of the *Reich* issued on the same day, were not removed from their offices, but rather stripped of the 'execution of the ongoing business of their office'. Moreover, the commissioners of the *Reich* envisaged by the decree of 20 July were appointed in their place, and have in fact taken over the official business of the Prussian ministers. A responsibility of the commissarial government towards the Prussian parliament was explicitly rejected by the chancellor of the *Reich*, in a letter of 19 August 1932 directed to the president of the Prussian parliament.

The meaning of the decree of the president of the *Reich*, executed by the chancellor of the *Reich*, is clear: in order to compel the *Land* of Prussia to fulfil certain duties, which have not been specified in particular, but which are incumbent upon it according to the constitution of the *Reich* and according to federal laws, and which, in the opinion of the president of the *Reich*, Prussia did not fulfil, and, at the same time, in order to restore public order and security in the territory of the *Land* of Prussia, which are, in the view of the president of the *Reich*, considerably disturbed and endangered, the complete power – or, put juristically – the whole competence of the Prussian government is transferred to the *Reich*, or more precisely, to certain organs of the *Reich*: to the chancellor of the *Reich* and to the commissioners he appointed and who are under his command. One could also express the matter by saying that certain powers of the *Reich* and of Prussia are being united in one hand. But in so doing, one would have to note [**67**] that this concentration of power takes place in the hands of the *Reich*. On the basis of article 48 paragraph 1 and 2, the whole executive competence of a *Land* (with the exception of adjudication) is transferred to the *Reich*. This means no more and no less than that the two basic organizational principles of the Weimar Constitution, the principle of federalism and the principle of democracy, are suspended for the largest German *Land* in the sphere of executive power, and the first of these two principles also in the sphere of legislation.

The federal state, from the point of view of organizational technique, is a particular form of decentralization. The competences of legislation and execution are divided between a central and several local authorities. In the field of execution, the principle of federalism expresses itself in the existence of a local government that is different from and independent of the central government, and in some cases also in a participation of the local governments in the execution of federal laws; in the field of legislation, in the existence of a local parliament that is different from and independent of the central parliament, and in particular in the participation of the local parliament or the local government in the central process of legislation. According to the constitution of the German *Reich*, the participation of the local authorities in central legislation and execution, a participation that is quite essential to federalism as a form of organization of the state, takes place in the *Reichsrat*, where the *Länder* are represented by members of their governments. Now, if the chancellor of the *Reich* and the commissioners appointed by him and subject to him insert themselves into the place of a Prussian government that is different from and independent of the government of the *Reich*, the principle of federalism is abolished for Prussia, and Prussia is no longer a '*Land*' in the sense that the constitution of the *Reich* gives to the term, but rather a mere federal province that, insofar as the function of local legislation has not, as yet, been transferred to a commissioner of the *Reich* (or to the federal parliament), enjoys a limited autonomy restricted to this sphere alone. But since this autonomous province does not have a government elected by the Prussian people or by the Prussian parliament, but rather one that has been appointed by a central federal authority outside of Prussia and that is thus not responsible to the Prussian parliament, the principle of democracy has likewise suffered a very considerable restriction, and has been eliminated completely in the area of execution. The fact that the chancellor of the *Reich*, [**68**] who has been charged with the exercise of governmental authority in Prussia, is appointed by the president of the *Reich*, and hence by an organ that is elected by the whole of the German people and therefore has a democratic character, is irrelevant, since what is at issue here is the realization of the principle of democracy in a constituent state of a federal state. Here, the principle of democracy and the principle of federalism are inseparably connected. Within a community that forms part of a larger community, democracy essentially requires autocephaly. A constituent state can be said to be organized democratically only insofar as the functions of government are discharged either immediately by the populace of the constituent state, or else by organs chosen by and from that populace, whether through election or lot. Centralization of the functions is inevitably at the same time de-democratization.

As far as the consequences of the decree of 20 July for the principles of federalism and democracy in Prussia are concerned, it is insignificant that, in the execution of this norm, only some of the Prussian ministers were altogether removed from their 'offices', while the others were merely barred from 'executing the competences of their office'. It is equally insignificant whether the chancellor of the *Reich* and the federal commissioners appointed by him and subject to him have, in the execution of the same decree, merely laid claim to the right of the Prussian ministry to represent Prussia in the *Reichsrat* or whether they have in fact exercised that right. It cannot, in seriousness, be doubted that these organs of the *Reich* are, according to the decree of the president of the *Reich*, which transfers to the chancellor of the *Reich* and to the persons chosen and appointed by him and subject to him 'all competences' of the Prussian government, entitled to represent Prussia in the *Reichsrat*. Of course, whether the decree of the president of the *Reich* is constitutional or not is a different question; it is the question the *Staatsgerichtshof* had to answer.

How, then, has the court answered this question? What is the legal opinion of the *Staatsgerichtshof*?

II

The *Staatsgerichtshof* initially declares that the condition under which article 48 paragraph 1 can come to be applied: the non-fulfilment of a duty incumbent upon Prussia according to the constitution of the *Reich* or federal statutes, is not satisfied in the present case and that the decree of 20 July therefore cannot be based on this provision of the constitution of the *Reich*. The *Staatsgerichtshof* does not expressly declare it, [**69**] and the point does not, moreover, figure explicitly in the tenor of its judgment. But the reasons offered for the judgment undoubtedly imply that the federal execution against Prussia, as which the decree presents the removal from office of the Prussian ministry as well as the transfer of its functions to the chancellor of the *Reich* and to the organs of the *Reich* appointed by him and subject to him, is incompatible with the constitution or, in other words, that this whole action is unconstitutional as a federal execution. However, the *Staatsgerichtshof* declares the very same action to be, in principle, not unconstitutional insofar as it is based on article 48 paragraph 2, i.e. insofar as it is qualified as a measure for the restoration of the severely disturbed and endangered public security and order. Here it is noteworthy, to begin with, that the *Staatsgerichtshof*, if not expressly then at least implicitly, takes it to be possible, in agreement with the decree of 20 July, that one and the same act can be a federal execution under article 48 paragraph 1 as well as a measure for the restoration of public security and order under article 48 paragraph 2. The judgment of the *Staatsgerichtshof* does not say – though one might have expected it to do so – that a transfer of the functions of the government of a *Land* to the *Reich* cannot be classified as an attempt to compel a *Land* to fulfil its non-fulfilled duties 'with the help of armed force'. It only says that the condition under which the action described in the decree of 20 July may be employed against Prussia as a federal execution does not obtain.

Now, while the *Staatsgerichtshof* takes itself to be entitled, without any hesitation, to ascertain whether the preconditions for an application of article 48 paragraph 1 are satisfied, it declares that it has never taken a position 'on the question whether the *Staatsgerichtshof* is called upon, in a disputed case, to inquire into the presence of the preconditions of article 48 paragraph 2 of the constitution of the *Reich* or whether it is bound, in such a case, to base its decision on the opinion of the president of the *Reich*', and it claims that it is equally unnecessary for the court to take a position on this question in the present case. However, already in the very next sentence, the court inquires whether the preconditions for an application of article 48 paragraph 2 are satisfied, and decides to answer the question affirmatively, by declaring – strangely enough as a justification for its claim that it does not have to take a position on the question at issue – 'It is obvious that the decree of 20 July was enacted during a time of severe disturbance [**70**] and endangerment of public security and order.' And the court explicitly points out: 'The preconditions for an intervention on the basis of article 48 paragraph 2 were therefore clearly given.' In making this claim, the *Staatsgerichtshof* recognizes as a sufficient condition for an application of article 48 paragraph 2 that the measures prescribed by this constitutional provision take place 'during a time' when public security and order are exposed to severe disturbance and endangerment. In its more detailed explanations, the court does not in any way address the question of whether the disturbance and endangerment of public security and order that it assumes existed in fact afflicted the area at which the measure was directed. The assumption of the *Staatsgerichtshof* that the condition for the application of article 48 paragraph 2 existed not merely temporally, but also spatially, namely in the *Land* to which the measures for the restoration of public security and order referred, is expressed only indirectly, in the court's rejection of the objection made by the Prussian government that circumstances similar or comparable to those in Prussia obtained in other German states, though article 48 paragraph 2 was not applied against these other states.

It cannot seriously be doubted that the *Staatsgerichtshof*, just as it is competent to review whether the conditions for an application of article 48 paragraph 1 are satisfied, is equally competent to review the conditions for an application of article 48 paragraph 2. In both cases, the court has to ascertain whether a matter of fact determined by the constitution obtains or not. In the one case, the fact in question is the violation of a duty on the part of a *Land*, in the other it is that of a disturbance or endangerment of public security and order. That a question of law comes into play, in addition to the question of fact, in the first of these two cases – namely the question of whether the duty the violation of which is alleged is indeed laid down in the constitution or a federal law – cannot change the fact that the *Staatsgerichtshof* must, if it is competent to review the conditions for an application of article 48 paragraph 1, decide on questions of fact in just the same way as it will have to do if it is to review the conditions for an application of article 48 paragraph 2. Besides, the court would be barred, in case of a dispute over whether an application of article 48 paragraph 1 or 2 conforms to the constitution, from examining the conditions of this application only if such a restriction was explicitly contained in the constitution or in a statute implementing the constitution. But that is not the case. Article 19 of the constitution of the *Reich* confers on the *Staatsgerichtshof* the right to decide [**71**] the entire constitutional dispute at hand, without adding any restrictions. And in a constitutional dispute, the question of fact can have an even larger significance than the question of law; or, put more accurately, the question of law can consist in a question of fact, since even the so-called question of fact is a question of law. Whether it is useful to concede such an extensive competence to a constitutional court is a question *de lege ferenda*. *De lege lata*, there is no restriction on the question of law in the narrower sense, though such a restriction is considered desirable by some. In particular, there is no basis in positive law for differentiating, with a view to introducing that restriction, between a constitutional dispute under article 48 paragraph 1 and a constitutional dispute under article 48 paragraph 2.

III

The *Staatsgerichtshof* believes that it can and that it ought to evade the question, fundamental for its judgment in the present case, of whether public security and order were severely disturbed and endangered, although it is in fact unable to do so and has indeed answered the question. The court is all the more certain, on the other hand, that it is permitted to decide which measures may be employed, according to the constitution, for the restoration of public security and order. And accordingly, it pronounces the following proposition of law: it is permissible 'not only to put the police powers of Prussia into the hand of the *Reich*, but also to unite the *Reich's* and the state of Prussia's entire means of power in one hand and thus to direct the policies of the *Reich* and of Prussia onto the same track'. The term 'means of power' is used ambiguously in this sentence. It is employed in its central and narrower sense where the court speaks of the police powers as 'means of power'. The police – as the epitome of the armed organs of security – are a central means of the state's exercise of power. However, where the talk is of 'all the state's means of power', the court cannot be referring only to such means of the exercise of power, given that the unification of all of the 'means of power' of the *Reich* and of the state of Prussia in one hand is supposed to have the effect of directing 'the policies of the *Reich* and of Prussia onto the same track'. The 'entire means of power' of a *Land* include a lot more than its police powers. The entire policies of the *Reich* and of the respective *Land* could not possibly be directed onto the same track through a mere subordination of the organs of police in the narrower sense [**72**] to federal administrative institutions. A state's 'means of power', apparently, is supposed to refer here to the fullness of a state's power, to all its competences or functions. The *Staatsgerichtshof* wanted to express the view that the transfer of the entire competence of the Prussian government to the *Reich*, as it was ordered by the decree of the president of the *Reich*, is not unconstitutional, or at least not unconstitutional in principle. A little later, the court itself speaks of 'ministerial spheres of business', and thus of ministerial competences, as means of a state's power in the relevant sense. But the function of the Prussian minister for science, etc., is not a means of power in the same sense as are the forces of the armed police. If the transfer of that function to the *Reich* is also to be covered by the formula 'unification of the means of power of the *Reich* and of the state of Prussia', then 'means of power' must signify as much as 'fullness of power'. But if that is the case, the proposition of law expressed by the *Staatsgerichtshof* goes far beyond the decree of 20 July. The state's 'means of power', in the sense of the state's fullness of power, after all, include not only the competence or function of execution, in particular as it pertains to the state's government, but also that of legislation, i.e. the competence of the Prussian legislature. The proposition of law initially formulated by the *Staatsgerichtshof* declares it to be permissible to transfer to the *Reich* 'all the means of power' of a *Land*, and hence, on the basis of article 48 paragraph 2, to transfer the competences of the Prussian legislature, as well as the competences of the state's executive, to the chancellor of the *Reich*, or to a commissioner of the *Reich* appointed by and subject to the chancellor, or to some other organ of the *Reich*. And indeed, it is not clear why, assuming it is permissible to transfer the competences of a state's government to the *Reich* under article 48 paragraph 2, it should be impermissible to take a similar measure with regard to the competences of a state's legislature. If the activities of a government of a *Land* led by certain persons can stand in the way of the restoration of public security and order, so can the activity or inactivity, and all the more so, of a legislature of a *Land* that is composed in a certain way. A differentiation of legislative and executive competences, with regard to their transferability to the *Reich*, cannot be deduced from article 48 paragraph 2.

In any case, according to the first formulation of the legal opinion of the *Staatsgerichtshof* [**73**] on the permissibility of measures under article 48 paragraph 2, the content of the decree of the president of the *Reich* of 20 July must be regarded as constitutional in its entirety. However, the judgment of the *Staatsgerichtshof* declares, at the same time, that this is not the case.

IV

In a subsequent part of its explanation of its judgment, the *Staatsgerichtshof* offers a second formulation of its legal opinion which is somewhat weaker than the first. According to this version, it was permissible only to 'unify the means of power of the *Reich* and of the largest German *Land* in one hand and to homogenize the internal Prussian policies and the policies of the *Reich* to the extent possible'. Here, the court no longer talks of all of the state's means of power, and the internal policies of Prussia are to be homogenized with the policies of the *Reich* only 'to the extent possible'. However, in the further course of its explanation of its judgment, the *Staatsgerichtshof* abandons even this modified, second formulation of its legal opinion. It declares that 'the measures of article 48 paragraph 2 must, however, not only conform to the purpose of the restoration of public security and order, but must also remain within the intangible limits that result from the connection of this prescription with other provisions of the constitution of the *Reich*'. And the court expresses the view, as its 'permanent' opinion, that 'the president of the *Reich* remains bound, with the exception of the seven basic rights that he is free to suspend temporarily,* to all provisions of the constitution of the *Reich* that do not merely concern the distribution of competences between the *Reich* and the *Länder* or that delimit the competences of the several organs of the *Reich*'. This means that to the provisions of the constitution of the *Reich* that may be suspended under article 48 paragraph 2 belong (i) the provisions of those articles of the second part of the constitution of the *Reich* that are explicitly enumerated in article 48 paragraph 2 and (ii) the provisions of the constitution of the *Reich* that 'delimit the competences of the *Reich* and of the *Länder* and the competences of the several organs of the *Reich*'. The first point is not at issue here; it is only point (ii) that is relevant. With it, the *Staatsgerichtshof* returns once again to the first, far-reaching formulation of its legal opinion. The 'entire means of power of a state', in the wider sense of competences, and thus the authority of a *Land*, is based on the delimitation of the competences of the *Reich* and of the *Länder* established by the constitution of the *Reich*. [**74**] The *Länder* possess all those competences, and thus all those means of state power, in the sense of a fullness of power or authority to use power, that the constitution does not reserve to the *Reich*. The whole principle of federalism, and the principle of democracy that is essentially connected to it, insofar as it is supposed to be realized in the *Länder*, depends on the delimitation of the competences of the *Reich* and the *Länder*, as has already been shown. If the executive competence that is, according to the delimitation of competences in the constitution of the *Reich*, left to the *Länder* is transferred to the *Reich* by way of a measure under article 48 paragraph 2 – if, in other words, the provision of the constitution of the *Reich* that concerns the delimitation of competences is suspended – the two essential principles of the first, organizational part of the constitution of the *Reich* are thereby annulled. If one interprets article 48 paragraph 2 in this extensive sense, it will hardly be possible to speak of 'intangible limits' that restrict the application of article 48 paragraph 2. If the delimitation of the competences of the *Reich* and of the *Länder* can be removed by a measure under article 48 paragraph 2, then there simply are no constitutional limits to action under article 48 paragraph 2 that might somehow have to be observed. Article 48 paragraph 2 would include not just the opportunity to suspend certain articles that belong to the second part of the constitution of the *Reich*, and that are exhaustively enumerated in the article itself. Rather, it would also entail a power to annul the decisive provisions of the first part of the constitution, as far as these concern the position of the *Länder*.

However, the *Staatsgerichtshof* does not want its third formulation, a formulation that goes extraordinarily far if interpreted literally, to be understood in this sense. Rather, the court tries to decisively restrict it by claiming that 'the determinations concerning the position of the *Länder* within the *Reich* and the constitutional structure of the *Länder*, in particular those contained in articles 17, 60, and 63* of the constitution of the *Reich* belong to the constitutional provisions that do not mainly contain mere delimitations of competence'. This is evidently incorrect. If article 17 provides that every *Land* must have a democratic constitution – and it is this provision in particular to which the *Staatsgerichtshof* refers – and if this is to be understood so as to imply that this democratic constitution – as the *Staatsgerichtshof* itself also explicitly pronounces – guarantees 'to every *Land* the existence of an indigenous government of the *Land* that is formed in the *Land* itself', then article 17 must mean that the competences not reserved to the *Reich* [75] are to be exercised, as competences of the *Land*, exclusively by organs of the *Land* and not by organs of the *Reich*. The constitution of the *Reich* separates not only the material sphere of competence of the *Reich* from that which pertains to the *Länder*. It also determines the boundaries of the personal competence of the *Reich* in relation to that of the *Länder*, as well as the personal competence of the *Länder* in relation to that of the *Reich*. If the constitution, in article 17, guarantees 'to every *Land* the existence of an indigenous government of the *Land* that is formed in the *Land* itself', as the judgment of the *Staatsgerichtshof* rightly points out, it thereby guarantees nothing other than the personal competence of the *Land*. In other words, it guarantees to certain organs of the *Land* that are 'formed in the *Land* itself', and that are, for this precise reason, 'indigenous', the competence – a competence that excludes the competence of organs of the *Reich* or of other organs of the *Land* and that is, in this sense, personal – to exercise the material competence that the constitution grants to the *Land*. The material competence that a federal constitution grants to a constituent state is necessarily connected with a personal competence that is to be exercised by certain organs of the constituent state. The *Staatsgerichtshof*, when it speaks of 'competence', identifies it with material competence without paying heed to the issue of personal competence, which must lead to very troubling consequences, especially in the field of the constitutional law of a federal state. That article 17 constitutes a rule of personal competence already follows from the fact that this article can be violated through a mere transfer of the competence of a government of a *Land* to an organ of the *Reich*, since the power of government in the *Land*, in that case, is no longer exercised by an 'indigenous' government of the *Land*, as provided for by article 17, but rather by the government of the *Reich*. It is self-contradictory to declare, on the one hand, that 'a mere shift of competence, in the form of a transfer of business and powers from the government of the *Land* to an organ of the *Reich*' is permissible, but to demand, on the other hand, that the provision of article 17 be respected which guarantees to every *Land* its own government formed in the *Land* itself. Articles 60 and 63 of the constitution of the *Reich* referenced by the *Staatsgerichtshof* exhibit the same character. It belongs to the material competence of the *Land* to participate in the legislation and administration of the *Reich*, and we are faced with a provision that concerns personal competence when the constitution of the *Reich* confers this participation [**76**] of the *Land* in the central process of legislation and execution to the members of the governments of the *Länder*, in determining that the *Länder* are to be represented in the *Reichsrat* by the members of their own governments (and not by members of the government of the *Reich* or by members of the governments of other *Länder*). The representation of the *Land* in the *Reichsrat* thus falls within the competence of the governments of the *Länder*, as determined by the constitution of the *Reich*. If, as the decree of 20 July states, 'all competences' of the Prussian government are transferred to organs of the *Reich*, and thus also the competence to represent Prussia in the *Reichsrat*, then the decree amounts to a suspension of articles 60 and 63 of the constitution of the *Reich*, precisely because the measure brings about a shift of competences. It is therefore a contradiction in itself for the *Staatsgerichtshof* to declare that a mere shift of competences, in the form of a transfer of the business and the competences of the government of a *Land* to an organ of the *Reich*, is permissible, and yet to demand, on the other hand, that the provision of the articles 60 and 63 of the constitution of the *Reich* be respected according to which the *Länder* are to be represented in the *Reichsrat* by the members of their own government alone, i.e. by members of a government appointed in accordance with the constitution of the *Land*. The *Staatsgerichtshof* plainly goes wrong in speaking of a 'mere' shift of competence, and in speaking of provisions of the constitution of the *Reich* that 'merely' delimit the competences of the *Reich* in relation to the competences of the *Länder*. These provisions regarding the distribution of competence are by far the most important determinations of the constitution of a federal state. One must not forget, after all, that even the provisions of the constitution of the *Reich* that grant a right of legislation to the *Länder* 'merely' draw a line between the competences of the *Reich* and the competences of the *Länder*. Therefore, if the *Staatsgerichtshof* is of the opinion that the constitution's 'determinations with regard to the position of the *Länder* within the *Reich*' must not be affected by a measure under article 48 paragraph 2, it cannot, at the same time, hold to the opinion that such measures may be used to bring about a 'shift of competences' between the *Reich* and the *Länder*.

And the *Staatsgerichtshof* in fact concurs with the view that the shift of competences, namely the shift of the personal competences of the Prussian government to the government of the *Reich*, is a violation of article 17 of the constitution of the *Reich*, when it declares that 'no other organ can be put in the place of this government of the *Land*, not even temporarily'; to put one organ in the place of another, after all, [**76**] is the same thing as to bring about a shift of competences. The same holds for the violation of articles 60 and 63 of the constitution of the *Reich* which the *Staatsgerichtshof* declares in the following words: 'To strip a *Land* of its representation in the *Reichsrat* on the basis of article 48 paragraph 2 of the constitution of the *Reich*, and to transfer the right to represent the *Land* to a commissioner of the *Reich*, amounts to a substantial infringement of the position of the *Land* within the *Reich* as well as to a change in the composition of the *Reichsrat* that conflicts with its very nature; it is therefore impermissible to appoint a commissioner of the *Reich* as the *Land's* government and to remove the constitutionally appointed ministers of the *Land* from their offices'. This violation of articles 60 and 63 is nothing other than a transfer of the competence of the government of the *Land* to a commissioner of the *Reich*, and thus a shift of personal competence. But precisely what the *Staatsgerichtshof* here characterizes as a violation of articles 17, 60, and 63 is what the decree of 20 July presumed to do. The decree would, therefore, in accordance with the final formulation of the legal opinion of the *Staatsgerichtshof*, have to be regarded as unconstitutional, precisely insofar as it purports to transfer the constitutionally guaranteed competence of the government of a *Land* to organs of the *Reich*; insofar, in other words, as it is a 'mere shift of competences'; while it would have to be regarded as constitutional from the point of view of the first formulation of the legal opinion of the *Staatsgerichtshof*, according to which a transfer of the whole competence of the government of a *Land* to organs of the *Reich* is permissible, insofar as it is a necessary consequence of the unification of all the means of power of the *Reich* and of a *Land*.

V

A compromise between these two legal opinions that completely exclude one another would appear to be impossible. And yet, the *Staatsgerichtshof* has tried to offer such a compromise. After having pronounced that no other organ may be put, not even temporarily, in the place of the government of the *Land*, and that it is impermissible to install a commissioner of the *Reich* as the government of a *Land* as well as to remove the constitutionally appointed ministers from their offices, the *Staatsgerichtshof* declares of the decree of 20 July that did appoint a commissioner of the *Reich*, and that authorized the latter to function as the government of the *Land* and to remove the constitutionally appointed ministers from their offices: 'The decree, however, can be justified insofar as it is merely a shift of competences, [**78**] within the limits that arise from this character of the measure.' Since the whole decree amounts to nothing other than a shift of competences it would, again, have to be considered as constitutional, and as constitutional in its entirety. But the *Staatsgerichtshof* does not come to this conclusion. It says: 'It was possible to separate the competences of the Prussian ministers in matters relating to the *Land* from the sum of the powers of the Prussian state, and to transfer them to the commissioner of the *Reich* as an organ of the *Reich*, while leaving the current ministers in possession of their offices.' After having initially declared that, under article 48 paragraph 2, all the means of power of the state of Prussia – that is, as has already been shown, all the competences of all the organs of the *Land* of Prussia – may be transferred to organs of the *Reich*, the *Staatsgerichtshof* now attempts to distinguish between competences that may and competences that may not be taken from the government of the *Land* on the basis of article 48 paragraph 2. The distinction that is made here – or so it seems at first glance – to accomplish this end, between competences in 'matters relating to the *Land*' and other competences of the Prussian government, cannot really be drawn, for the reason that the ministers of a *Land* do not have any competences other than such as relate to matters of the *Land.* Every competence they are invested with as ministers of a *Land* is a competence of the *Land* and hence a competence in matters relating to the *Land.* The *Staatsgerichtshof* declares the following to be competences that may not be taken from the government of the *Land*: 'The representation of the *Land* towards the *Reich*, in particular in the *Reichsrat* and in the *Reichstag*, as well as the representation of the *Land* vis-à-vis other *Länder*, moreover the constitutional rights and duties towards the other highest organs of the *Land*'. However, there can be no serious doubt that the competence under article 60 and 63 to represent the *Land* in the *Reichsrat* is a matter relating to the *Land.* We are faced here with a matter that is of concern to the *Land* in the most eminent sense of the word, namely with the participation of the *Land* in the legislation and administration of the *Reich.* This is the function through which the *Land* as such takes the stage as a constituent member of the *Reich*, as a local institution that stands in contrast with the central government. The same goes for the representation in the *Reichstag* as well as for the representation towards other *Länder*. As far as the 'the constitutional rights and duties towards other highest organs of the *Land*' are concerned, these must, without a doubt, likewise be regarded as matters relating to the governance of the *Land.* [**79**]

The *Staatsgerichtshof*, however, justifies the inalienability of all these competences of the government of a *Land* not merely with the claim that they are not matters relating to the governance of the Land (that this justification is in play must be assumed because it would otherwise make no sense, in this context, to speak of 'competences of the Prussian ministers in matters relating to the governance of the *Land*'); the inalienability of the competences named above is justified above all with the claim that they are 'indispensable for the preservation of the independence of the *Land* and of its position within the *Reich*'. The view that only the competences listed above are indispensable, and not also the other competences in matters relating to the governance of the *Land*, in particular the whole inner administration of the *Land* (and perhaps also its legislation), is the less justified the more it is clear that the competences declared to be inalienable by the *Staatsgerichtshof* cannot even be exercised without the others, and in particular not without the competence to direct the administration of the *Land.* How is the government of a *Land* supposed to represent the *Land* in the *Reichsrat* or vis-à-vis another *Land*; how is it supposed to exercise its constitutional rights and duties towards the legislature of the *Land*; how, in particular, is it going to discharge its political responsibility to the legislature of the *Land*, if it has been stripped of the basis of all these rights and duties, if it can no longer exercise its main function, that of the direction of the administration of the *Land*, since the latter has been transferred to organs external to the *Land*, namely to organs of the *Reich*? The boundary that the *Staatsgerichtshof* tries to draw with this distinction between competences that may and competences that may not be taken away through measures to be enacted under article 48 paragraph 2 is not only altogether impossible practically, it also lacks even the slightest basis in positive law. It leads to the construction of ministers of a *Land*, a construction possible neither under the constitution of the *Reich* nor under the constitution of Prussia, whose constitutional competence is totally hollowed out, with the exception of a completely insignificant remainder that has been determined on altogether arbitrary grounds. To be sure, the *Staatsgerichtshof* declares: 'The constitutional government of the *Land*, within the framework of the constitution of the *Land*, must remain in existence.' At the same time, though, the court holds it to be permissible to deprive this government of the *Land* of almost all of its constitutionally conferred and therefore legally essential functions. According to the final legal opinion expressed by the *Staatsgerichtshof*, a measure taken under article 48 paragraph 2 finds its limit in the existence of a Prussian prime minister whom it cannot depose. [**80**] However, the provisions of articles 46 and 47 of the Prussian constitution, according to which the prime minister determines 'the guidelines of the policy of the government' and directs the business of the ministry of state, are not supposed to apply to this prime minister whose existence must be preserved even during a restoration of public security and order. But these are functions essential to the office of prime minister, and an organ that is not permitted to exercise these functions can no longer be regarded as a prime minister in the sense intended by the Prussian constitution. According to the legal opinion of the *Staatsgerichtshof*, there have to be Prussian ministers even while an action under article 48 paragraph 2 is taking place, and these must not be removed by the action as such; but the provision of article 46 of the Prussian constitution which determines that 'every minister of state independently leads the branch of administration committed to his care', within the guidelines set by the prime minister, is not supposed to apply to them. But persons that have been deprived of this essential function of a Prussian minister of state cease to be ministers in the sense intended by the Prussian constitution. A ministry of state, as it is characterized by the judgment of the *Staatsgerichtshof*, does not exist, neither under the constitution of the *Reich* nor under the constitution of the *Land* of Prussia. And even if it was possible to create organs that had only the competences which, according to the judgment of the *Staatsgerichtshof*, mark the absolute minimum due to members of the Prussian ministry of state, these organs could no longer be referred to as 'prime minister' or as 'minister of state' in the sense these words are given by the Prussian constitution. The Prussian constitution could no longer form the legal basis of their functioning. That basis would have to be the same as that of the commissioners of the *Reich*, to whom the competences of the Prussian ministry of state have been transferred almost completely: article 48 paragraph 2 and the decree of the president of the *Reich* issued in its execution. This so-called prime minister and these so-called ministers of state remain organs of the *Land* – however paradoxical this may appear – only with a view to their original appointment. Their competence no longer rests, in contrast to that of the real Prussian ministry of state, on the constitution of the *Reich* as well as on the Prussian constitution. Rather, it depends exclusively and solely on a norm of federal law: the decree of the president of the *Reich*; and, from this point of view, they would, strictly speaking, have to be regarded as organs of the *Reich*. [**81**] Provided, of course, that they are left with some remnant of competence, however small, which ought to be the case according to the judgment of the *Staatsgerichtshof*, but which is not the case according to the decree of 20 July.

VI

The construction of the *Staatsgerichtshof* – according to which the chancellor of the *Reich* and the commissioners of the *Reich* appointed by him and subject to him are the Prussian government and are legally entitled to conduct its business, while the person elected prime minister by the Prussian parliament and the persons appointed by him in accordance with the Prussian constitution are still to be referred to as the government of the *Land*, alongside the chancellor and his commissioners, though they are left with nothing but an insignificant remainder of competence that they cannot even exercise in a proper way, notwithstanding the fact that they are still to be responsible towards the Prussian parliament – must lead not only, as the *Staatsgerichtshof* itself fears, to 'tensions between the commissioner of the *Reich* and the government of the *Land*'; it must also lead to a legally as well as politically altogether untenable situation in which a 'harmonious co-operation for the benefit of the *Land* and the *Reich*' – a wish whose expression probably goes beyond the competence of the *Staatsgerichtshof* – clearly cannot be achieved. This is especially so if the sword of Damocles, in the form of the threatened sanction of the article 48 paragraph 1, hangs above one of the two 'governments', and only above one, namely above that which is a government of the state of Prussia only in name. The *Staatsgerichtshof*, after all, declares: 'If the government of the *Land* was to conduct its business, within the sphere of competence that remains in its possession, in a way that would have to be regarded as a violation of its duties towards the *Reich*, the president of the *Reich* could, on the basis of article 48 paragraph 1, initiate further interferences with the rights of the *Land*.' But how could the so-called government of the *Land* conduct its business in a way that would have to be regarded as a violation of its duties towards the *Reich*, given that it is no longer permitted to exercise the core powers of government? The only power that might become relevant, in this respect, is the participation in the legislation and administration of the *Reich*, through which the members of the government of the *Land* represent the *Land* in the *Reichsrat*, and which, according to the *Staatsgerichtshof*, is to be left to the Prussian government. But is a violation of a duty towards the *Reich* even possible in this context? Such a violation could only consist in making a proposal, or in voting on one. And is the *Land*, [**82**] insofar as it is supposed to be represented by its own government, not altogether free in this regard, according to the constitution of the *Reich*? It is difficult to think of a form of violation of duty towards the *Reich* other than the one that consists in an attempt, on the part of the members of the so-called government of the *Land* of Prussia, to create moral-political difficulties for the commissioner of the *Reich*, by refusing to engage in what the *Staatsgerichtshof* calls a 'harmonious co-operation'. But is that a violation of a legal duty under the constitution of the *Reich*? And what if the refusal to co-operate occurs on the side of the commissioner of the *Reich*? That is truly a *societas leonina*. In what, moreover, is the federal execution against the *Land* of Prussia to consist, which is to take place in case of a violation of duty on the part of the so-called government of the *Land*? This *Land*, after all, does not exist anymore. It has been turned, by the measures to restore public security and order, into a mere federal province administered directly by the *Reich*. A federal execution in the form of the use of armed force would make no sense here, if only for the reason that the persons against which it could be directed no longer dispose of any means of power and are therefore incapable of putting up violent resistance the suppression of which might require the use of armed force. This federal execution could only consist in a further shift of competence, namely in a decision on the part of the commissioner of the *Reich* – a decision that, according to the decree 'concerning the restoration of public security and order in the territory of the *Land* of Prussia' that is now in force, he is in any case already authorized to take – to deprive the so-called members of the government of the state of Prussia of their right, a right that is already practically unusable, to represent Prussia in the *Reichsrat* and in the *Reichstag* and to transfer that right to an organ of the *Reich*. This federal execution would have no other meaning than that of depriving a province of the *Reich* of even the last appearance of a '*Land*', in the sense intended by the constitution of the *Reich*, an appearance that the measure that was taken for the restoration of public security and order would still have left it, if it had been enacted in accordance with the judgment of the *Staatsgerichtshof*.

VII

For the most part, the *Staatsgerichtshof* expresses its legal opinion on the decree of the president of the *Reich* of 20 July and on the measures that are permissible, in general as well as in particular, under article 48 paragraph 1 and paragraph 2 only in the opinion justifying its judgment, but not in the judgment itself. The latter does not even contain the central findings; [**82**] in the first place, it does not contain the decision on the question of whether the action ordered by the decree of the president of the *Reich* is to be recognized as what it is referred to by the decree itself, namely as a federal execution against Prussia; whether, in other words, it can be based on article 48 paragraph 1 or not, and therefore whether it is constitutional insofar as it purports to be a federal execution. The *Staatsgerichtshof* decisively denies that question, but only in its opinion. Now, one may certainly disagree over the question of whether the *Staatsgerichtshof*, in a case where it deems the preconditions for an application of article 48 paragraph 1 not to have been present, must express its legal opinion – the opinion that the *Land* that appealed to it, and against which the execution had been directed, did not violate any duty towards the *Reich* – in the tenor of the judgment itself. One can reasonably take the view that this belongs in the justification of the judgment; but into the justification of a judgment that clearly states that the federal execution was unconstitutional and that it is – insofar as it still continues – unconstitutional. If for no other reason, this is necessary in order to make possible the execution of the judgment envisaged in the last paragraph of article 19.* It is only the judgment that can be executed, not the legal opinion that justifies it. And in executing a judgment of the *Staatsgerichtshof*, the president of the *Reich* is obliged to discontinue a federal execution held to be unconstitutional only if it has been declared to be unconstitutional in the judgment of the *Staatsgerichtshof*, i.e. in the tenor of this judgment. One surely cannot reproach the organ tasked with the execution of a judgment if, in taking the required action, it keeps strictly to the judgment itself, i.e. to the tenor of the judgment, and not to the opinion justifying the judgment, an opinion that – as the judgment of the *Staatsgerichtshof* itself clearly illustrates – need not always be very unambiguous. Accordingly, the president of the *Reich* is under no obligation, in the present case, to discontinue the federal execution that the *Staatsgerichtshof* has qualified as unconstitutional in its opinion, but not in its judgment. The president, in other words, is under no obligation to rescind his decree of 20 July insofar as it invokes article 48 paragraph 1. With respect to this point, the decree still remains valid, and the action taken pursuant to it, therefore, remains in force as a federal execution against Prussia, notwithstanding the fact that the *Staatsgerichtshof* has declared – though only in the justification of its judgment – [**84**] that Prussia did not violate any duty towards the *Reich*.

With regard to the application of article 48 paragraph 2, the *Staatsgerichtshof* likewise failed to declare in the tenor of its judgment that the decree of 20 July is unconstitutional. The judgment states, rather, that the decree 'is compatible with the constitution of the *Reich*'; but it adds, 'insofar as it appoints the chancellor of the *Reich* as a federal commissioner for the *Land* of Prussia and insofar as it authorizes the chancellor temporarily to deprive the Prussian ministers of their competences and to exercise these competences himself or to transfer them to other persons acting as federal commissioners. But this authorization could not permissibly go so far as to deprive the Prussian ministry of state and its members of the right to represent the *Land* of Prussia in the federal parliament, in the *Reichsrat*, or towards the *Reich*, towards the legislature of the *Land*, the Prussian council of state, or towards other *Länder*.' This is apparently meant to express the view that the decree of 20 July, while constitutional, is constitutional only in part. A distinction is drawn, it appears, between a constitutional part of the decree and another part that is qualified, not directly but indirectly, as unconstitutional. The possibility of judging a statute or a decree that is submitted for review to a constitutional court to be partially constitutional and partially unconstitutional may well be given, under certain circumstances; for instance, in cases where only particular provisions, provisions that can be externally delimited or separated, such as individual sentences or words of the statute or the decree, and that can be taken out of the context of meaning constituted by the text as a whole, fail to be compatible with the constitution, whereas the other provisions in the statute or decree conform to the constitution. But the case is different if the statute or the decree in question cannot be divided into constituent parts that are open to differing legal evaluation, if it is unconstitutional in its entirety, because it goes farther in a particular direction than the constitution permits, and if it thus would have to be given a completely different wording, one that would restrict its material scope, in order to become constitutional. In this case, the constitutional court is not permitted to declare the statute or the decree in question to be one part constitutional and one part unconstitutional.

The difference between these two cases is of essential importance for the legal effect of the judgment. [85] The latter must consist – if the judgment of the *Staatsgerichtshof* is to have any legal effect at all – in the annulment of the norm qualified as unconstitutional, be it that the cassation is brought about immediately by the judgment itself, or be it that it is performed by an organ charged with the execution of the judgment, with effect *ex nunc* or *ex tunc*. Absolute, *a priori* nullity as opposed to mere annullability of the unconstitutional norm (i.e. the nullity that, for example, attached to the directives that were issued by the captain of *Köpenick**) obtains only if the norm in question never enjoyed any legal validity at all, and if, consequently, an act of public authority, and in particular a judgment of a constitutional court, is not needed to declare its 'nullity' or, in other words, to bring about its annulment. Since neither the constitution of the *Reich* nor the statute concerning the *Staatsgerichtshof* endow the judgments of this tribunal, judgments which decide constitutional disputes under article 19 of the constitution of the *Reich*, with an immediate power to annul general legal norms, of the kind that the statute implementing article 13 of the constitution of the *Reich** (of 8 April 1920, RGBl. p. 510) attributes to the relevant judgments of the *Reichsgericht* by providing the latter with 'statutory force', one would have to assume that a decree that is held to be unconstitutional by the *Staatsgerichtshof* is not immediately annulled by the court's judgment itself, but that its annulment requires a subsequent act of the president of the *Reich* who, according to article 19, is responsible for the execution of the judgment. This would have to apply, in particular, to legal acts that have been issued on the basis of the norm that is judged to be unconstitutional, and to which the judgment of the *Staatsgerichtshof* does not directly refer. The prevailing opinion, admittedly, leans toward the view that decisions of the *Staatsgerichtshof* such as that of 25 October are to be regarded as declaratory judgments that do not stand in need of execution, since they merely state the nullity, in purely declaratory terms, of the norm that has been recognized as unconstitutional. However, using that language, one expresses – in a way that is not very correct from a legal-scientific point of view – that these judgments annul the norm that has been recognized as unconstitutional with effect *ex tunc*. After all, one clearly cannot regard as *a priori* null a decree, such as the decree of 20 July, that the president of the *Reich* enacted within the apparent limits of his competence, on the basis of article 48 paragraph 2, and that was executed by the administrative organs of the *Reich* and of the *Länder* in numerous particular legal acts. If the decree is unconstitutional, i.e. if it is claimed, by some party or other, that the decree is unconstitutional, for the alleged reason that it incorrectly applies article 48 paragraph 2, [**86**] one will have to keep in mind that the constitution appoints the president of the *Reich*, in the first place, to apply and thus to interpret article 48 paragraph 2; and that the president's legal opinion, insofar as it is expressed in his decree, remains binding until it is declared to be unconstitutional by some other institution that is authorized by the constitution to apply and to interpret article 48 paragraph 2, namely by the *Staatsgerichtshof*, whose judgments, and not those of just anyone, can alone overturn the presumption of the legality of the president's actions. One cannot claim that the judgment of the *Staatsgerichtshof* merely states the nullity of the decree of the president of the *Reich* in purely declaratory fashion, and that the decree was already null before the court rendered its judgment, if one is forced to concede that this 'nullity' enters the sphere of the law only with the judgment. Unless the judgment is to be completely superfluous, one is forced to concede as well that the view that the decree is null can, in advance of the judgment, be no more than a private opinion; just like any other opinion expressed by a person other than the one who is authorized by legal order to declare that some judgment taken by a court is legally incorrect. If, in other words, one has to concede that an act of public authority is necessary, that appeal needs to be made to the

Staatsgerichtshof, and that the latter has to declare the unconstitutionality of a decree for the so-called 'nullity' of the decree to take effect, and if the *Staatsgerichtshof* judges this 'nullity' to be a partial one only, then one cannot reasonably uphold the claim that the decree was null even before the court rendered its judgment. The judgment by which the *Staatsgerichtshof* pronounces the incompatibility of the decree of the president of the *Reich* with the constitution has – though it appears with effect *ex tunc* or, rather, the more so because it appears with effect *ex tunc* – a decidedly constitutive character; just as every act that has a legal effect, and thus qualifies as a legal act, is constitutive, and just as any act that has no legal effect is no legal act and moreover completely superfluous.

Regardless of what effect one attributes to the judgment of the *Staatsgerichtshof*, regardless of whether one takes it to bring about only a mediate or rather an immediate cassation of the norm that is found to be unconstitutional, the judgment must, in any case, announce in unambiguous terms whether the decree is unconstitutional in its entirety, and is therefore annulled, or to be annulled, as a whole; or it must, if the court holds only a part of the decree to be unconstitutional, make clear which of its parts – that is, what paragraphs or sentences or even only words of the decree – are annulled as unconstitutional, or to be annulled as unconstitutional, and which are left standing, or to be left standing. If the unconstitutionality of the decree consists in the fact that the decree as a whole goes beyond a line drawn in the constitution, [**87**] and if the decree thus has to be annulled as a whole, and to be replaced with a differently worded decree, in order to restore a situation conformable to the constitution, then the judgment of the *Staatsgerichtshof* must declare the decree as a whole to be unconstitutional, so that the president will annul it as a whole, or so that he replaces it with another decree – in case the original decree is to be regarded as having already been annulled, with effect *ex tunc*, by the judgment itself – that stays within the limits that the constitution, in the opinion of the *Staatsgerichtshof*, imposes on such decrees. In the present case, the *Staatsgerichtshof* has determined these limits in the tenor of its judgment, but it has neglected to declare the decree to be unconstitutional, and, in order to avoid such a declaration, it has characterized the relationship of the decree to the constitution with the formula: 'constitutional, insofar as . . . ', although this formula is altogether inapplicable, given the legal opinion that the *Staatsgerichtshof*, after some vacillation, finally expresses in its opinion. According to this legal opinion, the decree is altogether unconstitutional, since the latter does not merely authorize the chancellor of the *Reich*, whom it appoints as a federal commissioner, 'temporarily to deprive the Prussian ministers of their powers of office' but rather to 'remove the members of the Prussian ministry of state from their offices', and to do so with permanent effect – this is how the *Staatsgerichtshof* itself understands the decree – and since it authorizes the chancellor of the *Reich* to strip the Prussian ministry of state and its members of all their official competences. The decree, consequently, includes an authorization to deprive the Prussian ministry of state and its members of the right to represent the *Land* of Prussia in the *Reichsrat*, and towards the *Reich*, the Prussian legislature, the council of state, or towards other *Länder*, which the judgment of the *Staatsgerichtshof* expressly declares to be impermissible. That the *Staatsgerichtshof* states, in its judgment, what content the decree would have to have in order to be constitutional is perhaps very useful politically, but such a statement is superfluous from a legal-technical point of view. In this particular case, such a statement is even highly questionable, since the judgment is capable of applying the inappropriate formula 'conformable with the constitution of the *Reich* insofar as . . . ' (i.e. in part constitutional, in part unconstitutional) only because the court engages in the fiction that the content of a decree conformable to the constitution, as it is set out in its own opinion, [**88**] already enjoys legal force as the constitutional part of the existing decree that the court had to review. Since the judgment of the *Staatsgerichtshof*, with the help of this formula, which in no way conforms to the true state of affairs, avoided the pronouncement that the decree is unconstitutional, a pronouncement essential to its legal effect, the president of the *Reich*, if he keeps closely to the wording of the tenor of the judgment – as is his right and perhaps even his duty – is not, strictly speaking, under an obligation to rescind his decree of 20 July. If one assumes, by contrast, that such an annulment on the part of the president is superfluous, for the reason that the decree is annulled by the judgment of the *Staatsgerichtshof* itself, and with effect *ex tunc* (if one holds, that is, that the judgment merely 'declares' the 'nullity' of the decree, as some authors think), then it is altogether unclear, what exactly is to be regarded as 'null', according to the judgment of 25 October. Clearly not the decree as a whole. Hence, a part of the decree only. But which part? The judgment does not make that clear, and it could not have done so, since its true meaning, though it is not explicitly stated, is after all the following: that the decree of 20 July is 'null' in its entirety, and that some other decree is valid, a decree the content of which is described in the judgment of the *Staatsgerichtshof*, but that has not, so far, been enacted by the president of the *Reich*. If one wanted to reach the conclusion that the state of affairs judged to be constitutional by the *Staatsgerichtshof* has already been brought about by the judgment itself, and if one is not content to identify that state of affairs with the annulment of the decree of 20 July, but takes it to consist, rather, in the fact that there already exists a decree that conforms to the legal opinion expressed in the judgment of the *Staatsgerichtshof*, then one would have to assume that the original decree automatically transformed itself into the decree judged constitutional by the court; even though one will find no traces of such a metamorphosis in the text published in the RGBl. I, p. 377. It would, then, be altogether impossible to inform oneself about the content of the new decree by reading it in the *Reichsgesetzblatt*. Rather, one would have to draw that content, by way of interpretation, from the judgment of the *Staatsgerichtshof*, a judgment that is not even published in the *Reichsgesetzblatt*. And this legal metamorphosis would also have to have taken place with regard to the legal acts enacted in accordance with the decree of 20 July, acts to which the tenor of the judgment of the *Staatsgerichtshof* does not even refer in any way. With all this, one would attribute to the judgment of the *Staatsgerichtshof* not merely a power to annul general legal norms, but also a power to reform them, [**89**] i.e. a power to replace a decree that the court judges to be unconstitutional, and thus annuls *ex tunc*, with another decree, a decree the content of which is determined by the court itself. This view, consequently, implies a right on the part of the *Staatsgerichtshof* to issue decrees, a right that competes with the competence of the president of the *Reich* based on article 48 paragraph 2. That the constitution provides no basis whatsoever for such a judicial right to issue decrees should be self-evident. But it is to be suspected that the *Staatsgerichtshof* – since it follows the prevailing opinion on the effect of its judgments – expects its decision to have precisely this effect.

The juristic critique of the *Staatsgerichtshof's* judgment thus leads to a rather unsatisfactory result. But it would be unjust to make the *Staatsgerichtshof* responsible for that result, either exclusively or even only for the most part. The root of the problem lies in the technical insufficiency of the Weimar Constitution* itself.

The latter created a very complicated federal system with a finely balanced distribution of competences between the *Reich* and the *Länder*, but it did not consider it necessary to fit this system with effective guarantees for its own preservation. The constitution neglected, in particular, to create a purposefully constructed system of constitutional adjudication. The design that the *Staatsgerichtshof* – which, of course, can take action only in a very limited range of cases – has in fact been given shows very clearly the distaste that German jurisprudence has always had for such a judicial control of the 'political' sphere, a sphere that it takes to be outside of the law. The constitution's provisions concerning the *Staatsgerichtshof*, as a result, are little more than a makeshift improvisation. The questions most important from a technical point of view, for example that of the effect of the judgment, were left open, which has created ample room for the most contradictory interpretations. The gravest technical deficiency, however, afflicts the formulation of article 48, and in particular of its paragraph 2, precisely the constitutional article that is in especially urgent need of a judicial control of its application if the system of federalism is to be preserved. This article provides the president of the *Reich* with a right to take measures for the restoration of public security and order, and thus to interfere with the competences of the *Länder*, without limiting the scope of such interference in an unambiguous way. The determination of this limit, a most important issue which is decisive for the whole structure of the constitution, [**90**] is left to an implementing statute. The consequence of this legal technique is that the organs that are called upon to apply article 48 enjoy an altogether unbounded discretion, as long as the implementing statute has not been enacted, with respect to one of the most essential questions of the constitution: the question of the extent to which the competences of a *Land* may be transferred to the *Reich*. The intention of the authors of the Weimar Constitution must surely have been directed at restricting the measures to be taken under article 48 paragraph 2, and hence the transfer of competences of the *Land* to the *Reich* that goes along with the latter, as far as possible. Certainly, the framers did not in the least contemplate the possibility, under the title of a restoration of public security and order, of a transfer of the whole competence of a *Land*, as provided for by the rest of the constitution, or even only of the essential elements of that competence, to organs of the *Reich*. It should be clear that an interpretation conformable to the intentions of the legislator must not take the measures that are permitted under article 48 paragraph 2 to include anything more than the function of securing public order, in the narrowest sense of the word. The constitution, however, expressed the intention of its authors which stands behind its text – an intention that, needless to say, can never be determined with the same degree of objectivity as the content of a statutory text, and that is, even if it can be determined, not a means of interpretation exclusive of others – in a manner that is altogether deficient from a legal-technical point of view. It created no guarantees whatsoever to ensure that only a restrictive, but not an extensive interpretation of article 48 paragraph 2 can acquire the force of law. As long as the limits within which any measures that may have to be taken to restore public security and order are to remain not clearly determined by a general legal norm that bears the character of a constitutional statute, the legal possibility of a presidential decree – and thus also of a judgment of the *Staatsgerichtshof* – through which *Land*-competences, and not just those of one *Land* only but possibly those of all the *Länder*, are claimed by the *Reich* to an even greater extent than in the decree of 20 July or in the judgment of the *Staatsgerichtshof* of 25 October is not excluded. As long as the constitution itself does not prevent it, it is the constitution itself that creates the possibility of transforming the *Reich* from a federal state into a unitary state by way of an application of article 48 paragraph 2.* It would be a form of self-deception [**91**] to close one's eyes to this possibility and to put one's trust in an 'intentional' interpretation of a constitutional article whose wording provides the opportunity to annul the most important organizational determinations of other articles. The judgment of the *Staatsgerichtshof* provides the least occasion for optimism in this regard. Leaving aside the fact that its somewhat restrictive interpretation of the decree of the president of the *Reich* applies to no more than one single case, the court's attempt to construct the limits for measures to be taken under article 48 paragraph 2 by way of exegesis must be regarded as a complete failure. Such a limit cannot, in principle, be gained by way of interpretation; it can only be created by way of constitutional legislation. The interpretation that comes to expression in the decree of 20 July is no less plausible, within the wide frame of article 48 paragraph 2, than the interpretation put forward by the *Staatsgerichtshof*. No person thinking reasonably will be able to deny that the former clearly merits preference to the latter from a legal-political point of view, since it creates a situation that, while being radically centralistic, is at least feasible from the point of view of administrative technique. The *Staatsgerichtshof*, however, in its humanly understandable desire to forge a compromise between the two extremes of an extensive interpretation, of the sort that grounds the decree of 20 July, and of a restrictive one, as it was advocated by the government of the *Land* of Prussia, managed only to increase the confusion of the legal situation. The constitution of Weimar has not been saved on the path of the golden middle sought out by the judgment of the *Staatsgerichtshof*.

NOTES

Chapter 1

[**1486**] *conception of the relationship*: For Kelsen's critique of the traditional understanding of the separation of powers see Kelsen (1924); Kelsen (1925), 255–61; Kelsen (1945), 269–82. On the theory of legal hierarchy compare Kelsen (1934), 55–75; Kelsen (1945), 123–35.

[**1487**] *the thoroughly legal nature of the functions of the state*: Kelsen argued that an act can only be attributed to the state if it is legally authorized. See Kelsen (1914). Hence, he held that it is impossible for an act of state to be altogether lawless (as opposed to being legally defective and therefore annullable). Kelsen arrived at the conclusion that the state, from a legal-theoretical point of view, must be regarded as identical to its legal order. See Kelsen (1928a), 114–204; Kelsen (1934), 99–106.

[**1488**] *the well-known monarchical principle*: The principle in nineteenth-century German public law that a monarch remains sovereign even in a constitutional monarchy. The principle portrays the constitution as a monarchical concession and constitutional restrictions on monarchical government as a voluntary and revocable self-restraint. See Stolleis (1992), 102–5.

[**1489**] *ministerial responsibility*: The principle of ministerial responsibility required that an act issued by the monarch, to be valid, had to be countersigned by a minister who assumed legal and political responsibility for the act. See Stolleis (1992), 105–6, 111.

[**1489**] *concept of the constitution*: See for Kelsen's concept of constitution Kelsen (1925), 248–55; Kelsen (1945), 124–8, 258–69 and Alexy (2005).

[**1490**] *the constitution in the material sense . . . is also the constitution in the formal sense*: To clarify, the constitution in the material sense is made up of norms that determine the process of legislation. The constitution in the formal sense, by contrast, consists of norms protected by a special procedure of amendment. Every polity possesses a constitution in the material sense, but not every polity has a constitution in the formal sense. Where the norms that determine the process of legislation are protected by a special procedure of amendment, the constitution in the material sense will be (or be a part of) the constitution in the formal sense. The constitution in the formal sense can, in addition, contain norms other than those that determine the process of legislation, for instance basic rights that limit the permissible content of legislation. See also Kelsen (1925), 251–3; Kelsen (1945), 124–8.

[**1491**] *enacted as a constitutional statute*: Enacted as a *Verfassungsgesetz*, i.e. in the form of a constitutional amendment.

[**1491**] *the constitution . . . authorizes the ordinary legislator to restrict these freedoms*: In German constitutional monarchies of the nineteenth century, basic rights were often protected by constitutional provisions that made limitations of rights depend on a statutory basis (and thus on parliamentary approval). The Weimar Constitution's bill of rights still relied on this technique (see articles 109 *et seq.*). A constitutional provision of this sort has no protective effect against a parliamentary majority, at least unless further restrictions on legislative interference with rights are added. Hence, many Weimar-era constitutional scholars argued that at least some of the rights-provisions of the Weimar Constitution were empty ('*leerlaufend*'). See Anschütz (1933), 517–20.

[**1494**] *the primacy of an individual state's legal order*: Kelsen argued that national and international law must, on pain of logical inconsistency of one's description of a legal system, be conceived as parts of one, encompassing legal system. But he held that this monist view of a legal system is open to two different ways of legal-theoretic construction: Either, legal theory can take a national monist point of view and regard international law as valid only insofar as it is incorporated into national law or legal theory can take an international monist point of view and regard national law as validated by norms of public international law. See Kelsen (1934), 111–25; Kelsen (1945), 363–88; and von Bernstorff (2010), 104–7.

[**1497**] *the civil liability of the organ that enacted the legally defective act*: See Kelsen (1914); Kelsen (1925), 277–8, 285–301; and Kelsen (1945), 159–61 for further discussion of the distinction between nullity and annullability.

[**1498**] *annulment ... with effectiveness ex tunc*: An annulment with retroactive effect.

[**1504**] *sovereignty ... must be an attribute of the order of the state*: Kelsen argued in Kelsen (1920) that the only coherent way to conceive of sovereignty is to understand sovereignty as a property of normative order, namely as the normative independence of a legal order. If the state is identical to its legal order, it follows that sovereignty can also be described as an attribute of the state, but never as a power that originally inheres in a particular organ of state. See also Kelsen (1925), 102–15.

[**1511**] *the legal-technical development of contemporary international law*: For Kelsen's advocacy of international adjudication see von Bernstorff (2010), 191–220.

[**1516**] *simply the expression of certain group-interests*: For Kelsen's view of justice and his critique of natural law see, for instance, Kelsen (1957) and Kelsen (1928b).

[**1525**] *in the sense of an alternative*: This is Kelsen's doctrine of normative alternatives, which appears to claim that the constitution equally authorizes legal and legally defective acts of state. See also Kelsen (1934), 71–5, 117–19. The context in which the doctrine is introduced here suggests that Kelsen is not, as some commentators have argued, indifferent to the alternative of constitutional legality/illegality. See Paulson (1980); Kletzer (2005); Vinx (2007), 78–100.

[**1525**] *to deny its legal character altogether*: For a radical example that Kelsen may have had in mind see Erich Kaufmann (1911). Schmitt (1926b) comes close to a denial of international law.

[**1527**] *in a federal state*: For Kelsen's theory of federalism, which conceives of both levels of government as equally subject to the constitution but independent from one another, see Kelsen (1925), 207–25; Kelsen (1927), 128–46; Wiederin (2005).

[**1528**] *the law of the Reich breaks the law of the Land*: German public law doctrine traditionally distinguishes between confederate states (*Staatenbund*) and federal states (*Bundesstaat*). It assumes that sovereignty must either, in a *Staatenbund*, rest with the constituent states or else, in a *Bundesstaat*, be vested in the federal government, so that the laws of the latter override the laws of constituent states in case of conflict. See Stolleis (1992), 364–8. The principle that the law of the *Reich* breaks the law of a *Land* was affirmed by the Weimar Constitution (in article 13).

[**1529**] *federal execution of the constitution*: For the German '*Reichsexekution*', i.e. the enforcement of the constitution of a federal state against the government of a constituent state, if need be with coercive means. The powers of the president of the Weimar Republic under article 48 paragraph 1 were an example of a power of federal execution. Compare Kelsen (1927).

[**1529**] *Guidelines of the co-rapporteur*: At the meetings of the *Vereinigung der Deutschen Staatsrechtslehrer*, two authors would give presentations on the same topic, which were then discussed by the other scholars present at the conference. At the meeting in 1928, Kelsen gave the second presentation on constitutional adjudication, after Heinrich Triepel had already spoken about the same topic. Hence, Kelsen is referred to as the co-rapporteur (to Triepel). The summary of his paper offered here is apparently Kelsen's own.

Chapter 2

[**12**] *the Reichsgericht . . . in its decision of 4 November 1925*: RGZ 111, 320 ff. In this decision, the *Reichsgericht* reviewed the constitutionality of a statute that provided for the partial revaluation of debts which had been devalued by hyperinflation. Its argument for the existence of such a right was rather thin. The court held that the fact that the constitution did not explicitly deny the existence of a right of review implied that such a right existed. Schmitt discusses the *Reichsgericht's* argument for a power of constitutional review in detail in Schmitt (1929b), 89–96.

[**13**] *a jurisdictional state*: For Schmitt's distinction between legislative, administrative, and jurisdictional states compare Schmitt (1932a), 3–14; 75–77 above in this chapter.

[**13**] *Staatsgerichtshof . . . Staatsgerichtsbarkeit*: Literally, a court/judicature in matters of state. The term is used here to refer generically to a special constitutional court of the Continental European type.

[**15**] *Reichsfinanzhof, Reichsversorgungsgericht, Preußisches Oberverwaltungsgericht*: The 'Federal Court of Finance' (that dealt with appeals against the administration of federal taxes), the 'Federal Court of Provision' (that dealt with appeals against administrative decisions concerning social security), and the Prussian Superior Administrative Court, respectively.

[**16**] *article 76 of the constitution of the Reich*: The article determined the procedure for enacting constitutional amendments. Under article 76, the Weimar Constitution could be amended by the *Reichstag* with a majority of two-thirds.

[**16**] *important question in constitutional law*: Schmitt defended the view that the Weimar Constitution contained limits to constitutional amendment that could make formally valid constitutional amendments materially unconstitutional. See Schmitt (1932a), 39–58 and Schmitt (1928), 72–4, 79–81, 150–8. This view had no basis in the text of the constitution, and it was rejected by most other Weimar-era constitutional lawyers. See, for instance, Anschütz (1933), 402–6; Thoma (1932), 153–5.

[**16**] *apocryphal acts of sovereignty*: Hidden or concealed acts of sovereignty. Compare Schmitt (1928), 154–6. Schmitt uses the term to refer to the Weimar-era practice of enacting statutes that violate the constitution under the procedural form of a constitutional amendment, but without making any change to the constitutional text.

[**17, n. 14**] *note 5 on pp. 9–10*: Schmitt points out that a parliament can, in a constitutional monarchy, come to occupy the role of a guardian of the constitution against the executive. See Schmitt (1931a), 9–10.

[**17**] *article 105 and article 109*: Article 105 determined that extraordinary courts are impermissible. Article 109 protected the equality of all Germans before the law.

[**19**] *the situation of normality that is presupposed by any norm*: Compare Schmitt (1934a); Schmitt (1922), 5–15.

[**19**] the *Freirechtsbewegung*: Literally, the 'free law movement'. Anti-formalist legal-theoretical movement in late nineteenth- and early twentieth-century Germany that emphasized the indeterminacy of law and advocated the use of judicial power for social reform. See Rückert (2008).

[**22**] *as I have shown several times*: See for constitutional law Schmitt (1929b) and for international law Schmitt (1926b).

[**22**] *difference between constitution and constitutional statute*: Schmitt argued that a constitution, in the primary sense, is not a set of constitutional laws but rather a fundamental political decision, taken by the constituent power, for a certain form of social and political order. Schmitt held that the content of that decision is legally inviolable by any act of any constituted power, including any act of the constitutional legislator acting under a constitution's amendment procedure. See Schmitt (1928), 75–81.

[**22**] *a statute in the formal or political sense*: Schmitt refers to a standard distinction in German public law theory of the Wilhelmine and Weimar periods. Roughly, a statute in the material sense must be a general legal norm that is addressed to the subjects of the state and that affects their individual rights and duties. By contrast, any decision taken by the legislature qualifies as a statute in the formal sense, even if it does not amount to the enactment of a general legal norm affecting the rights and duties of subjects. For instance, where the decision on a budget is to be taken through the legislative process, the resulting budget would be a statute in the formal sense, but it would not be a statute in the material sense. See Thoma (1932), 124–7 for a Weimar-era definition of the distinction and Caldwell (1997), 16–25 for an account of its historical origins. Schmitt suggests elsewhere that the parliamentary enactment of norms that are statutes merely in the formal sense undermines the separation of powers and the rule of law and should be restricted as much as possible. See Schmitt (1928), 181–96. Compare also chapter 3 above at [128] *et seq.*, where Schmitt uses the distinction to argue that the president has the power to enact financial emergency decrees without parliamentary approval.

[**25, n. 29**] *see also p. 142 below*: Schmitt claims that Otto Bauer's democratic theory, like Kelsen's, is unconsciously Millian, and thus liberal rather than truly democratic. Schmitt's view that democracy presupposes homogeneity was accepted, from a Marxist perspective, by Max Adler, whose views formed a negative foil for the development of Kelsen's pluralist theory of democracy. See Somek (2001).

[**25**] *the outvoted minority has made a mistake concerning its own true will*: Compare Rousseau (1988), 151 [Book IV, chapter 2]. Schmitt frequently invokes Rousseau as an authority for the claim that democracy consists in the identity of ruler and ruled and must therefore be based on a substantive homogeneity of the citizenry. See Schmitt (1926a), 8–15, 22–32 and Schmitt (1928), 257–67.

[**28**] *the Prussian conflict of 1862–6*: The conflict arose, in 1862, from a refusal of the Prussian parliament to approve a budget that would have included a sharp increase

in military expenditure. The Prussian government under Bismarck's leadership argued that the king, as sovereign, was obliged to continue to operate the state even without a budget authorizing the necessary expenditures. The theory was successfully put to the test, and parliament backed down in 1866 by passing a 'law of indemnity' retroactively authorizing the expenditures that had been made. See Caldwell (1997), 16–19.

[**29**] *the president of the Reich dissolved the Reichstag*: The *Reichstag* had on 16 July 1930 rejected a bill introduced by Brüning that was to stabilize public finances by lowering public expenditures and raising taxes. After the *Reichstag* had voted the bill down, Brüning issued an emergency decree containing the relevant provisions of the bill. On 18 July 1932, the *Reichstag* demanded the annulment of the decree, under article 48 paragraph 3 of the Weimar Constitution. Brüning retaliated by instantly dissolving the *Reichstag*, and then issued a new emergency decree with the same content. See Mommsen (2009), 358–61; Kolb and Schumann (2013), 132–4.

[**31**] *quis iudicabit*: Compare Schmitt (1922), 30–5.

[**33**] *will still have to speak . . . of a federal organization of the state*: Schmitt argues (see Schmitt (1931a), 54–60) for a narrow interpretation of the competences of the *Staatsgerichtshof* under article 19 of the Weimar Constitution. That article provided the *Staatsgerichtshof* with jurisdiction over constitutional conflicts within a *Land* and over disputes between several *Länder* or between a *Land* and the *Reich*, provided these were not grounded in private law. Schmitt is concerned to restrict the jurisdiction of the *Staatsgerichtshof* to the enforcement of the Weimar Constitution's provisions concerning the internal political organization of the *Länder*. He rejects the view that a private person or social group should have the right to appeal to the *Staatsgerichtshof* against organs of a *Land*.

[**33**] *Reichsabgabenordnung*: A federal framework law on taxation, enacted in December 1919 (RGBl. 1919, 1993).

[**34**] *so-called Dawes plan*: The Dawes plan was a plan of payment for the reparations Germany was obliged to pay under the treaty of Versailles. It was put in place in 1924 after Germany had defaulted on its reparations payments in 1923. See Kolb and Schumann (2013), 66–9. Under the Dawes plan, Germany's *Reichsbahn* or public railway was transformed into a *Reichsbahn* corporation under international control, so that its profits might be used to contribute to the reparations payments. However, the federal government did retain some influence on the governance of the *Reichsbahn*, and in particular on the setting of tariffs. The *Reichsbahngericht* was a court responsible for deciding conflicts between the *Reich* and the *Reichsbahn* corporation. See Kohl (1991), 99–101.

[**35, n. 49**] *conflict between the President of the Reichsgericht, Dr Simons, and the government of the Reich*: Simons objected to what he perceived as the interference on the part of the government of the *Reich* with a trial pending at the *Staatsgerichtshof* and complained to the president of the *Reich*. Simons resigned from his position as president of the *Reichsgericht* after the president had refused to take action on his complaint. See Kolb (1999), 133–5.

[**41**] *article 131 or article 153 of the constitution*: Article 131 regulates the liability of the state in case a public servant violates his official duties towards a third person in the exercise of his official powers. Article 153 guarantees the right of private property, subject to limitations based on statute.

[**44**] *dilatory compromises*: A compromise that does not decide a conflict but merely defers it. Schmitt complained that the Weimar Constitution contained too many such dilatory compromises. See Schmitt (1928), 84–8.

[**44**] *paragraph 1 and paragraph 2 of article 146*: The first paragraph of this article implies that confessional schools are impermissible, while the second seems to allow them.

[**46**] *decisionism*: Compare Schmitt (1912), 44–55; Schmitt (1922), 5–35; Schmitt (1934a).

[**46, n. 64**] *p. 103 below*: Schmitt describes several different measures that were employed in the Weimar Republic to bring technical expertise into the policy-making process. He expresses scepticism that such moves can lead to a genuine political decision. See Schmitt (1931a), 103–11. Compare the note below for chapter 3, [151, n. 33].

[**60**] *distinction of contract and agreement*: For the German 'Vertrag' and 'Vereinbarung'. In Triepel's terminology, a contract is a mere exchange of rights based on mutual advantage, whereas an agreement is a public consensus on some point of law. Triepel argued in his work on public international law that only an agreement, but not a contract, can be a source of general norms of international law. See Triepel (1899), 35–62.

[**61**] *Verfassungsverständnis of the year 1843*: Literally the 'constitutional understanding' of 1843, an informal agreement between the Bavarian government and the Bavarian *Landtag* on how to interpret the clauses of the constitution that concerned the *Landtag's* right to approve the budget. See von Seydel (1887).

[**62, n. 70**] *the note on p. 144 below*: In the section referred to here, Schmitt draws an analogy between dispute resolution through mediation in international law and in labour law. The question whether a dispute between employers and employees can, if necessary, be authoritatively resolved by the president is declared to be a criterion of whether the state still exists as a political unity. See Schmitt (1931a), 141–9.

[**62**] *that we discussed in the previous section*: See on this section the note for p. [33] above.

[**62**] *Landbund*: The 'country league', the Weimar Republic's main agrarian interest group with a strongly conservative, anti-parliamentarian bent. See Kolb and Schumann (2013), 197–8.

Chapter 3

[**76**] *state of exception*: Compare Schmitt (1921); Schmitt (1922), 5–15.

[**83**] *article 130 paragraph 2*: The second paragraph of article 130 of the Weimar Constitution guarantees the freedom of political opinion and of association to public servants, while the first paragraph of the article states that public servants are servants of the whole and not of a party. The standard interpretation held that public servants had the right to publicly confess to a political opinion and to be members of parties, but that their rights of expression and association were restricted by their duties of loyalty to the state. See Anschütz (1933), 602–7.

[**84**] *Triepel's authority has shown*: See Triepel (1927).

[**84**] *Max Weber holds on to the definition of the party as an entity that is essentially 'based on free advertisement'*: Compare the definition of 'party' in Weber (1978),

p. 284: 'The term "party" will be employed to designate associations, membership in which rests on formally free recruitment [*Werbung*].' The German term '*Werbung*' can mean both 'recruitment' and 'advertisement'. Schmitt's use of the term, in contrast to Weber's, is closer to 'advertisement'. Weber's point would appear to be that a party is a formally voluntary association, whereas Schmitt implies that a party is (or ought to be) nothing more than a group united by a consensus in political belief.

[**89**] *'completely mouldy' basis*: See Thoma (1985), 80.

[**89**] *it attempts to restrict as far as possible the chance*: Pluralism, in Schmitt's view, is likely to lead to violations of the 'principle of equal chance', which demands that a sitting government must not use its power of incumbency to discriminate in any way against political competitors. Schmitt holds that this principle is necessary for the legitimacy of a 'legislative state'. See Schmitt (1932a), 27–36.

[**90**] *'plurality of loyalties'*: English in the original. Compare Schmitt (1932b), 40–5.

[**90**] *a political decision which puts the shared basis of . . . the constitution beyond doubt*: A reference to Schmitt's conception of the constitution as a basic political decision. Compare Schmitt (1928), 75–88 and see the second note above for chapter 2, [22].

[**128**] *decrees that replace a financial statute*: The question here is whether presidential decrees issued under article 48 can stand in for a budgetary law approved by parliament. The issue was hotly contested among Weimar public lawyers, though the majority opinion tended to deny the claim, for the reason that such a view was in apparent conflict with articles 85 and 87 of the Weimar Constitution. See Anschütz (1933), 285–8. Schmitt himself had initially denied that the presidential power of dictatorship could be used to enact decrees that replace statutes. See Schmitt (1924), 213–18.

[**135**] *auctoritas and potestas*: See Schmitt (1928), 458–9.

[**135, n. 21**] *Rechts- und Staatsphilosophie, 2nd edition, §§ 97–80*: This appears to be a mistake, as there is no work of Stahl's of that title. Schmitt probably meant to refer to Friedrich Julius Stahl, *Die Revolution und die konstitutionelle Monarchie*, 2nd edn (Berlin, 1849), pp. 93ff. Compare Schmitt (1928), 314.

[**139**] *conflict with the government of the Reich*: See the note above for chapter 2, [35, n. 49].

[**140, n. 28**] *Bavarian actions*: In the wake of the assassination of foreign minister Walther Rathenau in June 1922 by a right-wing terrorist group, the Bavarian government initially refused to implement a federal statute for the protection of the republic that was enacted in July 1922. The ensuing conflict was settled by way of negotiation between Bayern and the *Reich*. See Hürten (2013).

[**140**] *polycratic entity*: Schmitt uses this term to refer to the 'chaotic co-existence of a multitude of largely self-governed and autonomous agencies of public economic activity that are independent of one another'. Polycracy, according to Schmitt, prevents unified and coherent planning for public economic activity. See Schmitt (1931a), 91–4.

[**148**] *institutional guarantee*: In interpreting the Weimar Constitution, Schmitt distinguished between subjective constitutional rights and mere institutional guarantees that constitutionally protect the existence of an institution, but do not necessarily give rise to actionable individual claims. See Schmitt (1928), 208–12; Schmitt (1931b).

[**148**] *the great tradition of the German professional public service*: A reference to the special legal position of public servants (*Beamte*) in Germany. A *Beamter* holds his

position for life and the state is obliged to provide for the *Beamter* in old age and, if necessary, to support his/her children. In return, a *Beamter* has special duties of loyalty towards the state. A *Beamter*, for instance, may not go on strike. The special position of public servants was constitutionally protected by articles 129–31 of the Weimar Constitution.

[**149**] *article 130 and article 46*: Article 46 of the Weimar Constitution authorizes the president to appoint federal public servants and military officers. On article 130 see the note for [83] above.

[**151, n. 33**] *above pp. 111–15*: Schmitt distinguishes between two basic species of neutrality, one that 'leads away from a political decision' and one that 'leads towards a political decision'. These are then further subdivided into different forms. Schmitt's argument for presidential guardianship of the constitution appeals, as an instance of the second species, to 'the neutrality of the state's decision of conflicts within the state, in contrast to the splintering and division of the state into parties and particular interests, provided that the decision gives effect to the interest of the whole of the state'. In other words, the president's decision, according to Schmitt, is not neutral in the sense of being non-political or purely technical, but neutral in the sense of representing the unity of the state or the people. See Schmitt (1931a), 111–15.

[**151, n. 33**] *the privilege of Kolleggeld*: Literally 'college money'. The lecture fees paid by students to university lecturers.

[**152**] *pp. 100–1*: Schmitt discusses the tendency towards governance by experts or public servants not beholden to parties. These can only form a counterweight to the threat of the pluralist dissolution, in Schmitt's view, insofar as they are subject to presidential political leadership. See Schmitt (1931a), 100–1.

[**156**] *p. 114*: Compare the note above for [151, n. 33].

[**156, n. 42**] *p. 108 above*: Schmitt observes that calls for 'de-politicization' are directed against the crippling effects of a parliamentary pluralism that prevents decisive decision-taking as well as against the disregard, on the part of party politicians, for value-neutral technical expertise. He points out that these two complaints differ from one another and should not be confused. A solution to the first problem requires an institution with a capability for taking more intensely political decisions than can be expected from a parliament. Such intensely political decisions, Schmitt thinks, cannot be based on or be legitimated by appeals to technical expertise. See Schmitt (1931a), 108–9 and compare Schmitt (1929a).

[**158, n. 48**] *the note on p. 98 above*: Schmitt rejects the view that article 165 of the Weimar Constitution, which provided for the establishment of a *Reichswirtschaftsrat* or federal economic council, should be regarded as the core of an 'economic constitution' that might come to stand alongside the political constitution of the *Reich*. The *Reichswirtschaftsrat* contained representatives of workers councils elected by employees as well as representatives of the owners of industry. Article 165 endowed the *Reichswirtschaftsrat* with the right to introduce bills in the *Reichstag* and determined that it must be heard on legislative proposals of fundamental importance in the fields of social and economic policy. See Schmitt (1931a), 97–8, n. 1.

[**159**] *popular referendum triggered by popular initiative*: Article 73 paragraph 3 of the Weimar Constitution provided that a legislative proposal originating from a popular initiative had to be put up for a referendum if 10 per cent of the voters

supported the initiative. If the proposal was for a constitutional amendment, the majority of voters (and not merely the majority of those participating in the referendum) had to assent for the popular initiative to pass (article 76 paragraph 1). No referendum initiated by popular initiative was accepted throughout the existence of the Weimar Republic. Schmitt discusses the popular referendum by popular initiative in Schmitt (1927) and Schmitt (1928), 286–7.

Chapter 4

[**1535**] *deep affinity with theology*: Schmitt was not the only one who pointed out that the concepts of the traditional theory of the state are theological in origin. See Kelsen (1923); Kelsen (1928a), 219–53.

[**1536**] *Handelshochschule*: Literally, the 'High School of Business'. Schmitt accepted a position at this relatively non-prestigious institution in 1928 to be able to work in Berlin. See Mehring (2009), 223–30.

[**1536**] *article 85 and 87*: These articles of the Weimar Constitution provided that the budget as well as public loans must be approved by parliament in the form of a statute.

[**1537**] *the infamous paragraph 14 in Austria*: The Austrian Constitution of 1867 (*Dezemberverfassung*), in its 'Basic Law on the Representation of the *Reich*' (*Grundgesetz über die Reichsvertretung*, RGBl. 141/1867) authorized the government to issue financial emergency decrees while the parliament or *Reichsrat* was not in session. The government had to seek the approval of parliament within four weeks after the beginning of the next parliamentary session.

[**1539**] *rather for a collective body*: Article 50 of the Weimar Constitution determined that all orders or decrees issued by the president required the countersignature of the chancellor of the *Reich* or of the relevant minister.

[**1539**] *a political theory of the 'as if'*: Implicit reference to Hans Vaihinger's *Philosophie des Als Ob*. See Vaihinger (1922). Both Kelsen and Schmitt discussed the relevance of Vaihinger's theory of fictions for jurisprudence. See Kelsen (1919) and Schmitt (1912), 21–43.

[**1539**] *conceptual jurisprudence*: For the German 'Begriffsjurisprudenz', a designation for the alleged tendency in some German jurisprudence of the nineteenth century to think of the law as a gapless system of concepts capable of providing a determinate and logically deducible solution to any legal case. The use of the term was typically intended as a criticism and suggests legal-theoretical naïveté. See Haferkamp (2011). Kelsen's charge that Schmitt is engaged in conceptual jurisprudence is supported by Paulson (1995).

[**1548**] *Vienna School*: The term was commonly used, among German-speaking legal academics, to refer to Kelsen and the circle of pupils that had gathered around him in Vienna.

[**1569**] *according to the constitution of 1920*: Under the Austrian Constitution of 1920, half the judges on the Constitutional Court were to be elected by the *Nationalrat* or federal parliament, and half the judges were to be elected by the *Bundesrat*, i.e. by representatives of the several constituent states of the Republic of Austria. See Heller (2010), 183.

[**1569**] *a conflict … that threatened its very existence*: The so-called 'Dispensehen-Kontroverse'. Austrian law (influenced by Catholic doctrine) did not permit spouses who lived in separation from their partners to remarry. At the same time, the administrative authorities of some *Länder* claimed the authority, and came to use it increasingly in the 1920s, to issue dispensations that would permit remarriage. These dispensations, however, were not recognized by Austrian civil courts, which frequently proclaimed second marriages to be legally invalid. The Austrian Constitutional Court, led by Kelsen, eventually decided that the civil courts lacked the competence to overturn an administrative decision to issue a dispensation for remarriage. This decision was very unpopular with conservative politicians and press, and led to harsh personal attacks on Kelsen. In the course of a constitutional reform of 1929 all sitting judges, including Kelsen, were removed from the Austrian Constitutional Court, though they had been elected for life. The mode of appointment of judges was then changed, so as to ensure a future conservative majority that was expected to overturn the decision in favour of the validity of administrative dispensations. After his removal from the court Kelsen refused to be reappointed as judge and moved to the University of Cologne in Germany. See Walter (2005), 57–68; Neschwara (2005); Heller (2010), 198–206, 210–14.

[**1572**] *the mythology of Ormuzd and Ahriman*: The good god and the evil demon in Zoroastrianism. See Duchesne-Guillemin (1984).

Chapter 5

[**205**] *active legitimation*: The standing to bring a suit in the *Staatsgerichtshof*. The question as to who possessed that standing was disputed in the Weimar Republic. The reigning opinion held that the *Staatsgerichtshof* was not entitled to hear complaints by individual citizens against infringements of their constitutional liberty rights. Rather, standing was seen as limited to organs of government, other public institutions, and possibly individuals, who claimed that their rights of active participation in the process of the will-formation of the state had been violated. See Anschütz (1933), 165–70.

[**205**] *article 19*: Compare the second note above for chapter 2, [33].

[**206**] *arm in arm with the Land of Bavaria and the Land of Baden*: In addition to the state of Prussia, represented by its government, the following parties brought suits against the *Preussenschlag* before the *Staatsgerichtshof*: the Centre Party and the Social Democratic Party in the Prussian *Landtag*, the individual members of the Prussian government who had been removed from their offices, and the states of Baden and Bayern, who argued that their constitutional rights were affected by the federal government's claim to represent Prussia in the *Reichsrat*.

[**206**] *devious trick*: See the introduction to this volume at p. 3.

[**208**] *article 17, as an independent norm of competence*: Article 17 paragraph 1 of the Weimar Constitution determined that every *Land*, like the Reich itself, must have a republican constitution, with a parliament elected in general, equal, direct, and secret elections, using an electoral system of proportional representation. It also provided that every *Land*, like the *Reich* itself, must have a parliamentary system of government. Anschütz argued before the *Staatsgerichtshof* that article 17 did not merely require a *Land* to be internally democratic but that it also guaranteed a democratically elected government responsible to parliament in every *Land*. Hence,

von Papen's wholesale removal of the Prussian government had, in Anschütz's view, been unconstitutional. See Brecht (1933), 301–7. Schmitt's claim that article 17 is an independent norm of competence figured prominently in his reply to Anschütz. See ibid., 311–22.

An independent norm of competence (*selbständige Zuständigkeitsnorm*), is a power-conferring constitutional norm that is not derived from other norms of competence in the same constitution. Article 48 paragraph 2 of the Weimar Constitution was commonly acknowledged to be an independent norm of competence. In other words, the president's power of dictatorship was taken to be a separate and self-standing competence, not reducible to the president's rights of participation in the ordinary process of legislation. Hence, it was regarded as a power whose exercise could affect the normal distribution of competences between the *Reich* and the *Länder*. As Grau put the point (see Grau (1932), 276–7), article 48 paragraph 2 empowered the president, 'within the frame of the purpose of dictatorial action' to 'take action in areas that, with respect to their material content, belong to the sphere of competence of the *Länder*'.

Schmitt relied on the claim that article 48 paragraph 2 is an independent norm of competence to argue that the guarantee that Anschütz had read into article 17 could not be invoked against the *Preussenschlag*. According to Schmitt, the primary purpose of article 17 is to ensure that there is homogeneity in political form between the federal government and the governments of the *Länder*. The president, consequently, must be permitted to use his power of dictatorship to interfere with the internal governance of a *Land*, so as to ensure that it lives up to the requirements of article 17. Hence, even if article 17 is itself an independent norm of competence – like article 48, one that guarantees to each *Land* the competence to organize its own constitutional affairs as it sees fit within the constraints of article 17 – it cannot, in Schmitt's view, be brought into play against a presidential act of dictatorship. A *Land's* competences, rather, are shielded against interference under article 48 only on the condition that the president judges that the *Land's* internal governance is in compliance with article 17.

To bolster this case, Schmitt repeatedly suggested, in Leipzig, that the Prussian caretaker government under Otto Braun did not qualify as a legitimate government within the constraints of article 17, or at least that the president had not been guilty of an abuse of discretion in judging that it did not. In particular, Schmitt claimed that the fact that Braun's government seemed to depend on the toleration of the communists in the Prussian *Landtag* had undermined the political homogeneity between Prussia and the *Reich*. See, for instance, Brecht (1933), 39–41. Hence the suggestion, in Schmitt's closing statement, that the deposed caretaker government should no longer be regarded as a Prussian government. Schmitt's argument was roundly rejected in the decision of the *Staatsgerichtshof*. The court adopted Anschütz's claim that article 17 implied that the president lacked the power to remove, even temporarily, the duly elected government of a *Land*. See Brecht (1933), 515–16 and Anschütz (1933), 770–2.

[**208**] *confirmed by Walter Jellinek*: In Jellinek (1932).

[**209**] *federal execution of the German Bund against Prussia*: The Austro-Prussian war of 1866 had taken the form of a federal execution of the *Deutscher Bund* (the confederation of German states) against Prussia. See Clark (2007), 531–46. Hindenburg had fought in the war on the Prussian side.

Chapter 6

[**66**] *articles 57 and 58 of the Prussian Constitution*: These two articles of the Prussian Constitution of 1920 provided that members of government are responsible to parliament and must resign upon a successful vote of no confidence and that the *Landtag* has the right to accuse ministers of a 'culpable violation of the constitution or of statutes' in a (Prussian) *Staatsgerichtshof*.

[**73**] *that he is free to suspend temporarily*: Under article 48 paragraph 2 of the Weimar Constitution, the president was authorized to suspend seven specifically enumerated basic rights. This provision raised the question of whether all or some non-enumerated constitutional provisions were consequently to be regarded as immune to the presidential power of dictatorship. The scholarly discussion remained inconclusive. See Grau (1932), 282–7; Anschütz (1933), 285–90; Schmitt (1924), 191–4.

[**74**] *articles 17, 60, and 63*: On article 17 of the Weimar Constitution, see the first note above for chapter 5, [208]. Articles 60 and 63 provided for the creation of the *Reichsrat* or federal council, through which the *Länder* participated in the Weimar Republic's federal process of legislation. They also regulated the mode of appointment to and the distribution of votes among the states in the *Reichsrat*.

[**82**] *the last paragraph of article 19*: The paragraph determined that the President of the *Reich* is to execute the judgments of the *Staatsgerichtshof*.

[**85**] *the captain of Köpenick*: The captain of *Köpenick* was an impostor who, in 1906, put on the uniform of a Prussian captain, entered the mayoralty of the Prussian town of *Köpenick*, and ordered the city's cashier to hand over all the available cash. The cashier complied and the false captain made off with a substantial sum of money. See Clark (2007), 596–9. The episode is Kelsen's preferred example for a pretended act of state that is absolutely null.

[**85**] *article 13 of the constitution of the Reich*: Article 13 of the Weimar Constitution determined that the law of the *Reich* takes precedence over the law of a *Land*. It also made the *Reichsgericht* responsible for deciding doubts and disagreements over whether a norm of the law of a *Land* conflicted with the law of the *Reich*.

[**89**] *technical insufficiency of the Weimar Constitution*: Compare Kelsen (1927), 167–75 for a more detailed analysis of this insufficiency.

[**90**] *by way of an application of article 48 paragraph 2*: This assessment appears to concur with Schmitt's analysis of the powers of the president under article 48 paragraph 2. See the first comment for ch. 5 [208] and compare Dyzenhaus (1997), 123–32.

BIBLIOGRAPHY

Alexy, Robert (2005) 'Hans Kelsens Begriff der Verfassung' in Stanley L. Paulson and Michael Stolleis (eds.), *Hans Kelsen. Staatsrechtslehrer und Rechtstheoretiker des 20 Jahrhunderts* (Tübingen: Mohr Siebeck, 2005), 333.

Anschütz, Gerhard (1933) *Die Verfassung des Deutschen Reiches vom 11. August 1919* (Berlin: Georg Stilke).

Anschütz, Gerhard and Richard Thoma (1932) (eds.), *Handbuch des Deutschen Staatsrechts*, 2 vols. (Tübingen:, Mohr Siebeck), II.

Baume, Sandrine (2012) *Hans Kelsen and the Case for Democracy* (Colchester: ECPR Press).

Beaud, Olivier and Pasquale Pasquino (2007) (eds.), *La Controverse sur 'Le guardien de la constitution' et la justice constitutionnelle. Kelsen contre Schmitt* (Paris: Éditions Panthéon-Assas).

Bernstorff, Jochen von (2010) *The Public International Law Theory of Hans Kelsen. Believing in Universal Law* (Cambridge University Press).

Berthold, Lutz (1999) *Carl Schmitt und der Staatsnotstandsplan am Ende der Weimarer Republik* (Berlin: Duncker & Humblot).

Brecht, Arnold (1933) (ed.), *Preußen contra Reich vor dem Staatsgerichtshof. Stenogrammbericht der Verhandlungen vor dem Staatsgerichtshof in Leipzig vom 10. bis 14. Oktober und vom 17. Oktober 1932* (Berlin: J. H. W. Dietz).

Breuer, Stefan (2012) *Carl Schmitt im Kontext. Intellektuellenpolitik in der Weimarer Republik* (Berlin: Akademie Verlag).

Caldwell, Peter C. (1997) *Popular Sovereignty and the Crisis of German Constitutional Law: The Theory and Practice of Weimar Constitutionalism* (Durham and London: Duke University Press).

Clark, Christopher (2007) *Iron Kingdom: The Rise and Downfall of Prussia 1600–1947* (London: Penguin).

Cristi, Renato (1998) *Carl Schmitt and Authoritarian Liberalism: Strong State, Free Economy* (Cardiff: University of Wales Press).

(2011) 'Schmitt on Constituent Power and the Monarchical Principle', *Constellations*, 18 (2011), 352.

Croce, Mariano and Andrea Salvatore (2013) *The Legal Theory of Carl Schmitt* (Abingdon: Routledge)

Diner, Dan and Michael Stolleis (1999) (eds.), *Hans Kelsen and Carl Schmitt: A Juxtaposition* (Gerlingen: Bleicher Verlag).

Dreier, Horst (1990) *Rechtslehre, Staatssoziologie und Demokratietheorie bei Hans Kelsen* (Baden-Baden: Nomos).

Duchesne-Guillemin, Jacques (1984) 'Ahriman' in Ehsan Yarshater (ed.), *Encyclopaedia Iranica* I/6–7, 670–3; available online at www.iranicaonline.org/articles/ahriman (accessed 15 February 2014).

Dyzenhaus, David (1997) *Legality and Legitimacy: Carl Schmitt, Hans Kelsen, and Hermann Heller in Weimar* (Oxford University Press).

(2006) *The Constitution of Law: Legality in a Time of Emergency* (Cambridge University Press).

Ehs, Tamara (2009) (ed.), *Hans Kelsen. Eine politikwissenschaftliche Einführung* (Vienna: Facultas).

Grau, Richard (1932) '*Die Diktaturgewalt des Reichspräsidenten*' in Gerhard Anschütz, and Richard Thoma (eds.), *Handbuch des Deutschen Staatsrechts*, 2 vols. (Tübingen: Mohr Siebeck, 1932), II, 274.

Gümplová, Petra (2011) *Sovereignty and Constitutional Democracy* (Baden-Baden: Nomos).

Haferkamp, Hans Peter (2011) 'Begriffsjurisprudenz' in Thomas Gutmann, *et al.* (eds.), *Enzyklopädie zur Rechtsphilosophie*; available online at: www.enzyklopaedie-rechtsphilosophie.net/inhaltsverzeichnis/19-beitraege/96-begriffsjurisprudenz (accessed 14 February 2014).

Hartmann, Bernd J. (2007) 'Das richterliche Prüfungsrecht unter der Weimarer Reichsverfassung' in Thomas Vormbaum (ed.), *Jahrbuch der Juristischen Zeitgeschichte* (Berlin: Berliner Wissenschafts-Verlag, 2007), 154.

Heller, Kurt (2010) *Der Verfassungsgerichtshof. Die Entwicklung der Verfassungsgerichtsbarkeit in Österreich von den Anfängen bis zur Gegenwart* (Vienna: Verlag Österreich).

Herrera, Carlos-Miguel (1995) (ed.), *Le Droit, le politique autour de Max Weber, Hans Kelsen, Carl Schmitt* (Paris: Éditions L'Harmattan).

(1997) *Théorie juridique et politique chez Hans Kelsen* (Paris, Éditions Kimé).

Hippel, Ernst von (1932) 'Das richterliche Prüfungsrecht' in Gerhard Anschütz, and Richard Thoma (eds.), *Handbuch des Deutschen Staatsrechts*, 2 vols. (Tübingen: Mohr Siebeck, 1932), II, 546.

Hofmann, Hasso (2002) *Legitimität gegen Legalität. Der Weg der politischen Philosophie Carl Schmitts* (Berlin: Duncker & Humblot).

Hürten, Heinz (2013) 'Kabinett Lerchenfeld, 1921/22' in Bayerische Staatsbibliothek (ed.), *Historisches Lexikon Bayerns*; available online at: www.historisches-lexikon-bayerns.de/artikel/artikel_44522 (accessed 10 February 2014).

Jellinek, Walter (1932) 'Zum Konflikt zwischen Preußen und dem Reich', *Reichsverwaltungsblatt und Preußisches Verwaltungsblatt*, 53 (1932), 681.

Jestaedt, Matthias and Oliver Lepsius (2006) 'Der Rechts- und der Demokratietheoretiker Hans Kelsen. Eine Einführung' in Hans Kelsen, *Verteidigung der Demokratie. Abhandlungen zur Demokratietheorie*, ed. Matthias Jestaedt and Oliver Lepsius (Tübingen: Mohr Siebeck, 2006), vii.

Kaufmann, Erich (1911) *Das Wesen des Völkerrechts und die clausula rebus sic stantibus* (Tübingen: Mohr Siebeck).

Kelsen, Hans (1914) 'Über Staatsunrecht' in Hans R. Klecatsky, René Marcic, and Herbert Schambeck (eds.), *Die Wiener rechtstheoretische Schule. Schriften von Hans Kelsen, Adolf Merkl, Alfred Verdross*, 2 vols. (Vienna: Verlag Österreich, 2010), I, 785.

(1919) 'Zur Theorie der juristischen Fiktionen' in Hans R. Klecatsky, René Marcic, and Herbert Schambeck (eds.), *Die Wiener rechtstheoretische Schule. Schriften von Hans Kelsen, Adolf Merkl, Alfred Verdross*, 2 vols. (Vienna: Verlag Österreich, 2010), II, 993.

(1920) *Das Problem der Souveränität und die Theorie des Völkerrechts. Beitrag zu einer Reinen Rechtslehre* (Tübingen: Mohr Siebeck).

(1923) 'Gott und Staat' in Hans R. Klecatsky, René Marcic, and Herbert Schambeck (eds.), *Die Wiener rechtstheoretische Schule. Schriften von Hans Kelsen, Adolf Merkl, Alfred Verdross*, 2 vols. (Vienna: Verlag Österreich, 2010), I, 131.

(1924) 'Die Lehre von den drei Gewalten oder Funktionen des Staates' in Hans R. Klecatsky, René Marcic, and Herbert Schambeck (2010) (eds.), *Die Wiener rechtstheoretische Schule. Schriften von Hans Kelsen, Adolf Merkl, Alfred Verdross*, 2 vols. (Vienna: Verlag Österreich), II, 1331.

(1925) *Allgemeine Staatslehre* (Berlin: Julius Springer).

(1926) 'Demokratie' in Hans Kelsen, *Verteidigung der Demokratie. Abhandlungen zur Demokratietheorie*, ed. Matthias Jestaedt and Oliver Lepsius (Tübingen: Mohr Siebeck, 2006), 115.

(1927) 'Die Bundesexekution. Ein Beitrag zur Theorie und Praxis des Bundesstaates, unter besonderer Berücksichtigung der deutschen Reichs- und der österreichischen Bundesverfassung' in Zaccaria Giacometti and Dietrich Schindler (eds.), *Festgabe für Fritz Fleiner zum 60. Geburtstag* (Tübingen: Mohr Siebeck), 127.

(1928a) *Der soziologische und der juristische Staatsbegriff. Kritische Untersuchung des Verhältnisses von Staat und Recht* (Tübingen, Mohr Siebeck).

(1928b) 'Natural Law Doctrine and Legal Positivism' in Hans Kelsen, *General Theory of Law and State*, trans. Anders Wedberg (Cambridge, MA: Harvard University Press, 1945), 389.

(1929a) 'Wesen und Entwicklung der Staatsgerichtsbarkeit' in Hans R. Klecatsky, René Marcic, and Herbert Schambeck (eds.), *Die Wiener rechtstheoretische Schule. Schriften von Hans Kelsen, Adolf Merkl, Alfred Verdross*, 2 vols. (Vienna: Verlag Österreich, 2010), II, 1485.

(1929b) *The Essence and Value of Democracy*, ed. by Nadia Urbinati and Carlo Invernizzi Accetti, trans. Brian Graf (Lanham, MD: Rowman & Littlefield, 2013).

(1931) 'Wer soll der Hüter der Verfassung sein?' in Hans R. Klecatsky, René Marcic, and Herbert Schambeck (eds.), *Die Wiener rechtstheoretische Schule. Schriften von Hans Kelsen, Adolf Merkl, Alfred Verdross*, 2 vols. (Vienna: Verlag Österreich, 2010), II, 1533.

(1932a) 'Das Urteil des Staatsgerichtshofs vom 25. Oktober 1932', *Die Justiz*, 8 (1932), 65.

(1932b) 'Verteidigung der Demokratie' in Hans Kelsen, *Verteidigung der Demokratie. Abhandlungen zur Demokratietheorie*, ed. Matthias Jestaedt and Oliver Lepsius (Tübingen: Mohr Siebeck, 2006), 229.

(1934) *Introduction to the Problems of Legal Theory: A Translation of the First Edition of the Reine Rechtslehre or Pure Theory of Law*, trans. Bonnie Litschewski Paulson and Stanley L. Paulson, introduction Stanley L. Paulson (Oxford University Press, 1992).

(1942) 'Judicial Review of Legislation: A Comparative Study of the Austrian and the American Constitution', *The Journal of Politics*, 4 (1942), 183.

(1945) *General Theory of Law and State*, trans. Anders Wedberg (Cambridge MA: Harvard University Press).

(1957) 'What is Justice?' in Hans Kelsen, *What is Justice? Justice, Law, and Politics in the Mirror of Science. Collected Essays by Hans Kelsen* (Berkeley: University of California Press, 1957), 1.

(2006) *Verteidigung der Demokratie. Abhandlungen zur Demokratietheorie*, ed. Matthias Jestaedt and Oliver Lepsius (Tübingen: Mohr Siebeck).

Kennedy, Ellen (2004) *Constitutional Failure. Carl Schmitt in Weimar* (Durham and London: Duke University Press).

Klecatsky, Hans R., René Marcic, and Herbert Schambeck (2010) (eds.), *Die Wiener rechtstheoretische Schule. Schriften von Hans Kelsen, Adolf Merkl, Alfred Verdross*, 2 vols. (Vienna: Verlag Österreich).

Kletzer, Christoph (2005) 'Kelsen's Development of the *Fehlerkalkül*-Theory', *Ratio Juris*, 18 (2005), 46.

Kohl, Wolfgang (1991) *Das Reichsverwaltungsgericht: ein Beitrag zur Entwicklung der Verwaltungsgerichtsbarkeit in Deutschland* (Tübingen: Mohr Siebeck).

Kolb, Eberhard (1999) 'Die Reichsbahn vom Dawes-Plan bis zum Ende der Weimarer Republik' in Lothar Gall and Manfred Pohl (eds.), *Die Eisenbahn in Deutschland. Von den Anfängen bis zur Gegenwart* (Munich: C. H. Beck, 1999), 109.

Kolb, Eberhard and Dirk Schumann (2013) *Die Weimarer Republik* (Munich: Oldenbourg).

Koller, Peter (2005) 'Zur Theorie des rechtlichen Stufenbaues' in Stanley L. Paulson and Michael Stolleis (eds.), *Hans Kelsen. Staatsrechtslehrer und Rechtstheoretiker des 20 Jahrhunderts* (Tübingen: Mohr Siebeck, 2005), 106.

Lagerspetz, Eerik 'The Value of Democracy: Kelsen's Two Arguments' in Andityas Soares de Moura Costa Matos and Carlos Miguel Herrera (eds.), *Kelsen and Schmitt Today* (forthcoming).

Lagi, Sara (2012) 'Hans Kelsen and the Austrian Constitutional Court (1918–1929)', *Co-herencia*, 9 (2012), 273.

McCormick, John P. (1997) *Carl Schmitt's Critique of Liberalism. Against Politics as Technology* (Cambridge University Press).

(1998), 'The Dilemmas of Dictatorship: Carl Schmitt and Constitutional Emergency Powers' in David Dyzenhaus (ed.), *Law as Politics. Carl Schmitt's Critique of Liberalism* (Durham and London: Duke University Press), 217.

(2004), 'Identifying or Exploiting the Paradoxes of Constitutional Democracy? An Introduction to Carl Schmitt's Legality and Legitimacy' in Carl Schmitt, *Legality and Legitimacy* (Durham and London, Duke University Press, 2004), xiii.

Mehring, Reinhard (2009) *Carl Schmitt. Aufstieg und Fall* (Munich, C. H. Beck).

Mommsen, Hans (1984) *Max Weber and German Politics 1890–1920* (University of Chicago Press).

(2009) *Aufstieg und Untergang der Republik von Weimar 1918–1933* (Berlin: Ullstein).

Neschwara, Christian (2005) 'Kelsen als Verfassungsrichter. Seine Rolle in der Dispensehen-Kontroverse' in Stanley L. Paulson and Michael Stolleis (eds.), *Hans Kelsen. Staatsrechtslehrer und Rechtstheoretiker des 20 Jahrhunderts* (Tübingen: Mohr Siebeck, 2005), 353.

Nino, Carlos Santiago (1996) *The Constitution of Deliberative Democracy* (New Haven and London: Yale University Press).

Öhlinger, Theo (2003) 'The Genesis of the Austrian Model of Constitutional Review of Legislation', *Ratio Juris*, 16 (2003), 206.

Olechowsky, Thomas (2009) 'Der Beitrag Hans Kelsen's zur Österreichischen Bundesverfassung' in Robert Walter, Werner Ogris, and Thomas Olechowsky (eds.), *Hans Kelsen: Leben – Werk – Wirksamkeit* (Vienna: Manzsche Verlags- und Universitätsbuchhandlung, 2009), 211.

Paulson, Stanley L. (1980) 'Material and Formal Authorization in Kelsen's Pure Theory', *Cambridge Law Journal*, 39 (1980), 172.

(1995) 'Arguments conceptuels de Schmitt à l'encontre du contrôle de constitutionnalité et réponses de Kelsen. Un aspect de l'affrontement entre Schmitt et Kelsen sur le gardien de la constitution' in Carlos-Miguel Herrera (ed.), *Le Droit, le politique autour de Max Weber, Hans Kelsen, Carl Schmitt* (Paris: Éditions L'Harmattan, 1995), 243.

(2003) 'Constitutional Review in the United States and Austria: Notes on the Beginnings', *Ratio Juris*, 16 (2003), 223.

Paulson, Stanley L. and Michael Stolleis (2005) (eds.), *Hans Kelsen. Staatsrechtslehrer und Rechtstheoretiker des 20 Jahrhundert* (Tübingen: Mohr Siebeck).

Radbruch, Gustav (1946) 'Statutory Lawlessness and Supra-Statutory Law', trans. Bonnie Litschewski Paulson and Stanley L. Paulson, *Oxford Journal of Legal Studies*, 26 (2006), 1.

Rossiter, Clinton L. (1948) *Constitutional Dictatorship. Crisis Government in the Modern Democracies* (Princeton, NJ: Princeton University Press).

Rousseau, Jean-Jacques (1988) *On Social Contract, in Rousseau, Jean-Jacques, Political Writings*, ed. Alan Ritter and Julia Conaway Bondanella (New York: W. W. Norton & Company), 84.

Rückert, Joachim (2008) 'Freirechtsbewegung' in Albrecht Cordes, Heiner Lück, and Dieter Werkmüller (eds.), *Handwörterbuch zur deutschen Rechtsgeschichte*, 2nd edn, 2 vols. to date (Berlin: Erich Schmidt Verlag), I, 1772.

Scheuerman, William E. (1999) *Carl Schmitt. The End of Law* (Lanham, MD: Rowman & Littlefield).

Schmitt, Carl (1912) *Gesetz und Urteil. Eine Untersuchung zum Problem der Rechtspraxis* (Munich: C. H. Beck, 1969).

(1921), *Dictatorship. From the Origin of the Modern Concept of Sovereignty to Proletarian Class Struggle*, trans. Michael Hoelzl and Graeme Ward (Cambridge, Polity Press, 2014).

(1922) *Political Theology. Four Chapters on the Concept of Sovereignty*, trans. and introduction George Schwab (Chicago: University of Chicago Press, 2005).

(1924) 'The Dictatorship of the President of the Reich according to Article 48 of the Weimar Constitution' in Carl Schmitt, *Dictatorship. From the Origin of the Modern Concept of Sovereignty to Proletarian Class Struggle*, trans. Michael Hoelzl and Graeme Ward (Cambridge, Polity Press, 2014), 180.

(1926a) *The Crisis of Parliamentary Democracy*, trans. and introduction Ellen Kennedy (Cambridge, MA: MIT Press, 1985).

(1926b) 'Die Kernfrage des Völkerbundes' in Carl Schmitt, *Frieden oder Pazifismus? Arbeiten zum Völkerrecht und zur internationalen Politik 1924–1978*, ed. Günther Maschke (Berlin: Duncker & Humblot, 2005), 73.

(1927) *Volksentscheid und Volksbegehren. Ein Beitrag zur Auslegung der Weimarer Verfassung und zur Lehre von der unmittelbaren Demokratie* (Berlin and Leipzig: Walter De Gruyter & Co.).

(1928) *Constitutional Theory*, trans. Jeffrey Seitzer, introduction Jeffrey Seitzer and Christopher Thornhill (Durham and London: Duke University Press, 2008).

(1929a) 'The Age of Neutralizations and Depoliticizations' in Carl Schmitt, *The Concept of the Political. Expanded Edition*, trans. and introduction George Schwab (University of Chicago Press, 2007), 80.

(1929b) 'Das Reichsgericht als Hüter der Verfassung' in Carl Schmitt, *Verfassungsrechtliche Aufsätze aus den Jahren 1924–1954. Materialien zu einer Verfassungslehre* (Berlin: Duncker & Humblot, 1958), 63.

(1931a) *Der Hüter der Verfassung*, 4th edn (Berlin: Duncker & Humblot, 1996).

(1931b) 'Freiheitsrechte und institutionelle Garantien der Reichsverfassung' in Carl Schmitt, *Verfassungsrechtliche Aufsätze aus den Jahren 1924–1954. Materialien zu einer Verfassungslehre* (Berlin: Duncker & Humblot, 1958), 140.

(1932a) *Legality and Legitimacy*, trans. Jeffrey Seitzer, introduction John P. McCormick (Durham and London: Duke University Press, 2004).

(1932b) *The Concept of the Political. Expanded Edition*, trans. and introduction George Schwab (University of Chicago Press, 2007).

(1932c) 'Die Verfassungsmäßigkeit der Bestellung eines Reichskommissars für das Land Preußen', *Deutsche Juristen-Zeitung*, 37 (1932), 953.

(1932d) 'Schlußrede vor dem Staatsgerichtshof in Leipzig in dem Prozeß Preußen contra Reich' in Carl Schmitt, *Positionen und Begriffe im Kampf mit Weimar – Genf – Versailles 1923–1939*, 3rd edn (Berlin: Duncker & Humblot, 1994), 204–10.

(1934a) *On the Three Types of Juristic Thought*, trans. Joseph Bendersky (Westport, CT: Praeger Publishers, 2004).

(1934b) *Staatsgefüge und Zusammenbruch des zweiten Reiches. Der Sieg des Bürgers über den Soldaten* (Berlin: Duncker & Humblot, 2011).

(1938) *The Leviathan in the State Theory of Thomas Hobbes. Meaning and Failure of a Political Symbol*, trans. George Schwab and Erna Hilfstein (University of Chicago Press, 2008).

(1958) *Verfassungsrechtliche Aufsätze aus den Jahren 1924–1954. Materialien zu einer Verfassungslehre* (Berlin: Duncker & Humblot).

(1967) *Die Tyrannei der Werte* (Berlin: Duncker & Humblot, 2011).

Schmitz, Georg (1981) *Die Vorentwürfe Hans Kelsen's für die österreichische Bundesverfassung* (Vienna: Manzsche Verlags- und Universitätsbuchhandlung).

Seiberth, Gabriel (2001) *Carl Schmitt und der Prozess 'Preußen contra Reich vor dem Staatsgerichtshof'* (Berlin: Duncker & Humblot).

Seydel, Max von (1887), 'Das Budgetrecht des bayerischen Landtages und das Verfassungs-Verständniss von 1843' in Max von Seydel, *Staatsrechtliche und politische Abhandlungen. Neue Folge*, ed. Karl Krazeisen (Tübingen: Mohr Siebeck, 1902), 278.

Somek, Alexander (2001) 'Das Mehrheitsprinzip in der Demokratie. Überlegungen zu einer Kontroverse zwischen Max Adler und Hans Kelsen', *Deutsche Zeitschrift für Philosophie*, 49 (2001), 397.

Stolleis, Michael (1992) *Geschichte des öffentlichen Rechts in Deutschland. Zweiter Band: Staatsrechtslehre und Verwaltungswissenschaft 1800–1914* (Munich: C. H. Beck).

(2002) *Geschichte des öffentlichen Rechts in Deutschland: Weimarer Republik und Nationalsozialismus* (Munich: C. H. Beck).

(2003) 'Judicial Review, Administrative Review, and Constitutional Review in the Weimar Republic', *Ratio Juris*, 16 (2003), 266.

Stone-Sweet, Alec (2000) *Governing with Judges: Constitutional Politics in Europe* (Oxford University Press).

Thoma Richard (1932), 'Die Funktionen der Staatsgewalt: Grundbegriffe und Grundsätze' in Gerhard Anschütz, and Richard Thoma (eds.), *Handbuch des Deutschen Staatsrechts*, 2 vols. (Tübingen: Mohr Siebeck, 1932), II, 108.

(1985) 'On the Ideology of Parliamentarism' in Carl Schmitt, *The Crisis of Parliamentary Democracy*, trans. and introduction Ellen Kennedy (Cambridge, MA: MIT Press, 1985), 77.

Triepel, Heinrich (1899) *Völkerrecht und Landesrecht* (Leipzig: C. L. Hirschfeld).

(1927) *Die Staatsverfassung und die politischen Parteien. Rede bei der Feier der Erinnerung an den Stifter der Berliner Universität König Friedrich Wilhelm III. in der alten Aula am 3. August 1927 gehalten von Heinrich Triepel* (Berlin: Preußische Druckerei- und Verlags-Aktiengesellschaft).

(1929) 'Wesen und Entwicklung der Staatsgerichtsbarkeit' in Vereinigung der Deutschen Staatsrechtslehrer (ed.), *Veröffentlichungen der Vereinigung der Deutschen Staatsrechtslehrer*, issue 5 (Berlin and Leipzig: Walter De Gruyter & Co., 1929), 2.

Troper, Michel (1995) 'Kelsen et le contrôle de constitutionnalité' in Carlos-Miguel Herrera (ed.), *Le Droit, le politique autour de Max Weber, Hans Kelsen, Carl Schmitt* (Paris: Éditions L'Harmattan, 1995), 157.

Vaihinger, Hans (1922) *Die Philosophie des Als Ob. System der theoretischen, praktischen und religiösen Fiktionen der Menschheit auf Grund eines idealistischen Positivismus* (Leipzig: Felix Meiner).

Vereinigung der Deutschen Staatsrechtslehrer (1929) (ed.), *Veröffentlichungen der Vereinigung der Deutschen Staatsrechtslehrer*, issue 5 (Berlin and Leipzig: Walter De Gruyter & Co.).

Vinx, Lars (2007) *Hans Kelsen's Pure Theory of Law: Legality and Legitimacy* (Oxford University Press).

(2013a) 'Carl Schmitt and the Analogy between Constitutional and International Law: Are Constitutional and International Law Inherently Political?', *Global Constitutionalism*, 2 (2013), 91.

(2013b), 'The Incoherence of Strong Popular Sovereignty', *International Journal of Constitutional Law*, 11 (2013), 101.

Walter, Robert (2005) *Hans Kelsen als Verfassungsrichter* (Vienna: Manzsche Verlags- und Universitätsbuchhandlung).

Weber, M. *Economy and Society. An Outline of Interpretive Sociology*, ed. G. Roth and C. Wittich (Berkeley: University of California Press, 1978).

Wiederin, Ewald (2005) 'Kelsen's Begriff des Bundesstaats' in Stanley L. Paulson and Michael Stolleis (eds.), *Hans Kelsen. Staatsrechtslehrer und Rechtstheoretiker des 20 Jahrhunderts* (Tübingen: Mohr Siebeck, 2005), 222.

INDEX

For EU product safety concerns, contact us at Calle de José Abascal, 56–1°,
28003 Madrid, Spain or eugpsr@cambridge.org.

www.ingramcontent.com/pod-product-compliance
Lightning Source LLC
LaVergne TN
LVHW011524200926
848484LV00001B/141
* 9 7 8 1 1 0 7 0 9 2 6 8 6 *